THE TWILIGHT OF SOUTHERN STEAM

THE UNTOLD STORY 1965 - 1967

THE TWILIGHT OF SOUTHERN STEAM

THE UNTOLD STORY 1965 - 1967

DON BENN

PEN & SWORD
TRANSPORT

First published in Great Britain in 2017 by
Pen & Sword Transport
an imprint of
Pen & Sword Books Ltd,
47 Church Street,
Barnsley,
South Yorkshire.
S70 2AS

A CIP record for this book is available from the British Library.

ISBN 978 1 47386 306 4

Printed and bound in India by Replika Press Pvt. Ltd

Pen & Sword Books Ltd incorporates the Imprints of Pen & Sword Aviation, Pen & Sword Maritime, Pen & Sword Military, Wharncliffe Local History, Pen & Sword Select, Pen & Sword Military Classics and Leo Cooper.

For a complete list of Pen & Sword titles please contact
Pen & Sword Books Limited
47 Church Street, Barnsley, South Yorkshire, S70 2AS, England
E-mail: enquiries@pen-and-sword.co.uk
Website: www.pen-and-sword.co.uk

Contents

Preface

This book is first and foremost the story of the enginemen and their steeds which brought the steam era to an end on the Southern Region of British Railways. It is therefore primarily about locomotive performance, but enlivened by stories about how that was achieved and also about the band of young men who followed the exploits of men and machines, day and night, over those last two and a half years. The photos are those taken mainly on the platforms and in the locomotive depots, snatched between runs and therefore the variety and quality is not perhaps what you would expect if this book were primarily a photographic record of the last years, which it is not. In any case that has been done many times elsewhere. I have wanted to write this book since the end of Southern steam in July 1967, but have only found the time recently actually to do so. As the years slip by I know that if I do not do it now then I never will; and even so memories are fading, but hopefully not enough to compromise accuracy. In any case I still have my trusty old notebooks which tell the story of those last two frantic years plus a few negatives. I have also stayed in touch with many of the friends made at that time and their help has been invaluable. Some are still active on the steam scene as are a few of the enginemen from those days, one of whom has contributed to this book. My equipment used to record times and speeds may be regarded today as antiquated,

but the ex-government one tenth of second stop watch was accurate enough when linked to sharp young eyes. Most of the logs of runs in this book have anyway been substantiated by others, if not also recorded by them. I have deliberately chosen the last thirty months as this was the period ingrained most on my mind and leads naturally through to the finale, even if some epic performances in the earlier years have had to be excluded. The book starts with a short chapter setting the scene, followed by a description of the engines and enginemen involved. Then follows the three core chapters describing the events and best runs of each year from 1965 to the end of steam in July 1967, then a chapter on footplate experiences including a substantial contribution from an ex Nine Elms fireman who is still in touch via my email group. I have used the 12-hour clock throughout as to me that seems appropriate to that era. I have also refrained from a detailed description of the routes involved and their gradients as this information is available elsewhere and the main gradient profiles are shown in Appendix L. Any mistakes are mine and mine alone, so with that in mind I hope the reader will enjoy this offering which is a tribute to the enginemen and their engines which performed near miracles in the very different world of the mid-nineteen-sixties railway.

CHAPTER ONE
SETTING THE SCENE

Although I had the occasional foray into the land of steam-hauled trains out of Waterloo in 1960, it was not until the summer of 1961 that any serious interest was shown in the last one hundred percent steam worked main lines from Waterloo to Salisbury and Exeter and to Bournemouth and Weymouth. Even then my time was mainly spent on the lineside, photographing the constant procession of steam hauled trains at locations within cycling distance of my home in Shirley, near Croydon. Serious train timing was only possible when travelling with a friend who owned a stop watch and until 1964 was confined mainly to Southern rail rovers, both the Area two-day tickets and the weekly £5 all system variety. This, together with the avid scrutiny of the various railway periodicals and Ian Allan publications, resulted in the acquisition of a reasonable knowledge of the routes, trains and locomotives used. My first log of train running which can be relied on as being reasonably accurate was timed in 1960 and appropriately was a run from Waterloo to Woking on Saturday 6th August 1960 behind H15 class 4-6-0 No.30491.

By 1964 I was spending more time out with my newly bought stop watch and also by then learning which drivers to seek after for good runs and I enjoyed my first footplate ride in April that year. Fraternising with like-minded enthusiasts also helped in gaining knowledge of what the future held for steam, and not all news was good as it became clear that the takeover of the lines west of Salisbury by the Western Region would mean the end of the fastest steam hauled train, the *Atlantic Coast Express*. At that time it had the only mile a minute timings of any steam hauled train in the UK and was the subject of much of my attention during the spring and summer of 1964. Also in September 1964 the Government

gave the go-ahead for electrification of the line through to Bournemouth via Basingstoke and Southampton which was due to be completed by June 1967. This announcement introduced a new sense of urgency into proceedings and I was determined to maximise the mileages travelled behind as many different engines as possible and to seek out the best drivers with the aim of recording the top performances. I was not alone in this and so gradually a small group of like-minded enthusiasts emerged who between them managed to record a vast number of high quality runs behind the ever dwindling steam locomotive fleet. As the number of steam worked trains diminished it is doubtful if many good runs went unrecorded and one of the problems I have had is choosing which runs to include and how to present them in a way which does not disrupt and overwhelm the flow of the script, but instead complements it. The solution was to describe all the best runs within the text and show the logs of the very best in the main Appendix in tabulated form. A separate publication, *Southern Steam Twilight-Supplement* is available setting out all the 400 approximately runs covered in full tabulated form, together with more photos and script. This is being printed and despatched to order by CreateSpace at Amazon.

Many of us worked for the railway at that time and so the cost of travelling around was a lot less than those who had none of the privileges which that gave. Then there was the time element of having to buy tickets for each journey and I got round this by having a season ticket which covered the core part of the route from Waterloo to Bournemouth, though trips on the remaining steam hauled trains to Salisbury required add-on tickets to be bought.

My season ticket was actually valid from

Elmers End, then my home station and I remember being stopped at Charing Cross one day where my ticket was carefully scrutinised by one of an inspection team, who muttered 'well covered but not good enough' and charged me 2d (two old pennies) excess from Waterloo East! There was, though, a culture amongst some of the enthusiasts to regard chasing after steam as not to be a genuine journey and therefore a reluctance to buy a ticket for each trip. This practice involved evading the army of travelling ticket inspectors and was known as 'nethering'. It worked a lot of the time but some of the inspectors, especially the more senior men (known as 'Golden G's':- G=Gripper) were wise to what was happening and some of the miscreants were caught. Other inspectors became very well known to us and one who stands out in the memory was of Asian extraction and who we fondly called 'Pundit' (Nehru). He was a very cheerful character who would throw open the compartment door and gleefully ask us what we were up to on that particular day.

Inevitably various groups of enthusiasts formed centred around their main areas of interest and they tended to travel together or at least on the same trains depending often on what the 'fast' drivers were working. Some groups were known by nicknames such as 'The Reading Mob' or the 'Gresleyites', neither of which needs much explaining. My 'group' were the died-in-the-wool Southern or Bulleid fans who really formed the nucleus of those closest to the action and whose enthusiasm bordered at times on fanatical, especially towards the end when every spare minute was spent recording proceedings and travelling behind the remaining locomotives. After Nine Elms men took over the up Weymouth fast train due at Waterloo at 8.40 pm, later 8.51 pm this train became almost a Mecca and many of the best runs were

Some of our group on the Club Train, the 8.51 pm arrival at Waterloo , on 11th February 1967. From the left, standing Roger Price, Paul Rowe, John Clifford and Bryan Benn. Seated Keith Farr, Tony Leaver. Alan Heyes, Les Kent, David (Squire) Huntley, John Braybrook, Graham Clark and John Evans. *John Tiley*

Maunsell U class 2-6-0 No. 31806 at Bournemouth Central with The Mogul Train, the 6.51 pm to Woking. *Author*

recorded on it. In theory we had to travel down on the 4.35 pm from Waterloo in order to be at Southampton in time to catch it at 7.16 pm as the 5.30 pm down, also a Nine Elms duty, would not have connected as it did not arrive until 7.15 pm (7.25 pm after 14th June 1965), but in practice sometimes it did and on more than one occasion the stopping time of the 5.30 pm down train was recorded after the departure time of the 7.16 pm up train! This involved practices which today would be impossible and meant a dash across the footbridge to board the already moving up train having jumped off the still moving down train. One such occasion was on 9th June 1965, during the 'Race to Basingstoke' week. The 8.51 arrival became known as 'The Club Train' and the picture shows some of the group on it on 11th February 1967. It was not always like that, and what I regard as my best 100 mph behind steam, with No. 35028 *Clan Line,* was on a cold damp December night when only a few of us were present (12th December 1966). Other trains almost became institutions as

well, notably the 'Mogul train' and also the last Weymouth, the former because it was the last regular booked turn for one of Maunsell's fine 2-6-0s until the timetable change in June 1965. It also provided a steam hauled alternative to the 'Club Train' and the last Weymouth especially on the evenings when I caught the 6.30 pm down or if the 5.30 pm down did not connect with the 'Club Train'. The latter because it stayed steam hauled to the end and because it provided many of the best performances including the highest speed at Roundwood summit and the fastest known speed with Southern steam. The 'Mogul Train' provided the opportunity for drivers from Guildford shed to make sure that their colleagues at Nine Elms did not get it all their own way in the speed stakes and for a while in May 1967 the battle was on to see who could set the fastest time from Basingstoke to Hook start to stop. This is discussed in more detail in Chapter Six. By then of course the Maunsell Moguls had all gone but during their long reign on this train, the 6.51 pm from Bournemouth to Woking, they gave me many runs, of which the extract shown in the log is typical. Table 1 – *See page 19.*

The last Weymouth though was the train which perhaps attracted the most attention as apart from a short time at the beginning of 1967 it stayed steam to the end. Its 6.30 pm (later 6.15 pm) departure from Weymouth enabled even those working until quite late to catch it somewhere en route and for most this was a decision made based on which Nine Elms driver was booked to work the train. Many of the best runs are discussed later in the book but here is one perhaps more typical of the day to day running on this train in 1965. It was in fact the same night as the run from Eastleigh on the 'Mogul Train' shown above. The driver, Fred Prickett was a true engineman and a lovely person who always had time to talk to us. Table 2 – *See page 20.* We had gone down that evening on the 6.30 pm from Waterloo behind one of my favourite engines, No.34037 *Clovelly.* This was also a good run as the train was booked for Merchant Navy haulage but Bournemouth driver Hardy turned in a competent performance keeping time with the 12 coach, 435 ton load reaching the first stop at Winchester in 69 minutes 49 seconds from Waterloo or 65 minutes net for the 46.55 miles with a maximum speed of 84 mph past Wallers Ash after a very good minimum speed of 61 mph at Wootton from 68 mph at Basingstoke.

The dedication and enthusiasm manifest itself in different ways. My own aim, apart from being on the best runs, was to record the highest mileage possible behind Bulleid pacifics and inevitably this led to some engines and indeed drivers becoming favourites. Others, like my brother Bryan, decided to try for the highest mileage in a week behind steam and after he had spent much of the last part of the summer term at school poring over the timetable, had worked out that 5,000 miles behind steam within a week was attainable. This was only possible by travelling day and night, making use of the night time paper and mail trains most of which carried passenger coaches and enabled continuous travel by changing trains

and direction in the middle of the night. This resulted in extreme tiredness through lack of proper rest and of course detailed recording of train running became secondary. On part of his 5,000 mile attempt he was accompanied by Paul Rowe and I remember that we met them on an up train at Basingstoke one day and had to restrain Paul, fully attired in overcoat with bag over shoulder, from disembarking as he insisted that we were at Waterloo and he had to get off to catch another train! This sort of behaviour was referred to as 'Rover Rot'. Bryan takes up the story of the 5,000 miles in a week:-

'One of the great pleasures of an approaching summer term end was the reducing level of homework allowing the time to be more usefully employed planning what steam trips could be undertaken over Southern Region metals during the lengthy holiday. Although the word 'holiday' was perhaps a bit of a misnomer in my case as for 1965 I would be utilising three of those wonderful week long £5 Southern Region Rail Rovers, paid for by working alternate weeks at the garage managed by dad. Always looking for something different and with others talking of having done close to 4,000 miles of steam haulage in a week utilising those rovers, I had found that, even with the much slower schedules now in force due to the Bournemouth line electrification, it was just possible to get to 5,000 miles. So late on the evening of Saturday 24th July I was on the last up train from Elmers End to Waterloo clutching a small and already battered case filled with some changes of clothes, a few packs of sandwiches made by mum along with notebook, pens, stopwatch and of course the vital SW division timetable. Complete with hand written insert detailing the trains I would need to catch for my continuous seven days and seven nights of steam haulage. Oh, and a carton of milk so thoughtfully secreted into a tight corner of the case by mum. More of that later on!

My plan was to time as many of the runs as possible, grabbing sleep mainly on the up mail train due into Waterloo each morning at 3.48 am. That was some way off as I boarded the 2.25 am paper train to start my 5,000 mile attempt, which being a Sunday, meant a non standard schedule for the day compared with the fixed routine I would follow for the weekdays. I left that train at New Milton to catch an up local to Eastleigh, then another to Woking before finally arriving at Waterloo in time to catch the 8.30 am back to Southampton. That started me off on the 'fast trains' that would form the vast bulk of my schedule, although being forced to stick to a fixed schedule meant I was unable to pick and choose which crews I timed runs behind. With the result that I timed seven days of mainly uninteresting and often quite boring runs. Good for the 5,000 mile target and for getting sleep, but not much in the way of excitement. That fixed schedule started after chasing the Sunday service to get as many miles as possible ending on the up mail into Waterloo at 3.48 am on Monday morning. Then it was five days of the 5.30 am Waterloo to Basingstoke, returning on the 7.05 am for an eight minute connection onto the 8.30 am Weymouth 'express'. But far from a true express as I only once risked the tight connection at Dorchester due to late running, catching the 11.30 am ex Weymouth at Wareham instead. Up for the 3.30 pm Waterloo to Bournemouth to catch the 5.35 pm Weymouth which got me nicely onto the 9.20 pm back down. New Milton should have been fine for the turnaround onto the up mail but most nights Brockenhurst was the safe option: presumably the Bournemouth crews had no incentive to run to time as the railway club and a cold beer would be shut regardless of when they got home. So overtime seemed to be their preferred option.

Most sleep was on the up mail, but far from enough meaning a steady deterioration into severe 'rover rot' as the week progressed, giving such highlights as leaving my battered and by now very smelly case behind at least once on a train just left - resulting in a panic stricken rush back to collect it. That smell got worse and worse, my initial assumption being that it was linked to the reason I always got a window seat with a space next to it as minimal washing in the toilets took its toll. That eventually forced me to decide to change my underwear. Which I had to abort, finding the smell had come from mum's packed milk carton which had burst open and was making a very rich cheese nestled in amongst my spare pants - ably helped by the rocking motion of the train. Don appeared from time to time to check I was still on schedule for the 5,000 miles, which I was monitoring very carefully, especially as I had those two early turn-arounds each day to cope with. And then he also checked on more trivial matters such as me being still alive and needing a top-up on mum's sandwiches. With further milk cartons politely declined! Other than those sarnies, my staple diet was pork pies from station buffets and some vile sparkling lime drink that was available from a dispenser at such as Waterloo. With hindsight it did mean I was at least getting one of my 'five a day'. Lack of drink and resulting dehydration was probably equally responsible with tiredness for 'rover rot' which on one day I thought had reached terminal level as an LMR Black 5 4-6-0 hauled the 11.30 am Weymouth into Wareham were I was waiting for the train. But no, one was down there for a short time and I got miles behind it. Miles that contributed to a week that ended with a BR Standard class 5 hauling me up from Brockenhurst to Waterloo on the 6.30 pm ex Weymouth, and a total of 5,020 miles for that exhausting week.

Exhausting it may have been, and with very few decent runs but I must have caught the bug as I did two more week long rovers during those summer holidays with a week's work in between to pay for them. I kept away from a full seven days continuous travel again but with just a couple of nights at home for each rover they still netted 4168 and 4171 miles respectively, gaining me in excess of 13,000 miles of steam in three weeks for a total of around £15. Nor perhaps what the marketing department of the old SR had intended when they introduced those tickets. Was it all worth the effort? Why yes. But not until 50 years later when Don asked me to right this short report on it!'

There were more civilised interludes though, such as the frequent visits to 'The Lancaster Grill' outside Waterloo station for sustenance at this seemingly ever open cafe, now replaced by a group of bus stops. And who could forget the buffet on the up side at Southampton Central where the large pasties were consumed accompanied by copious quantities of beer by those so inclined. After May 1965 the trick was to be able to drink a pint in 8.6 seconds,

this being the time that No. 35005 took to cover its fastest quarter mile on the night of 15th May. And then there was the Long Bar at Waterloo which may have been the reason why the last Weymouth due in at 10.56 pm was rarely late and often early, as the bar closed at 11 pm. This explained why the relief crew were often in charge of the engine by the time we had walked to the front of the train as the men who had brought us up from Southampton had disappeared at high speed! The slightly idiosyncratic tendencies of some of us were also manifest in other ways. One of our group decided that the tiny LSWR mileposts were too small to be seen properly, especially at night and so he walked the track from Brookwood to Basingstoke painting them white and at the same time daubing some of the over bridges near Winchfield with the exhortation 'In the roof', referring to the position of the engine regulator needed for optimum performance.

Others became obsessed with riding on the footplate and although my own mileage in that respect was reasonable and some is shown in Chapter Seven, it was nothing compared to some. This element became more prevalent as the end approached and there are some hair raising (literally) stories of what happened. One night a member of our group was travelling on the footplate of the engine hauling the last Weymouth, the 10.56 pm arrival at Waterloo, which was steam hauled to the end and his face was seriously burned when the engine slipped on wet rails at Roundwood summit during the course of a record attempt causing a blow back. This was of course hushed up as nearly all the footplate riding was unofficial. Other occasions were less serious and a little story from another of our group, Les Kent, is quite amusing. The engine was No. 34052 *Lord Dowding* working the 5.09 pm Waterloo to Basingstoke semi fast commuter train on 8th May 1967 with Jim Evans driving and Graham Pack

8th May 1967. Jim Evans on the footplate of No. 34052 *Lord Dowding* on the 5.09 pm to Basingstoke at Waterloo, talking to Les Kent. *Author*

On 8th May 1967, the evening of Les Kent's ride on the 5.09pm down with Jim Evans, some of the group returned to Waterloo behind No. 34037 *Clovelly* on the 7.32 pm Basingstoke to Waterloo. Here we see, from the left Andrew (Clackers) Clark, Alan (Nobby) Heyes, Les (Lurch) Kent, John (Shunter) Braybrook, Bob (Doze) Thompson, Richard (Joe) Jollife and George from Cardiff at Waterloo. No. 34037 lasted until the end of steam. *Author*

firing. Les was invited up onto the footplate at Farnborough and Les continues:

'Jim threw me his rag and told me I was driving to Basingstoke! He asked me if I could stop at Winchfield with the cab positioned under the footbridge. Not sure why but with a great deal of luck I managed it. Then all was revealed when he told me to look up. A slatted footbridge with all those young ladies returning home after a day at the office!! Great days.'

Most of the group returned to Waterloo with the same crew on the 6.38 pm from Salisbury semi fast which had No. 34037 *Clovelly* on eight coaches and three vans. Jim Evans ran up from Basingstoke to Waterloo in an overall time of just over 54 minutes for the 47.8 miles including a stop at Woking, arriving nearly seven minutes early after doing 81 mph at Hersham and running

in from Clapham Junction in just six minutes 15 seconds with 61 mph at Queens Road, a typical Jim Evans finish. No 34037 lasted until the end of steam. On another occasion when the much liked John 'Boy' Gaffney also known as 'The New Cross Lip' invited Les up onto the footplate 5.09 pm down. The train overshot the platform at Fleet leading to a verbal altercation with a stockbroker type in the front coach, which was non corridor stock. He was invited to jump down and walk back to the platform rather than the train being reversed, to which the city gent exclaimed 'I'll swing for you'. In view of what Gaffney's response was, we assumed that he had not yet been for his customer care training! John Gaffney was the only driver to give me a 100 mph run with a Bulled pacific in original condition. Les has many anecdotes and another is set out below in his own words:

Les Kent at the regulator of a Bulleid pacific. *Les Kent collection.*

Brian Smith on the footplate of West Country class pacific No.34015 *Exmouth* at Southampton Central on the 8.35 am Waterloo to Bournemouth on 14th September 1966. *Terry Jackson*

30th March 1966. Brian Smith with some of us at Basingstoke in front of No. 34032 *Camelford* **which had worked the 6 pm from Waterloo with driver John 'Boy' Gaffney. From the left:- John Evans, Paul Rowe, Les Kent, Brian Smith, Terry Jackson and Peter Trapp.** *Author*

'Pete Gyles of Nine Elms lived close to me in Balham so I had quite a few rides with him. On one occasion I was in the station buffet at Southampton waiting for the 7.15 pm nonstop to Waterloo. It duly arrived with 34001. John Braybrook and I boarded the loco and off we set. After a few moments I looked round but could not see the fireman. I enquired as to where he was and Pete said he was travelling in the train!! John and myself managed to fire 'ok' with a maximum of 78mph and no stop for a blow up!

The other one with him which came to light was I think one Sunday evening. A footplate run on, I think, the 17.00 ex Waterloo with a Warship to Salisbury. The return was the Seaton Jnc to Vauxhall Milk tanks. D6527. We set off at a reasonable speed without incident. I had a drive in the pitch black with dim semaphore signals. On approach to Andover Junction Pete said 'well , I am going for a coffee now with the guard in the back cab', leaving John and myself alone. Eventually he returned when we were approaching Basingstoke. Luckily we managed to read all the signals correctly!'

Les Kent was probably the one amongst us who identified most with the footplate crews and who enjoyed many miles on the footplate. If you needed any 'gen' on which train to go for then it was always a safe bet to ask Les. Recently he wrote to me that: 'Those few years we had were, apart from the family, the best of my life. What a fantastic time we had. I was very lucky in working at Waterloo so being able to chat up the Nine Elms crews. Hopefully I did my small bit to help with the fine performances we experienced.' Many of us around at that time would I am sure agree with those sentiments. This was <u>our</u> railway, they were <u>our</u> steam locomotives; they were <u>our</u> trains and <u>our</u> engine crews. This was <u>our</u> time and how lucky we were to have lived at the right time to have been there.

During 1965 I became aware of somebody else who was often seen on the footplate especially on the best runs with the fast drivers. He was known as 'that man from Clapham', one Brian Smith, who had an official role on the railway as a member of the Loco Testing Section at Brighton. This section was responsible for steam loco problems that were either causing issues in maintenance or steaming problems on the road. The former was certainly important in the 1950's, but not a big problem in the 1960's as steam was on the way out. The ability to raise steam was an issue to ensure trains as far as possible ran to time. Thus Brian was around a lot of the time and, as time went by, he became a friend and the source of much useful information on the drivers and enginemen and was the one who drove us home the night of Gordon Hooper's epic run on the 9.20 pm down on 15th May 1965 (see Chapter Four). He is seen in the photo of some of the group at Basingstoke. Others worked in the diagram

office at Wimbledon and thus were able to supply information on forthcoming changes to engine workings; very useful to us train timers. Also, in 1966 I worked in the Materials and Progressing section at Waterloo moving the stocks of spares around between depots in order to keep the ever declining steam fleet mobile. This was a thankless task as trade suppliers either no longer stocked what we wanted or did not want to know, so we became very reliant on what the stores clerks at the depots had hidden away. Small things like injector cones could be moved around by train, sometimes requiring my assistance at Waterloo and other things could be given to engine crews or moved by lorry. If all else failed then I would phone Freddie Butcher at Salisbury who could nearly always find what we wanted. He would answer the phone: 'Hub of the Universe-how can I help'! On such things and on so few people in that office at Waterloo and in the remaining steam sheds did the operation of steam hauled trains during those last years depend. Salisbury always looked after their engines and even found time to clean

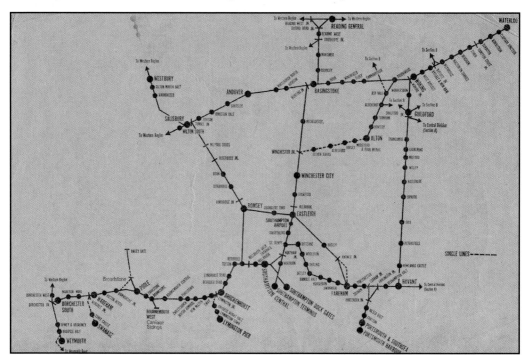

Map of South Western Division Main Lines

them. That tradition of care continues to this day as the class 159 diesel fleet allocated there is the most reliable of its type anywhere on the rail network. Working at Waterloo enabled me to see such things as Working Timetables, Engine Diagrams and Special Traffic notices, some of which survive in my archives today and which were very useful when planning which trains to catch and which engines to follow. Appendix A shows the complete set of the final engine diagrams which applied from 12th June 1967 together with a note of the engines which worked each diagram for selected days, where I was able to gain this information from observation or from information gleaned from others. It is probably the most comprehensive summary of what happened over those last four weeks in existence. The next chapter discusses the engines and their work over those last few years and the image shows the lines over which they worked.

Tables

Table 1

EASTLEIGH TO BASINGSTOKE

Date	29th March 1965	
Train	651 pm Bournemouth to Woking	
Loco	Maunsell U class 2-6-0 No. 31809	
Load	3 coaches and 2 vans, 145 tons tare, 155 tons gross	
Recorder	DB	

	miles	sched	mins	secs		speed
Eastleigh	0.00	0.00	00	00		
Allbrook Box	0.86		02	17		36
Shawford	3.81		06	57		41
Shawford Jct	4.66		08	05		44
St Cross	5.70		09	32		48½
Winchester	6.95	12.00	11	41		
	0.00	0.00	00	00		
Winchester Jct	2.10	5.30	04	32		41
Wallers Ash Box	4.80		08	11		48½
Weston Box	6.30		10	00		51
Micheldever	8.43	15.30	13	11		
	0.00	0.00	00	00		
Roundwood Box	1.87		04	07		38
Waltham Box	2.97		05	44		50
Steventon Box	4.12		07	04		56½
Wootton Box	5.57		08	38		61/56½
Worting Jct	7.80	10.00	11	02		61
MP 49½	8.57		11	45		63
Basingstoke	10.42	14.00	13	58		
	depart 4 late arrive 1 late					

Table 2

BASINGSTOKE TO WATERLOO

Date	29th March 1965
Train	630 pm Weymouth to Waterloo
Loco	Rebuilt West Country Class 4-6-2 No.34098 *Templecombe*
Load	4 coaches and 7 vans, 297 tons tare, 325 tons gross
Crew	Fred Prickett Nine Elms MPD
Recorder	DB

	miles	sched	mins	secs		speed
Basingstoke	0.00	0.00	00	00		
Newnham Siding	4.10		05	56		63
Hook	5.59		07	23		66
Winchfield	7.92		09	34		68/73
Fleet	11.27		12	25		72/75
Farnborough	14.55		15	07		74½
Sturt Lane	15.60		15	58		75½
MP 31	16.75		16	58		75
Pirbright Jct	18.26		18	05		80
Brookwood	19.76		19	17		82½
Woking Jct	23.00		22	22		49* sigs/56
Woking	23.46	26.00	23	19		
	0.00	0.00	00	00		
West Byfleet	2.61		04	55		56
Byfleet & New Haw	3.89		06	13		64
Weybridge	5.14		07	29		65/63
Walton	7.21		09	20		70½
Hersham	8.38		10	17		75
Esher	9.90		11	36		76
Hampton Court Jct.	10.95	12.00	12	27		77
Surbiton	12.25		13	32		74
Berrylands	13.31		14	27		71
New Malden	14.51		15	33		64
Raynes Park	15.65		16	39		63½
Wimbledon	17.10		17	57		66
Earlsfield	18.71		19	29		69
Clapham Junction	20.36	22.00	21	14		43*
Queens Road	21.48		23	19		25* tsr
Vauxhall	22.98		25	53		39/24* sigs
Waterloo	24.29	29.00	29	47		
						* brakes
	net time Woking to Waterloo 28 mins					
	Basingstoke 5 late, Waterloo 1 late.					

CHAPTER TWO
THE ENGINES

In this chapter I am going to look at the engines which survived into those last few years, their characteristics, shed allocations and the work they did. Although the good performances in later chapters were primarily produced by Bulleid's pacifics, and indeed some may think that this book should just be about them, other classes played their part. In particular the sturdy BR Standard Class 5 4-6-0s turned in some excellent runs even when in very poor condition. At times it was a case of the engine crew taking one of these on a turn booked for a Bulleid pacific or the train didn't run!

In the Spring of 1965 some 285 locomotives were still on the books from no less than fourteen different classes and allocated to nine motive power depots. This compares with the 565 engines at the end of 1962, after the purge of ex Southern Railway types. These were at Nine Elms, Feltham, Guildford, Eastleigh, Salisbury, Bournemouth, Weymouth, Redhill and Ryde (Isle of Wight). The Southern Region sheds with number code 72 at Yeovil Town and Exmouth Junction had been transferred to the Western Region in 1963 and although some steam hauled trains ran west of Salisbury in the summer of 1965 they used engines from Southern sheds which were serviced on the Western Region. The normal service from Waterloo to Salisbury and Exeter was worked by Western Region Warship class diesel hydraulics, but there were occasional steam substitutions as on 19th April 1965 when Bulleid West Country class pacific No. 34007 *Wadebridge* worked the 9 am from Waterloo, at least as far as Salisbury. There were still some survivors from pre Second World War designs by Maunsell in the form of S15 class 4-6-0s and N and U class 2-6-0s plus of course the venerable Adams 1889 built O2 Class 0-4-4 tanks on the Isle of Wight. Redhill remained open to provide BR Standard Class 4 2-6-4 tanks for remaining work on freight and parcels trains and for working the line from Tunbridge Wells to Eastbourne via Hailsham until it closed on 13th June 1965, though steam hauled passenger services on the lines between Tonbridge and Guildford finished on 3rd January 1965. On 2nd

On 11th December 1965, near to the end of its working life, Maunsell U Class 2-6-0 No 31809 takes water at Basingstoke with a down freight. The engine was withdrawn in January 1966 so this may have been its last working. *Author*

May 1965 BR Standard Class 4 tanks 80068 and 80094 were noted at Redhill as was Maunsell U Class 2-6-0 No. 31791. Other than those two exceptions all the sheds were associated with the South Western Division lines out of Waterloo. In addition until the end of 1965 ex GWR Hall Class 4-6-0s from Banbury or Oxford sheds worked through to Bournemouth on the daily train from YorkSometimes LMS Black 5s also appeared on this train and this was maybe the reason that No. 44915 from Rugby shed found itself purloined to work the 7.05 am from Basingstoke to Waterloo and 3.35 pm Waterloo to Bournemouth on 19th April 1965. The table

BR Standard Class 4 2-6-0 No. 76016 from Eastleigh shed stands at Southampton Central with the 1.09 pm Bournemouth West to Eastleigh stopping train on Sunday 30th June 1963. Hampshire DEMUs on services to and from Portsmouth can be seen, although the BR Class 4s continued to work the Portsmouth to Cardiff services until June 1965. *Author*

shows the allocation of Southern locomotives by shed in May 1965. Table 3 – *See page 55.*

1965 was the last year of the old timetable before extra time was added to the steam worked main line services in June for electrification work. It was also the last year when the Maunsell U and N Class 2-6-0 Moguls had any booked work. This was on the 6.51 pm Bournemouth to Woking 'Mogul Train', though some lasted into 1966. My last recorded run on that train with a Maunsell Mogul was with No. 31873 on 8th June 1965. Table 4 – *See page 56.* The Maunsell engines were also noted on 27th and 29th March (31809), 5th April (31803), 21st April (31866), 25th May (31873) and 26th May (31639). They also appeared on other trains from time to time, notably the 7.54 pm Waterloo to Basingstoke semi-fast service which could indeed produce almost anything and on 19th May No. 31873 appeared and turned in a half decent performance. Table 6 – *See page 57.* N class No.31858 was also turned out for this train on 23rd February but it was in appalling condition and struggled throughout with no higher speed than 46 mph and lost no less than 21 minutes to Basingstoke. The remaining S15 class 4-6-0s had all been withdrawn by the

end of the year. In terms of number of engines allocated, perhaps surprisingly Eastleigh shed dominated the scene with the mighty Nine Elms only having 36 allocated, the same number as Bournemouth. Eastleigh shed provided the BR Standard Class 4 2-6-0s in the 76xxx series for the inter Regional services from Portsmouth to Cardiff until it was dieselised from 14th June 1965 and these engines also worked local services to and from Bournemouth. The train running log shows a run from 1963 on the same day as the photograph was taken, though with No. 76018 rather than No. 76016. Table 8 – *See page 58.* Salisbury was home to just 24 engines, though 19 were Bulleid light Pacifics, including some of the best maintained. Weymouth had the lion's share of the Merchant Navy pacifics with the rest at Bournemouth and none at Nine Elms which meant that men from the London shed always worked the Merchant Navy duties on a 'Merchant' from one of the other two sheds. This carried on until the final reallocation of the remaining Merchant Navies to Nine Elms when Weymouth shed was downgraded to a stabling point in April 1967. It was of course the Bulleid pacifics which hauled most of the main line expresses and, ably supported by

Weymouth based Merchant Navy Class 4-6-2 No. 35005 *Canadian Pacific* **at Eastleigh on 23rd May 1965, just eight days after its record breaking run from Waterloo to Basingstoke and after reaching 105 mph down Roundwood bank.** *Terry Jackson*

The elusive Merchant Navy No. 35015 *Rotterdam Lloyd* in a busy scene passing Basingstoke on 1st July 1963 with the 7.20 am Bournemouth West to Waterloo . This was the only Merchant Navy that I didn't get hauled by. *Author*

the BR Standard Class 5s, produced the bulk of the runs described in Chapters Four, Five and Six, including some epic performances in 1965 before the timetables changed in June. Immediately after the extra time had been added to the schedules work began to upgrade the main line for the new electric services and this resulted in the end, for the time being at least, of the very fast start to stop times being achieved by steam. There was also a decline in operating standards to the extent that on the really bad days I gave up timing and resorted to some linesiding to watch the passing scene as in 1965 and the early part of 1966 nearly all Bournemouth line trains to and from Waterloo were still steam hauled. The proceedings on one such day at Basingstoke are shown in Table 10 – *See page 59*. and it can be seen just

how busy it was with 30 steam movements in less than four hours, even though I did not record all trains due to moving locations between the station and the over bridge on the London side.

Note how relatively good timekeeping was and the incursion by Class 33 diesels in the summer of 1965, though one of their turns was being covered by a BR Standard Class 2-6-0, which was doing rather well running two minutes early.

I had ended up at Basingstoke after trying the 9.30 am down with 'Spot' King, Nine Elms top link on Rebuilt West Country No. 34097 *Holsworthy* with 12 coaches for 435 tons, which had struggled a bit barely reaching 60 mph before Woking and then decamping onto the 9.54 am semi-fast behind BR Standard class 5 No. 73080 which proved to be much better,

Basingstoke Saturday 10th July 1965. After being stopped by signals by the engine shed at the country end of the station, rebuilt Battle of Britain class pacific No. 34090 *Sir Eustace Missenden, Southern Railway* accelerates vigorously towards London with the 12 noon Bournemouth West to Waterloo. *Author*

Basingstoke Saturday 10th July 1965. MN pacific No. 35010 *Blue Star* in very poor condition heads the 1.30 pm Waterloo to Weymouth on the slow line approaching its stop running five minutes early. The Bournemouth crew must have done well with the 12 coach load even on the revised schedules which applied from June that year. Surprisingly this engine lasted until September 1966. Note the chalked on smokebox number and WR Grange Class No. 6870 *Bodicote Grange* on the left waiting to take over the late running 1.11pm Portsmouth Harbour to Wolverhampton Low Level. *Author*

Standing in for the booked Merchant Navy, rebuilt Battle of Britain class light pacific No. 34050 *Royal Observer Corps* approaches Basingstoke with the down Bournemouth Belle on Saturday 10th July 1965. *Author*

regaining all but one minute of a 12 minute late departure from Woking, an altogether excellent performance with an unknown Nine Elms crew.

By January 1966 the active steam fleet was down to 220 locomotives with Eastleigh losing the most but Bournemouth having a net gain of just one and Guildford remaining almost static though losing nearly half of its Maunsell Moguls and its sole USA Class 0-6-0 tank in favour of 13 Standard class 5 4-6-0s. By then Redhill shed had closed. Table 18 – *See page 65.* At the beginning of 1966 nearly all trains between Waterloo, Southampton, Bournemouth and Weymouth were steam worked with the Merchant Navy pacifics in theory anyway covering the most demanding turns, though since the schedules had been slowed in June 1965 for electrification work, little distinction appears to have been made between these and the Bulleid light pacifics. The table shows the principle dimensions of the two classes.

Table 7 – *See page 57.*

All 30 of the Merchant Navy pacifics had of course been rebuilt by this time as had 60 of the

Merchant Navy pacific No. 35005 *Canadian Pacific* on shed at Eastleigh on 23rd May 1965 after working a Warwickshire Railway Society special from Waterloo. 35005 reached 105 mph on the 9.20 pm from Waterloo on 15th May 1965. *Mike Hodges*

Rebuilt Merchant Navy Class 4-6-2 No. 35023 *Holland Afrika Line* at Southampton on 17th October 1964 hauling the 10.30 am Waterloo to Weymouth. No. 35023 was one of the engines to reach 100 mph, in 1966. *John Tiley*

On 10th October 1964 No. 35022 *Holland America Line* on an up West of England express at Berrylands. *John Tiley*

110 light pacifics and the rebuilt engines were very handsome locomotives. 16 Merchant Navy pacifics survived to the beginning of 1966, seven at Bournemouth and nine at Weymouth.

The rebuilt engines were also much easier to maintain and drive as two of the problematical original features, the oil bath containing Bulleid's valve gear and the ratchet reversing lever had been abandoned in favour of more conventional designs. Nevertheless there were many, myself included, who thought that the unconverted engines were freer running and they were still good looking engines. The rebuilt engines never quite seemed to have the characteristic of the original engines, which when accelerating on favourable gradients seemed simply to sail effortlessly away. They could also be the equal of the rebuilt engines climbing banks, and perhaps bettered them, though the evidence for this is inconclusive. This partly depended on the driver being able to master the cut off lever. I can clearly remember asking Dave Parsons on the footplate of No. 34006 *Bude* what the cut off was. His reply

was that it showed 20% but could actually be anywhere between 15% and 30%. However, he had left it where the lever settled and that would be good enough to get us up to 100 mph as the engine sounded right! At the beginning of 1966, of the 54 remaining light pacifics, 14 were still in their original form and these were: 34002, 34006, 34015, 34019, 34023, 34038, 34041, 34057, 34064, 34066, 34076, 34079, 34086 and 34102. No. 34064 *Fighter Command* was fitted with a Giesl ejector in 1962 and many of the drivers, including Gordon Hooper, thought that this engine was almost equal to a Merchant Navy. Certainly some of the performances supported this view. The log shows part of a run on the 9.30 am down. It was a good clean start from Woking with no slipping and whilst not exceptional is noteworthy for the rapid acceleration from Brookwood to the summit at Milepost 31 and also after Hook where the free running characteristics of the original pacifics is clearly shown. No. 34064 ran well all the way to Bournemouth and the Eastleigh crew maintained the good work of the Nine Elms men who took the train as far as Eastleigh. My notebook is full of comments such as 'good clean exhaust' and 'no slipping on the starts'.

Table 5 – *See page 56.*

All the principle main line trains were booked to be hauled by the Bulleid pacifics and the sample diagram sheets from those applying from 13th June 1966 show examples of the work that they performed.

At the beginning of 1966 there were 31 BR Standard Class 5 4-6-0 workhorses still in service, of which 22 were at Guildford and

Eastleigh. They covered secondary work on the main line and stepped in for Bulleid pacifics from time to time. Although best suited to lighter trains they could tackle anything and some of their epic performances are shown in later chapters. However they did well on the secondary expresses as this train running log from 1965 shows. The net time of 83 minutes would have been good enough to have kept the schedule of the two hour trains, which were all booked for Bulleid pacifics.

Table 11 – *See page 60.*

SOUTH WESTERN DIVISION – MONDAYS TO FRIDAYS.   18.

NOS. 230 to 233 NOT USED.

EASTLEIGH DUTY NO.234
7P/6F (West Country Class)
M.X. Off No.238

	Eastleigh Loco	04 45‖
xx	Eastleigh Mar. Yd.	05 23F
08 20	Bournemouth Ctl Gds	08 39‖
08 46	Bournemouth Loco	09 50‖
10 17	Branksome	10 18‖
10 19	Branksome Loop	10 50‖
10 51	Branksome	10 52E
11 00	Bournemouth Ctl	11 07P
14 17	Waterloo	15 07E
15 17	Clapham Jn	15 45‖
16 00	Nine Elms Loco	
	Stage for No.235	

EASTLEIGH MEN.
(1) 1st set on duty 03 45, work and relieved Bournemouth Loco home passenger.
BOURNEMOUTH MEN.
(2) Off No.238 perform requirements and work 09 50‖ and rlvd at Bournemouth Ctl. 11 05 rlve No.420 at 11 35 work and rlvd at 12 50.

WEYMOUTH MEN.
(3) Off No.430 assist requirements 08 50 to 09 50.NI
NINE ELMS MEN.
(4) Off No. 235 relieve at Bournemouth Central 11 05, work and relieved at Waterloo 14 16.
(5) Off No. 433 relieve at Waterloo 14 16 work and dispose, assist requirements No.385

EASTLEIGH DUTY NO.235
7P/6F (West Country Class)
M.O. Off No. 235 SUNDAY
M.X. Off No. 234

	Nine Elms Loco	07 35‖
07 48	Waterloo	08 10P
11 39	Weymouth Jn8	xx‖
xx	Weymouth Loco	15 50‖
xx	Weymouth Jn	16 23P
	(16 00 Quay)	
19 45	Waterloo	20 56E
21 06	Clapham Jn	21 35‖
21 50	Nine Elms Loco	
	Work No.236	

NINE ELMS MEN.
(1) 1st set on duty 06 30 work and relieved at Bournemouth Ctl. 10 33 relieve at No. 234 at 11 05 work and relieved at Waterloo 14 16.
WEYMOUTH MEN.
(2) Off No.430 relieved at Bournemouth Ctl 10 33 work and relieved in depot.
(3) 1st set on duty 14 40 work and relieved Southampton Ctl 1755; (FO from 27.5.66.) relieved No. 240 at 21 36 and work to depot (other dates) home as ordered.
EASTLEIGH MEN.
(4) 1st set on duty 16 45, pass to Souton Ctl, relieved at 17 51, work and rlvd at Waterloo at 19 45, pass to Clap Jn. relieve No.5 at 20 30 work, rlvd at Basingstoke at 22 30 and home pass.

NINE ELMS MEN.
(5) 2nd set on duty 15 40 (FX) dispose No. 239 (FO) rlve No. 254 in depot and assist requirements for 17 57‖ prepare and work No.240 and rlve at Waterloo 1935 other dates) as ordered (DAILY) Rlve this duty at Waterloo at 19 45 work and dispose.

SOUTH WESTERN DIVISION — MONDAYS TO FRIDAYS   44.

BOURNEMOUTH DUTY NO.383
8P (Merchant Navy Class)
Large Tender
MO — Off No.385 Sunday
MX — Off No.382

	Nine Elms Loco	09 59‖
10 12	Waterloo	10 30P
13 45	Weymouth	xx‖
xx	Weymouth Loco	16.50‖
16 55	Weymouth	17 30P
20 51	Waterloo	21 25
21 40	Nine Elms Loco	

Stable for No.384

BOURNEMOUTH DUTY NO.383 CONTINUED
NINE ELMS MEN
(1) 1st set on duty 08 54 work and relieved
at Waterloo 10 20 relieved No.430 at 11 02
work and dispose relieve No.103 in depot
at 14 00 work and relieved at Claphma Jn.
16 30.
(2) 2nd set — on duty 09 50 relieve at
Waterloo 10 20 work and relieved Bournemouth
Cen 12 45, relieve No.385 at 14 30, and
work Waterloo 17 10.

BOURNEMOUTH MEN
(3) 1st set — on duty 12 25 relieve at
12 45 work to Weymouth Loco prepare and work
No.276 16 00‖ and relieved at Bournemouth
Cen 18 45 to depot perform requirements and
work No.277 20 00‖ and relieved at Station
20 10.

WEYMOUTH MEN
(4) Off No.236 prepare for 16 50‖
(5) 1st set on duty 16 35 work and relieved
at Southampton Cen 19 14 relieve No.442 at
20 00 work and relieved in depot.

EASTLEIGH MEN
(6) 1st set — on duty 17 42 pass 18 12 via
St. Denys to Southampton Cen relieve at
19 14 work and relieved at Waterloo 20 51
home as ordered.

NINE ELMS MEN
(7) Off No.385 relieve at Waterloo 2051
work and dispose.

On 13th May 1965, when this duty was covered by Eastleigh men, BR Standard Class 5 No. 73110 brings the 6.09 pm from Waterloo into Basingstoke . *Author*

```
SOUTH WESTERN DIVISION      - MONDAYS TO FRIDAYS.               15.

GUILDFORD DUTY NO.161                GUILDFORD DUTY NO.161 (CONTD)
5 M.T. (standard)                    BASINGSTOKE MEN. (CONTD).
MX - Off No. 164                     (4) Off No. 313 assist requirements
01 35 (MX) Guildford Loco (B) 03 30   and work 07 40 relieved at station
03 53      Woking        04 32PV     08 20.
       (03 40 Waterloo)              SALISBURY MEN.
05 27      Basingstoke      xx       (6) 1st set on duty 06 24 pass 06 49
  xx       Basingstoke Loco 07 40    to Basingstoke relieve at 08 20, work
07 45      Barton Hill      xxE      and dispose, home as ordered.
  xx       Basingstoke      08 23P
09 42      Waterloo         09 55    GUILDFORD MEN.
10 10      Nine Elms Loco 17 32      (7) No. 5 prepare and work 17 32 and
      (COUPLED TO NO. 461)           relieved at Woking 18 43 home passenger
17 47      Waterloo         18 09P   (8) 1st set on duty 17 53 passenger to
19 28      Basingstoke      xx       Woking relieve at 18 43 work and rlvd
  xx       Basingstoke      22 40    Basingstoke 19 30, as ordered, relieve
  xx       Basingstoke               No. 276 at 21 10, work & dispose.
    C. Shunting 19 30 - 20 30
                21 30 - 22 35        BASINGSTOKE MEN.
                22 50 - 00 20        (9) Off No. 313 relieve at station at
                00 40 - 01 00        19 30 work and relieved in depot.
      Basingstoke      01 00         (10) (tues to Sat) Off No. 313 dispose.
01 05      Basingstoke Loco -
Stable No. 162
(B) - Convey men for No. 164.
GUILDFORD MEN.
(1) 1st set on duty 01 10 (MO) as    GUILDFORD DUTY NO.162
ordered, prepare (MX) perform        5 M.T. (Standard)
requirements, (DAILY) work, relieved MO - Off No. 162 Saturday.
at Woking at 04 23 pass, 04 32 to    MX - Off No. 161
Basingstoke, relieve D.M.M.U. at 07 00 BASINGSTOKE LOCO.
work 07 50 to Woking, relieved at 08 32 As ordered
& home pass.                         Work No. 163 next day.
BASINGSTOKE, MEN.
(2) Off No. 164, relieve at Woking
04 23, work and relieved in depot
(3) 1st set on duty 02 00, as ordered
relieve this duty in depot, perform
requirements for 07 40 prepare and
work No. 282 and relieved in depot
09 30.
```

An example of the work they did is shown in the diagram.

The BR Standard Class 4 4-6-0s did not seem to have a useful role and only 10 remained at the beginning of 1966, all at Eastleigh. Although they had specific work, five diagrams, they seemed to be used indiscriminately with the smaller BR Standard Class 4 2-6-0s. For instance, although the 'Mogul Train' was booked for a 75xxx Standard after the Maunsell engines were displaced, it was just as often worked by a 76xxx Standard in 1966, thus continuing the 'Mogul Train' tradition. They did not often appear on anything other than local trains, including the Waterloo to Basingstoke semi fast trains which were first stop Woking and they performed well on these. In May 1964 I timed the most extraordinary run behind No. 75072 with a young Nine Elms crew on the lightly loaded 1.54 pm from Waterloo. This run on a bank holiday Monday is believed to be the fastest ever time with steam from Waterloo to Woking start to stop. Table 13 – *See page 62.*

The smaller BR Standard Class 4 2-6-0s were more widespread with 26 remaining of which 14 were at Eastleigh. These engines covered trip work and local services to and from Bournemouth. They were good reliable engines and often strayed onto the semi fast trains to and from Waterloo. The run with 76066 found it somewhat overloaded on the 6.38 pm Salisbury to Waterloo, a train which by January 1967 should have been worked by a Nine Elms BR Standard Class 5 4-6-0, instead of a Salisbury based BR Standard Class 4 2-6-0. Table 14 – *See page 63.* Even more BR Standard Class 4 2-6-4

tanks remained, 33 in total spread out between all the depots except Guildford and Weymouth. They had a variety of duties including empty stock working to and from Waterloo, the postal workers trains between Clapham Junction and Kensington Olympia and the Lymington and Swanage branch trains, the latter until that line was turned over to DEMU working on 4th September 1966. They also worked a few local passenger trains in the Eastleigh area. Eight of the smaller BR Standard Class 3 2-6-2 tanks remained at Nine Elms for empty stock and trip working. The LM equivalent 2-6-2 tanks were by June 1966 restricted to Bournemouth and Weymouth from where they shared trip

On 18th May 1964 BR Standard Class 4 4-6-0 No. 75072 leaves Woking after its record breaking run from Waterloo. On the right fellow recorder and good friend John Evans records the scene. *Author*

SOUTH WESTERN DIVISION : MONDAYS TO FRIDAYS   32.

EASTLEIGH DUTY NO.276
4 MT (STANDARD) (75000 Class)
  MO Off No. 277 Saturday
  MX Off No. 273
    Bournemouth Loco 05 51‖
  (Coupled Trailing No. 434)
DAILY
05 53	Bournemouth Ctl	05 56‖
	(Coupled)	
06 11	Bournemouth West Jn. Up Line	06 16‖
06 19	Bournemouth W.Sdgs	06 48E
06 53	Branksome	07 01‖
07 02	Branksome Loop	07 19‖
07 20	Branksome	07 23E
07 31	Bournemouth Ctl	07 37P
09 02	Eastleigh	09 20‖
09 35	Southampton Terminus	10 12P
12 02	Bournemouth Ctl	13 08P
14 27	Weymouth	14 40‖
14 45	Weymouth Loco	16 00‖
16 05	Weymouth	16 47P
18 05	Bournemouth Ctl	18 51P
21 59	Woking	22 20‖
22 30	Guildford Loco Stable No. 277	

BOURNEMOUTH MEN
(1) 1st set on duty 04 51 work and relieved Bournemouth Central 12 03.

EASTLEIGH DUTY NO. 276 (CONT'D)

WEYMOUTH MEN
(2) Off No. 442 relieve at Bournemouth Ctl. 12 03 work and relieved in depot
BOURNEMOUTH MEN
(3) Off No. 383 prepare and work 16 00‖ and relieved at Bournemouth Ctl. 1845 to depot perform requirements and work No. 277 20 00‖ and relieved at Station 20 10.

EASTLEIGH MEN
(4) Off No. 277 relieve at 18 45 work and relieved at Eastleigh 20 21.
(5) 1st set on 17 00 as ordered dispose No.245 relieve this duty at 20 21 work and relieved at Basingstoke 21 10 relieve No. 9 at 21 36 work and berth and berth No. 24.

GUILDFORD MEN

(6) Off No. 161 relieve at Basingstoke 21 10 work and dispose.

Continued.....

On 19th September 1965 whilst waiting for the up Excursion at Winchester this Eastleigh based BR Standard Class 4 No. 76018 appeared at 6.29 pm with the 3.15 pm Parcels train from Waterloo to Eastleigh, comprising 17 vans including bogie stock, a heavy train for this moderately sized engine. The run on the up Excursion with No. 34042 included one of the best ever climbs to Roundwood and is included in Chapter Four. *Author*

SOUTH WESTERN DIVISION - MONDAYS TO FRIDAYS   29.

EASTLEIGH DUTY NO.271

4 M.T. (STANDARD)

MONDAYS ONLY

| | Eastleigh Loco | 01 25‖ |
| 01 30 | Eastleigh | 01 57PV |

MONDAYS EXCEPTED

Off No.271 previous day

	Eastleigh	
	S.Shunting 00 01 to 01 40	
	Eastleigh	01 57PV
(01 34	Southampton Ctl)	

DAILY

02 47	Portsmouth Hbr	03 05E
03 13	Fratton Yd (B)(G)	04 05‖
04 18	Havant	04 55V
05 05	Fratton (Turn)	05 46E
06 05	Fareham	06 30P
06 50	Eastleigh	07 05‖
07 10	Eastleigh Loco	10 20‖
xx	Eastleigh Mar.Yd	10 50F

MONDAYS, TUESDAY AND THURSDAYS

| 11 45 | Winchester City | 12 10‖ |
| 12 38 | Eastleigh Loco | 23 15‖ |

WEDNESDAYS AND FRIDAYS

11 45	Winchester City	12 15F
12 35	Micheldever	
	F.Shunting 13 00 to 14 00	
	Micheldever	14 15F
14 50	Eastleigh E.Yard	xx‖
xx	Eastleigh Loco	23 15‖
	C.Shunting 23 30 to 23 50	

WORK NO.271 NEXT DAY

(B)   Shunt own train
(G)   Convey Guard Fratton
       Station to Havant.

EASTLEIGH DUTY NO.271 (CONT'D)

EASTLEIGH MEN

(1)   1st Set (MO) - On duty 00 40 work
      and dispose.

(2)   (MX) Off No.271 previous day work and
      relieved 00 15 relieve No.238 at
      00 44 work and dispose (DRIVER), work
      No.347 from 04 15 to 06 00 (FIREMAN)
      ride on No.346 and NO.347 Duty engines.

(3)   2nd Set (FX) - On duty 23 45 relieve
      at 00 15 work and dispose.

(4)   3rd Set - On duty 09 35 work and
      dispose, to carr sidings relieve No.270
      at 16 50 work and dispose.

(5)   4th Set - On duty 22 30 prepare and
      work 23 15‖ and relieved at 00 15,
      relieve No.238 at 00 44 work and
      dispose ; (DRIVER) work No.347 from
      04 15 to 06 00 ; (FIREMAN) ride on
      No.346 and 347 duty engines.

NO.272 - NOT USED

In August 1966 No. 80085
sits at the buffer stops at
Swanage with a train from
Wareham. *Bob Randall*

SOUTH WESTERN DIVISION : MONDAYS TO FRIDAYS 2.

NINE ELMS DUTY NO. 100.
4 M.T.T. (STANDARD)
MONDAYS ONLY

	Nine Elms Loco	08 20‖
08 50	Clapham Jn	09 26M

TUESDAYS AND WEDNESDAYS.
Off No. 105.

	Nine Elms Loco	06 15‖
06 45	Clapham Jn	07 12E
07 22	Waterloo	08 01‖
08 11	Clapham Jn	09 26M

OTHER DATES.
Off No. 105

	Nine Elms Loco	08 20‖
08 50	Clapham Jn	09 26M

DAILY.

13 54	Waterloo	14 34E
14 45	Clapham Jn	15 47E
15 56	Waterloo	16 37‖
16 50	Nine Elms Loco	19 00‖
19 38	Walton-on-Thames	19 58V
	(via E.P.)	
21 15	Clapham Jn	22 30E
22 40	Waterloo	01 17‖
01 30	Nine Elms Loco	02 30‖
	Work No. 105.	

NINE ELMS DUTY NO. 100 (Continued).

NINE ELMS MEN.
(1) 1st set on duty 05 25 work and rlvd at Vauxhall 13 10.

(2) Off No. 434 rlve at Vauxhall 13 10 work and rlvd Clapham Jn. 14 45 rlve No. 101 at 14 55 work and rlvd in depot.

(3) 2nd set on duty 14 15 rlve at Clapham Jcn 14 50 work and rlvd at Clapham Jcn. 21 50.

(4) 3rd set on duty 21 20 rlve at Clapham Jcn 21 50 work and perform requirements No. 105 for 02 30‖, as ordered prepare No. 463 for 05 00‖

Continued..

SOUTH WESTERN DIVISION : MONDAYS TO FRIDAYS. 3.

NINE ELMS DUTY NO. 101.
3.M.T.T. (STANDARD).
MONDAYS ONLY.
Off No. 100 Sunday

01 30	Nine Elms Loco	02 20‖
02 50	Clapham Jn	03 19E
03 29	Waterloo	04 45‖
04 55	Clapham Jcn	05 47E

MONDAYS EXCEPTED.
Off No. 102.

03 05	Nine Elms Loco	04 45‖
05 15	Clapham Jn	05 47E

DAILY.

05 56	Waterloo	
	C. shunting 07 25 to 08 00	
	Waterloo	08 05E
08 15	Clapham Jn	10 43V
10 52	Waterloo (SRE)	12 25E
12 36	Clapham Jn	
	C. shunting 13 30 to 14 30	
	Clapham Jn	14 57E
15 07	Waterloo	15 38‖
15 48	Clapham Jn	17 25E
17 35	Waterloo	18 22‖
18 34	Nine Elms Loco	20 20‖
20 50	Clapham Jn	21 19E
21 29	Waterloo	--
	C. shunting 23 20 to 23 35	
	23 50 to 23 59	

Work No. 102.

NINE ELMS DUTY NO. 101 (CONTINUED).

NINE ELMSMEN.
(1) (MO) Off No. 100 (SUN) work 04 05‖ and relvd Waterloo 07 00.
(2) (MX) Off No. 102 work and rlvd Waterloo 07 00
(3) 1st set on duty 06 30 rlve at Waterloo at 07 00 work and rlvd at Clapham Jn at 14 55
(4) Off No. 100 rlve at Clapham Jn 14 55 work and rlvd in depot.
(5) 2nd set on duty 18 00 perform requirements, work, and rlvd at Waterloo 01 10 (No. 102)

Continued.

SOUTH WESTERN DIVISION - MONDAYS TO FRIDAYS   53.

BOURNEMOUTH DUTY NO.404
2 M.T.T. (L.X. CLASS)
STABLED OFF NO.410 Sunday/404 previous
day.

	Lymington Loco	05 45‖

MONDAYS ONLY
05 47	Lymington Town	06 06P

MONDAYS EXCEPTED
05 47	Lymington Town	06 02P

DAILY
06 17	Brockenhurst	07 04P
07 21	Lymington Pier	07 30P
07 44	Brockenhurst	07 56P
08 32	Bournemouth Ctl.	08 38E
08 46	Branksome	08 54‖
09 05	Bournemouth W. Sdgs.	09 55E
10 00	Branksome	10 08‖
10 23	Poole	10 30P

(BANK)
10 49	Bournemouth Ctl.	10 58‖
11 00	Bournemouth Loco	13 18‖
13 45	Bournemouth West	14 25Q
	Goods Yard(DEPARTMENTAL)(OR‖)	
14 35	Branksome Yard	

F. Shunting 14 35 to 15 50
(including trip to Pottery Siding)
	Branksome Yard	16 23F
16 33	Poole Yard	16 35‖
	(coupled to No.406 MXFO)	
16 48	Bournemouth Loco	17 2‖
18 4	Brockenhurst	18 48P
19 02	Lymington Pier	19 13P
19 31	Brockenhurst	20 00P
20 15	Lymington Pier	20 35P
20 50	Brockenhurst	21 00P
21 10	Lymington Town	xx‖
xx	Lymington Loco	

FX work No.404 next day
FO Work No.411 Saturday

BOURNEMOUTH DUTY NO.404 (CONTD.)
LYMINGTON MEN
(1) 1st set on duty 05 00 work and change
with No.400 at Brockenhurst 07 50 work &
rlvd at Lymington Town 13 17.
BOURNEMOUTH MEN
(2) Off No.400 change over at Brockenhurst
07 50 work and dispose.
(3) 1st set on duty 12 33 work and assist
requirements for 17 42‖ to Station rlve
No.5 (L.M.R.) at 18 31 work and dispose.
(4) 2nd set on duty 1657 perform
requirements work and change with No.400
at Brockenhurst 18 30 work and rlvd in
depot.
LYMINGTON MEN
(5) Off No.400 changeover at Brockenhurst
18 30 work and dispose.

work and the Lymington and Swanage branch passenger trains, though the only booked work at Weymouth in June 1966 was one diagram which included banking the 6.15 pm Weymouth to Waterloo train as far as Bincombe tunnel. The train running logs show an interesting comparison between the work of one of the LM 2-6-2 tanks and the bigger BR Standard tanks. No 41312 was clearly struggling on the 1-in-70 gradients to the summit near to Milepost 96½ even with its light load. See tables 16 and 17 – *See page 64*. The 40 mph branch line speed limit was often exceeded going downhill towards Lymington, though nothing approaching the 68 mph I timed with heritage unit 1497 in 2008

was ever seen! The three Q1 Class 0-6-0 Bulleid freight engines, Nos. 33006, 33020 and 33027 shown as still on the books on 1st January 1966 had no work and indeed were all withdrawn that month. However no less than six of the unique USA Class 0-6-0 tanks remained, of which one was shed pilot at Guildford and the other five performed trip work in the Eastleigh area where they had three booked turns. Last but not least 1966 was the last year for Maunsell's solid and reliable Moguls. On 1st January 1966 four each of classes N, Nos 31408, 31411, 31866 and 31873 and U, Nos 31639, 31791, 31803 and 31809 remained and of these 31408, 31639 and 31791 lasted longest, being withdrawn finally in

No. 41230 at Corfe Castle on a train from Wareham on 15th August 1966. *Bob Randall*

SOUTH WESTERN DIVISION - MONDAYS TO FRIDAYS   41.

EASTLEIGH DUTY NO.327
3 F.T. (U.S.A. Class)
        Eastleigh Loco   07 15‖
07 20   New Loco Works
Shunting 07 20 to 15 30 (Workshops
               a/c)
(Less 30 minutes meals and E.R.)
        New Loco Works   15 42F
15 54   Eastleigh M. Yd.   **‖
  **   Eastleigh E. Yd. 16 22F
16 31   New Loco Works
Shunting 17 00 to 18 00 (Workshops
             A/C)
        Loco Works   18 00‖
18 10   Eastleigh Loco   -

EASTLEIGH MEN
(1) 1st set on duty 06 30 work and
relieved at 14 00.
(2) 2nd set on duty 13 30 relieve
at 14 00 work and dispose prepare
No. 116 for 20 10‖ and as ordered.

EASTLEIGH DUTY NO. 329
3 F.T. (U.S.A. Class)
        Eastleigh Loco   07 15‖
        (via South Jn. Exit)
07 20   Carriage Works
Stores etc. shunting 07 30 to 17 30
        (Workshops a/c)
(Less 1 hour meals and E.R.)
        Carriage Works   17 30‖
17 40   Eastleigh Loco

EASTLEIGH MEN
(1) 1st set on duty 06 30 work and relieved
13 45.
(2) 2nd set on duty 13 00 relieve 13 45
work and dispose as ordered prepare and work
No.270 20 35‖ and relieved 21 00.

NO.328 NOT USED

NOS. 330 TO 379
SEE DIESEL LOCOMOTIVE ROSTERS

On 3rd May 1964, USA Class 0-6-0 tank No. 30064 stands at Woking having been brought there for reasons unknown at 3 pm by MN Class 4-6-2 No. 35013 *Blue Funnel*. *Author*

June 1966. Prior to that Nos. 31791 and 31639 had worked a farewell special from Waterloo to the Longmoor Military Railway at Liss. An interesting arrival in March 1966 was a single BR Standard Class 2 2-6-0 No. 77014 which was allocated to Guildford Shed from where it worked two return trips on Mondays to Fridays from Woking to Farnham. It also strayed onto other things especially at weekends and perhaps the most extraordinary working was on 18th September 1966 when it piloted Bulleid No. 34102 *Lapford* on the down *Bournemouth Belle* over 'the Alps' from Alton during a Sunday diversion. No doubt the Diagram Office at Wimbledon had a hand in this. Later the same day No. 77014 piloted No. 34087 *145 Squadron* on the 4.30 pm Waterloo to Weymouth. Table 19 – *See page 66.* No 77014 also at least two railtours.

So the summer of 1966 was the last when all Bournemouth line trains were steamed hauled and before the decline towards electrification began. The table lists all the Bournemouth and

Salisbury line departures from Waterloo in June 1966.
Table 20 – *See page 66.*
Note in particular that all Bournemouth line trains were booked for steam haulage on Mondays to Fridays though the incursion of the Class 33 diesels on summer Saturdays which applied in the previous year as shown in the table of observations on 10th July 1965 continued and in fact increased. The West of England trains shown as DL hauled were covered by WR Warship class diesel hydraulics. By June 1965 the Waterloo to Basingstoke semi-fast trains had nearly all gone being replaced by WR DMMUs and a connection at Woking to and from a Waterloo to Portsmouth fast train. This helped to keep so much steam going as well as aiding the major track work going on between Brookwood and Basingstoke. An afternoon's observation at Fleet on Saturday 3rd September 1966 showed the extent of cover by the Class 33 diesel fleet. On this day of the 38 trains seen, just 16 were steam hauled, five

Maunsell farewell. On a fine and warm 30th April 1966 Maunsell U Class No. 31791 pilots another U Class No. 31639 on the RTCS special 9.59 am Waterloo to Liss. The pair were going very well passing Weybridge. *Author*

were hauled by WR Warship diesel hydraulics and no less than 16 by Class 33 Type 3 diesels. The remaining train, remarkably had Peak D56 *The Bedfordshire and Hertfordshire Regiment (TA)* at its head! This train is thought to have been a Portsmouth Harbour to Sheffield summer Saturday special which ran via Woking and Chertsey after being diverted from the more normal Reading line from July 1966. There were occasions, however, when the end of steam seemed a long way off and steam still reigned supreme, as a period of observation at Brockenhurst on the Friday before the spring bank holiday in 1966 demonstrated. Table 12 – *See page 61.* On some days though the situation regarding available steam power was dire and an example from 29th August 1966 is shown here when no less than 33 engines were stopped for a variety of reasons. Table 15 – *See page 63.*

This shortage of serviceable motive power

saw the arrival of the first of seven Brush Type 4 diesel electric locomotives in September 1966. These were numbered D1921 to D1926 and D1928, of which D1923 was the first. From 3rd October 1966 they were allocated to Eastleigh Diagrams 90 and 91 which covered the trains as shown on the attached. This meant the end of steam on two of the most popular trains, the 8.30 am and 5.30 pm from Waterloo. The latter in particular was a big blow as this meant that the choice of an evening's steam 'bashing' was much more limited as the 4.35 pm down was also diagrammed for a Brush Type 4 and the 6.30 pm down was covered by Bournemouth men who, with a few exceptions, did not enter into the spirit of showmanship and fast running shown by the Nine Elms men and to a lesser degree those from Eastleigh, preferring to end their days on steam quietly. The Brush Type 4s were very unreliable at first and not all men were

SOUTH WESTERN DIVISION – MONDAYS TO FRIDAYS   2

NOS. 1 – 89

SEE DIESEL LOCOMOTIVES

EASTLEIGH DUTY NO.90
(D.1500 CLASS)

	Eastleigh D.Depot	05 20‖
05 25	Eastleigh	05 49P
07 35	Bomo Ctl	07 51P
09 10	Weymouth	10 13P
11 37	Bomo Ctl	11 53‖
12 01	Branksome	12 02‖
12 03	Branksome Loop	12 18‖
12 19	Branksome	12 22E
12 30	Bomo Ctl. (1118 Weymouth)	12 35P
14 52	Waterloo	15 35‖
15 40	North Sdgs	15 55‖
16 00	Waterloo	16 35P
19 10	Bomo Ctl.	19 16P
20 15	Weymouth	20 30‖
20 35	Weymouth Loco (Fuel)	21 30‖
21 35	Weymouth	22 13P
23 28	Bomo Ctl.	23 37P

TUESDAY TO FRIDAY

04 11	Waterloo	05 15V

SATURDAY ONLY

04 11	Waterloo	05 30P

TUESDAY TO SATURDAY
Work No. 91
(505 MILES)

BOURNEMOUTH MEN
(1) Off 91 previous day prepare and work 05 20‖ and relieved Bournemouth Central 07 35.
(2) Off No. 381 relieve at Bournemouth Central 07 35, work and relieved at Bournemouth Central at 12 30.
(3) 1st set on duty 12 15, relieve at 12 30, work and relieved at Waterloo 16 25, relieve No. 430 at 18 20, work and relieved at Bournemouth Central 20 52.

EASTLEIGH DUTY NO. 90

NINE ELMS MEN
(4) 1st set on duty 15 55, relieve at Waterloo 16 25, work and relieved at Bournemouth Central 19 10, relieve No. 464 at 19 35, work and relieved at Waterloo 22 56.

BOURNEMOUTH MEN
(5) Off No. 283 relieve at Bournemouth Central 19 10, work and relieved at Bournemouth Central 23 35.
(6) 2nd set on duty 23 20, relieve at 23 35, work and relieved at Eastleigh 01 35, to depot, as ordered, prepare and work No. 90 (next day) and relieved at Bournemouth Central 07 35.

EASTLEIGH MEN
(7) 1st Set (Tuesday to Saturday) on duty 01 05, relieve at 01 35, work and change to No. 462 at Waterloo 04 30, work and relieved Basingstoke 07 30 home passenger.

trained for some time and so steam substitutions were quite common though the steam fleet was getting depleted. In addition BR Standard Class 5s were frequent substitutions for Bulleid pacifics, even for Merchant Navies. On 21st November No. 73085 was asked to cover for one and had take 13 coaches for 475 tons on the 1.30pm down. It really struggled losing 21 minutes to Basingstoke with a maximum speed of 53 mph after Hook being the highlight. I returned to Waterloo behind another Class 5 No. 73020 on the 12.59 pm Bournemouth to Waterloo, running 30 minutes late and covering for a Brush Type 4 which meant of course that the 5.30 pm down was also steam in the form of rebuilt West Country pacific No.34093 *Saunton*. Bert Hadley from Nine Elms top link did quite well with the Class 5 and Alf Hurley also from

```
SOUTH WESTERN DIVISION - MONDAYS TO FRIDAYS                    3

EASTLEIGH DUTY NO.91                    EASTLEIGH DUTY NO. 91 (CONT'D)
      (D.1500 Class)                    EASTLEIGH MEN
MONDAYS ONLY                            (1) Off No. 90 changeover with No. 462 at Wloo
          Off 90 Sunday                 04 30 work and relieved at Basingstoke 07 30
04 11    Waterloo           04 55||     home pass.
05 25    Stew. Lane Depot   07 15||     NINE ELMS MEN
          (Fuel )                       (2) Off No. 462 change over Waterloo
MONDAYS EXCEPTED                        04 30 work and relieved Waterloo 08 20
          Off No. 90                    (3) 1st set - on duty 07 50 relieve at
04 11    Waterloo           05 15V      Waterloo 08 20 work and relieved at
05 25    Clap. Jn.          05 55||     Bournemouth Central 10 45 (UNTIL 14/10/66
06 10    Stew. Lane Depot   07 15||     and from 3/4/67) home pass as ordered
DAILY          (Fuel)                   (FROM 17/10/66 until 31/3/67) relieve
07 45    Waterloo           08 30P      No. 145 at 11 05, work and relieved at
10 03    Souton Ctl         10 07P      Waterloo 14 17.
10 45    Bournemouth Ctl    10 48||     BOURNEMOUTH MEN
10 50    Bournemouth Loco   12 05||     (4) Off No. 143 relieve at Bournemouth
12 07    Bournemouth Ctl    12 59P      Central 10 45 work and relieved at 12 10
16 09    Waterloo           16 30||     to depot, perform requirements No. 412
16 35    North Sidings      16 55||     for 14 05||
17 00    Waterloo           17 30P      NINE ELMS MEN
19 10    Eleigh             19 12P      (5) Off No. 136, relieve at 12 10, work
20 30    Branksome          20 52||     and relieved at Waterloo 16 09.
21 02    Bournemouth Ctl.     -         (6) 2nd set on duty 15 39, relieve at
   C.Shunting 21 05 to 21 25            Waterloo 16 09, work and relieved at
         Bournemouth Ctl.    21 26P     Eastleigh 19 10, relieve No. 280 at 19 45
          (20 15 Weymouth)             work and relieved at Clapham Junction
22 24    Southampton Ctl    22 30||     23 00.
22 35    Northam Yd         23 10V      EASTLEIGH MEN
00 14    Portsmouth & S                 (7) 1st set on duty 18 47 relieve at
              (SRE)         01 30V      19 10 work and relieved.
01 40    Fratton Yard       02 10||
03 00    Eastleigh D.Depot    -
      (420 MILES)


                    NOS. 92 - 100

                 SEE DIESEL LOCOMOTIVES


              Continued.....
```

the top link at Nine Elms only lost two minutes to Basingstoke on the 5.30 pm with 12 for 435 tons, despite being very short of steam.

These were desperate days and it must have been a nightmare for roster clerks trying to find any available engine to cover trains, though I cannot recall any cancellations. It was therefore no surprise to find that nine steam engines withdrawn on 29th October 1966 were reinstated on 9th December 1966. These were Nos 34005, 34026, 34032, 73087, 73088, 73089, 73169, 76016 and 76057. It was much

more of a surprise though for me to record my best 100 mph run with steam on 12th December 1966 behind the now preserved No. 35028 *Clan Line.* Full details of this run are in Chapter Five. I recorded runs behind two of the reinstated engines before their final withdrawal at the end of the year, Nos 34032 and 73169. Both put in creditable performances belying their ghostly existence!

So into 1967 and the final few months of steam. On 1st January just 122 engines remained in service. **Table 21** *– See page 68.*

SOUTH WESTERN DIVISION - MONDAY TO FRIDAY   65.

WEYMOUTH DUTY NO.431

8P (Merchant Navy Class) Large
          Tender
MX - Off No.435

	Weymouth Loco	08 35‖
08 40	Weymouth	09 21P
13 03	Waterloo	13 32‖
13 43	Nine Elms Loco	16 58‖
17 12	Waterloo	17 30P
20 28	Bournemouth Ctl.	20 37E
20 45	Branksome	20 57‖
21 07	Bournemouth Loco	23 10‖
23 12	Bournemouth Ctl.	23 37P
	(22 13 Weymouth)	

TUESDAYS TO SATURDAYS

04 11	Waterloo	04 58‖
05 10	Nine Elms Loco	
	WORK NO.432	

WEYMOUTH MEN

(1)   Prepare for 08 35‖

BOURNEMOUTH MEN

(2)   Off No.442 work 08 35‖ and
      relieved at Bournemouth Central
      10 21

NINE ELMS MEN

(3)   Off No.463, relieve at
      Bournemouth Central 10 21 work
      and relieved at Waterloo 13 03

(4)   Off No.108 relieve at Waterloo
      13 03 work and dispose.

(5)   1st Set - On duty 15 53 work
      and relieved at Eastleigh
      19 12 to depot work No.116
      20 10‖ and relieved in depot.

                Continued.....

WEYMOUTH DUTY 431 (CONT'D)

EASTLEIGH MEN

(6)   1st Set - On duty 18 42, relieved at
      19 12 work and relieved at Bournemouth
      Central 20 28 to depot work No.434
      21 00‖ and relieved at Eastleigh 00 50
      and as ordered.

BOURNEMOUTH MEN

(7)   1st Set - On duty 19 15 prepare No.434
      to Station relieve this duty at 20 28
      work and relieved Bournemouth Central
      23 35 to depot dispose No.385

(8)   2nd Set - On duty 23 20 relieve at
      23 35, work and relieved at Eastleigh
      01 32 to depot, prepare and work
      No.244 (next day) 05 20‖ and relieved
      at Bournemouth Central 07 36

EASTLEIGH MEN

(9)   2nd Set (Tues to Sat) On duty 01 02
      relieve at 01 32, work, change with
      No.112 at Waterloo 04 30 work and
      relieved Basingstoke 07 30 home
      passenger.

NINE ELMS MEN

(10) MX - Off No.112 change over at
      Waterloo 04 30 work and dispose.

The remaining ten Merchant Navy pacifics were all allocated to Weymouth. These were Nos. 35003, 35007, 35008, 35012, 35013, 35014, 35023, 35026, 35028 and 35030. Feltham shed had closed and Nine Elms had acquired some light pacifics, nine in total, increasing their total steam allocation to 27, mainly at the expense of Eastleigh whose fleet had declined from 71 at the beginning of 1966 to 33. In total 36 Bulleid light pacifics remained and the images show Nos 34015, 34040, 34044, 34087 and 34089 in previous years. There were no longer any Maunsell engines, the Q1s had gone and the two remaining O2s on the Isle of Wight were simply engaged in clearing up operations following the closure of the lines for electrification on 31st December 1966. Remarkably five USA class tanks were still at Eastleigh with just one diagram to cover which was coal shunting at Eastleigh MPD. All five were to last to the end of steam. Inevitably the steam fleet reduction and new diagrams applicable from 2nd January

1967 meant a reduction in the number of steam hauled trains so that from the 27 steam hauled departures from Waterloo on Mondays to Fridays in June 1966 shown in the earlier table, there were now just 12, 14 on Fridays. These were as follows:

2.30 am 70A Bulleid light pacific

4.40 am 70A Standard 5

7.18 am 70D Standard 4 75xxx

8.35 am 70A Bulleid light pacific

10.30 am 70A Bulleid light pacific

11.30 am 70E Bulleid light pacific

1.30 pm 70G Merchant Navy

3.30 pm 70A Bulleid light pacific

5.09 pm 70E Bulleid light pacific

5.23 pm Fridays only, 70A Bulleid light pacific

6.22 pm Fridays only, 70D Bulleid light pacific

6.30 pm, 70G Merchant Navy

6.54 pm 70A Bulleid light pacific

10.35 pm.70E Bulleid light pacific

The 12 arrivals in the up direction were at 8.22 am, 9.16 am, 9.34 am, 10.22 am, 11.57 am, 12.10 pm, 1.03 pm, 2.17 pm, 4.52 pm, 8.25 pm, 8.36 pm and 8.51 pm. So a good day out with steam could still be had but more importantly the scope for evening excursions after work was much diminished, being restricted to the 5.09 pm down to Basingstoke, returning on the 8.25 pm or 8.36 pm arrivals, or the 6.30 pm down to Southampton, returning on the Mogul train to Woking, which could produce almost any class of steam engine, or the 6.54 pm to Woking returning on the 8.25 pm or 8.36 pm arrivals. To catch the 8.51 pm 'Club Train' arrival, which produced many of the finest runs in 1967, meant catching the 4.35 pm down behind a Brush Type 4, though this still had occasional steam substitutions. By May 1967 though the 4.35 pm down had become an Electro Diesel (EDL) plus Trailer Control (TC) set of coaches working and steam substitutions finished. The 6.30 pm down was worked by Bournemouth top link men, most of whom were quietly winding down

to retirement and so rarely produced anything of note. The train was booked 78 minutes to the first stop at Winchester but par for the course was 80 to 90 minutes, with or without delays. Typical was a run with No. 35023 on 9th January 1967 when we took 88 minutes 4 seconds, with no higher speed than 71 mph and that was downhill after Wallers Ash. There were temporary speed restrictions at Earlsfield and Micheldever and for many miles speed was in the late 50s declining to 40 mph at the top of the climb at Wootton. Fortunately from 6th March 1967 the last up Weymouth, 6.15 pm, arriving at Waterloo at 10.56 pm reverted to steam and this greatly improved matters as this was the train that not only gave us the highest known speed with Southern steam (106 mph with No. 35003) but also the highest recorded speed at Roundwood summit (83 mph with No. 34087). At the same time the 2.45 am down also became steam hauled again.

There were a total of 53 diagrams which applied on Mondays to Fridays from 2nd January 1967. Nine Elms had 16 diagrams for its 27 locomotives, Guildford had six for its 11 engines, Eastleigh had 33 engines to cover 10 diagrams, Bournemouth 21 engines also for 10 diagrams, Weymouth four diagrams for 14 engines and Salisbury 12 locos for six diagrams. In theory there was a lot of spare cover but in practice the condition of engines, now on minimum maintenance meant that depots still struggled. The other work for steam included empty stock to and from Waterloo, the Kensington Olympia postal workers' trains, empty stock working in the Bournemouth area, local services in the Eastleigh/Bournemouth/Weymouth areas and the last steam worked branch from Brockenhurst to Lymington Pier. These kept the smaller BR Standard and the LM class 2s occupied. Sadly the *Bournemouth Belle* had succumbed to the Brush invasion and was rostered both ways for one of the Type 4 diesels. One piece of history was in the form of the first diagrammed use of an electric multiple unit. This was the 5.41 pm from Waterloo to Basingstoke commuter train and was covered

SOUTH WESTERN DIVISION - MONDAYS TO FRIDAYS - 33

WEYMOUTH DUTY NO.430
8P (Merchant Navy Class)

	Weymouth Loco	08 35||
08 40	Weymouth	09 16P
10 18	Bournemouth Ctl	10 26||
10 34	Branksome	10 35||
10 36	Branksome Loop	10 48||
10 49	Branksome	10 52E
11 00	Bournemouth Ctl	11 07P
14 17	Waterloo	14 37||
14 50	Nine Elms Loco (M)	17 55||
(FO - Coupled to No.254)		
18 13	Waterloo	18 30P
21 58	Weymouth	xx||
xx	Weymouth Loco	

(M) To be changed with No.431
for maintenance as and when
required.

BOURNEMOUTH MEN

(1) (MO) Off No.442 (Sunday) prepare
and work 08 35\|\| and relieved at
Bournemouth Ctl 11 05

(2) (MX) Off No.280 prepare and
work 08 35\|\| and relieved at
Bournemouth Ctl 11 05\|\|

NINE ELMS MEN

(3) Off No.135/91 relieve at
Bournemouth Central 11 05 work
and relieved at Waterloo 14 17

(4) Off No.433 relieve at Waterloo
14 17 work and dispose.

(5) 1st Set - On duty 16 50 work
and relieved at Waterloo 18 20
as ordered, relieve No.113 at
20 36, work and dispose.

BOURNEMOUTH MEN

(6) Off No.91 relieve at Waterloo
18 20 work and relieved at
Bournemouth Ctl 20 52

WEYMOUTH MEN

(7) Off No.166 relieve at
Bournemouth Ctl 20 52 work and
relieved in depot.

WEYMOUTH DUTY NO.431

8P (MERCHANT NAVEY CLASS)

Stabled at Nine Elms Loco for Maintenance
purposes. Change-over with No.430, 432
and 433 as and when required.

430 - 431

not by one of the new REP/TC units but by a 10 coach set of HAP/HAL two car units. I was on the first one on 2nd January and the running, though good enough for timekeeping, was no better than steam had achieved. For the record the unit numbers were 5675, 6032, 6107, 6166 and 6088. From 3rd April 1967 there was a further reduction in the number of steam hauled trains so that only eight departures from Waterloo remained on Mondays to Thursdays, ten on

A lovely study of No. 35023 *Holland Afrika Line* in Clapham Cutting on 23rd June 1963 heading the 9.30 am Waterloo to Bournemouth West. *Author*

Fridays. These were at 2.30 am, 2.45 am, 4.40 am, 7.18 am, 8.10 am to Weymouth Quay, 8.35 am, 5.09 pm, 5.23 pm (Fridays only), 6.22 pm (Fridays only), and 6.54 pm. At the same time the remaining eight Merchant Navy pacifics, Nos 35003, 35007, 35008, 35012, 35013, 35023, 35028 and 35030 were all transferred to Nine Elms and Weymouth was reduced to a stabling point. Steam on the Lymington branch also finished. Regular electric working started to Bournemouth though steam still substituted for the new REP units and for the Brush Type 4s on a regular basis. For instance the 11.57 am arrival and 4.35 pm down trains were worked by No.35007 for the whole of the week from 20th April 1967 and on 4th May No. 34057 worked the up *Bournemouth Belle*.

Steam should have finished on 11th June but

there were insufficient electric units available to run the full service so a reprieve was won with yet another new set of diagrams applying until the final day on 9th July. On the 1st July there were still 72 engines in service, 25 of which were at Nine Elms. **Table 9** – *See page 58*. There were 41 diagrams for steam in total on Mondays to Fridays, sixteen at Nine Elms, six at Guildford, nine each at Eastleigh and Bournemouth and just two at Salisbury. There were fewer on Saturdays but remarkably still sixteen on Sundays though most of these were standby duties to cover failed electric units and Brush Type 4s. Appendices A, B and C show all the final weekday diagrams for those last two weeks with the engines I recorded working them. This is probably the most comprehensive record of the last four weeks to have been

The BR Standard Class 5s featured well in the final years of steam and one in particular stood out for me being responsible for some fine runs, often deputising for a Bulleid pacific. Here No. 73022, originally allocated to the Western Region and built at Derby in October 1951, is seen arriving at Southampton Central on 4th April 1965 with the Sunday 2.15 pm Weymouth to Waterloo. It was withdrawn in April 1967 and I travelled 451¼ miles behind it, the most with a Standard 5. *Author*

No 35022 *Holland America Line* looks quite superb in the winter sun after arrival at Southampton with the down 'Bournemouth Belle on a cold and frosty 28th November 1965. This was another engine which gave me many fine runs especially in 1965. I travelled 2,319½ behind this excellent engine before its premature withdrawal in May 1966 and initial period of storage at Weymouth shed, my highest behind a steam engine of any sort. It just always seemed to be there. It wasn't scrapped but is now preserved though not yet restored for use. *Author*

A lovely study of Battle of Britain class No.34057 *Biggin Hill* on the turntable at Bath on 6th March 1966 whilst working the final S&D railtour. This engine gave me some great runs during the course of a total of 880 miles travelled including the highest power output I recorded behind a Bulleid light pacific in original condition. It was withdrawn in May 1967. *John Tiley*

Gordon Porter takes No. 34057 *Biggin Hill* out of Southampton Central with a down train in 1965. *Les Kent collection*

published and is taken mainly from the notes I made at the time, assisted by records kept by others from the days of steam. There were also some extra steam workings and substitutions for diesel and electric power and these are referred to in Chapter Six.

During the last years a few engines stood out as turning in consistently good performances, amongst them No's 34013, 34057, 34102, 35003, 35007, plus 35022, until its withdrawal in 1966 and 73022. There were also the really outstanding 100 mph engines of which there were eight, No's 34008, 34013, 34042, 34102, 35003, 35005, 35007, 35008, 35023 and 35028. No. 34102 *Lapford* was the only

Bulleid in original condition to achieve the magic 'ton' and it performed consistently well to the end, but No. 35003 *Royal Mail* must take the honours as despite it is apparent appalling condition with much clanking of the motion it was recorded reaching 100 mph no less than six times, including the 106 mph maximum speed which is believed to be the highest recorded by a Southern engine. The table summarises the 100 mph efforts, full details of which are in the following chapters. **Table 22** – *See page 69.* Photographs of these engines end this chapter with some of their story in extended captions. We move next to the enginemen who produced the runs set out later in the book.

Salisbury based Bulleid Rebuilt West Country Class 4-6-2 No. 34013 *Okehampton* stands at Southampton Central on the down Bournemouth Belle in 1964. This was another of the 100 mph engines, having been credited with two authenticated runs. It was delivered new to Exmouth Junction shed on 30th October 1945 and withdrawn from Salisbury shed at the end of steam on 9th July 1967, having been rebuilt in October 1957. It covered a total of 944,928 miles. Its last light casual overhaul was in July 1966 and for its last four years was looked after by the excellent staff at Salisbury shed. I travelled 1,372 miles behind it during the course of which it gave me many good runs including one of the 100 mph runs.
John Tiley

On 3rd June 1963 No. 35028 *Clan Line* speeds past Pirbright with the 9.21 am Weymouth to Waterloo. *Clan Line* entered traffic at Bournemouth shed on 23rd December 1948 and was rebuilt in October 1959 after it had run 401,500 miles. It had a light casual overhaul in July 1966 and was therefore still in good condition when it gave me my best 100 mph run reaching 103 mph near Fleet on 12th December 1966. It lasted to the end of steam and was withdrawn from Nine Elms shed on 9th July 1967 having run a total of 794,391 miles. I travelled 1,595 3/4 miles behind No. 35028 prior to its withdrawal. It went straight into preservation and was back on the main line in 1974 and has since produced many fine performances. Its use on the main line is quite restricted and it is highly regarded by engine crews and by the public. *Author*

On 17th July 1964 high speed machine No. 35005 *Canadian Pacific* at Lymington Junction on the up 'Bournemouth Belle' . No 35005 gave me my first 100 mph run with steam during the course of a 65 minute net time run from Waterloo to Southampton on 15th May 1965, a day which is celebrated annually by those of us on board when the maximum of 105 mph was reached. It was delivered new to Salisbury shed in January 1942 and was rebuilt in May 1959. It was withdrawn quite early on 10th October 1965 from Weymouth shed having done a total of 976, 806 miles, its last heavy intermediate overhaul being in February 1964. I travelled just 262 miles behind her but that included not only the 100 mph run but another quite phenomenal effort on the 5.30 pm down. I consider this engine to be my all time favourite for what it achieved. No 35005 is preserved and though it has been in the main line it now resides on the Mid Hants Railway. *John Tiley*

No. 35007 *Aberdeen Commonwealth* waits at Waterloo on the 4.35 pm 'Royal Wessex' to Weymouth. This engine gave me many fine runs including a near miss 98 mph on the Club Train. It was though another of the 100 mph engines, reaching this speed the night before my 98 mph run. I travelled 1,911 1/2 miles behind No. 35007 which lasted until the end of steam, having travelled a total of 1,318,765 miles. *John Tiley*

On 5th April 1964 Rebuilt Merchant Navy No. 35003 *Royal Mail* enters Woking on the 4 pm Waterloo to Exeter. Towards the end of steam this engine proved to be the fastest of the remaining Bulleid pacifics despite sounding and looking really run down. It is credited with no less than six separate speeds of 100 mph or more including three on one run and also with the highest known speed with Southern steam, 106 mph on 26th June 1967. It entered traffic at Salisbury shed on 13th September 1941 and was rebuilt in August 1959 and withdrawn from Nine Elms shed in July 1967, having lasted to the end and with a total of 1,131,793 miles on the clock. Its last works attention was on 5th January 1967 and prior to that it had a light intermediate overhaul in July 1965, so no wonder it sounded run down! I travelled 1,637 miles behind this engine, mainly in 1966 and 1967. *Author*

West Country Class pacific No. 34102 *Lapford* arriving at Southampton Central on 4th February 1967 heading the 1.30 pm Waterloo to Bournemouth with driver Hockaday of Bournemouth at the regulator. No. 34102 produced the only 100 mph run in the 1965-67 period with a Bulleid pacific in original condition, though the maximum speed is disputed by some. It was delivered new to Stewarts Lane shed in March 1950 and lasted to the end of steam, running a modest total of 593,438 miles. I travelled 545 1/2 miles behind *Lapford*. *John Tiley*

No 35023 *Holland Africa Line* was responsible for the most high profile 100 mph run in the period covered by this book, on 15th October 1966, whilst working a special from Waterloo to Salisbury. It was delivered new to Exmouth Junction shed on 6th November 1948 and rebuilt in February 1957 having run 433,833 miles. Its last heavy casual overhaul was in May 1966 and it lasted to the end of steam having run a total of 941,326 miles. It was the engine which gave me my last run with Southern steam on 8th July 1967 and I recorded 1,305 1/2 miles behind this superb machine. In this fine study the engine is at Weymouth shed on 17th September 1966. *John Tiley*

On 17th April 1965 Merchant Navy No. 35008 *Orient Line* is seen arriving at Southampton Central on the 9.21 am Weymouth to Waterloo. I travelled 1,386¼ behind her but with no particularly outstanding performances though this was another of the 100 mph pacifics, the only one reaching this speed with a non Nine Elms driver, De'Ath from Basingstoke shed. No. 35008 was delivered new to Salisbury shed on 16th June 1942 and was rebuilt after 730,712 miles in May 1957. It was another engine which lasted to the end of steam and had accumulated no less than1,286,418 miles when withdrawn, the highest mileage of any Bulleid pacific. *Author*

Rebuilt West Country class No. 34008 *Padstow* at Basingstoke on 13th May 1965 while working the 4.55 pm Bournemouth West to Waterloo. The train is signalled from the up slow line to the up fast. It was one of the 100 mph engines which feat it performed down Roundwood bank on the 2.45 am from Waterloo in August 1966. No.34008 was delivered new to Exmouth Junction shed as 21C108 on 10th September 1945. It was rebuilt in June 1960 and had done 961,734 miles when it was withdrawn from Nine Elms shed on 25th June 1967, so not quite lasting to the end. I travelled 1,047 miles behind it, my last run being on the 6.15 pm from Weymouth on 2nd May 1967. *Author*

Tables

Table 3

SOUTHERN REGION STEAM FLEET MAY 1965

			NINE ELMS 70A	FELTHAM 70B	GUILDFORD 70C	EASTLEIGH 70D	SALISBURY 70E	BOURNEMOUTH 70F	WEYMOUTH 70G	RYDE 70H	REDHILL 75B	TOTALS
MN		4-6-2						9	12			21
BB/WC		4-6-2	4			36	19	7				66
U		2-6-0			8							8
N		2-6-0			10							10
S15		4-6-0		6								6
USA		0-6-0T				6						6
Q1		0-6-0			6							6
O2		0-4-4T								16		16
BR 5	73XXX	4-6-0	8			21			6			35
BR 4	75XXX	4-6-0	6			5						11
BR 4	76XXX	2-6-0		2		20	5	6				33
BR 4	80XXX	2-6-4T	5			12		7			11	35
BR 3	82XXX	2-6-2T	13									13
LM2		2-6-2T			4	3		7	5			19
TOTALS			36	8	28	103	24	36	23	16	11	285

Table 4

WINCHESTER TO BASINGSTOKE

Date	8th June 1965
Train	651 pm Bournemouth to Woking
Loco	Maunsell N Class 2-6-0 No. 31873
Load	3 coaches and 2 vans, 156 tons tare, 165 tons gross
Recorder	DB

	miles	sched	mins	secs		speed
Winchester	0.00	0.00	00	00		
Winchester Jct	2.10	5.30	04	24		38
Wallers Ash Box	4.80		08	33		40
Weston Box	6.30		10	42		41
Micheldever	8.43	15.30	14	15		
	0.00	0.00	00	00		
Roundwood Box	1.87		03	45		43½
Waltham Box	2.97		05	08		54
Steventon Box	4.12		06	17		62
Wootton Box	5.57		07	39		63
Worting Jct	7.80	10.00	09	51		62/63
MP 49½	8.57		11	37		60
Basingstoke	10.42	14.00	13	09		
depart 1 min late arrive 2 mins early						

Table 5

WOKING TO BASINGSTOKE

Date	9th January 1965
Train	930 am Waterloo to Bournemouth
Loco	Battle of Britain Class 4-6-2 No. 34064 *Fighter Command*
Load	9 coaches, 298½ tons tare, 320 tons gross
Driver	Unrecorded
Recorder	DB

	miles	sched	mins	secs		speed
Woking	0.00	0.00	00	00		
Woking Jct	0.46		01	33		26
Brookwood	3.70		07	32		41
Pirbright Jct	5.20		09	40		50
MP 31	6.75		11	15		55½
Sturt Lane	7.86		12	30		61
Farnborough	8.91		13	29		63½
Fleet	12.19		16	28		68/72
Winchfield	15.54		19	22		69/66½
Hook	17.87		21	28		70/68
Newnham Siding	19.36		22	49		72/74
Basingstoke	23.46	29.00	26	46		

Table 6

WATEROO TO WOKING

Date	19th May 1965
Train	754 pm Waterloo to Basingstoke
Loco	Maunsell N Class 2-6-0 No. 31873
Load	5 coaches and one van, 183 tons tare, 195 tons gross
Driver	Godden Nine Elms No. Four link
Recorder	DB

	miles	sched	mins	secs	speed
Waterloo	0.00	0.00	00	00	
Vauxhall	1.29		03	14	33
Queens Road	2.81		05	18	44
Clapham Junction	3.93	7.00	07	21	34*
Earlsfield	5.58		10	08	40
Wimbledon	7.24		12	32	43
Raynes Park	8.64		14	23	48
New Malden	9.78		15	48	51
Berrylands	10.98		17	12	53
Surbiton	12.04		18	25	56
Hampton Court Jct	13.34	18.30	19	47	59
Esher	14.39		20	50	60
Hersham	15.91		22	23	61
Walton	17.08		23	33	58½
Oatlands Box	18.10		24	38	55
Weybridge	19.15		25	42	59
Byfleet & New Haw	20.40		26	59	63
West Byfleet	21.68		28	13	60
Woking	24.29	31.00	31	54	to local line
					* brakes

Table 7

BULLEID PACIFICS-PRINCIPLE DIMENSIONS

	MERCHANT NAVY	LIGHT PACIFICS
CYLINDERS	(3) 18 in X 24 in	(3) 16 5/8 in X 24 in
DRIVING WHEELS	6 ft 2 in	6 ft 2 in
BOILER PRESSURE	250 lb	250 lb
HEATING SURFACE	3,273 sq ft	2,667 sq ft
GRATE AREA	48½ sq ft	38¼ sq ft
TRACTIVE EFFORT	33,495 lb	27,715 lb
LENGTH, WITH TENDER	69 ft 7¾ in	67 ft 4¾ in
LOCO WEIGHT	97 tons 18 cwt	86 tons 0 cwt (Original)
		90 tons 1 cwt (Rebuilt)

Table 8

SOTON TO FRATTON

Date	Sunday 30th June 1963					
Train	246 pm Southampton to Fratton					
Loco	BR Standard Class 4 2-6-0 No. 76018					
Load	3 coaches, 95 tons tare, 100 tons gross					
Recorder	DB					
Weather	Cloudy					

	miles	sched	mins	secs		speed
Southampton	0.00	0.00	00	00		
St Denys	1.93		05	07		27
Bitterne	2.65		06	27		50
Woolston	4.29		09	03		20*
Sholing	4.90		10	15		32
Netley	6.78		12	42		57
Hamble Halt	7.43		13	21		63
Bursledon	8.80		14	52		47*
Swanwick	10.79		17	26		44/58
Fareham	14.50	25.00	22	34		
	0.00	0.00	00	00		
Portchester	3.18		05	08		62 max
Cosham	5.78	9.30	08	35		
	0.00	0.00	00	00		
Hilsea Halt	1.41		03	28		47 max
Fratton	3.77	9.00	07	01		
						* brakes

Table 9

LOCOMOTIVES REMAINING FOR LAST WEEK OF STEAM 3rd to 9th JULY 1967

Class	Numbers	Total
Merchant Navy 4-6-2	35003/7/8/23/28/30	8
Rebuilt Light Pacifics	34001/4/13/18/21/24/25/36/37/52/60/87/89/90/93/95	16
Unconverted Light Pacifics	34023/102	2
BR Standard class 5 4-6-0	73020/29/37/43/65/80/92/93/118/155	10
BR Standard class 4 4-6-0	75074/75/76/77	4
BR Standard class 4 2-6-0	76005/6/7/9/11/26/31/64/66/67	10
BR Standard class 4 2-6-4 tank	80011/15/16/133/134/139/140/143/146/152	9
BR Standard class 3 2-6-2 tank	82019/29	2
BR Standard class 3 2-6-0	77014	1
LM Class 3 2-6-2 tank	41224/41298/41312/19/20	5
USA class 0-6-0 tank	30064/67/69/71/72	5
TOTALS		72

Table 10

OBSERVATIONS AT BASINGSTOKE SATURDAY 10th JULY 1965

Time	Train	Engine	Load	Notes
morning				
1120	1020 am Waterloo to Southampton Docks	34064	10	Ocean Liner Express
1123	923 am B'th West to L'Pool and Manchester	34085	13	Right time
1128	953 am Bournemoth Central to Waterloo	35004	9	Right time. Non stop
1133	1030 am Waterloo to Weymouth	35028	11	6 late
1139	1045 am Waterloo to Swanage	D6512	10	6 late
1148	1004 am Bournemouth West to Waterloo	34102	12	Right time
1159	1035 am Lymington Pier to Waterloo	D6527	10	Right time
afternoon				
1205	Light Engine up local	76011	-	
1209	925 am Weymouth to Waterloo	34103	11	4 early
1210	1100 am Waterloo to Exeter Central	D6521	12	7 late
1215	1105 am Waterloo to Bournemouth West	73088	9	4 late
1221	1115 am Waterloo to Weymouth	35017	8	Right time
1224	Southampon Docks to Waterloo	34076	12	Ocean Liner Express
1225	9 am Exmouth to Waterloo	D825	10	6 late
1232	1130 Waterloo to Weymouth	D6530	11	3 early
1252	Southampon Docks to Waterloo	34077	13	Ocean Liner Express
112	1042 am Poole to Sheffield Midland	34044	10	3 late
115	1055 am Bournemouth West to Waterloo	35011	11	2 late
119	1214 pm Waterloo to Bournemouth West	34036	10	2 late
125-130	1110 am Bournemouth West to Newcastle	35003/NR	11	Right time. Changed engines
128	1230 pm Waterloo to Bournemouth West	34050	11	Right Time. Bournemouth Belle
132	1150 am Lymington Pier to Watero	76026	10	2 early
134	1235 pm Waterloo to Weymouth	34009	12	4 early
137	1035 am Exeter St Davids to Waterloo	D801	10	16 late
155	1200 Bournemouth West to Waterloo	34090	10	Right Time*
157	Unidentified down train	73169	12	
159	100 pm Waterloo to Exeter Central	D816	10	2 early
159	1120 am Swanage to Waterloo	34004	12	Right time. 75 mph
200	Light engine	73110	-	
204	1117am Weymouth to Waterloo	35012	12	Right Time. 80 mph
226-233	Relief train.Possibly Portsmouth to Birmingham	34040	11	
228	130 pm Waterloo to Weymouth	35010	12	5 early
241-249	111 pm Portsmouth Hbr to Wolverhampton LL	73117/6870	10	13 late. Changed engines
253	Down freight	76011	54	
257	128 pm Portsmouth Hbr to Wolverhampton LL	6937	10	Right time
304	125 pm Lymington Pier to Waterloo	D6524	11	9 late
307	1145 am Wolverhampton LL to Poole	7914	11	16 late

Time	Train	Engine	Load	Notes
309	101pm Bournemouth West to Waterloo	34053	12	Right time
323	1000 am Manchester Pic to B'th West	35027	11	15 late. Pines Express
				* stopped by shed and then thrashed away to reach 55 mph by bridge

Table 11

SOUTHAMPTON TO WATERLOO

Date	5th June 1965
Train	220 pm Bournemouth West to Waterloo
Engine	BR Standard Class 5 4-6-0 No. 73092
Load	8 coaches, 267 tons tare, 285 tons gross
Driver	Jackson, Nine Elms MPD
Position	Back of train
Recorder	DB

	miles	sched	mins	secs		speed
Southampton	0.00	0.00	00	00		
Northam Jct	1.05	3.30	03	33		16*
St Denys	2.11		05	25		38
Swaythling	3.45		07	22		47/51
Eastleigh	5.80	10.00	10	16		41* sigs
Allbrook Box	6.66		11	27		47½
Shawford	9.61		14	59		52
Shawford Jct	10.48		15	54		52½
St Cross Box	11.50		17	08		52½
Winchester City	12.70		18	36		53
Winchester Jct	14.85		21	02		53½
Wallers Ash Box	17.55		24	11		51½
Weston Box	19.05		25	54		51
Micheldever	21.18		28	19		53
Roundwood Box	23.05		30	26		54
Waltham Box	24.15		31	41		59
Steventon Box	25.30		32	49		63
Wootton Box	26.75		34	11		64
Worting Jct	28.98	37.00	36	22		60*
Basingstoke	31.50		38	33		72½
Newnham Siding	35.55		41	48		77½
Hook	37.08		43	03		71½
Winchfield	39.41		45	03		70
Fleet	42.76		47	53		72
Farnborough	46.05		50	45		68
Sturt Lane Jct	47.05		51	40		66½
MP 31	48.25		52	46		64½

	miles	sched	mins	secs		speed
Pirbright Junction	49.60		53	59		70½
Brookwood	51.25		55	19		72/63½
Woking Jct	54.50	61.00	58	20		67
Woking	54.95		58	43		70½
West Byfleet	57.56		60	56		73
Byfleet & New Haw	58.84		62	04		67½
Weybridge	60.09		63	15		64
Oatlands Box	61.15		64	10		66
Walton	62.16		65	04		71
Hersham	63.33		66	01		74
Esher	64.85		67	19		73
Hampton Court Jct	65.90	71.00	68	10		74½
Surbiton	67.20		69	16		73/70½
New Malden	69.46		71	08		72½
Raynes Park	70.60		72	19		23* tsr
Wimbledon	72.05		75	21		37
Earlsfield	73.66		77	44		51
Clapham Junction	75.31	81.00	79	53		43*
Queens Road	76.43		81	30		54
Vauxhall	77.93		83	04		43*
Waterloo	79.24	88.00	85	50		
	net time 83 minutes * brakes depart 9½ mins late, arrive 7 mins late					

Table 12

OBSERVATIONS AT BROCKENHURST

Date   FRIDAY 27th MAY 1966

Time	Train	Engine	Notes
646 pm	435 pm Waterloo to Weymouth	35003	3 mins late. Driver Harry Pope, Nine Elms
650 pm	Shunting vans	80085	
725 pm	651 pm Bournemouth to Woking	76016	Right time. The Mogul train
726 pm	713 pm from Lymington Pier	41230	5 mins early
732 pm	523 pm Waterloo to Bournemouth	73115	Right time.
759 pm	530 pm Waterloo to Bournemouth	35026	7 mins late
802 pm	8 pm to Lymington Pier	41230	2 mins late
806 pm	615 pm Weymouth to Waterloo	34004	4 mins early
822 pm	614 pm relief Waterloo to Bournemouth	34108	
829 pm	622 pm Waterloo Bournemouth	73119	7 mins late
845 pm	630 pm Waterloo to Weymouth	34034	16 mins late
850 pm	Up vans	80085	
901 pm	725 pm Eastleigh to Bournemouth	73113	16 mins late

Time	Train	Engine	Notes
958 pm	724 pm Waterloo to Bournemouth	73086	21 mins late
1005 pm	815 pm Weymouth to Eastleigh	35028	3 mins late

Table 13

Waterloo to Woking

Date	18th May 1964
Train	154 pm Waterloo to Woking
Loco	BR Standard Class 4 4-6-0 No. 75072
Load	3 coaches 101 tons tare, 105 tons gross
Driver	Grainger Nine Elms
Recorder	John Evans and DB
Weather	hot and sunny

	miles	sched	mins	secs		speed
Waterloo	0.00	0.00	00	00		
Vauxhall	1.29		02	44		45
Queens Road	2.81		04	17		60
Clapham Junction	3.93	7.00	05	44		53
Earlsfield	5.58		07	36		62
Wimbledon	7.24		09	11		65
Raynes Park	8.64		10	25		69
New Malden	9.78		11	26		71
Berrylands	10.98		12	24		72
Surbiton	12.04		13	20		74
Hampton Court Jct	13.34	18.30	14	23		75
Esher	14.39		15	14		78
Hersham	15.91		16	29		77
Walton	17.08		17	24		74
Oatlands Box	18.10		18	16		72
Weybridge	19.15		19	07		77
Byfleet and New Haw	20.40		20	06		82
West Byfleet	21.68		21	02		80
Woking	24.29	31.00	23	53		
	depart right time arrive Woking 7 early					

Table 14

Basingstoke to Woking

Date	2nd January 1967
Train	635 pm Salisbury to Waterloo
Engine	BR Standard Class 4 2-6-0 76066
Load	8 coaches and 2 vans, 327 tons tare, 345 tons gross
Driver	J J Smith Nine Elms MPD
Recorder	DB
Position	Rear
Weather	Cold and dark

	miles	sched	mins	secs		speed	
Basingstoke	0.00	0.00	00	00			14 late
MP 46	1.75		03	36		49	
Newnham Siding	4.10		06	14		56½/55	
Hook	5.59		07	50		57½	
MP 41	6.75		09	06		56	
Winchfield	7.92		10	22		58	
MP 38	9.75		12	10		64½	
Fleet	11.27		13	36		62	
MP 35	12.75		15	6		60	
Farnborough	14.55		16	57		54	
Sturt Lane Jct	15.60		18	11		55½	
MP 31	16.75		19	31		54	
Pirbright Jct	18.26		21	00		60	
Brookwood	19.76		22	33		64/65½	
MP 27	20.75		23	30		63	
Woking Jct	23.00		25	56		51	
Woking	23.46	28.00	26	50			13 late

Table 15

ENGINES STOPPED		
29TH AUGUST 1966		
73043	35023	35003
34066	73022	35010
73087	34044	35007
82029	34019	75070
34036	73037	34089
34008	73020	30064
34047	35026	73171
34002	41301	75076
34021	76033	34023
34025	73092	34093
34104	76014	34088

Table 16

LYMINGTON PIER TO BROCKENHURST

Date	6th March 1967
Train	220 pm Lymington Pier to Brockenhurst
Loco	BR Standard Class 4 2-6-4 tank No. 80152
Load	2 coaches, 67 tons tare, 70 tons gross
Recorder	DB

	miles	sched	mins	secs		speed
Lymington Pier	0.00	0.00	00	00		
Lymington Town	0.52	2.00	01	29		
	0.00	0.00	00	00		
Ampress	0.97		02	24		32½
MP 98	1.15		02	47		37
MP 97½	1.65		03	35		38
MP 97	2.15		04	22		37½
MP 96½	2.65		05	14		34
MP 96	3.15		06	00		38½/41½
Lymington Jct	3.97	7.30	07	20		18*/37
Brockenhurst	4.94	10.00	09	30		
	* brakes					

Table 17

LYMINGTON PIER TO BROCKENHURST

Date	1st May 1965
Train	11.20 am Lymington Pier to Brockenhurst
Loco	LMS Class 3 2-6-2 tank No. 41312
Load	2 coaches, 64 tons tare, 66 tons full
Recorder	DB

	miles	sched	mins	secs		speed
Lymington Pier	0.00	0.00	00	00		
Lymington Town	0.52	2.00	02	02		
	0.00	0.00	00	00		
Ampress	0.97		03	02		23
MP 98	1.15		03	39		26½
MP 97½	1.65		04	42		30
MP 97	2.15		05	52		24
MP 96½	2.65		07	26		18½
MP 96	3.15		08	42		26/32
Lymington Jct	3.97	7.30	10	23		25*
Brockenhurst	4.94	10.00	12	41		
	* brakes					

Table 18

SOUTHERN STEAM FLEET JANUARY 1966

		NINE ELMS 70A	FELTHAM 70B	GUILDFORD 70C	EASTLEIGH 70D	SALISBURY 70E	BOURNEMOUTH 70F	WEYMOUTH 70G	RYDE 70H	TOTALS
MN	4-6-2						7	9		16
BB/WC	4-6-2	4			26	16	8			54
U	2-6-0			4						4
N	2-6-0			6						6
USA	0-6-0T			1	5					6
Q1	0-6-0			3						3
O2	0-4-4T								14	14
BR 5	73XXX 4-6-0	1		13	9			8		31
BR 4	75XXX 4-6-0				10					10
BR 4	76XXX 2-6-0				14	3	9			26
BR 4	80XXX 2-6-4T	9	6		7	4	7			33
BR 3	82XXX 2-6-2T	8								8
LM2	2-6-2T						6	3		9
TOTALS		22	6	27	71	23	37	20	14	220

Table 19

ALTON TO WINCHESTER

Date	18th September 1966				
Train	430 pm Waterloo to Weymouth				
Train Engine	Rebuilt Battle of Britain Class 4-6-2 No. 34087 *145 Squadron*				
Pilot Engine	BR Standard Class 3 2-6-0 No. 77014				
Load	11 coaches, 373 tons tare, 405 tons gross				
Driver Train Engine	Phillips, Bournemouth				
Pilotman	Ward of Guildford on No. 34087				
Driver Pilot Engine	Hutchings, Eastleigh				
Recorder	Terry Jackson				

	miles	sched	mins	secs		speed
Alton	0.00	0.00	00	00		
MP 50	0.85		03	07		26
MP 50½	1.35		04	05		31½
MP 51	1.85		05	06		28
MP 51½	2.35		06	22		22
MP 52	2.85		07	48		20½
MP 52½	3.35		09	23		17½
MP 53	3.85		11	10		16½
Medstead & Four Marks	4.45	12.00	13	06		16*/58
Ropley	7.50		17	06		55½/56½
Alresford	10.15	22.00	20	47		16*/54½
Itchin Abbas	13.80		26	00		50/53
Winchester Jct	16.95	31.00	31	26		16*/35
MP 66	18.45		detach 77014			0
Winchester City	19.05	34.00	39	16		
						* brakes

Table 20

BOURNEMOUTH AND SALISBURY LINE TRAINS FROM WATERLOO
Date   MONDAYS TO FRIDAYS IN JUNE 1966

Time	Train	Booked engine	Shed
115 am	Plymouth	DL	
230 am	Portsmouth Hbr	WC/BB	Eastleigh
245 am	Bournemouth Central	WC/BB	Eastleigh
440 am	Woking	Class 5	Nine Elms
530 am	Weymouth	WC/BB	Salisbury
718 am	Salisbury	Class 4 75xx	Eastleigh
810 am	Weymouth Quay	WC/BB	Eastleigh
830 am	Weymouth	MN	Bournemouth
835 am	Weymouth	WC/BB	Eastleigh
9 am	Exeter St Davids	DL	
930 am	Bournemouth Central	WC/BB	Eastleigh

Time	Train	Booked engine	Shed
1030 am	Weymouth	MN	Bournemouth
11 am	Salisbury	DL	
1130 am	Bournemouth Central	WC/BB	Eastleigh
1230 pm	Bournemouth Central	MN	Weymouth
1 pm	Exeter St Davids	DL	
130 pm	Weymouth	MN	Weymouth
3 pm	Exeter St Davids	DL	
330 pm	Weymouth	MN	Weymouth
335 pm	Bournemouth Central	WC/BB	Bournemouth
435 pm	Weymouth	MN	Weymouth
5 pm	Exeter St Davids	DL	
509 pm	Basingstoke	WC/BB	Eastleigh
523 pm*	Bournemouth Central	WC/BB	Eastleigh
530 pm	Bournemouth Central	MN	Weymouth
541 pm	Salisbury	WC/BB	Salisbury
6 pm	Salisbury	WC/BB	Salisbury
609 pm	Basingstoke	Class 5	Guildford
622 pm*	Bournemouth Central	WC/BB	Eastleigh
630 pm	Weymouth	MN	Weymouth
654 pm	Salisbury	WC/BB	Salisbury
7 pm	Exeter St Davids	DL	
730 pm	Weymouth	MN	Bournemouth
920 pm	Bournemouth Central	MN	Bournemouth
1035 pm	Weymouth	WC/BB	Eastleigh
* Fridays only			

Table 21

SOUTHERN STEAM FLEET JANUARY 1967

Class	No.	Wheel	NINE ELMS 70A	GUILDFORD 70C	EASTLEIGH 70D	SALISBURY 70E	BOURNEMOUTH 70F	WEYMOUTH 70G	RYDE 70H	TOTALS
MN		4-6-2						10		10
BB/WC		4-6-2	9		12	9	6			36
USA		0-6-0T		1	5					6
O2		0-4-4T							2	2
BR 5	73XXX	4-6-0	6	6	2			4		18
BR 4	75XXX	4-6-0			5					5
BR 4	76XXX	2-6-0		5	4	3	5			17
BR 4	80XXX	2-6-4T	8		4		5			17
BR 3	82XXX	2-6-2T	2							2
BR 3	77014	2-6-0		1						1
LM2		2-6-2T	2		1		5			8
TOTALS			27	13	33	12	21	14	2	122

Table 22

KNOWN 100 MPH RUNS WITH BULLEID PACIFICS 1965-1967

Engine	Train	Date	Load	Crew	Details
34008 *Padstow*	245 am Waterloo to Bournemouth	?.8.1966	?	Matthews, Nine Elms	100 mph at Weston
34013 *Okehampton*	6 pm Waterloo to Salisbury	01.12.1965	215 tons	Matthews and Davis, Nine Elms	100 mph at Hurstbourne
34013 *Okehampton*	649 am Salisbury to Waterloo	17.12.1966	135 tons	West, Nine Elms	100 mph at Hersham
34042 *Dorchester*	245 am Waterloo to Bournemouth	14.04.1965	270 tons	Hooper and Daley, Nine Elms	102 mph at Winchester Jct
34102 *Lapford*	638 pm Salisbury to Waterloo	14.06.1967	235 tons	Gaffney and Lee, Nine Elms	100 mph at Bramshot
35003 *Royal Mail*	638 pm Salisbury to Waterloo	19.04.1967	215 tons	Enticknapp and Gaffney Nine Elms	100 mph before Fleet
35003 *Royal Mail*	638 pm Salisbury to Waterloo	27.04.1967	245 tons	Chapman and Symon, Nine Elms	100 mph before Fleet
					101 mph at Bramshot
					100 mph before Brookwood
35003 *Royal Mail*	615 pm Weymouth to Waterloo	26.06.1967	180 tons	Burridge and Symon, Nine Elms	106 mph before Fleet
35003 *Royal Mail*	615 pm Weymouth to Waterloo	28.06.1967	180 tons	Burridge and Roscoe	105 mph before Fleet
35005 *Canadian Pacific*	920 pm Waterloo to Bournemouth	15.05.1965	355 tons	Hooper and Wilson Nine Elms	105 mph before Winchester Jct
35007 *Aberdeen Commonwealth*	530 pm Weymouth to Waterloo	15.11.1966	375 tons	Porter	102 mph after Winchfield
35008 *Orient Line*	638 pm Salisbury to Waterloo	05.07 1967		De'Ath Basingstoke	102 mph after Grateley
35023 *Holland Africa Line*	Spl Waterloo to Salisbury	15.10 1966	280 tons	Hooker and Deadman, Nine Elms	101 mph at Andover
35028 *Clan Line*	530 pm Weymouth to Waterloo	12.12.1966	375 tons	Porter and Lee, Nine Elms	103 mph before Fleet

Gordon Porter, driver on so many
good runs, at Southampton in 1967.
Les Kent collection

CHAPTER THREE
THE ENGINEMEN

In the early days of train spotting on the bridge at Bromley South we became aware that a certain Stewarts Lane driver by the name of Sam Gingell was probably the one responsible for some of the explosive starts by King Arthurs, BR Standard Class 5s and Maunsell D1 and E1 4-4-0s up the 1 in 95 gradient to Bickley. Such names as Bill Hoole on the A4 pacifics and driver Jack Swain with fireman Bert Hooker on Bulleid pacifics became legend, the latter following their exploits during the locomotive exchanges in 1948. It was also that pairing who were reputed to have reached the same speed as the number on the engine with Bulleid light pacific No. 34107 *Blandford Forum* whilst working an up express past Brookwood in the 1950s. Whatever the truth behind this story,

which came from an uncle who worked with the engines, Bert Hooker certainly acquired a taste for speed as he was one of the elite band of enginemen who were timed driving a Bulleid pacific at 100 mph or more in the 1965-67 period. In those last few years some of us youngsters became quite close to the 'fast' men who were treated with something approaching hero worship for their exploits. Tracking down the names of the men at the remaining steam depots and the work that they did has proved to be more difficult than delving into the history of the locomotives; but once again, with the help of some of my colleagues from the days of steam and using the information from my notebooks and from the engine duties I have been able to piece together a reasonable amount of data.

Ace fireman of so many good runs, Dave Wilson, on the footplate of Merchant Navy No. 35023 *Holland Afrika Line.*
Dave Wilson collection

8 P

35023

Nine Elms driver B. McLaggon on No.35003 *Royal Mail* **at Southampton in 1967.** *Les Kent collection*

In May 1965 there were four links at Nine Elms and inevitably as these crews covered the majority of turns from Waterloo, the names of these men feature in a significant number of the runs in Chapters Four, Five and Six. Men from Bournemouth MPD also featured well and there were still a few steam turns for the Salisbury men who had become well known to us for their work on the *Atlantic Coast Express* and other West of England expresses until the Western Region took over and downgraded the line west of Salisbury. Other depots whose crews were involved in 1965 were Eastleigh, Basingstoke, Guildford and Weymouth, though men from the latter did not work north of Southampton. The table shows the steam hauled departures and arrivals at Waterloo in May 1965 with the depot of the crews that worked them, where known. Table 23 – *See page 81.* This table has been put together from detail in my notebook and partly from memory and once again my old friends from the days of steam have been a great help. Total accuracy is not guaranteed though. So of the faster trains including the two hour

expresses, which lasted until the new timetable which applied from 14th June 1965, Nine Elms and Bournemouth more or less shared these. Notice that Nine Elms No.3 link had a lot of work including the 5.30 pm Waterloo to Bournemouth as far as Eastleigh, returning on the vans and empty stock train at 8.40 pm. It was on the 5.30 pm that so many good runs were recorded by such fast men as Gordon Porter and Eric (Sooty) Saunders and it was the latter who on in the last week of the old timetable tried every day to equal the rumoured 40 minute timing between Waterloo and Basingstoke of the new electric service which was to apply from June 1967, later amended to July. He also wanted to beat the fastest known steam time set on 15th May 1965 by Gordon Hooper on the 9.20 pm down. The fireman on the epic runs on the 5.30 pm that week was Dave Wilson who has written the footplate perspective in Chapter Seven. No 3 link also included driver Dave Parsons who gave me a number of very good runs on the footplate including 95 mph efforts with both the rebuilt and original versions of a

Nine Elms No. Two link driver Gordon Hooper on the footplate of rebuilt West Country class pacific No. 34036 *Westward Ho!* **whilst working the 9.33 am down Excursion on Good Friday 8th April 1966.** *John Tiley*

Bulleid light pacific. The drivers in Nine Elms Nos. 1 and 3 links at that time are shown in Table 24 – *See page 82.* I do not have full details of Nine Elms No 2 link at that time but it included Gordon Hooper and Bert Hooker, both 100 mph men and indeed Gordon Hooper was responsible for the only absolutely certain recorded 3,000 indicated horsepower from a Bullied pacific with No. 35012 *United States Line* and its 76 mph climb to Roundwood in April 1965. Other No 2 link men were Bill Anderson, Harry Pope, Dickey Budd, Bert Fordrey, Syd Cull, George Enticknapp, Reuben Hendicott, Jim Evans, Clive Groome and Bill Plumb. All of these were fast men and it was men from this link that produced most of the good runs in the final years. No 4 link also included some very good drivers including the aforementioned John (Boy) Gaffney, another 100 mph man. In the week beginning 3rd May

Bill Anderson on No. 34036 *Westward Ho!* **at Fareham on a diverted Waterloo to Bournemouth train in 1967.** *Les Kent collection*

Bert Fordrey at Southampton Central while working the 5.23 pm Friday only train from Waterloo to Bournemouth. Note his highly polished shoes. In the background are Les Kent and Terry Jackson. *Les Kent collection*

Harry Pope walks round No.34007 *Wadebridge* oiling up as the engine takes water at Salisbury on a down train in 1965. This is probably one of the steam hauled summer only trains from Waterloo which went west of Salisbury, possibly the 8 am Waterloo to Sidmouth. *Les Kent collection*

Jim Evans and Graham Pack on the footplate of Battle of Britain class pacific No. 34052 *Lord Dowding* about to leave Waterloo on the 5.09 pm to Basingstoke on 8th May 1967. *Author*

On 11th September 1965 Bill Kiff awaits the right away from Southampton on Battle of Britain pacific No. 34082 *615 Squadron* working the 1.25 pm Weymouth to Waterloo. *John Tiley*

1965, Harry Pope worked the 8.30 am down on the Monday, Wednesday and Friday returning on the train due back at Waterloo at 2.09 pm and Gordon Hooper on the Tuesday, Thursday and Saturday. His run down on 7th May with No. 35028 and back with No. 34089 are both described in Chapter Four.

The top link men at Nine Elms also included some who were happy to drive their engines hard and not just to keep time but to produce some good runs and these included Ted Male, Bill Kiff, 'Conker' Gee, Arthur Camp and George Holloway. 'Spot' King and Fred Prickett were real gentlemen who treated their engines with care but could still produce good runs and both always had time to talk to us youngsters often berating the way that the fast men thrashed the engines and exceeded speed limits. Amongst the lesser known men was Sid Nash and though I cannot trace a run behind him in my records

he clearly spent some time in the top link. All of them though would try to keep their trains to time, whatever the allocated engine and amongst them were some real characters. Ernie Harvey had an allotment next to the main line at Earlsfield and one abiding memory is of him standing by his patch holding two canes in the air in a victory sign as we passed with a fellow Nine Elms top link driver at the regulator of the 10.30 down. He was also the one who at Basingstoke one morning was heard to ask his fireman ''ain't you uncoupled yet'' in that unmistakable London voice of his. I could tell many stories about Bill Kiff but suffice it to say that he was one of the fast men who could always be relied on the produce a good run and without fail tried to get the last Weymouth back into Waterloo well before the Long Bar closed. The table shows the Nine Elms No 1 link and some of their allocated work for the week

On 3rd July 1965 at Bournemouth West Nine Elms No. One link driver Sid Nash with rebuilt Battle of Britain class pacific No. 34052 *Lord Dowding* **on the 2.13 pm to Waterloo.** *John Tiley*

Firemen John Roscoe and Barry Cox give a Bulleid pacific their attention. It was the firemen who did most of the work though the drivers sometimes swapped places with them. *Les Kent collection*

John (Boy) Gaffney in front of the departure board at Waterloo. *Peter Austin*

ending 1st May 1965. Table 25 – *See page 82* It has not been so easy to gather information on the fireman at Nine Elms during that time as so often it was the drivers who stole the limelight, but it should not be forgotten that it was the fireman who did most of the hard work. Some of the driver/firemen combinations were as follows:

Eric (Sooty) Saunders and Dave Wilson or Alan Roe

Reuben Hendicott and Bill Stanley or Ray McQuade Jim Robinson (Snr) and Pete Roberts

George Enticknapp and Norman Vidaurri

Gordon Hooper and Ray McQuade or Alan Cook

Gordon Porter and Tom Moult

Clive Groome or Peter Steward and Robbie Lee

George Holloway and Colin Gray

Bert Hooker and Alan Newman

John Gaffney and Tom Moult

That was all in May 1965 prior to the big timetable change in June of that year. By October 1965 Nine Elms had three links as shown in Appendices D, E and F. These show the complete rotas for the week beginning 25th October 1965 and are scans of the actual Enginemen's Roster posted at Nine Elms showing the complete driver/fireman combinations for that week and is surely the most comprehensive record available from that time. The driver links were reformed during the 1965/1966 period when No. 1 link was increased to 24 drivers and No. 2 link reduced to 16 and drivers of all four links are shown in Table 26 – *See page 83.* Towards the end of steam some men from the top link opted to retire or take local work so there was a fair amount of reshuffling amongst the links at that stage. Other Nine Elms drivers who were around at that time and not already mentioned or in one of the tables were Tommy Clarke, Jim Robinson (Jnr), Fred Smith, George Lloyd, Peter Shackleton, Tim Crowley, John Westgate, Snelling, Frank Morris, Phil Bassett, Dave Davis and Bob Payne.

As can be seen from Table 27 – *See page 84,* that men from Bournemouth top link had a hand in many of the faster trains in May 1965, including the prestigious *Bournemouth Belle* in both directions on Mondays to Fridays. This was also a two hour train at that time and with its normal load of ten Pullmans and a bogie van, grossing about 455 tons, was the hardest task on the main line, especially when a Merchant Navy pacific was not available and one of the smaller pacifics deputised. The full Bournemouth top link rota for the week ending 16th January 1965 is shown in the table. Bournemouth drivers received a lot of adverse comment in the last two or three years of steam as there were some who would not make the effort to keep time unless they had the right engine in good condition. An example of this was on 19th April 1965 when with Rebuilt West Country No. 34017 *Ilfracombe* in perfect condition and fresh from a light casual overhaul finished just ten days before, the Bournemouth top link driver who shall be nameless, lost nearly 11 minutes

Driver Ron Bennett and fireman Dave Deadman on No. 35023 *Holland Afrika Line.* *Les Kent collection*

unchecked from Southampton to Waterloo. When asked what the problem was he replied that it was the wrong class of engine. (The train was booked to be hauled by a Merchant Navy pacific). Equally there were some good drivers such as Jack Varney who with his regular fireman Condon turned in some great performances some of which are included in the next chapter. Others were Woods, Short,

Peyton, Young (No 1), Hutton with his mate Jones, and Hardy. It was Hutton who produced a truly brilliant run with BR Standard Class 5 No. 73117 with the 6.30 pm down on the evening of the Clapham Junction signal box collapse also shown in the next chapter. An example of the work of Woods on the heavy *Pines Express* is shown in Table 28 – *See page 85.* Bournemouth No. 2 link also had some good drivers, including Bill Sanson and French. Other No. 2 link drivers were Baker, Hockaday, Elliot and Roles. Footplatemen from Eastleigh shed also had turns to and from Waterloo, including the 'Club Train' until early 1966 off which they went home as ordered, the 10.35 pm down Mails off the 8.25 pm arrival for a time from June 1966, and the up *Channel Islands Express* until the end of steam. There were some very good drivers at Eastleigh including Roy Sloper, Shepherd and his regular mate Hill, Hoskiss, Lockhart, Bailey, Living, Jones and

Alexander. Roy Sloper gave me a number of footplate rides. He lived to the good age of 95. Driver Pearce from Eastleigh worked the last up *Channel Islands Express* on 8th July 1967. Even with the demise of steam on the faster west of England trains, Salisbury men still had work in 1965/66 which took them to Waterloo, including the 6 pm Waterloo to Salisbury and 6.54 pm Waterloo to Basingstoke. Table 29 – *See page 86,* shows the driver rota for these trains in the spring/summer of 1965. Fred Hoare was perhaps the best known as a result of his exploits on the *Atlantic Coast Express* up until September 1964, but other fast men still around from those glory days were Cox, Burton and Hooper. One story that I recall about Fred Hoare was that he was booked up to London one weekend and his return train was diverted because of engineering works via Southampton and Romsey for which he had a pilotman. He was another one of the older men who was

Weymouth crew Ted Murphy and Ray Wills on No. 35023 *Holland Afrika Line* **at Wareham in 1967.** *Les Kent collection*

always happy to talk to us youngsters and with his regular mate Pete Allen was still around working the 6 pm down until Nine Elms men took over this turn. Weymouth men knew the road as far as Southampton and worked the 'Club Train' that far until the end of steam. Drivers included Watts, Allen, Murphy and Phillips. Basingstoke and Guildford crews also had some main line turns in 1965/66. Basingstoke men worked the 'Mogul Train' from Basingstoke to Woking until the end of steam and the 6.29 am Basingstoke to Waterloo in 1966. They also covered the 5.09 pm Waterloo to Basingstoke in 1965. In June 1966 Guildford men worked the 6.09 pm from Waterloo to Basingstoke and also the 6.35 pm Salisbury to Waterloo as far as Woking in 1965. There were some very good drivers at these sheds including Harris, Warren, Ward, Earl, De'Ath and Ken Parker from Basingstoke plus Cobbett and Allingham from Guildford. Guildford drivers along with drivers from Fratton and Eastleigh provided pilotmen for drivers from other sheds when trains were diverted via the Portsmouth direct or Mid Hants lines due to engineering work. Even Feltham could claim a main line turn in the spring of 1965 in the form of the 7.54 pm Waterloo to Basingstoke and Fratton men had steam turns on local work. Now we move to the main chapters of the book covering the locomotive performance in the period 1965 until the end of steam in July 1967.

On 30th March 1964 fireman Les Hoath on Rebuilt West Country class pacific No.34009 *Lyme Regis* **awaits the right away at Woking on the 9.30 am Waterloo to Bournemouth.** *Author*

Tables

Table 23

STEAM HAULED TRAINS TO AND FROM WATERLOO-MAY 1965

Date   MONDAYS TO SATURDAYS WITH MPD RESPONSIBLE FOR ENGINEMEN

DOWN	UP		DOWN	UP	
215 am	934 am	Nine Elms No. 3 link on Mondays to Fridays	254 pm	1116 am	Salisbury
215 am	1000 am	Nine Elms No 3 link on Saturdays	330 pm MF	1154 am	Bournemouth No 1 link
230 am MF	751 am	Nine Elms No 3 link to Basingstoke	335 pm MF	815 pm	Nine Elms No 1 link to Eastleigh
230 am SO	822 am	Nine Elms No 3 link to Basingstoke	335 pm SO	1154 am	Bournemouth No 1 link
245 am	1050 am	Nine Elms No 2 link	354 pm	909 pm	Nine Elms No 1 link
440 am	1226 pm	Nine Elms No.1 link on Saturdays	435 pm	1056 pm	Nine Elms No 1 link
440 am	1226 pm	Nine Elms No 3 link on Mondays to Fridays	509 pm		Basingstoke
530 am	1246 pm	Nine Elms No 3 link	523 pm FO		Nine Elms No 3 link
720 am			530 pm	1107 pm	Nine Elms No 3 link
810 am			543 MF	821 pm	Nine Elms No 1 link
830 am	209 pm	Nine Elms No 2 link	554 SO		
835 am	409 pm	Nine Elms No 2 link	600 pm	326 pm	Salisbury
930 am		Basingstoke men to Eastleigh on Mondays to Fridays	609 pm		Guildford
		Nine Elms No 1 link to Eastleigh on Saturdays	622 pm FO		
		Eastleigh men from Eastleigh	630 pm	240 pm	Bournemouth No 1 link
954 am		Guildford	654 pm	534 pm	Salisbury
1030 am	626 pm	Nine Elms No 1 link	730 pm	440 pm	Bournemouth. No 2 link MF and No 1 link SO
1054 am		Salisbury	A/O	735 pm	Eastleigh
1130 am	859 am	Eastleigh	754 pm		Feltham
1154 am	942 am	Salisbury	854 pm	752 pm	Salisbury No 1 link
1230 pm	1000 am	Bournemouth No 1 link on Mondays to Fridays	920 pm	640 pm	Bournemouth No 1 link Mondays to Fridays
1230 pm	640 pm	Nine Elms No 2 link on Saturdays	920 pm	348 am	Nine Elms No 3 link on Saturdays
1235 pm SO	1000 am	Bournemouth No 1 link	A/O	840 pm MF	Eastleigh
1239 pm SO		Salisbury	1035 pm	348 am	Nine Elms NO. 3 link on Mondays to Fridays
1254 pm MF			1035 pm	821 pm	Eastleigh on Sturdays

DOWN	UP		DOWN	UP	
124 pm SO			1135 pm SO	840 pm SO	Eastleigh
130 pm	1149 am	Bournemouth No 1 link			
154 pm					
A/O: As ordered					
FO: Fridays only		SO: Saturdays only			
MF: Mondays to Fridays					

Table 24

NINE ELMS DRIVER LINKS 1966
Date   NINE ELMS DRIVER LINKS 1966 (EXACT DATE UNKNOWN)

NE 1	NE 2	NE 3	NE 4
Anderson	Evans	Adams	Aynsley
Blanchard	Gammon	Aplin	Bennett
Budd	Hendicott	Ball	Chapman
Cull	Hooper	Boyce	Coppard
Domm	Hughes	Burridge	Cummings
Doust	Jackson	Coles	Dente
Enticknap	Neville	Collison	Dominey
Fordrey	O'Dell	Conlon	Gaffney
Hadley	Plumb	Groome	Gale
Harvey	Robinson	Gyles	Hutchinson
Hawkins	Skinner	Hamlin	Matthews
Holloway	Slimmon	Harrington	McMail
Hooker	Steward	Knight	Payne
Hurley	Sullivan	McLaggon	Pearce
King	Sutton (A)	Mercer	Pilcher
Lloyd	Walker	Nott	Roycroft
Male		Parsons	Smith
Mills		Porter	Taylor
Pope		Prior	Thompson
Prickett		Saunders	Twyman
Roberts		Stonestreet	West
Robinson		Watford	Yardley
Sutton (C)		Wilton	
Turner		Wright	

Table 25

NINE ELMS DRIVERS MAY 1965

NO I LINK	NO 3 LINK
Male	Adams
Hurley	Aplin
Camp	Boyce
Cutting	Brown
McCarthy	Burridge
Holloway	Callow
Bowen	Coles
Harvey	Gammon
Gee	Hamlin
Kiff	Jackson
King	McLaggon
Prickett	Nott
Robinson	Neville
Sartin	O'Dell
Sutton (C)	Porter
Turpin	Prior
	Saunders
	Skinner
	Slimmon
	Steward
	Sullivan
	Sutton (AW)
	Walker
	Wright

Table 26

NO. 1 LINK DRIVERS ROSTER W/E 1ST MAY 1965 (INCOMPLETE)

	MONDAY	TUESDAY	WEDNESDAY	THURSDAY	FRIDAY	SATURDAY
Male						
Hurley						
Camp	543 pm/821 pm	543 pm/821 pm	543 pm/821 pm	543 pm/821 pm	543 pm/821 pm	
Cutting	354 pm/909 pm	435 pm/1056 pm	354 pm/909 pm	435 pm/1056 pm	354 pm/909 pm	435 pm/1056 pm
McCarthy						
Holloway	435 pm/1056 pm	354 pm/909 pm	435 pm/1056 pm	354 pm/909 pm	435 pm/1056 pm	354 pm/909 pm
Bowen						
Harvey						
Gee						
Kiff						
King						
Prickett	1030 am/626 pm		1030 am/626 pm		1030 am/626 pm	
Robinson		1030 am/626 pm		1030 am/626 pm		1030 am/626 pm
Sartin						1230 pm/640 pm
Sutton (C)						930 am/?
Turpin						

All times are at Waterloo; the first time being the down train and the second the up train

Table 27

BOURNEMOUTH TOP LINK DRIVER ROSTER W/E 16th JANUARY 1965

	MONDAY	TUESDAY	WEDNESDAY	THURSDAY	FRIDAY	SATURDAY
Sprague	-	240 pm/630 pm	-	Pines both ways	-	440 pm/730 pm
Adams	1149 am/1.30 pm	-	1154 am/330 pm	-	1000 am/1230 pm	-
Varney	640 pm/920 pm	-	240 pm/630 pm	-	Pines both ways	-
Langdon	-	1149 am/130 pm		1154 am/330 pm	-	York both ways
Woods	-	640 pm/920 pm	-	240 pm/630 pm	-	Pines both ways
Dean	1000 am/1230 pm	-	1149 am/130 pm		1154 am/330 pm	-
Short	Pines both ways	-	640 pm/920 pm	-	240 pm/630 pm	-
Young (1)	-	1000 am/1230 pm	-	1149 am/130 pm		1000 am/1235 pm
Beavis	-	Pines both ways	-	640 pm/920 pm	-	240 pm/630 pm
Hutton	1154 am/330 pm	-	1000 am/1230 pm	-	1149 am/130 pm	-
Young (2)	240 pm/630 pm	-	Pines both ways	-	640 pm/920 pm	-
Hardy	-	1154 am/330 pm	-	1000 am/1230 pm		1149 am/130 pm

All times are at Waterloo; the first being the arrival time of the up train and the second the departure time of the down train

Pines Express: 1000 am Bournemouth West to Oxford and 204 pm return

York: 1045 am Bournemouth West to Oxford and 403 pm return

Table 28

SOUTHAMPTON TO BOURNEMOUTH

Date	4th September 1965
Train	10 am Manchester Piccadilly to Bournemouth Pines Express
Loco	Rebuilt Merchant Navy class 4-6-2 No. 35029 *Ellerman Lines*
Load	13 coaches, 456 tons tare, 500 tons gross
Driver	Woods, Bournemouth No. One link
Fireman	not recorded
Recorder	DB
Weather	warm and sunny

	miles	sched	mins	secs	speed
Southampton Central	0.00	0.00	00	00	slipping
Millbrook	0.90		03	35	30½
Redbridge	2.65	5.00	06	05	49
Totton	3.30		06	50	51
Lyndhurst Road	6.15		10	06	53
MP 86	6.75		10	45	61½
Beaulieu Road	8.85		12	51	56
Woodfidley Box	10.45		14	23	66½
MP 90½	11.25		15	06	63
MP 92	12.75		16	25	70½
Brockenhurst	13.55		17	09	63
Lymington Jct	14.50	24.00	18	07	56
MP 94½	15.25		18	57	51
Sway	16.30		20	13	53
New Milton	19.30		23	21	60
MP 100	20.75		24	50	55½
Hinton Admiral	21.80		25	50	63
MP 103	23.75		27	47	58½
Christchurch	25.10		29	04	65
Pokesdown	27.05		30	59	54
Boscombe	27.60		31	41	50
			sigs stop		
MP 107½	28.25		33	02	0*
			39	00	
Bournemouth Central	28.80	47.00	40	59	
					* brakes
net time 34 minutes					

Table 29

SALISBURY TOP LINK ROTA FOR WATERLOO TRAINS 1965

326 pm/6 pm driver	week ending	534 pm/654 pm driver
Joslyn	02.04.1965	Sibley
Bowles	09.04.1965	Pistell
Emm	16.04.1965	Hooper
Singleton	23.04.1965	Phillips
Moore	30.04.1965	Cox
Sayer	07.05.1965	Simms
Blandford	14.05.1965	Hoare
Sibley	21.05.1965	Kelly
Pistell	28.05.1965	Burton
Hooper	04.06.1965	Joslyn
Phillips	11.06.1965	Bowles
Cox	18.06.1965	Emm
Simms	25.06.1965	Singleton
Hoare	02.07.1965	Moore
Kelly	09.07.1965	Sayer
Burton	16.07.1965	Blandford
first time is arrival at Waterloo and second is departure		

CHAPTER FOUR
1965

So now we come to the main purpose of this book which is to describe the locomotive performance during the final two years and just over six months of steam out of Waterloo. All the best runs that I have been able to find are included, and whilst most are timed by myself, others have searched their attics and archives and added many more including some which I knew about but had never seen tabulated before. In this respect Terry Jackson has been of immense help with his well organised record of that period which is probably the most comprehensive in existence.

First though a few words on conventions used and some technical aspects. Throughout the book I have used the 12 hour clock as this was still in use at the start of the period covered and also it seems more appropriate to that era. In the train running logs and descriptions I have used the terms slow line (SL) and fast line (FL) as this is what my old notebooks show, even though the working timetables referred to local (LL) and through lines (TL). Other terms referred to in the logs are shown below and apply to all logs in the book.

SVO: safety valves open (engine blowing off steam).

Asterisk * : brakes or speed restriction, either permanent or temporary.

tsr: temporary speed restriction, usually for track works

A word on mileages. The mileages I have used are from my old mileage books compiled at the time using my timing points on stations and at junctions and signal boxes and where possible checked against the Rail Performance Society database. They have been adjusted to take account of the cumulative mileage error which applies as far as Milepost 78 on the Southampton line where a correction takes place so that there is a short quarter mile of just 208 yards. There is a similar adjustment between Tunnel Junction and Salisbury. For consistency I have stuck to using these distances even though in some cases my recent calculations for locations which no longer exist (such as signal boxes) show that the likely actual mileages are slightly different, meaning that some speeds are not fully supported by the averages calculated from the mileages shown in the train running logs. However it is statistically likely that where the average speeds between two particular points for a large number of logs is inconsistent with the timed speeds then it is the mileage shown which is wrong and not the speeds. An example of signal box mileages showing the distances used against the likely actual distances is shown below.

DISTANCES FROM SOUTHAMPTON CENTRAL		
Roundwood Box	23.05	23.08
Waltham Box	24.15	24.23
Steventon Box	25.30	25.38

It should also be remembered that GPS did not exist then and runs were timed by sweep hand stopwatches; and whilst these were generally very accurate they relied on the good eyesight and consistent approach of the user in picking up the tiny LSWR mileposts, though at least the lineside was not in the overgrown state it is today. This and in some cases, doubtful mileage accuracy of stations, junctions and signal boxes were the reasons why I increasingly used full milepost times and speeds in addition to stations etc. The mileages shown in the contemporary Working Timetables and Sectional Appendices are the incorrect unadjusted mileages. The train running logs timed by Terry Jackson use his mileages which may differ slightly from those which I use.

From time to time I refer to the power outputs produced by the locomotives in terms of equivalent drawbar horsepower (EDBH) and indicated horsepower (IHP). This is a complex and much debated subject but essentially EDBH is the power exerted in moving the train taking into account the weight of the train, the speed and gradient, and whether the train is accelerating or slowing down. The resistance figures for rolling stock and basic formula for calculating EDBH figures are those published in the *Railway Magazine* in January and February 1968. IHP is the total horsepower including locomotive horsepower. The locomotive horsepower increases with speed and some years ago I constructed a graph from which can be read off the horsepower for each type (i.e. class 5, 7 or 8) at various speeds. Factors such as wind speed and direction, plus whether or not the track is jointed also affect the final figures; but I have not found a definitive way to allow for these so they are mentioned where relevant. These things can make enough of a difference to turn a very high output into a phenomenal one, a good example being the run on 12th December 1966, which may or may not have been the highest power output of any Bulleid pacific partly dependent on whether or not the track was jointed. So whilst this is not an exact science I have been consistent throughout in my method which aids comparisons. Regarding position in trains; normally on down trains from Waterloo I would be at the front but on up trains I chose the back, so start to pass times can be compared on a like for like basis.

I said earlier in the book that I would not describe the route in great detail but nevertheless in setting the scene with a quite ordinary run from Waterloo right through to Weymouth on 24th January 1965 with which I kick off this chapter I have described the main gradients and speed restrictions which the enginemen had to encounter. This was on the 1.30 pm

from Waterloo, which was actually a cut above normal for a Bournemouth driver, albeit one from No. 2 link as they tended to be younger and faster than the more senior men in the top link. I suspect the driver might have been Bill Sanson, but whoever it was he was a friendly type who invited me onto the footplate at Waterloo where I noted that the boiler pressure was 190 lb about ten minutes prior to departure. An Ocean Liner Express left at 1.24 pm and we were to catch this three times before our first stop at Basingstoke, though without any significant delay. With a modest load of 9 coaches, about 325 tons full, No. 35028 *Clan Line* got away on time up the initial tricky curved and uphill start before the dip past Queens Road and the restricted passage of Clapham Junction and the climb to milepost 5 saw us past Wimbledon at 58 mph before we got our first slight check from the 1.27 pm semi-fast train to Portsmouth and Alton which had no doubt caught the Ocean Liner Express. The easy gradients on to Hersham saw speed rise to 73 mph before another check at Walton, though we were up to 72 mph again into the dip at Byfleet Junction which is the foot of the 9.35 mile climb at 1-in-387/326/314/298/304 to Milepost 31, which was again interrupted by adverse signals after which the driver decided to take things easily along the largely level stretch to Milepost 38, where the line climbs to just beyond Winchfield. It was down this dip in the up direction that many of the maximum speeds were recorded, including the highest known speed with Southern steam, 106 mph on 26th June 1967. On the 1.30 pm down we continued to run easily on to the Basingstoke stop, past Hook and into the slight dip after Newnham siding which marks the foot of the 8 mile climb at 1-in-249 to just before Wootton Box. We stopped in Basingstoke in 53 minutes 39 seconds from Waterloo, a gain of a minute and a half in schedule and with a net time of 51½ minutes for the 47.75 miles. Here No. 35028 took water; and now well behind the boat train we were away three and a half minutes late for good run on to Winchester, reached two minutes inside schedule after a long relaying slack past

Worting Junction and with a maximum speed of 83 mph down the 1-in-252 which is almost uninterrupted from the middle of Litchfield tunnel following an undulating stretch from Wootton. This climb in the up direction produced some quite phenomenal feats of high power output, including the highest known with Southern steam as well as some of the 100 mph runs going down. Two and a half minutes late away from Winchester we ran smartly down the continuing 1-in-252 to Allbrook Box and on down easier gradients past St Denys to a signal stop at Mount Pleasant before a long speed restriction after Tunnel Junction saw us into Southampton Central just over six minutes late.

On to Bournemouth the line is interesting with many restrictions and varied changes of gradient from a level stretch as far as Totton, just before which the line crosses the Test estuary on a causeway, followed by a short sharp climb culminating at 1-in-200 to Lyndhurst Road. Then a downhill stretch before another sharp climb at 1-in-150 to Beaulieu Road after which the line falls past Woodfidley Box in the middle of an attractive undulating section through the New Forest at Brockenhurst. Here the line climbs at 1-in-176/200 to Lymington Junction steepening for the final mile of 1-in-103 to the summit at Milepost 94½. Then follows another varied stretch to Milepost 100 and downhill past Hinton Admiral to the foot of the bank over the river Avon just before Christchurch preceding a section of 1-in-99 to Pokesdown and a summit at Milepost 107½ before a final drop down into the curving platforms of Bournemouth Central. In the up direction this little climb made for some interesting starts with Bulleid pacifics on heavy trains and, in my view, the 32 minute booking to Southampton of the up fast trains was the hardest on the whole line and needed good enginemanship for timekeeping. It was probably my favourite stretch of line on the whole route and it was always exhilarating to get the initial climb behind us and sweep down to Christchurch with speed mounting rapidly. On the 1.30 pm down *Clan Line* did well to reach Bournemouth just under two minutes late

after being seven and a half minutes late away from Southampton, especially as the rain was now very heavy. The sure-footed climb away from Brockenhurst was particularly noteworthy. From Bournemouth we had a Weymouth crew and the train was now reduced to just three coaches, so the engine performance with such an excess of power was of little interest. Suffice it to say that from being slightly late away we arrived at Dorchester South two and a half minutes early, only to be held by signals at Dorchester Junction for over six minutes, presumably for a late running train off the Westbury line to clear and so final arrival at Weymouth was four minutes late.

I returned almost straight away on the 5.50 pm semi-fast train to Waterloo which had No. 34034 *Honiton* on six coaches for 215 tons full. From Weymouth the line is level for the first half mile and then climbs steeply to the north end of Bincombe tunnel, first at 1-in-187 to Radipole, then at 1-in-74 to Upwey and 1-in-50/52 for the remaining three miles to the top of the climb. The load limit for Bulleid light pacifics on the climb was 290 tons (about 7 coaches) and it is amazing to recount that driver Pete Roberts (ex Nine Elms fireman) took 11 coaches up this bank unaided with No. 34067 *Tangmere* on a main line special on 10th July 2009 after the banking diesel locomotive had failed! The line now drops at 1-in-91 past Moncton and Came to Dorchester South, situated on a slight hump and where at this time the up platform was separate from the down and had to be reached by reversal from the main line. From there the start was downhill for a short distance and then followed just over a mile of 1-in-200 up to Milepost 133 after which a lovely downhill stretch at 1-in-240/100/180 took us to Wareham, with a slight hump at Moreton and again before Worgret Junction. After Wareham easy gradients followed until the 1-in-60/130 climb of Parkstone bank after Poole took the line to Branksome and along to Bournemouth. On the 5.50 pm from Weymouth No. 34034 made a workmanlike climb of Upwey bank reaching 26 mph before falling to a minimum of 22 mph in the pouring rain, with no slipping noted. It was however the romp down Moreton bank which was the highlight of this run, speed reaching 82 mph before a stop for signals at Wool destroyed the prospect of an even time run to the Wareham stop. Another good climb of Parkstone bank would have seen us into Bournemouth just a few minutes down except for a long stop for signals outside. We left there 14 minutes late and were the same amount in arrears at Waterloo with our load now increased to 12 coaches for 435 tons full, after some unenterprising running and further signal checks, a common feature of the running at that time.

I have described these two runs in some detail including a route description in order to set the scene for what follows and, although all the runs will be touched on, only the best will be tabulated in detail. These are shown in the Main Appendix. On 26th February and 11th March I timed two good runs on the 6 pm Waterloo to Salisbury commuter train with identical times of 48 minutes 36 seconds for the 47.80 miles from Waterloo to Basingstoke from two of Salisbury's' finest enginemen, Messrs Cox and Hoare, with rebuilt light pacifics on good 11 coach loads of around 400 tons. Whilst No. 34089 was in tip top condition, No. 34012 was a bit run down and so the detail was different with No. 34089 giving the better climb to milepost 31 with a very good minimum speed of 66½ mph and a subdued finish after 78 mph at Fleet whereas No. 34012 kept going well right to the stop. Both trains were very early into Basingstoke though. In late February and early March I timed a selection of runs over the racing stretch from Basingstoke to Woking, 23.46 miles, where even time 60 mph start to stop runs were quite common even with heavy loads and with drivers who would not have been considered fast men. On 23rd February George Bowen had BR Standard 5 No. 73170 on the last Weymouth and produced a time of 23 minutes 15 seconds unchecked with 405 tons, maximum speed 78 mph and on 2nd March 'Spot' King had No. 34009 on the same train

with 330 tons and did the run in 23 minutes net, maximum 75 mph. Even Charlie Sutton, not known for fast running, produced a time of 23 minutes 47 seconds with No. 34077 on 395 tons on the 3.00 pm Bournemouth up, reaching 74 mph! George Bowen had an easier task on 26th February when he had No. 34026 on the 6.35 pm Salisbury and had a net time of 22½ minutes with 215 tons, maximum speed 77½ mph. During this period we were spoilt for choice for trains to catch after work but a very common combination was either the 5.30 pm or 6.00 pm down, both first stop Basingstoke, returning on the 8.15 pm or 8.21 pm arrivals at Waterloo, both at that time worked by Nine Elms top link men. The stopping pattern of the semi fast trains then in both directions generally included Eastleigh, Winchester, Basingstoke and Woking. No main line steam hauled trains called at Clapham Junction. This meant that

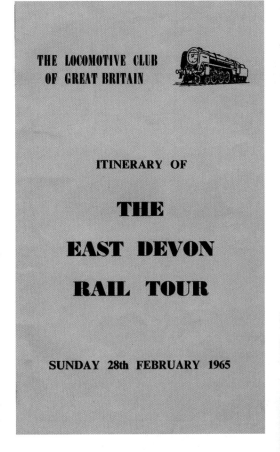

THE LOCOMOTIVE CLUB
OF GREAT BRITAIN

ITINERARY OF

THE

EAST DEVON

RAIL TOUR

SUNDAY 28th FEBRUARY 1965

The East Devon railtour was very popular and was repeated the following week. Here, No. 35022 stands at Axminster on 7th March 1965. *John Tiley*

the scope for fast times from Basingstoke to Woking was significant and some good times were recorded though not many in the same

Another shot of No. 35022 taking water at Yeovil Junction whilst working the East Devon railtour on 28th February 1965. *John Tiley*

league as in 1967 when enginemen were really going for it.

I was not a great one for going on special train trips but one I could not resist was the *East Devon Tour* on Sunday 28th February 1965. This was booked an unprecedented nonstop run from Waterloo to Yeovil Junction, 122.65 miles in 123 minutes. Remember there were no water troughs on the Southern so the only way it could be done safely was by using a Merchant Navy with a 6,000 gallon tender, as it turned out the excellent No. 35022 *Holland America Line,* limiting the train load to ten coaches and by careful driving. In fact as **65.01** shows we did not manage the run nonstop but the net time was well within the booking at 117½ minutes. Nine Elms driver Arthur 'Spot' King was the ideal choice as he was not one of the 'thrash' men and handled the engine perfectly aided by one of the best young firemen at Nine Elms, Dave Wilson. He had swapped turns in order to work this train and amazingly fired all day from start to finish apart from a midday break between the down and up trains. The running was fast downhill, with 90 mph attained at both Andover and Sherborne but really the story is about water conservation.

Dave takes up the story:

'There were dramas and incidents on the footplate of which the passengers knew nothing. For the crew the 'non-stop' didn't mean signal checks but actual stops - so for us this was a non-stop run. The one stipulation that I was given, as to whether we stopped or not, was that we had to have water 'in the tap' when we passed Worting. If there had been no water in the tap at Worting then we would have had to stop at Salisbury for water - this would have, for the crew, broken the non-stop aspect of the run.

The journey out to Worting could have been faster, but this would use more water, so it was always going to be something of a balancing act between speed and water consumption. I had taken every possible precaution, getting the engine ready myself and ensuring the tender was full to the brim and the boiler well filled before we left Nine Elms for Waterloo. I made up the fire in anticipation of what was to come and to try and avoid any blowing-off, which wastes a lot of water. I had never worked west of Salisbury - so for me once we passed Salisbury I was going to have to take advice on where and when we were going to need steam.''

The return run was also booked nonstop

No 35022 *Holland America Line* **takes water at Yeovil Junction on Sunday 28th February 1965 whilst working the East Devon Railtour. The run from Waterloo, ostensibly non stop, is shown in** 65.01 . *John Tiley*

On 7th March 1965, No.35022 *Holland America Line* stands at Seaton Junction with the second East Devon Rail tour. *John Tiley*

but once again this was not to be and we got back over half an hour late though with some fast running with 89 mph though Andover and 86 mph after Winchfield. This fast running didn't reflect the drama being seen on the footplate though and again Dave Wilson takes up the story:

'On the return journey everything was going well - though I did lose my seat to a footplate passenger. However, as we cleared Tunnel Junction disaster struck. A huge 'cob' of coal fell right across the shovelling plate and refused to budge. There was only one solution - I would have to go through the tender door and manhandle the lump through the door onto the footplate. Getting into the tender whilst on the move is not only a breach of company rules, it is a dangerous thing to do - but it was either this or stop in section and sort it out. Stopping wasn't a favoured option because we were already on the climb to Grateley. Between us Inspector Jupp and I managed to get the lump onto the footplate and even into the firebox. Thankfully there were no further incidents before we reached Waterloo and our relief crew. I had paid fireman Henning to swap turns - the passengers had had a whip-round for the crew - it covered what I paid fireman Henning with a little to spare! It wouldn't have mattered if it didn't - I'd still have done the job. It wasn't about the money but 'being there doing it' - a truly memorable trip and with light engine movements and the like, a journey of close to 400 miles - or Euston - Glasgow and I still had a couple of weeks to go before my 18th birthday!''

This trip was repeated on 7th March. After such a memorable trip we return to the reality of day to day running in 1965 with a couple of runs timed by David Foale on the cross Country route

On 7 March 1965, No. 35022 *Holland America Line* stands at Yeovil Junction with the second East Devon railtour from Waterloo. *John Tiley*

from Salisbury to Portsmouth. Many trains were still steam and the run behind No. 34066 on 320 tons on 16th January was particularly good with 76 mph attained on the level at Dean after five miles of gradients as steep as 1-in- 236 from Romsey, but No. 34077 also did well with a time of 24 minutes 7 seconds from Southampton over the heavily restricted 14.50 miles to Fareham. Basingstoke to Woking featured highly in my travels reflecting both my inability to stay away from that favourite section and also the lack of any great excitement at that time on the

faster limited stop trains. Different approaches to the lightly loaded 6.35 pm from Salisbury produced some variety as the table shows with Jim Robinson Snr producing a very fast start to stop average with No. 34052 and Ernie Harvey just keeping the schedule with No.34100 despite being three minutes late, and there were some good runs with heavier trains, the one with No. 34025 being remarkable as coming within a whisker of even time without exceeding 72 mph. There was another very fast run on the up Salisbury with the excellent No. 34032

BASINGSTOKE TO WOKING 23.46 MILES								
Date	05.03.65	11.03.65	12.03.65	13.03.65	24.03.65	27.03.65	29.03.65	21.04.65
Train	6.35 Sals	6.35 Sals	4.55 Bm	1.00 Bm	6.35 Sals	6.15 Wey	6.15 Wey	615 Wey
Engine	34052	34100	34041	34025	34032	34023	34098	34050
Load	215t	215t	385t	395t	210t	320t	325t	295t
Time	21/46	25/03	23/51	23/29	21/47	23/42	23/19	22/56
Net					21	23	22¾	22
Max	83	77½	77½	72	82	79½	82½	79½
Av	64.67				64.62		60.37	61.38

Camelford while there were three good even time actual or net time runs on the moderately loaded 6.15 pm last Weymouth up, all of them recovering lost time. The run with Fred Prickett in charge of No. 34098 was particularly pleasing for a driver not known for fireworks, but for good old fashioned enginemanship. Normally at the other end of the scale Frank Matthews seemed to be quite subdued with *Blackmore Vale* though maybe it was due to having problems with the valve gear as later in the run the engine dropped the inside set and became a failure at Wimbledon; one of only three failures on the main line that I experienced in over 75,000 miles behind Bulleid pacifics.

Saturday 13th March saw me on the 8.35 am semi-fast train to Southampton as the first part of a full day travelling behind steam which produced no less than four runs worthy of mentioning in this chapter. Gordon Hooper had Giesl-fitted No.34064 *Fighter Command* on a decent load of just under 400 tons on the 8.35 down. Gordon always reckoned that the Giesl-fitted engine was nearly as good as a Merchant Navy and as 65.02 shows this certainly seemed to be the case with some fast running after slowish starts and a lovely romp down Roundwood to reach 93 mph before the Winchester stop. I returned to London behind No. 35029 on the 12.46 arrival and Bournemouth men; a reasonable run ruined by signal checks from the preceding football excursion which left Southampton five minutes in front of us and then went down on the 1.30 pm with No. 35003 as far as Basingstoke before returning to London again behind No.34025 with Gordon Hooper, the Basingstoke to Woking section of which is discussed above. Arrival at Waterloo was slightly late but unabated I carried on back down to Southampton on the 4.35 pm behind No. 35029 and George Holloway on the regulator. This was a good solid performance with a ten coach 370 ton load and gave a net time to Winchester of just 63½ minutes without reaching 80 mph. Finally on that day of 412½ miles behind Bulleid pacifics came a very good 76 minute net run up from Southampton for the 79.24 miles behind No.35004 on 350 tons with

driver Bailey from Eastleigh in charge again without quite reaching 80 mph. The highlight was the excellent climb of Roundwood bank with no less than 69 mph at Winchester Junction before checks intervened. It is possible that we were following another train in from Worting Junction though there is nothing recorded to that effect in my notes. The eight minute late arrival at Waterloo was symptomatic of the poor operating at the time and a slightly sad end to a very good day. Gordon Hooper was beginning to feature increasingly in my travels and a typical run with him in charge was with No. 35007 on the 5.30 pm down on 18th March. Although very good the net time of 44¼ minutes was not exceptional for this train in view of what was to follow prior to the slowing down of the schedules in June. Recovery from the speed restriction through Woking up the 1-in-314/298/304 to Milepost 31 was however very good requiring 35% cut off and nearly full regulator. Early running could be a feature of this train though the semi- fast 5.09 pm down in front could sometimes be a problem as it ran fast line before transferring to the slow before Farnborough.

Amongst the Bournemouth drivers at that time Jack Varney was considered to be the best and he was almost always paired up with fireman Condon. It was always worthwhile sampling one of his efforts on a Bournemouth two hour train and so on Saturday 27th March I went down on the *Belle* behind No. 35007 in order to catch the 1.30 pm Weymouth from Southampton to Waterloo. The run down was spoilt by signal checks once again but No. 35027 had a good road as far as just after Clapham Junction passed in just 71 minutes 6 seconds for the 75.31 miles, six minutes early before checks and a long stop for signals outside Waterloo ensured a loss of time. On 10th and 21st April with No. 35023 and 35007 respectively he produced two more very good up runs to demonstrate just how consistently good he was. No. 35023 was obviously in top form and the time of 69 minutes 14 seconds to pass Clapham Junction was one of my fastest beaten only by the quite exceptional run on 4th

On 27th March 1965 a filthy No. 35007 *Aberdeen Commonwealth* leaves Southampton on the down Bournemouth Belle with driver 'Conker' Gee in charge. The run from Waterloo had been quite competent in a net time of 78 minutes, with a maximum speed of 81 mph at Winchester Junction, but was spoilt by many out of course delays so the train was about 10 minutes late leaving. *Author*

April. The average speed from Basingstoke to New Malden was 77.43 mph, maximum 87 at Fleet and with the engine eased after Woking. I have tabulated the return runs 65.03 and 65.04 on the 6.30 pm down with the Varney/Condon combination and once again both were very good, with *Aberdeen Commonwealth* on 12 for 435 tons. The second

In October 1964, No. 35023 *Holland Afrika Line* stands at Southampton Central on the 10.30 am Waterloo to Weymouth while No. 35022 *Holland America Line* arrives on the 10.42 am Poole to Sheffield Midland. *John Tiley*

run on 21st April 65.04 produced my fastest net time to Winchester but was unfortunately slightly spoilt by signal checks which could be a problem on this train. Notice the wonderful climbs to Milepost 31, topped at 70 mph on both runs, the first one recovering from 66½ mph through Woking and the quite exceptional average speed of 77.03 mph from Brookwood to Hook on this run, with speed maintained at 80 mph plus all the way from before Fleet until after Newnham Siding, against the collar. I estimate that the equivalent drawbar horsepower (EDBH) climbing from Woking to Milepost 31, where the average gradient is just a bit over 1-in-314, on the first run to be in the region of 1,700 or at that speed about 2,350 Indicated horsepower (IHP). To achieve this I estimate that Varney would have used full regulator and 22% from Woking, then probably dropping the lever back to around two thirds

after the summit. Just to show that it was not just Jack Varney who could put up a show amongst the Bournemouth men driver Hardy had charge of a rebuilt light pacific No. 34037 on 29th March on the full 12 coach 435 ton load on the 6.30 pm down. The net time was an excellent 65 minutes and the running throughout was consistently good with a particularly fine climb to Wootton, minimum 61 mph and an uninhibited dash down Roundwood, maximum 84 mph. Some of the men from that Dorset shed would deliberately lose time if given the wrong class of engine as recounted in Chapter Three. These three fine runs are a complete contrast to the dismal running on this train I suffered in the winter of 1966, after Jack Varney and some of the faster men had retired.

Now we come to one of the greatest performances ever produced by a Bulleid pacific, which in a way sets the scene for the final few weeks before the new timetables were introduced in June, when the opportunity for really high speed runs was to be much reduced until the final few months of steam. It was in this Indian summer of the old order from around the beginning of April until the middle of June that most of the heavy load fastest time and highest power output runs were produced. On the day of the up *Belle* run shown in 65.05, Sunday 4th April, I went down to Southampton on the 1.30 pm down with Bill Sanson doing his best with a poor steaming, rough riding but free running unmodified 34041 *Wilton* and two extracts are included here. Table 30 – *See page 128.* The first shows a very lively start from Waterloo to pass Surbiton in 15 minutes 32 seconds after

a late start, despite a speed restriction at Loco Junction, and the extract sets out a fast unchecked run from Winchester to Southampton. Table 31 – *See page 128.* The rest of the run was spoilt by engineering work though we were not that late into Southampton. I am not sure why I did not go through to Bournemouth but no matter my eyes were firmly on a run on the up *Belle* with Gordon Hooper, who the grapevine had whispered would be in charge. No. 35012 *United States Line* had the usual *Belle* load of ten Pullmans and a bogie van 455 tons full. It was therefore somewhat strange to discover later that only a few of us (just myself, Alan Wild and maybe one other?) were on board to time this extraordinary effort and it is just as

On 4th April 1965 West Country class light pacific No. 34041 *Wilton* **leaves Southampton on the 1.30 pm from Waterloo with Bournemouth driver Sanson at the regulator. The Winchester to Southampton section of the running of that train is shown in the extract in** Table 30 **. That was the day of Gordon Hooper's up Belle run.** *Author*

well that I was not alone as if I had been then perhaps I would not have believed my stop watch! We got away from Southampton just a fraction late and made a good clean start to pass Eastleigh inside schedule at 63 mph, where Hooper was using full regulator and 22% cut off. Brian Smith was firing from Southampton and maintaining boiler pressure at 240 lbs plus all the way. Not sure if that was taken as a hint but Gordon wound the cut off round to 27% at Winchester Junction where we were doing 71 mph and I was by now getting really excited as I had timed nothing like this before. The noise from No 35012 was quite fantastic and increased as speed continued to rise, to 73 mph by Weston box and 75 at Micheldever and finally to an unprecedented 76 mph at Roundwood summit. Table 32 – *See page 129.* Brian Smith told me recently that boiler pressure was being maintained at 245-250 lbs and he had to use the second injector for a short spell to stop the engine from blowing off steam, so if the engine had been opened up to say 35% cut off then I think we would have achieved 80 mph at the top of the 1-in-252 climb. As it was I had just timed what was probably the highest power output ever from a Merchant Navy class pacific, the calculated figures over the final stretch being 2,325 EDBH and an amazing 3,085 IHP, one of the very few times this magic figure has been reached by any British steam locomotive in normal service. And what a demonstration of the steaming qualities of Bulleid's boiler! In DW Winkworth's book *Bulleid's Pacifics*, comparisons with other big efforts by other British steam locomotives puts this climb to Roundwood second only to the supreme effort by LMS Princess Coronation No. 6234 on test, when compared on the basis of IHP per ton of engine weight set against duration. For the section of the climb from Winchester Junction, where cut off was increased to 27% to the summit the EDBH was 2,175 and the IHP 2,905. This was over a period of nearly seven minutes.

Gordon Hooper wasn't finished yet though and as if to show that No. 35012 was in no way

winded by this phenomenal performance we streaked away to reach 83 mph at Steventon before easing for the approach to Battledown where we had a severe signal check down to little more than walking pace, which I thought might be a prelude to more delays from engineering works. It was not though, and then followed a breathtaking headlong flight along the South Western main line, incredibly unchecked to give an average speed of 86.82 mph over the 30.12 miles from Hook to Surbiton which included 93 mph down Winchfield bank and 94 at Brookwood with an easing to 85 mph past Woking and a minimum of 81 at Weybridge. Adverse signals and a track relaying speed restriction after Clapham Junction could not prevent an arrival in Waterloo just over nine minutes early, in an actual time for the 79.24 miles from Southampton of 74 minutes 13 seconds at an overall average speed of 64.06 mph. I calculate the net time to have been 69½ minutes which would have been good enough to have kept the new electric schedules which applied from July 1967, and the fastest known time with steam. I have always regarded this run to be my best with steam, though others in 1965 came close.

Anything after that had to be anticlimax, however good, but I timed a particularly fine effort with a light pacific on the 5.30 pm down on 13th April with that ace driver Gordon Porter in charge of No. 34090 on the usual 11 coaches for 400 tons. Checks in the early stages provided the incentive for a very good climb to Milepost 31. The EDBH was 1,360 from Byfleet Junction to Milepost 31 (IHP 1,950) and 1,510 from Woking to Brookwood (IHP 2,100). Subsequent fast running produced a 46 minute net time to Basingstoke, one of my best with a light pacific. The next log 65.06 shows a very fine run timed by Brian Smith on the 2.45 am down paper train with No. 34042 where Gordon Hooper managed to get No. 34042 *Dorchester* up to 102 mph on the descent of Roundwood bank, the highest known speed with a Bulleid light pacific. Although with a moderate load, the whole run was a *tour de force* as it included a fast run to the Woking stop, a quite brilliant effort from Woking to

Basingstoke which included a maximum of 88½ mph after Newnham Siding and a very rare 90 mph down the bank from the New Milton start. The 5.80 miles to the Christchurch stop occupied only 6 minutes 16 seconds and it is likely that even time was reached before the stop. The next two logs, **65.7 and 65.08** show two good runs from Bournemouth to Southampton on the very tight 32 minute schedule for the 28.80 difficult but interesting and varied miles. The run with No. 35019 shows what was needed to keep time and Reuben Hendicott with No. 35011 was above par with a heavy load. Note that fireman Bill Stanley and also Brian Smith were both involved again on a good run. There were many unspectacular but solid performances from Nine Elms No.3 link drivers with rebuilt light pacifics such as on the Fridays only 5.23 pm down on 23rd April 1965 with No. 34017 and driver Adams which needed a good climb to Wootton and a fast descent to Winchester to recover earlier delays. One of the

better Eastleigh driver/fireman combinations of Shepherd and Hill were responsible for the two very good efforts from Southampton to Waterloo with the 'Club Train' on 23rd and 24th April turning in net times of 75 and 76 minutes on consecutive evenings and Gordon Hooper put up a typically good show on the 8.30 am down with No. 35016 on 30th April also with a net time of 75 minutes despite injector trouble for some miles. Bill Plumb coaxed a good run out of a light pacific No. 34097 on 1st May without exceeding 77½ mph and despite a restrained run down the bank still caught the usual checks in the Eastleigh and St Denys areas which made timekeeping to Southampton on the down two hour trains almost impossible. Net time was a very good 76 minutes. Bill Plumb had a nice side line making little black lunch boxes for the drivers at Nine Elms and elsewhere known of course as 'Plum Boxes!' The next table, **65.09**, shows the details the continuation of the up *Belle* run with No. 35011

The engine on Reuben Hendicott's up Belle run, No 35011 *General Steam Navigation* passé Basingstoke on Saturday 10th July 1965 working the 10.55 am Bournemouth West to Waterloo. *Author*

No. 34009 *Lyme Regis* stands at Waterloo on 22nd July 1965. A picture full of the atmosphere of Waterloo in the 1960s. This engine featured in runs shown in the book, one of them being my only even time run from Basingstoke to Waterloo. Although the disc is showing Duty 431, which was the 5.30 pm to Bournemouth, the engine wasn't in fact working that train and the quiet platform suggests it was pre evening peak so it may have been working the 4.22 pm relief to Bournemouth West, a view supported by the train length which looks to be about 8 coaches. *Terry Jackson*

shown in 65.08 when Reuben Hendicott and Bill Stanley turned in an actual time of 76 minutes 48 seconds from Southampton to Waterloo or 73 minutes net of checks, to arrive eight minutes early, apparently in response to Gordon Hooper's superlative effort with No. 35012 on 4th April. It was not until after St Cross that Brian Smith threw down the gauntlet and Reuben reacted by increasing the cut off first to 22% and then to 30% in an effort to beat Hooper's 76 mph at Roundwood but having been checked in the Eastleigh area and then leaving the challenge a little too late plus with an engine maybe not quite as good, he had to settle for a 'mere' 72½ mph. Over the 5.50 miles from Wallers Ash, where

cut off was increased to 30%, to Roundwood the EDBH was 2,030 which gives around 2,710 IHP, not far off Hooper's run with No. 35012 and at the summit around 2,185 EDBH and 2,910 IHP. The flying average from Hook to Surbiton was 81.41 mph with plenty of steam to spare. Good though this run was, it pales in comparison with Hooper's record breaking performance on 4th April.

In the late spring the up Channel Islands boat train only loaded to around six coaches and so although an even time run from Basingstoke to Waterloo required little effort from No. 34009 which turned in a very rare actual even time of 45 minutes 24 seconds for the 47.75 miles without exceeding 82 mph, though with a light load of 245 tons. 65.10 shows the fastest net time runs on both the Waterloo to Southampton and Southampton to Bournemouth sections that I have been able to find. The engine was *Clan Line* and it almost goes without saying that the crew was Gordon Hooper, Paul Daley and Brian Smith. With a late start and 13 on for 475 tons to Southampton you might have expected some fireworks and maybe a clear run, but unfortunately it was not to be, though the net time of 71 minutes is unrivalled by any other run that I can find as is the 28 minutes net on to Bournemouth which included a very good minimum of 61½ mph after Lymington Junction and a very unusual, if not unique, 94 mph down Hinton Admiral bank. Returning the same day with rebuilt light pacific No 34089 the same crew turned in a good performance from Basingstoke to Waterloo with this 430 ton load to recover time lost through checks and arrive at the terminus two minutes early. It is possible that the time of 10 minutes 33 seconds to pass Hampton Court Junction, 10.95 miles from Woking is a record with a light pacific and this load and the Basingstoke to Woking time of 20 minutes 50 seconds, 67.54 mph may also be. Off the beaten track again are two more runs timed by David Foale between Salisbury and Southampton. The little BR Standard class 4 2-6-0 No. 76010 with an ideal six coach load was rather fiery in the last days of the steam hauled Cardiff to Portsmouth trains and its time of 19 minutes 19 seconds from Salisbury to Romsey would nearly have kept today's schedule timed for 85 mph class 159 Sprinters. And finally as a prelude to one of my best weekends ever of steam locomotive performance we have in 65.11 a wonderful effort with one of the much underrated BR Standard Class 5 workhorses, in this case No. 73117. The train was the 6.30 pm down and the reason for this Class 5 substitution on a train booked for Class 8 haulage was disruption caused by the collapse of the signal box at Clapham Junction. The train had the usual 12 coaches for 435 tons full and Bournemouth top link driver Hutton was in no way put off by his underpowered steed as the net time of

69 minutes to Winchester would have kept the schedule for this train. We left five minutes late and lost more time as a result of checks in the Clapham Junction area. The '5' then struggled a bit with this big load but was worked very hard up to Milepost 31 with speed only falling from 59 at Woking to 52½ at the summit. Plenty of steam was evident at Fleet and now we had consistent noise from up front as Hutton got 73117 well up into the sixties before Basingstoke and then followed a good and noisy climb to Wootton and a lovely dash down Roundwood to reach a maximum of 84 mph before the Winchester stop. The schedule had been kept from Woking and my notebook simply states 'brilliant'.

With just one month to go before the schedules were slowed down for the electrification work, the weekend of 14th to 16th May 1965 stands out as including some exceptional runs and 15th May in particular is still celebrated by a few of us each year as being one of the best days for timing steam we ever had, including as it did the fastest known steam time from Waterloo to Basingstoke and a 105 mph maximum speed, both on the same train. We knew in advance that some of the top Nine Elms crews would be out and so the double overnight epic started with Gordon Porter and Dave Wilson taking unconverted West Country pacific No. 34006 *Bude* along in fine style on the 10.35 pm down mails. It was quite unusual to record a time of under 20 minutes from Basingstoke to Winchester, but this was achieved comfortably with speed rising to 95 mph at Winchester Junction. The return run on the up mails behind No. 34018 was good but not exceptional and got us onto the 4.40 am down to Woking behind No. 73043 with Charlie Sutton followed by a return to Waterloo and a visit to 'The Lancaster Grill' for breakfast. I suppose at some stage we may have grabbed some sleep as I was wide awake to time a very fine effort on the 8.30 am down two hour train with Bert Fordrey driving one of my favourite Bulleid light pacifics, No. 34008 *Padstow*, deputising for a Merchant Navy, though on 10 instead of the more usual 12 coaches. The run is notable for a very fast spell over the 33.13 miles from

Fleet to Shawford where we averaged 75.5 mph including no less than 75 mph through Basingstoke well over the 65 mph speed limit, after a slowish start, suggesting maybe a last minute engine substitution. The net time of 75 minutes was my personal best with a light pacific. We returned to London behind No. 35023 on the 10.15 am from Southampton, a nonstop train but not one of the two hour trains. Beavis of Bournemouth did well enough on a light load to get us into Waterloo just over a minute early and in good time to join the down *Belle* where another light pacific was covering for a Merchant Navy, in this case No. 34021 *Dartmoor*. The ten Pullmans and a bogie van adding up to 455 tons was a much sterner proposition for Billy Hughes to cope with compared to the 8.30 am down especially as the engine was very rough and struggling for steam throughout. Despite this *Dartmoor* did well enough to record a net time of 79 minutes to Southampton and 31½ minutes on to Bournemouth. No. 35017 *Belgium Marine* was noted standing outside Eastleigh works as we past, having that day just being out-shopped from a Light Intermediate overhaul, its last before withdrawal in July 1966. We could have done with that engine instead of our struggling light pacific but we did not have to wait long for it to turn in a superb performance on the 5.30 pm down in the last week of the current timetables, during the race to Basingstoke week. After a swift dash under the subway to the up platform, a Bournemouth crew took us back to London on the 2.40 pm up two hour train, behind yet another Merchant Navy substitution in this case No. 34004 *Yeovil*. We ran well enough with nothing exceptional to arrive three minutes late whereupon I decided that a brief return home for rest and victuals was in order before returning to London for what turned out to be one of the finest steam performances ever seen on Southern metals.

When we had got back into London after the run with Gordon Porter on the 10.35 pm down early that morning, somebody had asked him if he was going to take the 9.20 pm down that night. The 9.20 pm train was a Bournemouth turn during the week but on Saturday nights at that time it belonged to Nine Elms men. He replied that he could not due to the difficulties of getting home to Basingstoke early on Sunday morning and that night we would have Gordon Hooper driving. We could hardly believe this as Nine Elms number two link did not have any fast Basingstoke turns at that time and the prospect of getting Gordon Hooper on such a turn was mouth watering and not to be missed. Somebody phoned Brian Smith and so we had Gordon Hooper with Dave 'Dropgrate' Wilson firing, accompanied by Brian Smith. I know that we had been told to expect something special but I do not think any of us quite expected the extraordinary run that unfolded, shown in `65.12` especially as there was a speed restriction for track repairs at Wimbledon and one was also expected near Weston. In fact despite the Wimbledon check our time to Basingstoke of 43 minute 48 seconds, a start to stop average of 65.41 mph, turned out to be the fastest ever recorded with steam, although the net time of 41¼ minutes was equaled or possibly bettered later that year. Our load of 9 coaches and a van adding up to around 355 tons was ideal for a Merchant Navy to break records and No. 35005 *Canadian Pacific* was the engine to do it. It was in fine form at that time. The 89 mph at Byfleet Junction was my personal best though the 77½ mph minimum at milepost 31 was slightly disappointing in the context of the rest of the run, but was possibly the result of Dave needing to get some water into the boiler at that point. We carried on at a fantastic rate averaging 86.71 mph from Farnborough to Newnham Siding, including a very rare 90 mph maximum at the latter point. So we rolled into Basingstoke no less than 11¼ minutes early giving us excited youngsters time to recover before the next stage. Here one or two timers alighted - I think these were Bob Grainger and M.D Barrett, whose log appears in D.W.Winkworth's book. I recall that they needed to get to Swindon to work a night shift. That left just four of us timers on the train for one of the hundred mile an hour efforts of those last few years, and for most of us the first and always fondly remembered as the best.

No.35005 *Canadian Pacific* working the down 'Bournemouth Belle' at Raynes Park exactly one year prior to its epic run, on 15th May 1964. *Author*

(Technically it was not though - see December 1966). The four were Terry Jackson, John Evans, brother Bryan and myself. After a good start from Basingstoke Gordon Hooper set the regulator at about three quarters open and the cut off at 22% which was good enough to get us up to 76 mph at Roundwood and the descent of the 1-in-252 to the Winchester stop. By Micheldever we were doing 86½ mph and soon after passed Weston Box at 94 mph where the track gang were standing back and ready to start work with their lights on as the block came on at 10.30 pm. At this point boiler pressure was 210 lb and Gordon increased the cut off to 27% to take us on the train into uncharted

territory with the sound of the rail joints merging almost as one as speed rose to reach 100 mph just after Wallers Ash Box causing great excitement in our compartment and making it difficult for me to concentrate on seeing the mileposts as I tried to record the details of this epic run. Into the tunnel now and through the long cutting past milepost 63 with the quarter miles now consistently below nine seconds and finally a reading of 8.6 seconds for the best quarter (agreed by us all), or no less than 105 mph, before an easing to 102 mph at Winchester Junction. The average speed from passing Wallers Ash had been 102.1 mph and we had run the 18.80 miles from Basingstoke to

This is the actual speedometer of No. 35005 *Canadian Pacific* showing the maximum speed it attained of 105 mph on the night of 15th May 1965. It was not, of course, taken on that night but is the product of the marvels of digital photography, though take on the footplate of No. 35005. *Bryan Benn*

Winchester in 18 minutes 50 seconds, a fraction short of 60 mph start to stop. My notebook simply states 'this beats everything'. At Winchester a businessman walked up to the front and took a long hard stare at the loco and crew though I do not think any words were exchanged but he probably knew what had happened. I think Gordon Hooper intended to disconnect the speedo and report it as not working but in the end didn't do so. At that time although 90 mph was tolerated, 100 plus certainly was not as the blind eyes of the last few weeks were some two years away. The 83 mph maximum speed before the Southampton stop where we alighted with our engine crew is hardly worth a mention after that. It has been calculated that if we had run non stop from Waterloo the net time would have been in the region of 65½ minutes for the 79.24 miles, nearly five minutes inside the best schedule for the electric service to be introduced in July 1967. We returned to London on the up Mails with Gordon Hooper and Dave Wilson on No. 34089 *602 Squadron* producing another good run. The 20 minute net time from Basingstoke to Woking was considered to be good at the time but unexceptional compared with what was to come later with this sort of sub 300 ton load. Once back in London early on the Sunday morning Brian Smith offered to take some of us home and so we set off in his big Vauxhall Cresta and after dropping Gordon Hooper somewhere in the south London area we ended up at home in Shirley near Croydon, drinking tea in the front room at around 6 am. I have never forgotten the look on my old mum's face when she came downstairs to see this collection of tired and dirty young men, including one, Dave Wilson, who looked like a chimney sweep! It was indeed a fantastic and never to be forgotten night. It is worth seeing fireman Dave Wilson's take on the night as follows;

'It is strange how everyone has a slightly different recollection of that May night so long ago. I knew something was up when we had an Inspector - Brian Smith - on the footplate. However it wasn't made entirely clear to me that we were going to

be setting records. All I was told was we needed to be in good order with steam and water, which we were throughout. I wasn't even told we were going to attempt the ton on the run down to Winchester. Even in the dark I could tell we were motoring so I went over to look at the speedo; the needle had passed the 100 mark! The gout of flame which blew back through the 'closed' Ajax doors as we entered Wallers Ash tunnel at 100 plus reached half way to the tender doors. I don't know about the injector on the climb up to milepost 31 but I would have had one injector running pretty much most of the time after we cleared the slack through Clapham. I remember Brian working the firedoors and I remember riding round the streets of London in the wee small hours, back to my lodgings in Earlsfield, after tea with Don and co.

Remember Dave 'Dropgrate' was just 18 years old at the time. Although Brian Smith was often referred to as an inspector, strictly speaking he was not that, but was working with the engines to find ways of improving performance.

We now move on from that special weekend to the following one when once again I was out overnight, this time to sample the work of Eric 'Sooty' Saunders and fireman Phil Bassett on the 2.45 am down paper train returning on the 7.37 am Weymouth to Waterloo, off Bournemouth at 8.40 am with the same crew. No. 34086 did very well on the paper train, just failing to achieve even time from Woking to Basingstoke reaching 86 mph on the slow line after Newnham Siding and No. 35026 gave me my personal best time from Bournemouth to Southampton of 30 minutes 32 seconds followed by another best net time of 62½ minutes up from Winchester and this with a heavy 12 coach load of 450 tons. At Bournemouth we had a choice to make between our train and the 7.20 am up from Bournemouth West which had No. 35023 with Gordon Porter and fireman Ibbs in charge. We had photographed both drivers together on the footplate of No. 35023 at Bournemouth. As it turned out this would have been the better choice as this run was one of the best ever up from Winchester, turning in a net time of under 60 minutes, one of the very few occasions when this was done with steam. The actual start to stop average from the Winchester start to a signal stop just after Hampton Court Junction was 66.05 mph despite three moderate signal checks. 65.13 shows the details of this fine run, timed by David Sprackland, the highlight being the climb to Roundwood summit passed at 74 mph from the start with 400 tons, thus putting this run alongside the very few with a Merchant Navy to get close to 3,000 IHP. My calculations show that *Holland Afrika Line* was putting out just under 2,000 EDBH or 2,700 IHP from Wallers Ash to Roundwood, 5.50 miles and at the summit the figures were 2,150 EDBH and 2,910 IHP. This compares very closely with Reuben Hendicott's up *Belle* run on 2nd May but is just below Gordon Hooper's supreme effort with No.35012 on 4th April. The next day, a Sunday, I decided to sample the up *Belle* with a light pacific and driver Dickey Budd did well enough with No. 34087 on the usual 455 ton load, turning in a net time of 79 minutes up from Southampton.

Basingstoke men worked the 5.09 pm down commuter train and this nearly always produced a good competent performance when taken instead of the 5.30 down if the latter did not have an attractive enough engine or crew. BR Standard class 5 No.73043 with driver Harris is a good example with 380 tons reaching Woking in 27 minutes 24 seconds actual time or 26½ minutes net after a continuous slog along in the seventies from Hampton Court Junction reaching a maximum of 75 mph in the dip at Byfleet Junction. This train could cause delays to the following 5.30 pm down if it wasn't sharp enough to clear the main line at Farnborough. Later that evening of 25th May I returned to London on the last Weymouth up behind No. 34086 and with Arthur Camp in charge we produced an even time Basingstoke to Woking run despite 410 tons behind the tender. This had followed a dreary run down on the 6.30 pm

with a poor steaming No.34102 *Lapford* and sound effort on the Mogul train with No. 31873. Driver Hockaday turned in a good competent performance from No. 35017 on the Sunday 1.30 pm down on Sunday 30th May. In fact with no great effort this run gave me my second fastest time from Southampton to Brockenhurst of 15 minutes 48 seconds. The reason for the trip was because George Enticknapp was rostered to work the up *Belle* and he had No. 35019 which produced an above par run without anything exceptional. Time was kept to Southampton and then Roundwood passed at 65 mph, followed by good fast running though with checks preventing a strictly on time arrival, but with a 76 minute net time. My note book tells me that my Pullman ticket was number D30. No. 34013 *Okehampton* did well on the heavy 6 pm Waterloo to Salisbury, the only remaining down semi-fast steam hauled train on the West of England line on 2nd June, Driver Hooper of Salisbury MPD turned in a typically good run throughout. On 4th June the record breaking *Canadian Pacific* was on the 8.30 am down, this time with Reuben Hendicott and Bill Stanley and maybe, knowing about Gordon Hooper's run on 15th May, he was trying to get to Southampton in under 70 minutes as the time of 37 minutes 2 seconds to pass Hook is the fastest recorded with steam. With 400 tons rather than the 355 of 15th May, the running as far as Hook was nearly as good. Milepost 31 was topped at 75½ after 84 at Byfleet Junction and the average speed from Farnborough to Hook was 83.70 mph. Even with subdued running down the bank the net time to Southampton in this fine run was no more than 71½ minutes so a sub 70 minute run would have been quite possible. The time of 29 minutes 12 seconds on to Bournemouth is believed to be the fastest with steam involving a minimum of 60½ mph before Sway, 86 down Hinton Admiral bank and an exuberant and illegal 70 mph through Christchurch. Terry Jackson, who timed this superlative run thinks they were near enough right time away from Waterloo, but he has a memory of being told that Bill Stanley 'pointed

On 30th March 1965, No. 34032 *Camelford* runs into Basingstoke with the 5.43 pm Waterloo to Salisbury semi fast train. This Salisbury based engine appeared frequently and often features in run covered by this book. *Author*

out' to Reuben that they had the same loco as Hooper had on the 9.20 and that anything he could do…! The full detail is in 65.14 . The next day, Saturday 5th June saw No. 34087 on the same train, this time with Fred Smith and Ken Seaby in charge on the same 400 ton load. The light pacific did very well securing a net time to Southampton of 75½ minutes and after a Windsor line start got over Milepost 31 at 67 mph after 75 in the Byfleet dip. The time of 31 minutes 19 seconds from Southampton to Bournemouth is the fastest I can find with a light pacific. I missed both of these runs as I had

gone to Scotland overnight on the 3rd/4th June to enjoy some very good runs with A4 pacifics and Stanier black fives. On the way up I had seen A1 pacific N0. 60146 at Doncaster, my last sighting of one of these fine locomotives, withdrawn in October that year. Quite why I had chosen to go north just then is a mystery, with just ten days left before the timetables changed; but who knows how the mind of this twenty year old steam fan worked then. The main thing was I was back for the finalé of the race to Basingstoke which took place during the week beginning 7th June. First off that week

65.15 sets out a fantastic effort of Gordon Hooper with No. 34032 *Camelford* on the semi-fast 10 am Salisbury to Waterloo where some fastest times were set between stops on the Basingstoke to Woking stretch, two of them close to even time over very short distances. The start out of Woking was also very fast though the time of 3 minutes 38 seconds to pass West Byfleet was equaled by 34093 *Saunton* with over 100 tons more on 7th July 1966. But before we get to the runs on the 5.30 pm down that week, it is worth going back to late 1964 when the seeds of the race to Basingstoke were sown. Word was that the new electric schedules would include a time of 40 minutes from Waterloo to Basingstoke and a certain Nine Elms driver by the name of Gordon Porter reckoned he could do it with steam; not with a light load mind you but with a Merchant Navy pacific on 11 or 12 on the 5.30 pm down. It was known that provided the 5.09 pm Basingstoke semi fast was behaving itself and there was no 5.23 pm, then the 5.30 pm would normally get a good road and an unchecked run was quite possible. So on 26th October 1964 with No. 35024 and 11 coaches for 400 tons Gordon did indeed have a clear run, albeit with a Windsor line start, costing about minute, the actual time being 43 minutes 55 seconds, or 43 minutes net. The running was good throughout but was beaten on later runs, though these were checked. It is interesting to realise that without the Windsor line start the actual time would have been 43 minutes, beating Gordon Hooper's record set on 15th May 1965. Gordon had another go on 12th November 1964 No. 35017 but this was not in the same league and so it was left to Eric 'Sooty' Saunders to attempt to beat Gordon Porter's time, which he had been boasting about at 'The Elms'. Gordon had tipped off David Sprackland that Eric Saunders and Dave Wilson would be working the 5.30 pm down during the week before Christmas 1964 and that David should be there as Gordon Porter had wound 'Sooty' up to have a go after overcoming his initial reluctance to get involved. The run with No. 35024 on 400 tons was a determined effort and the time of 23

minutes 53 seconds to pass Woking after another Windsor line start was truly fantastic even if the 74 mph round the curve at Raynes Park caused a massive lurch and some concern on the train! The 82 mph at Surbiton is the highest speed in the down direction at that point known with steam. Checks spoiled the rest of the run as the 5.23 pm was running that evening and this had caught the 5.09 pm down. However the net time of 41¼ minutes equaled that of the run on 15th May, by dint of a very fast start. This was the trademark of the way 'Sooty' decided that Basingstoke could be reached in 40 minutes and we were to see it again on 7th June. No further improvement was made that Christmas week in 1964 though No. 35022 produced another good effort as shown on 23rd December with the full 12 coach 445 ton load.

It was 24 weeks before the roster found Eric Saunders once again on the 5.30 pm down for the week beginning 7th June. Alan Roe had just replaced Dave Wilson as Eric's regular fireman but it appears that both were on the footplate on the Monday and maybe for the whole of the week. On the Monday of that week Dave Wilson had wound Sooty up to have a go and got him to arrange with Len Trigg (the running shed foreman) to swap the booked engine for No. 35005 *Canadian Pacific* as this was in such fine form at the time and it was the ideal locomotive to set a new fastest time. With a full 12 coach load of 435 tons the start was quite brilliant and we were past Surbiton in 14 minutes 16 seconds doing 77½ mph. By Esher with a continuous roar from the engine we were up to 83 mph but then suddenly the brakes came on and we stopped at Mole Intermediate signal about half way between Esher and Hersham . There was much cursing both on the footplate and by us timers on the train but we restarted with a vengeance. Dave Wilson recalls:

'005 was steaming beautifully. I'd built a great fire and we were flying when I spotted the distant 'on'. It was one of those distant which the fireboy saw first, Sooty was forced to shut off and make a brake application. After we were checked I said

Record breaking *Canadian Pacific* which got close to 3,000 Indicated horsepower on the supreme effort on the 5.30 pm down shown in **65.16** is shown here at Eastleigh after working a special train on 23rd May 1965. *Terry Jackson*

to Sooty that we should try to accelerate all the way over Milepost 31-and we very nearly did'

And so indeed we nearly did as after 74 mph at Byfleet Junction we were up to 76 mph past Woking and no less than 78 on the 1-in-314 at Brookwood. This extraordinary effort required full regulator and 40% cut off so it was no great surprise that the cylinders were starting to beat the boiler and speed dropped slightly to 75 mph at the summit. The average speed from Byfleet Junction to Milepost 31 was 77.03 mph and over that whole stretch of nearly eight and a half minutes I calculate that the EDBH was 1,850 and the IHP 2,700. During the acceleration from Woking to Brookwood when 40% cut off was used these figures rise to 2,050

EDBH and 2,920 IHP, once again equaling the climbs to Roundwood on 2nd and 22nd May. Based on the actual running the net time joined the other top runs at 41¼ minutes, but I am quite sure that if we had not been stopped at Hersham the momentum of such a fast start and the determination of the footplate crew would have finally got us to Basingstoke in under 40 minutes. As Dave said: 'Given the engine, the road, and even with 12 on I still think it was more than possible to do it in 40 minutes start to stop'. **65.16** shows the detail of this wonderful run that will live in my memory for ever. It was Whit Monday so we returned on the up Excursion with No. 34017 which no doubt would have achieved 70 mph at Roundwood from the Winchester start if adverse signals hadn't intervened.

The next evening we all congregated on the 5.30 pm down again but this time the below par No. 35019 could 'only' produce a net time of 44½ minutes in the rain, despite an actual time of 46 minutes 39 seconds. Returning that evening I had my last run with a Maunsell 2-6-0 on the up 'Mogul Train' (see Chapter Two) and BR Standard 9F 2-10-0 made a rare sighting at Eastleigh. On Wednesday 9th June the 5.30 pm down was 11 coaches for 400 tons 65.17 and with No.35017 Belgium Marine in good condition Eric Saunders once again had high hopes of beating the record. As noted earlier in the chapter No.35017 was fresh from a light intermediate overhaul on 15th May and didn't need to be worked very hard at all; just 22% cut off except for 30% out to Surbiton. Unfortunately we started over the Windsor lines costing a few seconds but were up to a very unusual 61 mph after Queens Road to pass Clapham Junction in just 6 minutes 24 seconds so we had high hopes that this would be the evening that the record to Basingstoke was broken. 87 mph in the Byfleet dip and a time of 23 minutes 41 seconds to pass Woking reinforced that view, though we knew that our hopes were misplaced as that evening BR Standard class 5 No. 73092 on eight coaches had left at 5.23 pm on an Ocean Liner Express and cruelly we caught this at Woking and so suffered signal checks until it cleared the 5.09 pm down after Sturt Lane. Despite the best running of the week from Fleet to Newnham Siding, averaging 82.8 mph we could not quite beat Gordon Hooper's time on 15th May, though 44 minutes 21 seconds once again translates to 41¼ minutes net. The race to Basingstoke was over and with the benefit of looking back over the years with all the information now gathered in front of me, I have to conclude that it was honours even between those three great enginemen, Gordon Porter, Gordon Hooper and Eric Saunders.

\That evening of 9th June was one of those when we were able to sprint across the footbridge at Southampton and catch the 7.16 pm up two hour train despite that leaving on time after our arrival at 7.15 pm! The rest of the week was an anticlimax but I finished the period before the timetable change with a good run from Southampton to Bournemouth on 10th June with that ACE locomotive Canadian Pacific timed by Joe Joliffe. The time was 30 minutes 25 seconds, with a minimum of 60 mph after Lymington Junction.

From the timetable change on 15th June extra time was added to all schedules west of Woking and in particular the fast lines were shut in stages between Brookwood and Basingstoke for upgrading, plus there was a lot of single line working and closures between Worting Junction and Winchester with diversions via Alton or over the Portsmouth direct line at weekends. At the same time most of the semi-fast trains between Waterloo and Basingstoke were withdrawn being replaced by a Western DMU connection into and out of one of the Portsmouth semi-fast services. All this had an adverse effect on train performance and timekeeping and it is true to say that a lot of the interest was lost until the major part of the upgrading work had been completed. This was reflected in the reduced number of good runs for the second half of the year. The table shows the effect of the slowing down of the schedule on one of the former two hour trains.

	Pre June 15th	Post June 15th
Waterloo	1030	1030
Clapham Jct	1037	1037
Hampton Ct Jct	1048	1048
Woking Jct	1058	1058
Worting Jct	1122	1130
Winchester Jct	1136	1145½
Eastleigh	1143	1154
Northam Jct	1148	1159½
Southampton	1151	1203

A similar situation applied to the other fast trains in both directions and also of course to the semi-fast services. In practice the day to day upgrading work plus the very poor operating which now became the norm meant that many dreary runs were timed over the next few months an example being No. 35005 (again) on the 1.16 pm up from Southampton on 19th June which with Bournemouth driver Reggie Sprague and 12 coaches for 430 tons it took no less than 118 minutes and 40 seconds to get to Waterloo, where arrival was 24 minutes late, due to a succession of signal checks and restrictions for track work. Many drivers simply gave up trying to keep time though there were some bright spells such as driver Sullivan with No. 34019 *Bideford* on 13 coaches and a van for 500 tons as shown in **65.18**. Not only was there

a very fine climb to Roundwood on this big load but we managed an even time start to stop run on the slow line from Basingstoke to a signal stop outside Woking. Despite leaving Woking only seven minutes late after being 19 late off Winchester, we were 31 late into Waterloo due to a signal stop and then a door seen to be open on the train. It was not just the train crews who were disheartened but some of us timers were also and I spent some time in search of steam elsewhere including the remaining steam hauled trains out of Marylebone and a long spell in Scotland at the beginning of July. On my return I decided that some linesiding would be

A typical platform end scene at Southampton on 18th July 1965, with No. 34034 *Honiton* ready to go with the 11.30 am from Waterloo to Bournemouth West. Nine Elms driver Jim Evans had brought the train from Waterloo, arriving nearly three minutes early after running up to 78 mph down Roundwood bank. *Author*

After arriving at Southampton eight minutes early, the driver of No. 35012 *United States Line* takes the down 'Bournemouth Belle' on towards Bournemouth on Sunday 18th July 1965. This was the engine, with Gordon Hooper in charge, which set new records on the up 'Belle' on 4th April 1965. *Author*

worthwhile and so managed a couple of spells at Basingstoke where the high level of steam hauled trains was still evident. (See Chapter Two). There were some highlights though especially when the better drivers were around. On Sunday 18th July I went down on the 11.30 am behind No. 34034 *Honiton* and with Jim Evans from Nine Elms in charge we ran well and actually arrived in Southampton over four minutes early after 78 mph down the bank and a rare sub 17 minutes run from Winchester. It may be that I made the wrong choice of train though as the down *Belle* then ran in no less than eight minutes early behind No.35012 *United States Line* in a time of 84 minutes from Waterloo which would have included at the very least a fast/slow/fast weave between Brookwood and Basingstoke. This weekend was actually the start of quite a good spell of engine performance and Terry Jackson's log of No. 34024 *Tamar Valley* shows a very fine effort on the 7.15 am up from

Bournemouth on 17th July with a decent load of 365 tons. Having been thwarted in his attempt to wrest the Waterloo to Basingstoke record from Gordon Hooper, Eric Saunders appears now to have attempted to get the record from Winchester to Roundwood with a time of 11 minutes 50 seconds and 74 mph at the summit. Table 33 – *See page 129*. This would have required 1740 EDBH or 2260 IHP over the 8.25 miles from Winchester Junction to Roundwood and an extraordinary 1880 EDBH or 2510 IHP over the final stretch from Micheldever. These are the highest power output figures I have ever seen with a Bulleid light pacific. The net time from Winchester to Waterloo was about 63 minutes, the fastest I could find with a light pacific. Clearly I was in the wrong place that Saturday and should have been with Terry and not returning from Plymouth behind D1014, but that is a very different story! Terry adds to the story:

'Sooty was determined to see what could be done that morning. When we got to Waterloo I thanked him for a great run and told him that it was the highest speed I had recorded at Roundwood from a Winchester start with a light pacific and that load. I also said that I hadn't seen anything better in print. Later that year in September, I timed the same engine and crew with 11 coaches on one of the other early morning Bournemouths. The running was good reaching 65 before Roundwood before easing but obviously not up the same high level. On reaching Waterloo, I walked up to the engine to find Sooty and Alan having a discussion. Sooty asked if this was the engine they had on the earlier run and, when I said yes it was, he turned to Alan and said 'there, I told you it was the record breaker'. I think this really sums up the spirit at that time'.

The week beginning Monday 19th July saw Gordon Hooper on the 5.30 pm down and he showed what a consistently good performer he was almost irrespective of locomotive. 34087 and 34048 turned in net times to Basingstoke of 48 and 46 minutes respectively with 11 coach loads and then No. 35016 and 35007 both clocked 43 minutes net. 65.19 and 65.20 . The latter only had 10 on and was the only one that week with which Gordon got 90 mph. In practice he did not actually go much above that normally despite his reputation. The times from Winchester to Eastleigh on these four runs make for interesting comparisons. Table 34 – *See page 129.* In the summer of 1965 there were still a few holiday extras from Waterloo to Exmouth and Sidmouth as the Western Region still had not managed to kill off this trade and though these were all booked for diesel haulage (Warships) they were actually largely steam worked and so I decided to sample

a couple on Saturday 24th July. To find BR Standard class 5 No. 73022 at the head of the 8.00 am Waterloo to Sidmouth was however a bit of a surprise but Bill Kiff did his best with the ten coach load to Salisbury and despite 79 in the Hurstbourne dip and 84½ mph down Porton bank, a late start and checks meant we were 9 late into Salisbury where driver Hooper of that shed took over. He was faced with the impossibly tight 63 minute schedule for the 61.10 miles to Axminster but produced a valiant attempt to only lose just over two minutes. Inevitable more time was lost over Honiton bank despite the engine being worked very hard to sustain 27 mph. Altogether a heroic performance by a class 5 rated locomotive on fast diesel timings. I returned on the 11.15 am from Exmouth which had No. 34013 *Okehampton* also on ten coaches for 355 tons and driver Bevan did well despite two stops to sort out dragging brakes. The net time of 59 minutes for the 61.10 miles from Axminster to Salisbury required some very good uphill work, with 51 mph after Sherborne and 47½ at Semley. At Salisbury Bill Kiff and Jim Martin took over and gave me by far my fastest time to stop at Andover with a minimum of 60 mph up Porton bank and 87 mph before the stop. With plenty of steam available and the engine obviously in fine form we continued to run well and arrived at Waterloo nearly two minutes early. The EDBH on the 1-in-140 was about 1760 and the IHP 2210, more very high figures from a light pacific. A Warship would not have done any better. Details in 65.21 .

Things had gone quiet again on the performance front so it was more linesiding plus another visit to Scotland until on Sunday 8th August I sampled the 11.30 am down, once again with No. 73022 but this time with Bill Plumb. With 380 tons this was very good throughout and the net time of 47½ minutes to Basingstoke, reached nine minutes early being particularly noteworthy. On Saturday 14th August I decided on a another spot of linesiding at Basingstoke, Table 35 – *See page 130,* to capture the scene on cine film, but quickly cut the session short when Maunsell Mogul, U class No. 31803 turned up

In June 1965, No 34013 *Okehampton* is the centre of attention at Southampton Central whilst working an up train to Waterloo. Six months later it was timed at 100 mph at Hurstbourne on the 6pm from Waterloo to Salisbury. *Terry Jackson*

on the 9.40 am Birmingham to Portsmouth Harbour. I had gone down to Basingstoke on the 9.54 am from Waterloo which now ran on summer Saturdays only. No. 73018 put on a very good show with 76 mph at Byfleet Junction but was late away from Woking but over four minutes early at Basingstoke. Anyway I boarded the Birmingham to Portsmouth train and was rewarded with the very fine run shown in 65.22 . A week later I decided to cover the Exmouth and Sidmouth trains again and this time the 8.00 am was a Bulleid light pacific. However not only was No. 34077 *603 Squadron* in very poor shape but we had driver Charlie Sutton as far as Salisbury. Now good old Charlie could cope with a good engine on normal steam timings but had no hope with a poor engine on diesel times. Fortunately at Salisbury that ace man Fred Hoare took over though even his regular fireman Pete Allen could not work miracles and we took over 67 minutes to get to Axminster with no higher

speed than 73 mph. We had to bale out at Seaton Junction to be sure of catching the 11.15 am from Exmouth which had driver Jury of Exmouth Junction on No. 34026 *Yes Tor* on ten coaches for 355 tons who did very well to get us to Salisbury half a minute early despite a severe signal check at one of the worst possible places, Sherborne. Our return to Seaton Junction was diesel hauled on the 12 noon from Waterloo and this got us onto the 2.03 pm from Exmouth, the return working for No. 34077 with Fred Hoare and Pete Allen. Pete had worked hard on the fire and managed to break up the foot deep layer of clinker and so was able to turn in a very fine performance. With nine on for 325 tons only a slight signal check prevented an even time run from Axminster to Templecombe but we still kept the very tight booking of 34 minutes for the 32.6 miles. I had high hopes of an even time run on to Salisbury but it was not to be as we caught the late running Warship hauled 2.30 pm from Exeter after Gillingham and again at Dinton. I was able to record quite a lot of cine film (now copied to a CD) on this run including Fred Hoare alighting from the engine at Salisbury.

A measure of just how slow the schedules had become was shown by a run up from Southampton the next day, Sunday 22nd August when No.34103 *Calstock* on eight coaches for 285 tons managed to arrive at Waterloo two minutes early despite taking 107 minutes 22 seconds for the trip. The following week Ron Skinner was on the 5.30 pm down, putting up the usual fine running for this train, but without anything exceptional. On the 26th Harry Pope had BR Standard Class 5 No. 73119 on the 4.55 pm from Bournemouth and with 380 tons produced the very good run and on Saturday 28th August Gordon Porter decided to try his luck with No. 35022 on the 11.15 am down to such an extent that, though with only eight on for 285 tons, we were inside even time by West Byfleet having averaged 84.34 mph from Hampton Court Junction with 88 mph in the Byfleet dip. Checks ruined the rest of the run. At Southampton I transferred to the down *Belle* which had No. 34002 *Salisbury* on the usual load. However, the unconverted pacific was in very poor condition and although Harry Pope got us into Bournemouth two minutes early, he decided to fail the engine in the hope of being given something better for the return run. My notes do not record what his comments were when he discovered that he had been given BR Standard class 5 No. 73117 for the up *Belle*. Fortunately this was one of the better 5s and with hard work by fireman Norman Vidaurri plus Brian Smith on the footplate No. 73117 kept time and arrived at Waterloo over a minute early. The climb to Roundwood took its toll though and speed fell to 34½ mph at the top. However the time lost to Worting Junction had been recovered by Woking and a good spell of fast running up to 75 mph with this heavy train saw us home. Having started out on the 11.15 am down I decided to carry on through the night, including the 3.30 am paper train to Portsmouth with No. 34053 (poor) and back to Waterloo to find Harry Pope again on the 9.20

am down excursion with No. 34089. This was fast to Southampton and *602 Squadron* did well, more than keeping time despite the run being ruined by checks. I continued through the day with mediocre runs before finally succumbing to sleep on the 4.12 pm up from Southampton behind No. 73084 and 'Dick' Turpin driving.

As I was now footloose and free of a girlfriend, I decided that I would risk a double overnight to try to pick up some good runs, and this was successful to a degree. I started on the 5.30 pm down on Friday 3rd September behind N0. 35026 on 11 for 400 tons. Gordon Hooper and Graham Pack did well enough and at Southampton I decided to carry on to Weymouth on the 6.30 pm which had No. 35017 on 12 for 435 tons. Woods of Bournemouth recovered all six minutes of a late start to get us into Bournemouth on time and with a Weymouth driver and the load reduced to seven for about 250 tons we ran very well to arrive on time Table 36 – *See page 131.* No 34042 *Dorchester* took me back to Bournemouth on the 10.13 pm Mails, where No. 35026 took over to Waterloo with Ron Skinner keeping time. I then decided to fill in time by catching the 4.40 am to Woking which had No. 34089 *602 Squadron* with a light load but a very unusual stopping pattern, including Vauxhall! My notebook does not record what I did then but no doubt it was back to Waterloo in an EMU and breakfast at the Lancaster Grill, the next objective being the 10.30 down with Ted (Hedley) Male. We had No. 35026 on 10 for 365 tons and lost over seven minutes to Southampton due to checks but still managed 82½ mph at Wallers Ash. By far the best run of the weekend though was on to Bournemouth. This was top drawer throughout with 59 minimum at Lyndhurst Road, 75 before Brockenhurst, 61 minimum up the 1-in-103 before Sway, 85 mph down Hinton Admiral bank and an absolutely storming climb up the 1-in-99 to Boscombe cut short by a signal stop outside Bournemouth, still reached over two minutes early, an actual gain of 14 minutes on the (easy) schedule. Net time was 29½ minutes, my personal best. After a rest and some lunch

I returned to Southampton on the 2.40 pm to Waterloo with No. 34004 and Ted Male, but although this did well enough I decided to stay west that day and caught the down *Pines Express* with Woods of Bournemouth in charge of No. 35029. This regained nearly six minutes of a late start to arrive on time (see Chapter Three). After a short break I caught the 2.30 pm from Waterloo as far as Wareham with No.34095 *Brentor* changing to the 5.30 pm from Weymouth which had No. 35014 *Nederland Line* on five coaches and a van to Bournemouth and 11 plus the van on to Southampton. For some reason I then decided to wait for the last Weymouth even though I probably knew it was going to be 'Uncle' Ernie Harvey. He had No. 34024 *Tamar Valley* and contrived to arrive at Waterloo nine minutes early with no

higher speed than 72 mph at Hersham. So just when I needed a really late arrival to spin out time, I got the opposite. I do not recall how I filled in the time but my next train was another attempt at decent run on the 3.30 am paper train to Portsmouth, this time with some success. No 34004 *Yeovil* ran well enough to regain nearly eight minutes of the twenty-one we were late past Guildford with a nice 80 mph at Liss. Back to London on the first up EMU stopper at 6.08 and onto the 9.30 am down with No. 34042 *Dorchester* and driver Peter Gammon who took me in an entirely forgettable fashion to Southampton returning after under half an hour on the 12.11 pm up with No. 35012 which produced another uninspiring run to arrive over eight minutes early. When unchecked the slower schedules had a ridiculous amount of

On the evening of 19th September 1965, No. 34001 *Exeter* leaves Winchester with an up Ramblers Excursion. A few minutes later Gordon Porter would also leave the same platform driving No. 34042 *Dorchester* on its way to topping Roundwood at 72^1/$_2$ mph. *Author*

recovery time. I then decided to call it a day and went home to sleep. On that day, 5th September 1965, Bournemouth West closed but with the stupidity of youth I did not bother to go there during my two breaks at Bournemouth Central!

After another spell 'up north' to do the York to Aberystwyth mail and the Manor hauled *Cambrian Coast Express* I returned to the Southern on 17th September to find it in some disarray that evening. The 5.13 pm up from Bournemouth Central had arrived at Basingstoke behind No. 34095 *Brentor* which Bill Kiff had promptly failed and been given BR Standard 5 No. 73083. No. 73086 had also failed on the up relief Channel Islands express and there was also an engine failure on the 4.22 pm down on that black Friday. I gave up and went home returning on Sunday afternoon 19th September as word was that Gordon Porter and Tom Moult were working the up excursion and that they were going to have a go up Roundwood. It was a warm dry beautiful autumn evening in Winchester and I first watched No. 34001 *Exeter* pull away on a returning Ramblers excursion at 7.11 pm before No. 34042 *Dorchester* arrived . The memory of that great climb to Roundwood reached in 11 minutes 48 seconds at 72½ mph stays with me today as one of those very special runs with a special engine crew. There had been better climbs before and there would be better afterwards but somehow the combination of ingredients makes this one stand out for me. Full regulator and 30% cut off was needed and my notebook says that the engine was eased at Micheldever otherwise I think the speed at Roundwood would probably have been about 76 mph, very good with 340 tons. That there was no shortage of steam so maybe Gordon wanted to give Tom Moult a rest! The net time of 38 minutes for the 42.25 miles to the Woking stop and was good throughout.

The hot dry weather persisted and was still in evidence on 21st September when John Gaffney showed what *Tamar Valley* could do with 400 tons on the 5.30 pm down and again with No. 35029 on 23rd September, giving net times of 46½ and 43½ minutes respectively. That same week David Sprackland timed two very good runs on the 1.25 pm Weymouth up both with Norman Prior and the legendary Dave Davis. The net time of 72 minutes with No.35011 on 22nd needed 69-72 mph up the bank and 80-86 mph afterwards. This was one of the fastest recorded but the light pacific, No. 34001, was probably the better of the two, turning in 75 minutes net, the highlight being 65-69 mph up the bank on 400 tons. On 2nd October I had a very good run with No. 34059 *Sir Archibald Sinclair* on the up *Royal Wessex* and on the same day a lively snippet with BR Standard Class 4 2-6-0 No. 76014 on a local train from Southampton to Bournemouth, but one of the best runs of the year came the next day when Gordon Hooper and Robin Brown broke all sorts of records with No. 35022 *Holland America Line* on the LCGB special *Exeter Flyer* as shown in 65.23 . With the load limited to 8 coaches for 285 tons we were required to run nonstop and without taking water both ways over the 123.96 miles between Basingstoke and Exeter Central, timed in 122 minutes going down and 136 minutes return. Despite various checks we managed an even time run to a signal stop before Sturt Lane and a net time of 43½ minutes to Basingstoke, reached eight minutes early. After leaving there slightly early we were stopped by signals at Grateley and so were about four minutes late past Salisbury. From there Gordon really let fly and with 70 mph minimum over Semley after no more than 75 mph beforehand, we touched 88 at Gillingham and 87 mph on the level stretch after Buckhorn Weston, where the minimum was 75½. The engine was now being worked very hard and this took us over the 1-in-80/100 climb after Templecombe at a remarkable 72 mph minimum followed by a flight down through Sherborne at the only 90 of the day. No. 35022 continued in similar style with a superb 67½ minimum over Hewish after three miles of 1-in-80 and fairly restrained running down the long racing stretch past Axminster where we were nearly five minutes early. However we suffered a severe signal check down to walking pace at Seaton Junction but the recovery up the 1-in-80

No 35022 stands at Waterloo on the Exeter Flyer on 3rd October 1965. *John Tiley*

Holland America Line stands at Basingstoke on the Exeter Flyer on 3rd October 1965, whilst Inspector Smith is engaged in conversation. Maybe something like. 'Now, make sure Hooper sticks to the speed limits' *John Tiley*

Fireman Robin Brown carefully watches the hose as No.35022 takes water at Basingstoke on the Exeter Flyer on 3rd October 1965. *John Tiley*

to Honiton tunnel was both extremely noisy and speedy with speed reaching 50 mph at the top. A very swift descent through the woods at Broad Clyst and a clear road saw us standing at Exeter Central over four minutes early in an actual time of 118 minutes 54 seconds for the 123.96 miles, an average of 62.04 mph. Net time had been a remarkable 105 minutes equal to over 70 mph start to stop over this heavily graded route. The equivalent time from Salisbury to Sidmouth Junction would have been 63 minutes compared to the 75 minutes booking of the *Atlantic Coast Express* though this would have had 11 coaches for around 400 tons and sometimes more. Good though this run was, the accompanying table puts this into context when compared to my best run on the down *Atlantic Coast Express*. Table 37 – *See page 132.* I will leave readers to decide which of these runs was the better of the two, but on the face of it there really was not a lot of difference I suppose. We continued to Barnstaple Junction with double headed BR Standard class 4 2-6-4 tanks No. 80043 and 80039, whence No. 80043 took our four coach portion on to Ilfracombe, which was actually the wrong choice for me as I had been there before with steam in 1962 and should have been in the other portion of the train which went to Bideford and Torrington which I had not visited before. The train returned to Exeter in similar

fashion and Gordon Hooper and Robin Brown on No. 35022 then took over for our high speed dash back to Waterloo shown in 65.24 . We left on time in the rain at 5.20 pm and immediately set about pulverising the schedule to such an extent that despite a signal check down to 20 mph we were no less than 21 minutes early at Salisbury. As we crept through the platform at walking pace, Nine Elms driver Ron Skinner who was waiting to work an up service train was heard to shout at us enthusiasts on the train 'What's up with Hooper? Has he gone raving mad?'!! Indeed as we had covered the 88.05 miles from Exeter in 78 minutes 58 seconds, with an actual time from Sidmouth Junction of 63 minutes 28 seconds, or 61½ minutes net, as against the old *Atlantic Coast Express* schedule of 75 minutes. Highlights were 55½ mph at Honiton tunnel after no more than 61 mph following the signal check, 72½ minimum at Hewish, 61½ minimum after Sherborne and a brilliant 69 minimum at Semley after 88½ mph at Gillingham, the highest speed on the return run. Not surprisingly we were stopped for over five minutes at the foot of Porton bank which put paid to any more fireworks as clearly we had caught the 4.30 pm Exeter to Waterloo. Net time for the 123.95 miles from Exeter to Basingstoke was no more than 110 minutes and after taking water we left on time and ran well

Gordon Porter (right) and Tom Moult (left) bring down the coal on the tender of No.34071 on the 8.35 am down on 9th October 1965. *John Tiley*

No 34071 *601 Squadron,* with a footplate visitor, stands at Southampton Central during the course of a very fine run on the 8.35 am down on 9th October 1965, during which it reached 97 mph down Roundwood bank and set a new fastest time for steam from Waterloo to the Surbiton stop. *John Tiley*

to Waterloo arriving over seven minutes early after a day of breathtaking running, unequalled on the Southern on a special train before or since. No. 35022 followed me around for a time after that but without anything like the same level of performance.

The next weekend saw us out on the 8.35 am from Waterloo with Gordon Porter and Tom Moult on No. 34071 *601 Squadron.* This run with 345 tons full from Waterloo and 320 tons from Southampton gave me three personal best times; 14 minutes 40 seconds from Waterloo to Surbiton; 13 minutes 28 seconds from Surbiton to Woking; and 13 minutes 48 seconds from Winchester to Southampton. Some of these times may be records with steam. Acceleration was quite stunning, such as for instance from the 17 mph track relaying slowing at Steventon to 97 mph at Winchester Junction and the start from Winchester to pass Shawford in just four minutes six seconds at 76 mph. The long delay

at Beaulieu Road was due to single line working but a storming climb from Brockenhurst to Milepost 94½ ensured we were only two minutes late into Bournemouth. Brian Smith was assisting on the footplate and the details are shown in 65.25 . My notebook states that the engine was ex-works but I have been unable confirm this. We returned with the same crew on the 12.59 pm from Bournemouth which suffered a lot of checks. No. 34089 had a light load but even so the climb out of Winchester, the electric start from Basingstoke to pass Hook in 5 minutes 49 seconds, one of my fastest and the very fast time from Woking to Waterloo are of some merit. There were many dreary runs at that time and it was essential to know where the best drivers were to get a good performance. The next day I went down to Havant on the diverted 9.30 am from Waterloo with No. 34044 *Woolacombe* and this same engine features in a fast Woking to Waterloo snippet timed by Alan

A lovely study of record breaking No. 35005 *Canadian Pacific* **standing at Eastleigh after working a special train on 23rd May 1965.** *Mike Hodges*

Rawlings who recorded a time of 25 minutes 4 seconds with no higher speed than 78 mph at Hersham, but with a very fast finish, one of the trademarks of runs with Bill Kiff. The 10th October 1965 was a sad day indeed as record breaking No. 35005 *Canadian Pacific* was withdrawn. I did not travel many miles behind this locomotive but it was a case of quality over quantity.

The 5.30 pm down was still providing good performances, two of which were with John Gaffney driving 35014 (net time 46 minutes) and 35017 (net time 44 minutes, minimum speed 73 mph at milepost 31) on 15th and 16th October. Occasionally the BR Standard 5s could find a reasonably clear road and with a good driver such as Driver Cobbett of Guildford as far as Woking, 73018 did well, though with a light load, on the 6.35 pm Salisbury on 16th October. From Woking John Gaffney took over and produced a very fast time of just 10 minutes 5 seconds to pass Hampton Court Junction,

being inside even time as early as Hersham, 8.38 miles. At that time I tended to concentrate on the Waterloo to Basingstoke section as the early evening after work still gave a lot of options. During the week the 5.09 pm semi-fast commuter train was worked by Basingstoke men and the 5.43 pm semi- fast by Nine Elms top link men who returned from Basingstoke on the 6.35 pm from Salisbury, 8.29 pm arrival. Nine Elms top link men also worked the 8.25 pm arrival, 5.13 pm ex Bournemouth from Eastleigh having worked down on the 3.35 pm semi- fast. Nine Elms men (in theory No.3 link men) worked the 5.30 pm down to Eastleigh returning on the 8.40 pm empty stock and vans. Nine Elms men worked the 6 pm down through to Salisbury, Guildford crews had the 6.09 pm semi-fast and Salisbury worked the 6.54 pm semi-fast, so there was plenty of choice. Eastleigh men had the up 'Club Train' due at 8.51 pm and also the Channel Islands express fast up from Basingstoke at 7.30 pm though the times varied. Bournemouth men worked the 6.39 pm arrival and the 'Mogul Train' was still steam though usually a BR Standard class 5 at that time. The 'Club Train' was rather out of favour until Nine Elms men took it over early in 1966. One of my favourite short evening trips was to go down on the 5.30 pm which was nearly always good, go back to Hook on the 6.37 pm DMU and join the 5.43 pm down back to Basingstoke due at 7.02 pm and then choose which of the three possible up trains to catch back to London, depending on engine and crew. On Saturdays things were different as the Nine Elms crew came off the 5.30 pm down

at Basingstoke and then travelled to Woking on the cushions on the 6.35 pm Salisbury up, taking it over there from Guildford men. A lot of this changed with new rosters early in 1966. After another spell in Scotland chasing A4s on the three hour trains, I arrived back in London early on Sunday morning 31st October behind E3124 and decided to try my luck on the 9.30 am down, again diverted via Havant and driver Fred Burridge with the help of a Guildford pilotman from Woking on No. 34056 *Croydon* did well enough on 345 tons which I took through to Southampton. Unfortunately the return via the main line with the same driver on

On 31st October 1965 No. 34056 *Croydon* stands at Fareham on the 9.30 am from Waterloo diverted via the Portsmouth direct line. *Author*

No. 34079 *141 Squadron* was about as bad as it could be and I succumbed to sleep after a stop for a blow up at Micheldever. To show just how bad this engine was at the time Gordon Porter had it on the 7.01 am up from Bournemouth on 2nd November and with 12 on for 435 tons it slipped so badly starting and the valves were so far out that we took no less than five minutes 17 seconds to get past Boscombe, when four minutes was considered poor. It was put out of its misery and withdrawn on 27th February 1966. To show just how much spare time there was in the Sunday schedules, No. 34060 *25 Squadron* on eight coaches for 290 tons gained no less than 25 minutes to turn a 15 minute late start into a 10 minute early arrival! Gordon Hooper with No. 35030 *Elder Dempster Line* the same evening tried for the record at Roundwood

starting from Winchester but was thwarted by the weather on that dark wet and windy night. In between bouts of slipping the engine was worked very hard indeed and no doubt with the moderate 335 ton load could have reached 80 mph. On Saturday 13th November I went down to Southampton on the *Belle* with Bill Kiff and Paul Daley in charge of No. 34008 *Padstow,* one of my favourite light pacifics and it proved to be a good choice as we ran well, keeping time and turning in a net time of 80 minutes with this heavy load. The highlight of this run was the climb from Basingstoke to Wootton where speed fell only from 53 to 52 mph. It seems that Eric Saunders was still after the record time to Basingstoke as on the following Saturday 20th November he gave me one of my fastest net times with a light pacific and in doing so

The level of enthusiast interest being shown in No. 34008 *Padstow* suggests that this is a special occasion; but no, it was just another Saturday (13 November 1965) and steam still had nearly two years left. Bill Kiff was about to take the light pacific out on the 'Bournemouth Belle'. On the right a Warship has just set back onto the 1.00 pm to Exeter. *Author*

claimed the record fastest time to pass Woking (23 minutes 32 seconds) without exceeding 84 mph in the Byfleet dip. However, we were still doing 82 mph as we stormed past Woking with the whistle blasting amid much excitement in the train as the record was broken. The time to passing Milepost 31 was also a record, despite the engine being shut off ready for the speed restriction by then. The fast/slow/fast line weave of course robbed us of any chance of the long sought after Basingstoke record but it was exciting stuff amidst the gloom of so much poor

running and we still arrived at Basingstoke over 11 minutes early. The image shows what was happening on the main lines which caused the fast to slow and return weaves. This run was all the more surprising as No. 34090 *Sir Eustace Missenden SR* was considered to be a poor engine and at that time was known as 'The Milk Marketing Board' machine, or in other words an old crate (also known by some railwaymen as 'Useless Eustace' after a cartoon which I believe used to appear in the Mirror). Just as

On Sunday 14th November 1965 N class No. 31858 is engaged in Engineering duties on the recently relaid up main line near Fleet. The shot was taken from the 1130 am Waterloo to Weymouth on the down slow line being hauled by No. 73115 with George Enticknapp driving. *Author*

well the load was only 10 for 375 tons and not the weekday 12.

1st December saw the third recorded 100 mph run of the year and this was in most fortuitous circumstances. Firstly Frank Matthews (usually referred to as the 'Mad Monk'), Nine Elms spare link, was covering the 6.00 pm down for a Nine Elms top link driver that week and second, due to a coach defect, the train was only six coaches instead of the normal 11. So as shown in 65.26 No. 34013 *Okehampton* had just 215 tons with which to recover nine minutes of a late start from Basingstoke. Frank Matthews' intention was clear from the start as we were up to 58½ mph by Worting Junction passed in just 4 minutes 8 seconds and the full regulator and 30% there was left unchanged until we swept across the viaduct at Hurstbourne at exactly 100 mph, before easing for a relaying slack and stopping at Andover reached in even time

On Saturday 11th December 1965 No.35022 *Holland America Line* runs into Basingstoke with the 1107 am Bournemouth to Waterloo. The locomotive was very active at that time. I was in the middle of a mileage bash which included an overnight trip on the 2.45 am down and runs hauled by five different engines, none of which were particularly special though No. 34098 did produce 93 mph down Roundwood bank on the 2.45 am down. *Author*

from Basingstoke, the net time being just 16¼ minutes for the 18.60 miles. As we eased after the ton had been reached, one of our number in the compartment was heard to say 'Did anyone get any MORE than 100?', which remark was greeted with mirth. From Andover No 34013 was given no respite and had reached 69 mph on the climb to Grateley before a temporary speed restriction intervened, but Matthews still pushed on after that to reach 95 mph down Porton bank before running into Salisbury just 1¾ minutes late. Sadly he died in the West Brompton collision some years after the end of steam. On 9th December Terry Jackson had a very good run on the 7.24 am Bournemouth to Waterloo when Gordon Hooper had No. 35026 on a full 12 coach load of 440 tons. 70 mph at Roundwood was very good indeed with this load and some fast running in from Woking saw a gain of six minutes on the schedule and an excellent 61 minute net time for the 66.6 miles. Gordon Hooper was in action again on 11th December this time on the 2.45 am down with No. 34098 *Templecombe* on the usual load turning in some very fast start to stop times including a sub 15 minute run from Southampton to Brockenhurst. Eric Saunders and Alan Roe had No. 34052 *Lord Dowding*

on the up excursion making another attempt on the record to Roundwood from the Winchester start on 12th December but were beaten by the weather on an awful wet winter night, despite using 45% cut off in between some violent slipping. I have a particular memory of that run as the engine struggled away from the stops and Sooty described the light pacific as clapped out. BR Standard class 4 2-6-0 no 76016 did very well on the 6.35 pm Salisbury on 18th December and the Basingstoke to Winchester effort from No. 35030 on 22nd December is worthy of mention as we had a clear road and it was just sub 20 minutes, with a modest 88 mph maximum down the bank. Finally in 1965 Bill Plumb on Bank Holiday Monday 27th December did very well with light pacific No. 34048 *Crediton,* getting to Winchester on the 7.30 pm down in 64 minutes net. Good solid running with 355 tons, 76 at Byfleet, 62 over milepost 31 and 84 down Roundwood after a series of checks.

In 1965 I had a total of 588 runs behind steam locomotives for a total of 34,322 miles of which 524 were on the Southern covering 30,608 miles. Overall it was the best of the three final years.

Tables

Table 30

WATERLOO TO SURBITON

Date	4th April 1965
Train	130 pm Waterloo to Weymouth
Loco	West Country Class 4-6-2 No. 34041 *Wilton*
Load	9 coaches, 298½ tons tare, 325 tons gross
Driver	Bill Sanson, Bournemouth No. Two link
Weather	fine and warm
Recorder	DB

	miles	sched	mins	secs	speed	
Waterloo	0.00	0.00	00	00		7½ mins late
Vauxhall	1.29		03	22	36/32*	tsr
Queens Road	2.81		05	35	45	
Clapham Junction	3.93	7.00	07	28	41*	
Earlsfield	5.58		09	41	52½	
Wimbledon	7.24		11	27	61	
Raynes Park	8.64		12	45	65½	
New Malden	9.78		13	45	71½	
Berrylands	10.98		14	44	73	
Surbiton	12.04		15	38	75½	pass

Table 31

WINCHESTER TO SOUTHAMPTON

Date	4th April 1965
Train	130 pm Waterloo to Weymouth
Loco	West Country Class 4-6-2 No. 34041 *Wilton*
Load	9 coaches, 298½ tons tare, 325 tons gross
Driver	Bill Sanson, Bournemouth No. Two link
Weather	fine and warm
Recorder	DB

	miles	sched	mins	secs	speed	
Winchester	0.00	0.00	00	00		15½ mins late
St Cross Box	1.23		02	38	50	
Shawford Jct	2.47		03	49	61½	
Shawford	3.12		04	34	65	
Allbrook Box	6.06		07	05	75	
Eastleigh	6.96	9.00	07	46	72*	brakes
Swaythling	9.22		09	43	74½	
St Denys	10.63		10	53	71	
Northam Jct	11.71	14.30	12	43	22*	
Southampton Central	12.75	17.30	15	53		

Table 32

EXTRACT 4TH APRIL 35012

	miles	mins	secs	speed	
Winchester City	12.70	15	51	69½	
Winchester Jct	14.80	17	43	71	27% cut off
Wallers Ash Box	17.55	20	02	72	
Weston Box	19.05	21	14	73	
Micheldever	21.20	22	59	75	
Roundwood Box	23.05	24	28	76	
Waltham Box	24.15	25	22	80	
Steventon Box	25.30	26	12	83	

Table 33

EXTRACT 17TH JULY 1965 34024

	miles	mins	secs	speed	gradient
Winchester City	0.00	00	00		404 R
MP 66	0.60	01	48	23	249 R
MP 65	1.60	03	25	45	349 R
Winchester Jct	2.10	04	14	49	252 R
MP 64	2.60	04	39	52	252 R
MP 63	3.60	05	43	58	252 R
MP 62	4.60	06	42	61½	252 R
Wallers Ash Box	4.85	07	04	62½	252 R
MP 61	5.60	07	39	65	252 R
Weston Box	6.35	08	25	66	252 R
MP 60	6.60	08	35	67	252 R
MP 59	7.60	09	28	68	252 R
Micheldever	8.50	10	16	70	252 R
MP 58	8.60	10	19	70	252 R
MP 57	9.60	11	10	72½	252 R
Roundwood Box	10.35	11	50	74	252 R

Table 34

WINCHESTER TO EASTLEIGH

Date	Tuesday 20th July 1965	Wednesday 21st July 1965
Loco	No. 34087	No. 34048
Load	11 coaches, 374 tons tare, 400 tons gross	11 coaches 377½ tons tare, 405 tons gross
Driver	Gordon Hooper, Nine Elms MPD	Gordon Hooper, Nine Elms MPD

	miles	sched	mins	secs	speed	sched	mins	secs	speed
Winchester City	0.00	0.00	00	00		0.00	00	00	
St Cross Box	1.23		02	48	48		02	51	50

	miles	sched	mins	secs	speed	sched	mins	secs	speed
Shawford Jct	2.47		04	02	59		04	00	61½
Shawford	3.12		04	48	63½		04	42	68½
MP 71½	4.90		06	20	76		06	10	79
Allbrook Box	6.06		07	42	27*		07	20	24*
Eastleigh	6.96	11.00	09	40		11.00	09	24	

Date	Thursday 22nd July 1965	Friday 23rd July 1965
Loco	No. 35016	No. 35007
Load	11 coaches, 374 tons tare, 405 tons gross	10 coaches 331½ tons tare, 355 tons gross
Driver	Gordon Hooper, Nine Elms MPD	Gordon Hooper, Nine Elms MPD

	miles	sched	mins	secs	speed	sched	mins	secs	speed
Winchester City	0.00	0.00	00	00		0.00	00	00	
St Cross Box	1.23		03	02	49		02	36	55
Shawford Jct	2.47		04	15	61		03	41	68
Shawford	3.12		04	59	64½		04	22	73
MP 71½	4.90		06	30	76		05	46	85
Allbrook Box	6.06		07	46	24*		06	58	27*/39½
Eastleigh	6.96	11.00	09	51		11.00	08	51	

Table 35

OBSERVATIONS AT BASINGSTOKE 14th AUGUST 1965

Time	Train	Engine	Load
1124 am	923 am Bournemouth West to Liverpool and Manchester	35023	13
1124 am	953 am Bournemouth Central to Waterloo	35010	12
1125 am	1030 am Waterloo to Weymouth	35028	10
1146 am	955 am Bournemouth West to Manchester 'Pines Express'	35011	13
1150 am	1004 am Bournemouth West to Waterloo	35014	12
1155 am	843 am Wolverhampton Low Level to Portsmouth Harbour	6833 (vice DL)	11
1201 pm	Southampton Docks to Waterloo	34059	13
1212 pm	1105 am Waterloo to Bournemouth	73086	11
1219 pm	1115 am Waterloo to Weymouth	35017	8
1220 pm	925 am Weymouth to Waterloo	34097	11
1228 pm	1034 am Bournemouth West to Bradford Exchange	34037	11
1235 pm	Unidentfied through train from Reading line	6959	11
1250 pm	940 am Birmingham to Portsmouth Harbour	31803	10

Table 36

BOUREMOUTH TO WEYMOUTH

Date	3rd September 1965
Train	630 pm Waterloo to Weymouth
Loco	Rebuilt Merchant Navy class 4-6-2 No. 35017 Belgian Marine
Load	7 coaches 234 tons tare, 250 tons gross
Crew	Weymouth MPD
Weather	Fine
Recorder	DB

	miles	sched	mins	secs	speed	
Bournemouth Central	0.00	0.00	00	00		¾ min early
Gasworks Jct	2.20	5.00	04	33	46/39*	
Branksome	2.65		05	13	44	
Parkstone	3.96		06	49	56½/59	
Poole	5.76	10.00	09	31		
	0.00	0.00	00	00		
Hamworthy Jct	2.23		04	18	47/43*	
Holton Heath	4.99		07	20	64	
Wareham	7.10	10.00	09	36		
	0.00	0.00	00	00		
Worgret Jct	1.09	3.00	02	56	23/63	
Wool	4.99	8.30	07	31		
	0.00	0.00	00	00		
MP 128	2.23		04	17	49	
MP 129	3.23		05	29	51	
Moreton	4.45		07	59	62½	
MP 132	6.23		08	38	65½	
MP 133	7.23		09	34	67	
Dorchester South	10.03	13.00	12	57		
	0.00	0.00	00	00		
Dorchester Jct	0.30	1.30	01	14	24	
Bincombe Tunnel Box	2.55		04	24	48/46	
Upwey Wishing Well	3.38		05	17	56	
Upwey and Broadwey	4.50		06	18	75½	
Weymouth	6.86	11.00	10	21		right time

Table 37

COMPARISIONS SALISBURY TO AXMINSTER

Date	Sunday 3rd October 1965	Wednesday 22nd July 1964
Loco	No. 35022	No 35009
Load	8 coaches 285 tons gross	11 coaches 405 tons gross
Crew	Hooper and Brown Nine Elms MPD	Cook and Smith Exmouth Jct MPD

	miles	sched	mins	secs	speed	sched	mins	secs	speed
Salisbury	0.00	0.00	00	00	16*	0.00	00	00	
Dinton	8.30		10	25	75		11	14	76
Semley	17.60		18	00	70		19	00	68½
Gillingham	21.70		20	54	88/75½		21	58	92/75½
Templecombe	28.50	30.30	25	41	87/72		26	54	86/65½
Sherborne	34.55		30	11	90		31	43	94
Yeovil Junction	39.15	39.00	33	25	83/72½/88	40.00	34	58	81/67/84
Crewkerne	47.95		39	57	81/67½		41	56	62
Axminster	61.10	58.00	49	33	86½	61.00	52	02	86

CHAPTER FIVE
1966

1966 was the last full year of steam operation and although there were some good performances, including four more 100 mph runs, in general performance was still being affected by the ongoing engineering and electrification work and also by poor operating. However some 220 locomotives remained in service including a few of Maunsell's Moguls although they had no booked work. Most Bournemouth line trains were still steam worked and would remain so until the incursion of the Brush Type 4s in the autumn and although variety was diminished this chapter still encompasses 95 runs including some quite ordinary performances as I want to show the day to day scene as well as the spectacular. The Swanage branch was still steam worked, mainly by the LM 2P 2-6-2 tanks but with BR Standard class 4 tanks also appearing and these two snippets kindly provided by Bob Thompson show some of their work. Tables 38 & 39 – *See page 165.* The Lymington branch was also steam and would remain so

almost to the end of steam and once again Bob timed examples of above par runs on the branch in February 1966. Bob was perhaps unkindly known as 'Doze' and maybe now after over 50 years we can understand how this nickname was earned as he was maybe the most prolific timer of runs of all us, so no wonder he was always tired! Other nicknames abounded such as 'Lord Patchett of Liss', 'Adolf', 'The Squire' and 'Midland Bank' plus others which even with the passage of time are best not related.

The year started with one of the many 'last steam to Exeter' trips, this one organised by Derek Winkworth and Geoff Bloxham. The work of No. 34001 was unspectacular with driver Edwards of Guildford in charge as far as Salisbury, but good enough to keep time. The continuation to and from Exeter was behind unconverted light pacific No. 34015 and unenterprising running both ways caused the discontent amongst some of the fraternity to spill over into verbal criticism of the driver

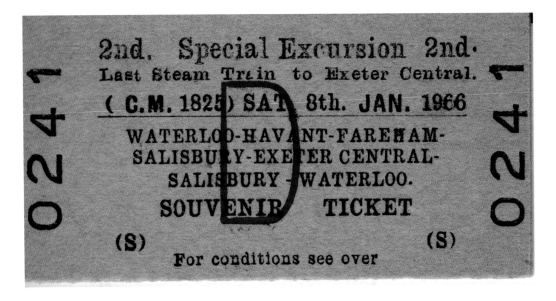

No. 34015 at Salisbury on 8th January 1966, ready to work the next leg of the 9.20 am special from Waterloo. *Terry Jackson*

being shown openly on the return to Salisbury. There was a reasonable effort made with another Salisbury driver taking No. 34001 back to Waterloo. Many Sunday evenings were spent timing the up Bournemouth excursion which was worked by Nine Elms crews and which I often caught from Southampton or Winchester having gone down on the 4.30 pm with a Bournemouth crew. Typically on 9th January driver Tommy Coles of Nine Elms turned in a good run from Micheldever to Waterloo with No. 34048 producing two sections close to even time after engineering work had disrupted the early stages. The week beginning Monday 10th January saw me on the 5.30 pm down on four evenings as Dave Parsons drove on three of those evenings and gave me footplate rides from Basingstoke to Winchester on all three nights. These are shown in Chapter Seven and the running to Basingstoke on 14th January with was a typically good run with Dave taking No.34026 along in fine style to achieve an excellent net time of 45½ minutes. On the three evenings speeds at Byfleet were 78½, 77 and 79 mph with No. 34036, 34012 and 34026 respectively and at Milepost 31 the minimum

speeds were 61½, 60½ (after a check to 53 mph at Brookwood) and 64½. Net times were all in the 45½ to 46½ minutes range, good consistent going with this heavy 410 ton train, taking us into Basingstoke on time or early every evening. On the evening of 14th January we made it across the footbridge at Southampton onto the 7.16 pm up 'Club Train' which had No. 35026 in charge and left 18 minutes late but was unable to regain any time to Waterloo, despite some good running at 60-64 up Roundwood and up to 79 mph after. The driver was Pearce of Eastleigh who would give me my very last steam hauled run into Waterloo on 8th July 1967. **66.01** shows the continuation of a run on the 10.30 down from Bournemouth to Dorchester with some lively running to regain six minutes of time lost earlier in the run. Although with a light load No. 35022 produced an even time section and some fast running. Arthur Camp had brought the train down from Waterloo and suffered many signal checks on the way though he still managed to run up to 86½ mph down Roundwood bank. The return run was also above par to Bournemouth with another 80 mph maximum speed. Generally though this wasn't a time for good runs as the fast to slow weaves between Woking and Basingstoke were still in place and the poor operating was causing a lot of signal checks. However there were some bright spots and I made up for the dull period to some extent by another visit to Scotland for the A4s and for Fairburn tanks working the local services between Glasgow and Paisley.

At this time Nine Elms crews were working the 6.00 pm Waterloo to Salisbury in place of Salisbury men, though even drivers like Gordon Hooper who worked the train on 14th February with No. 34032 could not get the Salisbury engines to perform as well as the Salisbury drivers did and it wasn't until after the train reverted to its rightful home shed in May that

performance improved again. However that same week saw one of my favourite Nine Elms crews rostered for the 10.35 pm down Mails and they were always worth missing a night's sleep for. 66.02 shows a superb effort with No. 34008 on a good load with Gordon Porter really going for it and producing a net time to Woking of 24 minutes, excellent with 375 tons, followed by another even time net run to Basingstoke, topped off with 91 mph below Wallers Ash tunnel after a severe track relaying slack at Steventon. I went down on the same train on the Friday night but as this was on the footplate the whole way, it is covered in Chapter Seven. Sections of the return runs on both nights on the 10.13 pm Weymouth up Mails were good as

No. 34098 *Templecombe* at Waterloo on 25th October 1966, heading the down Bournemouth Belle, with Les Kent in the shot. We all had our favourite locomotives and No. 98 was the one which Les had the greatest affinity for. *Author*

well, the one with No. 34026 being particularly noteworthy for the sharp running between stops after Woking. No.34098 produced a good effort in poor conditions on the 5.30 pm down on 23rd February with Bob Jackson of Nine Elms in charge, getting to Basingstoke in 48 minutes net and running down past Wallers Ash at 93 mph. McLaggon produced a rare even time run from Woking to Surbiton with No.34026 on 27th February with 325 tons, maximum 83 mph. I did another overnight stint on 3rd/4th March going down on the 10.35 pm with Bill Plumb driving No. 34093, returning with No. 34104, though the running was quite ordinary. I decided to forgo the Lancaster Grill so went down to Basingstoke on the 5.30 am behind No. 34052 with Alf Hurley driving and returned to Waterloo on the 7.05 am stopping service behind No. 73118 on 10 coaches with Nine Elms driver Bob Jackson. Once again nothing of note; but this train gave a comfortable turn round onto the 8.30 am to Weymouth which that morning had Gordon Hooper and Ray McQuade on No. 34047 and this was well up to GH's high standard as shown in 66.03 . It was misty and damp and the engine was inclined to slip but still kept time with the usual checks, giving an excellent net time of 74 minutes. The romp down past Shawford at 93 mph was as enjoyable as it was unusual at this point. It was turning out to be a good day as Gordon Porter was working the 8.35 am down that day and so I abandoned the 8.30 and joined the 8.35 at Southampton as far as Brockenhurst. This was a very lively effort from No.34038 (known by some as 'Stormy' Lynton). In fact the time of 15 minutes and 18 seconds, net 14½ minutes, was my fastest with steam over this stretch. As I wanted to catch the 11.07 from Bournemouth up with Gordon Hooper, I baled out at Brockenhurst and caught the Bournemouth to York train behind LM class 5 No. 45089 as far as Southampton, which was the usual dreary trundle for this train and waited for No. 35027 with Gordon Hooper. This was nothing special and badly checked so I finally caught the 12.59 pm up from Bournemouth with No. 34052

Eastleigh driver Roy Sloper on the footplate of LM class 5 No. 45186 in 1966. The LM 5s worked the York to Bournemouth train in 1966 and also had fill-in turns. *Peter Austin*

on 275 tons which Gordon Porter took from Woking to Waterloo in a net time of 24 minutes with a very fast time of 9 minutes 49 seconds to pass Hampton Court Junction after 88 mph at Hersham. I still was not finished that day though, as I caught the 4.35 pm down behind No. 35017 and Ernie Harvey driving, returning from Southampton behind No. 34088 on the 6.15 pm up, during which I gave up the battle to stay awake; so details were sketchy. Total steam mileage over the two days was 636½.

No. 35028 *Clan Line* passing Weybridge on 30th April 1966
with the 9.24 am Bournemouth to Waterloo. *Author*

Terry Jackson timed the runs covering the LCGB Somerset and Dorset last day railtour between Waterloo and Salisbury where No. 35028 turned in a very good net time of 73 minutes, albeit with a light load, an excellent run on the diverted down *Belle* where No. 34056 reached a very unusual 88 mph at Liss and a very good effort with unconverted No. 34006 on a heavy load also over the Pompey direct. The week beginning Monday 7th March brought Gordon Porter round to his turn on the 5.30 pm down for another series of top class performances, two of which are shown in 66.04 and 66.05 . On Monday 7th March he only had Standard 5 No. 73022 which struggled for steam but was uninhibited down the bank reaching 87 mph. There was the consistency of net times with 34057 and 34071, both achieving 45 minutes to Basingstoke and 20 minutes on to Winchester, and the very fast time from Winchester to Eastleigh with No.34071. It was No. 34057 *Biggin Hill* which stole the show for me though. The engine was in poor condition and priming at the start. The valves were way out of kilter and it seemed to be missing a

beat but Gordon Porter drove her very hard on full regulator and 45% cut off away from the permanent way slack at Walton to reach 70 mph by Woking and 72½ by Brookwood on the 1-in-314 climb, giving about 1,700 EDBH and 2,300 IHP. At that point the cylinders were beating the boiler and pressure was back to 160 lb. Poor Tommy Moult simply could not keep up! I have a tape recording of the climb and the noise plus the whistle screaming as we passed Woking is spine tingling and makes me misty eyed every time I play it. The 90 mph down the bank was reached with 200 lb of steam in the boiler, 160 lb in the steam chest and 25% cut off. Truly the Bulleid pacifics in their original condition were remarkable free running engines. On each of these three evenings we made the up 'Club Train' back from Southampton, despite the 5.30 pm down not being due there until 7.27 pm and the 'Club Train' due away at 7.15! Joe Jolliffe was on the 5.30 pm down on the Friday and the 96 mph down the bank was the best that week but the engine was No. 35003, even at that stage a very free running locomotive. 66.06 . Sunday 13th March saw me on the down *Belle*

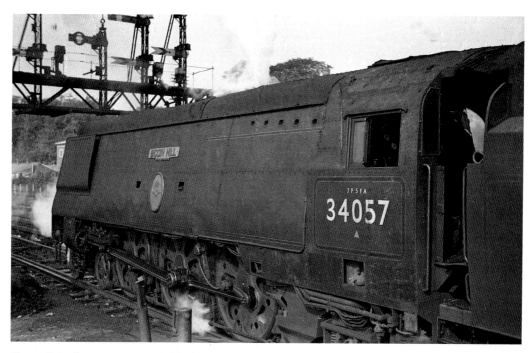

One of the best unconverted Bulleid pacifics, No. 34057 *Biggin Hill* stands at Southampton Central while working the 8.35 am down on 26th September 1966. *John Tiley*

behind No. 34017 diverted via the Pompey direct line and which did well despite being short of steam, recovering seven minutes of a late start from Guildford. Terry Jackson timed an excellent run on the 2.45 am down when No. 34077 ran Woking to Basingstoke in even time with Reuben Hendicott at the regulator. Despite my earlier comments there were a few decent runs on the 6.00 pm down, examples being with Bill Anderson in charge at the end of March. No doubt though he would have preferred to forget 28th March when No. 34108 failed at Farnborough with a hot box on the tender, one of only three failures with Bulleid pacifics, all with hot boxes. The 6.35 pm Salisbury was now being driven up from Basingstoke by the Nine Elms top link men from the 5.41pm down and we were getting some good runs with the moderate loads of this train. On 30th March Harry Pope had the Giesl ejector fitted No. 34064 and this engine showed again how free running it was, notably with a fast time from the Woking start to pass Hampton Court

Junction in 10 minutes 24 seconds. The 5.30 pm down features again in 66.07, this time with spare link driver Les Cummings teamed up with Tom Moult and producing a good overall performance with a free steaming No. 34021 *Dartmoor* racing down the bank to reach 97 mph before Winchester Junction and a fast time on to Eastleigh. I seem to recall that the rest of the group got off the 5.30 at Basingstoke that evening and so missed a high speed run. Once again the minus 12 minute 'connection' onto the 7.15 pm 'Club Train' was made and I returned to London behind No. 35013 which left at 7.33 pm and kept the schedule though regained no time despite a good run, because of many checks - typical of that train at that time. The Nine Elms men worked back to London on the 8.40 pm vans and empty stock from Eastleigh.

Saturday 2nd April saw another in the series of last steam trains to Exeter specials though the destination of this one was Exmouth, reached from Sidmouth Junction behind Hymek diesel D7069. I have tabulated one of the five

Giesel Ejector fitted 34064 *Fighter Command* at Basingstoke on 30th April 1966 prior to working the 7.05 am stopping service to Waterloo. Driver Conlon, Nine Elms No. 3 link is at the regulator. *Author*

sections of the day in **66.08** as the running was worthwhile, and whilst not brilliant west of Salisbury was certainly better this time with No.34006 compared to the poor performance alluded to earlier in the chapter. The 43 mph minimum over Honiton bank was very good even taking into account the moderate 325 ton load. But it was Bill Plumb with No.34032 who stole the show with a very good net time of 75 minutes to Salisbury, the highlight being the 70 mph minimum over Grateley from just 83 mph at Andover. This was a typical solid Bill Plumb performance. **66.09** covers a very good run on

the up *Belle* with light pacific No. 34005 doing well with Hendicott and Stanley on the footplate and No.34026 did very well on the 6.35 pm Salisbury up, this time with a Basingstoke crew. It was the Thursday before Good Friday and so a Saturday service was in operation, which explains the absence of Nine Elms men. I had a week off work from 11th April and covered a lot of trains including some overnight, but did not time anything of note except a little snippet with No.34026 turning in my one and only even time run with steam from Basingstoke to Farnborough, where the 10.13 up Mails called

No. 35013 *Blue Funnel* works the down Belle past Vauxhall on 24th May 1966 with driver Beavis of Bournemouth at the regulator. *Author*

Ted Male and his fireman on the footplate of No. 34056 *Croydon* after arrival at Basingstoke on the 6 pm from Waterloo to Salisbury on 20th April 1966, with No. 73171 behind on the 5.41 pm from Waterloo. An everyday scene in 1966. The run down had kept time but had been unexceptional and maybe there were problems with the fire as the fireman was examining the black smoke, often evidence of poor coal. *Author*

A lovely image of Salisbury light pacific No. 34089 arriving at Basingstoke with the 5.41 pm from Waterloo in July 1966. *Terry Jackson*

on Mondays only. Just to show that the 6.35 pm up from Salisbury did not have the monopoly of good up evening runs John Gaffney gave a good performance with No. 34089 on a 350 ton load on the 3.50 pm from Bournemouth on 20th April producing a net time of 20 minutes, maximum speed 87 at Brookwood. I had gone down to Basingstoke behind No. 34056 on the 6.00 pm with driver Ted Male. Gaffney had worked the 3.35 pm down in place of a top link man. Although the number of steam hauled trains continued at the same level, it was a quiet time for fast runs and I sometimes resorted to timing the local EMU worked services with SUBs, BILs and EPBs! Timekeeping had also improved somewhat with the end of the fast/

slow weaves though there was still a lot of track renewal going on. I had some good runs on the 8.30 am down with Ron Skinner and also on the up Channel Islands Boat train with Eastleigh men though this was quite lightly loaded in April and May. On 9th May, Dave Parsons and Ray McQuade worked the 5.41 pm down with No. 34032 and they gave me a footplate ride from Fleet to Basingstoke. This little snippet is shown here and was typical of the hard work by the Salisbury Bulleid pacifics on this train. Table 40 – *See page 166.* For the return run on the 6.35 pm Salisbury when we had No. 34006 *Bude* on 255 tons, Dave offered me a footplate ride as far as Woking, which I eagerly accepted. This is described in full in Chapter seven, and

12th May 1966, the occasion of the visit of BR Standard Britannia class pacific No. 70002 *Geoffrey Chaucer*. The Brit stands at Waterloo next to No. 34017 which was working the 9.30 am to Bournemouth. *Author*

it was excellent and gave me my fastest speed on the footplate with an unconverted pacific, 95 mph after Fleet. Thursday 12th May saw BR Standard Britannia No. 70002 *Geoffrey Chaucer* working the 9.20 am boat train from Waterloo to Southampton Eastern Docks, with Jim Robinson Snr in charge. The engine had worked down to Portsmouth the previous day with a troop train from Elgin. However as there were no servicing facilities on the LMR at this time, it returned to Nine Elms for servicing. It returned ECS to Clapham Junction and was then stopped at Nine Elms until the 19th May when it ran LE to Basingstoke before returning to the London Midland Region. While I was out of the office I took the opportunity to photograph No.35029 on the down *Belle* at Wimbledon, travelling there in 4EPB No. 5016 on the 12.22 pm Guildford New Line train (59 mph

max!) No. 34009 produced another good solid performance with a light pacific on the 8.30 am down on 14th May resulting in a 75 minute net time to Southampton, with the master Gordon Hooper in charge. On 16th May I went down to Basingstoke on the 5.30 pm with No. 34019 but it was a poor run, though the return on the 6.35 pm Salisbury with No. 34052 was much better with a maximum speed of just under 80 mph at Fleet. The evening of 18th May proved to be more productive as I went down on the 6.00 pm Salisbury with driver Sayer on No.34089 getting to Basingstoke four minutes early and came back behind No. 34032 giving a 65 mph start to stop run.

With only just over a year of steam to go it is easy to see how we got rather blasé about the amount of steam worked trains still to be seen at Waterloo in the early evening as the table shows

Jim Robinson Snr takes the Brit out of Waterloo on the 9.20 am boat train to Southampton Eastern Docks. *Author*

On 12th May 1966 No. 35029 is passing Wimbledon on the down Bournemouth Belle. *Author*

A busy platform end scene at Waterloo on 16th May 1966. No. 34108 is on the 5.41 pm semi fast to Salisbury and No.34019 *Bideford* heads the 5.30 pm to Bournemouth, which driver Steward of Nine Elms had the misfortune to drive as the engine was in poor condition and lost time to Basingstoke with nothing more than 58 mph anywhere. Engine Duty 381 was a Bournemouth turn booked for a Merchant Navy though the 5.30 pm down was actually Duty 383, though the engine progressed through Duties 381 and 382 to get to 383. Nobody had bothered to change the board! *Author*

with departures from Waterloo on Monday 23rd May.

- 4.35 pm to Weymouth 34090
- 5.09 pm to Basingstoke 34008
- 5.30 pm to Bournemouth 34021
- 5.43 pm to Salisbury 34032
- 6.00 pm to Salisbury 34089
- 6.09 pm to Basingstoke 73037
- 6.30 pm to Weymouth 35003

I went down on the 6.30 pm as it was the only train with a big pacific and driver Hutton, one of Bournemouth's better drivers, kept time with ease on 12 coaches for 435 tons, without exceeding 74 mph down Roundwood. The return with Harry Pope in charge of No. 34038 on the last Weymouth was equally competent. On 1st June, Joe Jolliffe timed a well above par run on the 5.30 pm up from Weymouth. Roy Sloper must have been working No. 34001 very hard to reach 68½ mph up the bank on 430 tons and ran very fast wherever he could afterwards to secure an excellent net time of 72½ minutes, one of the fastest seen with a light pacific 66.10. There were many good competent runs with Nine Elms men on the

No 35027 heading the 8.30 am down on 29th March 1966. *Author*

6.35 pm Salisbury up, and this included one when Les Cummings did well with a Standard 5 struggling the whole way for steam, with a maximum of 170 lb available. I went down on the 9.20 pm on 15th June behind No. 35026, followed by the up mails with 34008 to Eastleigh and 73085 from there and 5.30 am from Waterloo with No. 34025 the next day in order to catch the 6.56 am from Bournemouth up from Winchester as I knew that Ron Skinner had No. 35029 and he was always worth timing. With 11 for 395 tons we ran up into Waterloo over eight minutes early in a net time of 61½ minutes. This run is notable for a rare unchecked sprint over the 28.59 miles from Basingstoke to Weybridge in 21 minutes 32 seconds, an average of a fraction under 80 mph, including braking down to 74 mph before Woking. Perhaps Skinner sighted double yellows here but it is nice to speculate what the speeds might have been he had made full use of the excess steam available and the run had taken place a year later when drivers were throwing caution to the wind. We all had our favourite drivers and I seem to recall that Ron Skinner was Reg Elliot's in the same way that Roy Sloper and Gordon Porter were mine. We continued with No. 35013 on the 10.30 am and No. 35012 on the 11.25 Weymouth, all good timekeeping runs before succumbing to Warship haulage

(D823) on the 3.00 pm to Woking, returning behind No. 34025 on the 4.09 pm arrival with driver Tommy Coles in charge. Nothing special but an eight minute early arrival into Waterloo. Yet another Merchant Navy, No 35027 appeared on the 4.35 pm *Royal Wessex* which driver Arthur Wilton took down to Winchester six minutes early without exceeding 76 mph at Byfleet. I cannot remember the last time I had runs behind five Merchant Navy pacifics in less than 24 hours or when the operating had been so good. Hants DEMU No. 1112 took us to Eastleigh from where No. 73119 on the 3.50 pm from Weymouth hauled us to Basingstoke, Eastleigh driver Living keeping time. The final run of that very long 'day' was rather special as No.34009 gave me one of only a few sub 20 minute runs from Basingstoke to Woking, as shown in 66.11 .The actual time of 19 minutes 48 seconds gave a start to stop average of 71.09 mph and a flying average of 88.01 mph from Hook to Brookwood. Net time was 19 minutes, and 24 minutes on to Waterloo, where arrival was nearly eight minutes early. Overall we had only taken 53 minutes 14 seconds for the 47.75 miles from Basingstoke which included over six minutes standing at Woking. Les Cummings could nearly always be relied on for some high speed running and of course 260 tons is an ideal load to do this with a light pacific.

Unconverted light pacifics No. 34002 *Salisbury* and 34102 *Lapford* on Weymouth shed in 1966. *John Tiley*

No.34032 *Camelford* backs onto the 5.23 pm Fridays only train to Bournemouth at Waterloo on 29th April 1966. *Author*

David Foale timed a very good run with No. 34002 on a heavy load working the 8.30 am down west of Bournemouth on Saturday 16th June. To get 69 mph before Holton Heath was very unusual with any load and the 49 mph minimum up Moreton bank good with 360 tons. Dave Parsons was in good form again with No. 34001 on the 8.35 am down on 22nd June and the engine had to be worked in 40% cut off to reach 67½ mph at Milepost 31 from the Woking restart with 12 bogies. That day was a good one for timing as there were two excellent performances with light pacifics on heavy loads over the Bournemouth to Southampton stretch. No. 34090 takes the honours with a faster time of 32 minutes 25 seconds with 425 tons. The same engine had also done well up from Dorchester with the same Weymouth crew. The continuation to Waterloo with an Eastleigh crew was also good, with Roundwood climbed at a steady 55-57 mph and speed in the seventies all the way from below Basingstoke to a track relaying slack at Walton. We suffered three signal stops though and so were five late into Waterloo. Net time was approximately 79 minutes. The whole run demonstrated a solid performance with a rebuilt light pacific on a heavy train. Unlike the previous week there was not a Merchant Navy to be seen that day! Steam was though still very much in command during the week as the table shows.

TIMES TO WATERLOO		
Tuesday 28th June 1966		
8.22 am	arrival	34095
8.30 am	down	34001
8.35 am	down	34093
9.34 am	arrival	35023
10.11 am	arrival	35026
11.02 am	arrival	35012
11.57 am	arrival	34088
12.08 pm	arrival	34002
12.12 pm	arrival	34102
12.30 pm	down	35026
1.30 pm	down	34090

On 26th June there was another good run with unconverted light pacific No. 34002 *Salisbury* working yet another 'last train' to Exeter (in fact *The Devonshire Rambler*). Driver John Pilcher let this free running pacific have her head down to Andover at 89 mph through Hurstbourne and again with 93 mph down Porton bank, between which the minimum over Grateley was a very good 71½ mph, albeit with a light load. The net time to Salisbury was 80 minutes and David Foale timed this excellent run. 66.12 and 66.13 show the work of Salisbury driver Fred Hoare on the 6.00 pm down and though the running between Basingstoke and Salisbury produced almost identical times, No. 34026 was by far the better engine and did not need pushing as hard as No. 34032, which Fred described to me at Salisbury as short of steam, rough and 'unsafe'. These were my last runs with Fred Hoare driving as he retired soon afterwards and the 6.00 pm down went over to

Class 33 'Crompton' haulage at the beginning of September. Fred was one of those quiet spoken, knowledgeable and friendly enginemen who was easy to approach and always happy to talk to you. Ray Churchill who retired from driving steam for West Coast Railways in May 2016 reminded me very much of Fred Hoare. Gentlemen of the footplate both. The week before these runs, 'Mad Monk' Frank Matthews worked the 5.41 pm down and the 6.35 pm Salisbury back from Basingstoke and produced his usual crop of erratic and noisy runs. On the 7th July with No. 34093 he set what I think is the fastest start with steam out of Woking towards London with a decent load. The table shows the detail of the start and my notes state that the engine was worked in full regulator and 75% cut off to Milepost 22½, the 60% cut off to Milepost 22 and then 15%. Table 41 – *See page 167*. No wonder they were short of steam by that point as no fireman could possibly

No. 34036 *Westward Ho* at Southampton on the 9.33 am Excursion from Waterloo to Bournemouth on Good Friday 8th April 1966. Gordon Hooper in charge. *John Tiley*

SOUTH WESTERN DIVISION – MONDAY TO FRIDAY   65.

WEYMOUTH DUTY NO.431

8P (Merchant Navy Class) Large
                    Tender
MX – Off No.435
                    Weymouth Loco   08 35‖
08 40   Weymouth   09 21P
13 03   Waterloo   13 32‖
13 43   Nine Elms Loco   16 58‖
17 12   Waterloo   17 30P
20 28   Bournemouth Ctl.   20 37E
20 45   Branksome   20 57‖
21 07   Bournemouth Loco   23 10‖
23 12   Bournemouth Ctl.   23 37P
           (22 13 Weymouth)

TUESDAYS TO SATURDAYS

04 11   Waterloo   04 58‖
05 10   Nine Elms Loco
                    WORK NO.432

WEYMOUTH MEN

(1) Prepare for 08 35‖

BOURNEMOUTH MEN

(2) Off No.442 work 08 35‖ and
     relieved at Bournemouth Central
     10 21

NINE ELMS MEN

(3) Off No.463, relieve at
     Bournemouth Central 10 21 work
     and relieved at Waterloo 13 03

(4) Off No.108 relieve at Waterloo
     13 03 work and dispose.

(5) 1st Set – On duty 15 53 work
     and relieved at Eastleigh
     19 12 to depot work No.116
     20 10‖ and relieved in depot.

Continued.....

WEYMOUTH DUTY 431 (CONT'D)

EASTLEIGH MEN

(6) 1st Set – On duty 18 42, relieved at
     19 12 work and relieved at Bournemouth
     Central 20 28 to depot work No.434
     21 00‖ and relieved at Eastleigh 00 50
     and as ordered.

BOURNEMOUTH MEN

(7) 1st Set – On duty 19 15 prepare No.434
     to Station relieve this duty at 20 28
     work and relieved Bournemouth Central
     23 35 to depot dispose No.385

(8) 2nd Set – On duty 23 20 relieve at
     23 35, work and relieved at Eastleigh
     01 32 to depot, prepare and work
     No.244 (next day) 05 20‖ and relieved
     at Bournemouth Central 07 36

EASTLEIGH MEN

(9) 2nd Set (Tues to Sat) On duty 01 02
     relieve at 01 32, work, change with
     No.112 at Waterloo 04 30 work and
     relieved Basingstoke 07 30 home
     passenger.

NINE ELMS MEN

(10) MX – Off No.112 change over at
     Waterloo 04 30 work and dispose.

have kept up with the demands of a locomotive being (ill) treated in that way. He was the exact opposite of Fred Hoare who would be horrified at such actions, but it was exciting to travel in a train with him driving and all good fodder for the tape recordists amongst us. By the end of July the up Channel Islands Express was a heavy train and still running non stop between Basingstoke and Waterloo. On 27th July I recorded a good run with an Eastleigh crew on 13 bogies for 455 tons with No. 34036 when we ran up in a net time of 47 minutes with 80 mph

at Byfleet and the next day Richard (Joe) Jolliffe had another good run on the 5.30 pm down with light pacific 34087 in 46½ minutes net to Basingstoke and then a 90 mph effort with *Bude* on the 6.38 pm Salisbury up on 5th August. The 5.30 pm down continued to be worth timing for consistently good runs with Nine Elms men on heavy loads with light pacifics, despite being booked for Merchant Navy haulage. No. 34098 on 410 tons with driver McLaggon on 10th August was typical with 74 mph at Byfleet, 61½ over milepost 31 after a signal check to

44 before Woking and 74 mph again at Fleet before arriving at Basingstoke eight minutes early in 47½ minutes net from Waterloo. The commuters must have wondered if the promised new electric service could improve on this sort of timekeeping, day in day out. The BR Standard 5s were still doing well on the secondary trains and No. 73088 was above par on the Salisbury train on same day running the 23.46 miles from Basingstoke to Woking in 22 minutes 48 seconds (22 minutes net), maximum speed 79½ at Fleet. This was a very good even time run Basingstoke to Woking with a heavier 325 ton load than usual, arriving at Waterloo on time after an 8 minute late start. The driver was Ball of Nine Elms MPD. Joe Jolliffe recorded a very good run behind No. 34047 on the 12.59 pm from Bournemouth on 16th August. The start from Woking to West Byfleet was only 10 seconds slower than the mighty effort with No. 34093 shown earlier and the running continued at a very high standard as no doubt Gordon Porter had more consideration for his fireman and the engine than the driver of No.34093 had. Notwithstanding this comment about Gordon Porter being easier on engines he produced an extraordinary performance on the same train on 19th August with No. 34015 as shown in 66.14 . The engine must have been worked very hard to get to over 80 mph at Micheldever from the Winchester start even with the relatively light load and this required about 1,450 EDBH or 2,250 IHP. From Basingstoke an all out effort was made to get to 100 mph and no doubt this is what the speedometer on the engine showed, though the stop watch 'only' recorded 97 mph at Palelane after Winchfield. I had gone north on the 9.20 pm from St Pancras to secure some steam runs over Shap and so missed out on this highlight of unconverted Bulleid pacific running. Joe had gone down on the 8.35 am with the same crew and the running was hardly less impressive with rebuilt pacific No. 34034. Highlights were 56 mph at Wootton starting from Basingstoke, a close to even time run from Winchester to Southampton Airport, 82 mph twice before the Brockenhurst stop

and the very fast net time from Brockenhurst to Bournemouth involving 91 mph after Hinton Admiral.

It was beginning to be difficult to keep engines running due to a backlog of maintenance and lack of spares as these and the fleet were being run down. An example of the increasingly desperate situation taken from the daily record supplied to my office at Waterloo is shown here. No wonder so few Merchant Navy pacifics were seen pulling trains around that time as no less than eight were stopped!

ENGINES STOPPED FOR REPAIRS OR BOILER WASH OUT ON SUNDAY 14th AUGUST 1966

35003 35010 34024 76061 75070 34071 34004 30064 73118 73171 34023 34093 35029 73043 34036 73037 34021 34044 34008 35012 35014 35023 35026 73092 76033 73020 35028

On Saturday 20th August, as I was getting Brit haulage over Shap Terry Jackson was timing an extremely rare run with a BR 9F on the 10.42 am Poole to Sheffield between Bournemouth and Southampton and 2-10-0 coped very well. Back to the mundane, Gordon Porter turned in one of my best runs with a BR class 5 on the 6.35 pm from Salisbury on 22nd August, which is shown in 66.15 . No. 73087 was even better than its sister No. 73088 which worked the same train on 10th August. The overall time up from Basingstoke was just 49 minutes 33 seconds including nearly two minutes standing at Woking and the start to stop average from Basingstoke to Woking at 64.47 mph was my best with a Standard 5 on the Southern. A 15 minute late start was nearly all recovered by the fast running, smart running and good operating. Alongside it is a run with No. 34026 which makes a good comparison and Ted Dente had Pete Roberts firing who was no doubt a bit bemused by the driving style of Ted as it was a bit faster than his usual mate Jim Robinson Snr. It would have been even more of a shock to fire to 'Mad Monk' Frank Matthews on the 5.41 pm down with No. 34013 on 24th August especially on the section from Woking up

No. 34044 on an up train at Southampton on 29th October 1966. *Terry Jackson*

to milepost 31 where my log book has such comments as 'utter thrash'. The return run with No. 34006 produced a net time of 21 minutes from Basingstoke to Woking. I noted that Pete was back with his normal partner when working the 3.35 pm down with No. 73110 on 26th August. As a change from the Salisbury train No. 34005 with an Eastleigh crew turned in turned in an even time run with 370 ton without a lot of effort on 31st August on the 3.50 pm Weymouth with a maximum speed of just under 80 at Pirbright. On the evening of Ted Dente's up run he worked the 5.41 pm down with No. 34057 which I picked up at Hook having gone down on the 5.30 pm behind No. 35014 and Reuben Hendicott driving arriving its almost normal six minutes early. A rare appearance of a Merchant Navy pacific on this train. The table shows that *Biggin Hill* was driven very

hard but the effort came to nothing as we had a long signal stop outside Basingstoke. **Table 42** – *See page 167.* Then came two runs on the 8.35 am down with light pacifics; Gordon Porter with No. 34009 making yet another attempt to get to 100 mph but thwarted by a temporary speed restriction at Wallers Ash and the run with 34015 as far as Basingstoke was another fine run with Dave Parsons at the regulator. The highlight was the 70 mph at milepost 31 starting from Woking with 320 tons and even time net from Woking to Basingstoke. On 14th September I timed a run with No. 34032 from Woking to Waterloo, notable for a fast time to pass Hampton Court Junction in 10 minutes 19 seconds and by reaching 79 mph by Byfleet Junction. September continued with yet more runs on the up Salisbury, the one with No. 34013 included two 90 mph maxima at

Pirbright and Hersham, and I enjoyed Wilton's run with No. 34102 on the 5.30 pm down on 21st September as it again showed just how free running the unconverted pacifics could be. I suspect that the driver was happily going along without much effort when he suddenly realised that they had left over five minutes late and so opened up *Lapford* to produce a lovely little sprint averaging 76.7 mph between mileposts 35 and 46 to run into Basingstoke just under a minute early on a schedule which had been shaved by two minutes after the track work out to Basingstoke had been completed. I covered a lot of miles on Wednesday 14th September starting on the 8.35 am with No. 34015 and returning to Waterloo behind No. 34024 on 13 for 445 tons on the 1.03 pm arrival. Arthur 'Spot' King did not have to work *Taw Valley* at all hard to arrive over seven minutes early without exceeding 76 mph in a net time of 85 minutes from Southampton. Then it was back down on the 1.30 pm with No. 34005 and Bournemouth driver Cooper who managed to lose two minutes to Basingstoke without exceeding 59 mph, probably not able to lift the regulator more than a few inches from the stop block (unlike many Nine Elms men who would normally have the regulator at the opposite end of the quadrant). We returned to Waterloo with Dave Parsons driving No. 34057 and then must have adjourned to the Lancaster Grill or the Long Bar for our next run was on the 5.41 pm to Basingstoke with 70A crew West and Fred Davis, before enjoying a nice even time run back to Woking on the 3.50 pm from Weymouth behind No. 35026 on 380 tons, maximum 83 mph after Brookwood, changing at Woking onto the up Salisbury. Osborne of Eastleigh was the driver with 35026 and he was one of many good men from that good depot, though there were a few who had some of the characteristics of some of their Bournemouth cousins! At around this time Les Kent timed No. 34008 *Padstow* at 100 mph down Roundwood at Weston on the 2.45 am paper train and although it lacks some detail it is included here as one of the definite 100 mph runs. Table 45 – *See page 169.* Also in August 1966 Bob Thompson recorded quite a few runs on the postal trains between Clapham

Junction and Kensington Olympia, an example being with No. 80133 on 4 coaches for 143 tons gross on 10th August which did the run in 8 minutes 52 seconds, maximum speed 51 mph after Battersea.

Apart from the large number of engines stopped for various reasons at that time there were also mishaps on the road and my notebook tells me that No. 35010 blew a cylinder cover off at Clapham Junction on 8th September whilst working the 8.23 am from Basingstoke and was withdrawn forthwith. The motive power situation demanded some action to ease the situation and so six Brush Type 4 diesels were drafted in and from 3rd October had two diagrams which covered the following passenger trains:

5.49 am	Eastleigh to Weymouth	09.10 am
10.13 am	Weymouth to Bournemouth	11.37 am
12.35 pm	Bournemouth to Waterloo	2.52 pm
4.35 pm	Waterloo to Weymouth	8.15 pm
10.13 pm	Weymouth to Waterloo	4.11 am
8.30 am	Waterloo to Bournemouth	10.45 am
12.59 pm	Bournemouth to Waterloo	4.09 pm
5.30 pm	Waterloo to Bournemouth	8.30 pm
9.26 pm	Bournemouth to Southampton	

This was a big blow to the fraternity, although these diagrams were later amended and added to and at first the diesels were very unreliable and steam had to be substituted. It was though the beginning of the end and the scope for high daily mileages bashing steam and especially after work activities was much reduced. Both the 6.35 pm up Salisbury and 3.50 pm Weymouth plus the Channel Islands Express, the 'Club Train' and last Weymouth all remained steam and to access these the 5.09 pm, 5.41 pm and 6.30 pm were all still steam, for the time being at least. On 4th October the stock position was as shown in Appendix G. To summarise 123 engines remained plus ten class O2 tanks on the Isle of Wight. These included 10 Merchant Navies, 30 rebuilt light pacifics, seven in original condition and 20 BR Standard class 5 4-6-0s. In theory therefore there should have been no problems but as we have seen there was now a very high level of unavailable steam locomotives. The use of the Brush Type 4s did not entirely solve the crisis and nine steam engines withdrawn on 29th October 1966 were reinstated on 9th December 1966. These were Nos 34005, 34026, 34032, 73087, 73088, 73089, 73169, 76016 and 76057.

MERCHANT NAVY CLASS PACIFICS REMAINING ON 4TH OCTOBER 1966	
35003	Royal Mail
35007	Aberdeen Commonwealth
35008	Orient Line
35012	United States Line
35013	Blue Funnel
35014	Nederland Line
35023	Holland-Afrika Line
35026	Lamport and Holt Line
35028	Clan Line
35030	Elder Dempster Lines

However there were still some quite fantastic performances to be had amongst the gloom and one such was on Saturday 15th October. This was the day of the unofficially sanctioned 100 mph run on the Southern as Derek Winkworth's private excursion had been given a fast timing of just 78 minutes for the 83.7 miles, with the load limited to 8 coaches for 280 tons. I missed the run as on that day I was in Bridport for a family christening, but some of our group were there and I have chosen Terry Jackson's log shown in 66.17 to show the detail. The driver was Bert Hooker, veteran fireman of the 1948 locomotive exchanges and his fireman Alan Deadman, who is still around today. The running was brilliant throughout, the highlight for me being the 80 mph minimum over Grateley and the 101 mph down through Andover must have been an amazing experience. This was always my favourite part of the down *Atlantic Coast Express* as we swept round the reverse curves

On 17th May 1966 No. 35008 *Orient Line* gets majestically under way with the down Bournemouth Belle at Vauxhall. The train has the full consist of 11 Pullmans and a bogie van, around 500 tons gross. This is one of my favourite images of Southern steam and a large framed picture of it sits on the wall of my study in front of me as I write. *Author*

Another shot at Southampton taken on 29th October 1966. No 35013 has steam leaking from places it should not be and no doubt would be declared a failure if on the main line today. *Terry Jackson*

and dashed through the platform with whistle   screaming, though the maximum speed I ever

No 35023 at Southampton Central on a down train. *John Tiley*

No. 35023 *Holland Afrika Line* stands at Salisbury after arrival from Waterloo on its 100 mph run on 15th October 1966. Inspector Jupp is on the running plate possibly checking that everything is still in place! **66.17** shows the details of the run. *John Tiley*

No. 35026 is seen at Westbury waiting to take the railtour of 15th October on to Exeter. *Terry Jackson*

High speed pacific No. 35023 at Weymouth on 17th September 1966. *John Tiley*

recorded here was 94 mph. On the 15th October run it is said that Arthur Jupp, the Inspector, hung his hat over the speedometer so he could not see it! The net time of 71 minutes is the fastest recorded with steam. No. 35023 then took the train on to Westbury where No. 35026 took over to Exeter via Taunton. Terry Jackson comments about this section that 'the story at the time was that the Western Region were asked for a 75 minute timing from Westbury to Exeter but refused. However an excellent performance ensued and we did it in 75 minutes anyway'. No. 35026 worked the train back to Salisbury running non stop from Exeter Central as shown in 66.18 . Good though this was with a net time of 81¼ minutes for the 88.05 miles it did not compare with Gordon Hooper's run on 3rd October 1965 when, with the same load No.35022 covered the same stretch in an actual

time of 78 minutes 58 seconds, or 76 minutes net 65.24 . From Salisbury No. 35023 took over to take the train back to Waterloo and with Salisbury crew driver Pat Kelly and fireman Bacon in charge ran well with speed in the eighties for many miles, but with no heroics ran up in 75 minutes net. What a day it had been and there are some amongst us who still revere *Holland Afrika Line* as THE engine from the days of steam

Back to the normality of everyday running. My return from Bridport involved No. 35007 on the Sunday 2.11 pm from Weymouth (which was to be the last steam hauled train into Waterloo on Sunday 9th July 1967). With just 7 coaches of about 255 tons full, George Holloway and Colin Grey had no trouble running from Bournemouth to Southampton in 30¼ minutes net with 79 mph after Beaulieu

No 34100 *Appledore* runs into Basingstoke on the 5.41 pm from Waterloo in July 1966.
Terry Jackson

No. 34102 *Lapford* passing Raynes Park with an up boat train from Southampton Docks in June 1966. *Peter Austin*

Road and 73 minutes net up from Southampton after 74 mph up Roundwood and no more than 76 mph after Basingstoke. The struggle for motive power continued as, for example, on Wednesday 19th October I decided to avoid the Brush Type 4s by going down on the 3.35 pm which had No. 73118, piloted by D6511 for some reason, and we followed the 3.30 pm down which had another class 5 No. 73085 on 13 for about 460 tons so we were checked all the way to our Woking stop. At Basingstoke I transferred onto the 4.51 pm to Salisbury behind No. 34100 which managed to lose four minutes with a light load. I then returned on the 6.38 pm up behind No. 35026. It was very unusual to find a Merchant Navy on this train and there was nothing of note until John Gaffney took over at Basingstoke and gave us a 20½ minutes net run to Woking with 88 mph at Brookwood. Although the 5.30 pm down was now booked

for Brush haulage, No. 35026 was turned out for it on 26th October and I returned on the 3.50 pm Weymouth which was now Eastleigh men and had the good run with No. 34034 with 14 bogies for just under 500 tons. The 5.30 pm down was steam again on 31st October with No. 34102 but Fred Prickett had to fire as well as drive as he had been given a passed cleaner who had never fired anything bigger than a Black 5 and who had not been on the footplate for six weeks, so the run is best forgotten. On 1st November No. 35013 deputised for a Brush Type 4 on the 4.35 pm down and 34052 was on the 12.50 pm Bournemouth with No. 35023 on the 5.30 pm so both Brush diagrams were mainly steam that day. As the 5.30 pm down was now more often than not steam hauled it appears that the Brush diagrams had been changed though I cannot confirm this from my records. On days when the Type 4s were on their diagrams I often used

No 35013 *Blue Funnel* **at Southampton Central on an up express on 29th October 1966.**
Terry Jackson

the 6.30 pm down returning on the old 'Mogul Train'. To ring the changes and compensate for the reduction in evening services I was now spending time bashing up and down between Waterloo and Woking prior to going to my office above the concourse at Waterloo, without much success until the morning of 9th November when Les Cummings gave me the fine run with Standard class 4 4-6-0 No 75079 shown in 66.19 .Two days later he had No. 34013 on the same train and ran Woking to Surbiton in just over even time or 12 minutes net for the 12.25 miles with a maximum of 90 mph. 66.20 . I also had a run with No. 76007 on the 7.18 am down which I caught from Surbiton to Woking before returning to Waterloo behind No. 34087. I had started the day on the 6.25 am from Waterloo with an 8 coach set of 2Bil stock which produced a scintillating maximum speed of 54½ mph before Wimbledon.

The week beginning 14th November saw Gordon Porter booked to work the 5.30 pm Weymouth up 'Club Train' and I managed to be present for two of the runs, on Monday 14th 66.21 and Wednesday 16th 66.23 . Porter had his usual mate of Tom Moult and Gordon told me that he was going to get 100 mph at least once that week, which he did. This was on Tuesday 15th which I could not be there for but fortunately Les Kent was on the train and his log is shown in 66.22 . On the Monday we left Southampton nearly 15 minutes late and were then stopped by signals before Northam Junction and checked again at Eastleigh before getting 67 mph at Winchester before yet another signal check. I suspect we might have been following a boat train. No. 35007 then accelerated its 405 tons train to 71 mph at Roundwood summit before getting a very unusual 80 at Wootton and being stopped again before Basingstoke, thus ruining our chances of getting 100 mph on the racing stretch. In fact we got 93 after Winchfield and 94 at Pirbright before being turned slow line at Brookwood and stopped by signals in the platform at Woking. I wonder whether Gordon had in his mind to let No. 35007 run up to 100 mph past Brookwood, which would have been very unusual. The running on to Waterloo was slightly more subdued but this had been a fine run in an excellent and not often beaten net time of 71 minutes up from Southampton. 66.21 . 66.22 shows the 100 mph run. Les Kent cannot remember why progress was so slow up the bank but maybe Porter was hanging around in order to get a clear run through Basingstoke, notorious at that time for signal checks. If that was the plan then it worked and speed was up to 80 mph past Basingstoke and 96 at the foot of the 1-in-249/385 to Newham Siding before falling to 91 at Hook. With 96 mph again at Winchfield speed the rose to 102 at Milepost 38 passing Fleet at 101 mph before brakes brought speed down to more normal levels. This would have required about 1,380 EDBH or about 2,830 IHP. No less than three signal stops ruined the rest of the run and with so many variables calculating a net time would not really be realistic. On Wednesday 16th November I went down on the 4.35 pm with Ernie Harvey driving Brush Type 4 No. D1921, reaching Winchester over five minutes early without exceeding 76 mph. Gordon Porter again had No. 35007 on 400 tons and on a rotten night of rain and gales we had the usual crop of three signal stops, despite another late start. The engine was slipping up the bank and not being pushed but opened up audibly as we passed Worting Junction at 66 mph with a big lurch (speed limit was 60 mph), giving me high hopes of a clear run through Basingstoke. But no, on came the brakes and we slowed to a crawl before the station. Then, nothing daunted, as shown in 66.23 , we were away again with Gordon using full regulator and 40% cut off to get us up to 98 mph down Winchfield bank, EDBH 1470 or IHP 2750, before easing somewhat prior to be turned slow line and the stopped for signals before Woking. Then followed a nice sprint to another stop for signals before Wimbledon, the 16.75 miles from the previous stop being run in 16 minutes 12 seconds, an unexpected even time bonus. So I had been robbed of 100 mph after Winchfield again by poor operating but I would

NO 35007 ABERDEEN COMMONWEALTH			
	14.11.66	15.11.66	16.11.66
	405 tons	375 tons	400 tons
Hook	53m 27s 83 mph	47m 12s 91 mph	55m 04s 82.5 mph
Winchfield	55m 08s 87/93 mph	48m 40s 96/102 mph	56m 49s 88/98 mph
Fleet	57m 23s 90 mph	50m 43s 101 mph	58m 58s 95 mph
Winchfield to Fleet (average)	2m 15s 89.3 mph	2m 03s 98.05 mph	2m 09s 93.5 mph

not have to wait long for my turn in this series of high speed exploits by Porter and Moult in late 1966. The table shows a comparison of times and speeds for the three runs.

These were desperate times on the motive power front as my runs on Monday 21st November demonstrated. I started on the 1.30 pm down where the 13 coaches for 475 tons had nothing bigger than BR Standard class 5 No. 73085 and no banker at the start and so took nearly five minutes to get past Vauxhall and limped all the way to the first stop at Basingstoke, losing 20 minutes. The 4.09 pm arrival (12.59 pm Bournemouth) then had another class 5 No. 73020 in place of the booked Brush Type 4, ending up at Waterloo nearly half an hour late, followed by No. 34093 on the 5.30 pm down, again instead of a Brush diesel, though Alf Hurley kept time. No. 34013 then took me to Woking on the 6.38 pm Salisbury and finally Lockhart of Eastleigh had Merchant Navy No. 35014 on the 3.50 pm from Weymouth running 48 minutes late, due to an earlier engine failure. The next day driver Adams of Bournemouth, nearing the end of his footplate career had to cope with No. 34102, desperately short of steam on the 6.30 pm down, all of which prompted me to catch the up 'Mogul Train' hauled by BR Standard class 4 Mogul No. 76063, which ran well between Basingstoke and Hook with a maximum of 71 mph. As Thursday 24th November was his last run before retiring some of us decided to go down with Adams on the 7.30 pm and with No. 34060 on just 7 coaches for 245 tons he did quite well on a cold and very foggy night . As we went into December things looked up a bit and the table shows that the evening of 7th December was almost like old

times, except for the lack of Merchant Navies again. It would soon all be changed though as new rosters would apply from 2nd January and the first scheduled electric services would begin.

DEPARTURES FROM WATERLOO ON WEDNESDAY 7TH DECEMBER 1966
5.09 pm to Basingstoke: 34090
5.30 pm to Bournemouth: 34098 (for Brush Type 4)
5.41 pm to Salisbury: 34019
6.22 pm to Bournemouth: 34013
6.30 pm to Weymouth: 34052
6.54 pm to Basingstoke: 34095
7.00 pm to Exeter: 34089 (for class 42)
7.30 pm to Weymouth: 34104

The new month seemed to produce an uplift both in available Bulleid pacifics and in the quality of performance as all the runs tabulated were out of the top drawer, including two more 100 mph efforts, one of which I regard as being in my top five steam runs. Starting the remarkable series of runs. 66.24 shows a very fast run on the lightly loaded Saturday 7.05 am up from Basingstoke with No. 34077, timed by David Foale. This run has I believe the fastest ever time with steam from the Woking start to passing Hampton Court Junction, 9 minutes and 19 seconds. Next in 66.25 is one of my best ever runs with a Bulleid pacific, on the 'Club Train' with Gordon Porter this time partnered by Robert Lee. I had gone down on the 4.35 pm behind D1923 with Sydney Cull driving and for once in that year the train had the full 13 coach load. The 5.30 pm Weymouth was close to right time and we had fewer out of course checks than usual. My notebook states that main line running had improved by better operating and locomotive availability though this did not apply to the Brush Type 4s as again that evening the 5.30 pm down was steam hauled, this time by a Standard class 5. The reinstatement of the nine engines mentioned above undoubtedly would have helped. On the 'Club Train', No. 35028 had 11 bogies for 375 tons and after adverse signals all the way from after Swaythling to Allbrook, where we were turned slow line to pass a freight standing on the up fast, progress up the bank in the rain was good but not nothing of note with speed held at around 60 mph, as the engine was slipping and not being pushed. Steam was shut off just before Wootton and we drifted up onto Battledown flyover at 54½ mph. Steam was put on and we passed Worting Junction more or less on time at 62 mph. Smoke was laying back heavily on the milepost side in thick billows but as speed rose into the eighties (my stop watch reading for the three quarters of a mile across Basingstoke was 32.3 seconds) it lifted and we stormed past Basingstoke laying burning cinders along the down platforms, witness to the engine being worked hard. In fact Gordon was using full regulator and 20-25% cut off all the way to Fleet; none of this 'full and 40' needed here to get to 100 mph. I was standing by an open window in the corridor in order to ensure I could pick up the tiny LSWR mileposts in the dark and rain and I can still remember the next few exciting minutes when I realised that we were certain to get to the magic 'ton', which we did with 103 mph just after the foot of the bank at Palelane. We had taken one second less than two minutes from Winchfield to Fleet at an average of 101.36 mph and ran the 11 miles between Mileposts 46 and 35 at an average of 95.43 mph. The table shows the detail of this fine run. Table 43 – *See page 168.* Others were on the train that night and there was some disagreement concerning the maximum speed and also the power needed to achieve it. The notes that I made at the time show my best quarter mile readings to be 8.8 seconds from MP 38¼ to 38 and 8.7 seconds from MP 37¾ to 37½, followed by 8.9

seconds. It is the 8.7 seconds figure which has given rise to the controversy as if correct this means that the maximum speed would have been on level track. Another area of dispute is over whether or not the track was welded and by then the view is that it would have been. However my notes state 'the rail joints could just be heard, merging almost as one'. Some years ago Alan Wild did a detailed analysis of the high speed section the results of which suggest that *Clan Line* was producing around 3,000 IHP that night, another phenomenal performance from an engine in good condition and steaming well as 200-220 llb in the steam chest was used throughout. My calculation for the EDBH figure from Winchfield to Milepost 38 gives 1,545 or a magic 3,015 IHP. Adverse signals (the new colour light multiple aspect signals) were sighted in the distance at Fleet and so brakes brought speed back into the 70s before a long relaying slack all the way from Pirbright to below Brookwood but then away we went again accelerating brilliantly to 88½ mph at Byfleet Junction, falling to 85½ over the slight climb to Oatlands and racing away to 94 at Hersham prior to another temporary speed restriction and an arrival at Waterloo nearly 12 minutes early in an actual time of 82 minutes 50 seconds from Southampton or 72 minutes net, my second fastest. In calculating the net time I have assumed that we would have continued at around 80 mph from Farnborough to passing West Byfleet. The net time shown in DW Winkworth's book is in my view too slow for high speed before and after the restricted section. The log of this run in DW Winkworth's book shows the time as 83 minutes 15 seconds though Terry Jackson who was also on the train made it 82 minutes 54 seconds. The actual time in from Basingstoke had been just 42 minutes 43 seconds, also my second fastest. There was a story at the time concerning a comment made by the signaller in the new Basingstoke panel box and recently Terry Jackson recalled this:

'Shortly after this run, although I cannot recall exactly when, I was coming up from Soton on a semi-fast which stopped at

Basingstoke. The door of my compartment opened and in walked Gordon Porter who was on his way to NE. During our conversation on the way to Waterloo, he told me that he had visited the new power box at Basingstoke shortly after the 100 in December. The guy in the box was giving him a guided tour and showed him how they could now track an up service on the panel from where it entered Basing's domain to the start of Woking's domain. He then passed comment about the Club train which he had followed one night on the panel and the time it had taken from when it first showed on the panel until it left the Basing area. Apparently he couldn't believe how fast it was going. I think Gordon was taken aback when he realised that this was almost certainly his run on the 12th and by the fact that others were now able to see what had been going on.'

The next day, Tuesday 13th December I had a run behind one of the reinstated engines, BR Standard class 5 No. 73169 and it did well enough on the last Weymouth when Roberts of Nine Elms got 75 mph past Hampton Court Junction and ran into Waterloo on time. On the 14th I went down on the 4.35 pm again with Sydney Cull driving but this time we had No. 34014 in place of a failed Brush Type 4, but the run was not very good, The point was to catch the 'Club Train' again though the running with No. 35008 was more normal with nothing higher than 80 mph noted and Albert Wright of Nine Elms in charge. A spoof of the running that evening showing 100 mph plus speeds appeared for a while on the RPS database but was soon taken down. **66.26** shows a very fast run with No. 34089 on the 7.18 am down when West of Nine Elms produced what is thought to be the fastest actual time with steam from Surbiton to Woking, though his time out to Surbiton was beaten by the run shown in **65.25** with a much heavier load. Peter Trapp who timed this run was joined by Les Kent

on the 6.49 am up from Salisbury at Woking and the running on this light train produced another 100 mph, this time behind No. 34013 at the most unlikely place of Hersham, almost certainly the only time 100 mph was recorded there. **66.27** Jim Evans had some turns on the 6.38 pm Salisbury from Basingstoke, and on 21st December, having taken the 5.41 pm down with D813 (this train was booked to be diesel hauled for a short time before being turned over to electric traction at the beginning of 1967), he produced a near even time run from Woking to Waterloo with No.34057 on 21st December, maximum 84 mph. Driver Sauter of Eastleigh drove No. 34036 well enough to get an even time run from Basingstoke to Woking on 22nd December with 425 tons and without exceeding 76 mph. Finally Jim Evans on 29th December brought 1966 to a close **66.28** with a very fast run from Basingstoke to Woking in just 19 minutes 14 seconds, an average of 73.19 mph with No.34057 threatening to run away up to 100 mph before Jim touched the brakes just after we had passed Winchfield at 93 mph. We were inside even time by Milepost 41, though with a light load of 185 tons. Detail of the start from Basingstoke is shown in the table. **Table 44** – *See page 169.* My notes state that Jim used 35% cut off to Newnham Siding and then 20%. Steam pressure was 220 lb at Basingstoke falling to 160 lb from Winchfield to Woking and the engine was only fired once over the whole stretch. The start from Woking was also very fast to pass West Byfleet, 2.61 miles in 3 minutes 35 seconds at 70 mph and no doubt Waterloo would have been reached in even time had we not been checked. The start to West Byfleet was the fastest I recorded, beating by three seconds the big effort by Frank Matthews driving No. 34093 on 315 tons discussed earlier in the chapter, but was narrowly beaten by the run timed by David Foale shown in **66.24**. The 6.38 pm Salisbury up produced a good number of even time runs in 1966, some of which are shown in the table **Table 46** – *See page 170.*

Despite the reduction in the number of steam locomotives, my work move from Waterloo to East Croydon and my activities away from accumulating steam runs, I still managed to travel a decent distance behind steam for the last two months of 1966, as shown in the table.

STEAM MILEAGE FOR THE PERIOD FROM 10TH OCTOBER TO 15TH DECEMBER 1966	
Merchant Navy Pacifics	920
Rebuilt Light Pacifics	1335.5
Unconverted Light Pacifics	271.75
BR Standard class 5 4-6-0s	390.25
BR Standard class 4 4-6-0s	106
BR Standard class 4 2-6-0s	54.5
Total steam mileage	3077.75

And so ended another good year for steam performance, though not in the same league as 1965, still managing to produce another four 100 mph runs and two more huge efforts from Merchant Navy pacifics at the 3,000 IHP level. Once again the full tabulated versions of all the runs can be found in a separate publication.

On 29th April 1966, No. 34023 *Blackmore Vale* arrives at Basingstoke with the 6 pm Waterloo to Salisbury. Driver Mills of Nine Elms MPD was in charge. *Author*

16th May 1966 No. 34108 backs into Waterloo prior to working the 5.41 pm semi fast train to Salisbury. *Author*

No 34023 *Blackmore Vale* in absolutely filthy condition at Basingstoke working the 6.0 pm Waterloo to Salisbury on 29th April 1966. *Author*

Tables

Table 38

WAREHAM TO SWANAGE

Date	Saturday 14th May 1966
Train	1110 am Wareham to Swanage
Loco	LM Class 2P 2-6-2 tank No. 41295
Load	2 coaches, 75 tons gross approx
Driver	Woods, Bournemouth MPD
Recorder	Bob Thompson

	miles	sched	mins	secs	speed
Wareham	0.00	0.00	00	00	
Worgret Jct	1.08	3.00	03	36	22/15*/52½
Furzebrook Sdg			07	22	44½/54
Corfe Castle	6.05	12.00	11	33	
	0.00	0.00	00	00	
MP 132½ Summit					31 min/56 max
Swanage	4.99	9.00	09	50	
	* brakes				

Table 39

CORFE CASTLE TO WAREHAM

Date	Saturday 14th May 1966
Train	1140 am Swanage to Wareham
Loco	BR Standard class 4 tank No. 80011
Load	2 coaches, 75 tons gross approx
Recorder	Bob Thompson

	miles	sched	mins	secs	speed
Corfe Castle	0.00	0.00	00	00	
Furzebrook Sdg			04	32	38½/47
Worget Jct	4.97	8.30	06	53	41*
Wareham	6.05	11.00	09	13	
	* brakes				

Table 40

FLEET TO BASINGSTOKE

Date				Monday 9th May 1966					
Train				541 pm Waterloo to Salisbury					
Loco				Rebuilt West Country class 4-6-2 No. 34032 *Camelford*					
Load				11 coaches, 348½ tons tare, 380 tons gross					
Crew				Dave Parsons and Ray McQuade, Nine Elms MPD					
Recorder				DB					

	miles	sched	mins	secs	speed	regulator	cut off	boiler pressure (lb)	steam chest (lb)
Fleet	0.00	0.00	00	00	5¾ mns late	¼	75%	200	80
MP 37	0.50		01	45	25	¼	50%	205	80
MP 38	1.50		03	19	44	¾	25%	205	160
MP 39	2.50		04	29	53½				
Winchfield	3.35	6.00	05	55					
	0.00		00	00		¼	75%	215	80
			tsr		15*	¼	30%	210	50
MP 40¼	0.40		01	57	15*	¾	25%	210	170
MP 41	1.15		03	36	42½	¾	25%	215	170
Hook	2.33	5.00	05	34					
	0.00		00	00		¼	75%	215	80
MP 43	0.80		02	20	40	full	45%	210	200
Newnham Siding	1.49		03	16	51	shut/full	45%	200	200
MP 44	1.80		03	38	56	full	45%	195	185
MP 45	2.80		04	40	60	full	40%	180	170
MP 46	3.80		05	39	62½	full	30%	180	170
			sigs		37*	shut			
Basingstoke	5.59	10.00	09	03	2½ mins late				
					* brakes	slipped briefly at Newham Siding			

Table 41

FAST START FROM WOKING

Date	7th July 1966	
Train	635 pm Salisbury to Waterloo	
Loco	Rebuilt West Country class 4-6-2 No. 34093 *Saunton*	
Load	5 coaches and 6 vans, 286 tons tare 315 tons gross	
Crew	Frank Matthews and Ray McQuade Nine Elms MPD	
Recorder	DB	
Weather	Fine	

	miles	sched	mins	secs	speed
Woking	0.00	0.00	00	00	
MP 24	0.29		01	06	21
MP 23	1.29		02	25	55
MP 22	2.29		03	22	68½
West Byfleet	2.61		03	38	72½
Byfleet & New Haw	3.89		04	40	75
Waterloo	24.29	33.00	26	20	

Table 42

HOOK TO BASINGSTOKE

Date	Monday 5th September 1966	
Train	541 pm Waterloo to Salisbury	
Loco	Battle of Britain class 4-6-2 No. 34057 *Biggin Hill*	
Load	11 coaches, 361 tons tare 365 tons gross	
Crew	Ted Dente and Pete Roberts, Nine Elms MPD	
Recorder	DB	

	miles	sched	mins	secs	speed	
Hook	0.00	0.00	00	00		2 mins late
MP 43	0.80		02	11	37½	
Newnham Siding	1.49		03	05	51	
MP 44	1.80		03	27	56	
MP 45	2.80		04	28	64	eased/SVO
MP 46	3.80		05	24	65	
			sigs stop			
MP 47¼	5.05		08	39	0*	
			13	29		
Basingstoke	5.59	10.00	16	05		

Table 43

12TH DECEMBER 1966 714pm SOUTHAMPTON TO WATERLOO
DETAIL FROM WORTING JUNCTION TO FARNBOROUGH

Date	12th December 1966
Train	530 pm Weymouth to Waterloo
Loco	MN Class 4-6-2 No. 35028 *'Clan Line'*
Load	9 coaches + 2 bogie vans, 348 tons tare, 375 tons gross
Driver	Gordon Porter
Fireman	R Lee
Timed by	Don Benn
Weather	dark, damp, light rain falling, light SW wind

	miles	sched	mins	secs	speed	
Worting Jct	28.98	39.30	38	05	62	
MP 49	30.25		39	11	76	
Basingstoke	31.50		40	07	83½	over ¾ mile
MP 47	32.25		40	39	86	
MP 46	33.25		41	20	93	
MP 45	34.25		41	59	92	
MP 44	35.25		42	38	95	
Newnham Siding	35.55		42	51	94	
MP 43	36.25		43	16	92	
Hook	37.08		43	48	93	
MP 41	38.25		44	34	95	
Winchfield	39.41		45	19	98	
MP 39	40.25		45	49	99	
MP 38	41.25		46	25	102/103	
MP 37	42.25		47	00	101	
Fleet	42.76		47	18	100	
MP 35	44.25		48	15	93	off
			brakes			sigs
Farnborough	46.05		49	40	74	
	average speeds:- Winchfield to Fleet=101.35 mph MP 41 to MP 35=97.74 mph MP 46 to MP 35=95.42 mph Basingstoke to Fleet full regulator 20-25% cut off 210 lbs of steam in steam chest					

Table 44

DETAIL OF START FROM BASINGSTOKE

Date	Thursday 29th December 1966
Train	638 pm Salisbury to Waterloo
Loco	Battle of Britain class 4-6-2 No. 34057 *Biggin Hill*
Load	4 coaches and 2 vans, 179 tons tare 185 tons gross
Crew	Jim Evans and Dave Davis, Nine Elms MPD
Recorder	DB

	miles	mins	secs	speed	
Basingstoke	0.00	00	00		
MP 47	0.79	01	43	40	
MP 46	1.79	02	52	63	35% cut off
MP 45	2.79	03	46	70½	
MP 44	3.79	04	35	77	
Newnham Siding	4.10	04	47	82½	
MP 43	4.79	05	20	83	20% cut off
Hook	5.59	05	52	86	

Table 45

Basingstoke to Winchester

Date	August 1966
Train	245 am Waterloo to Bournemouth
Loco	Rebuilt West Country class 4-6-2 No. 34008 *Padstow*
Load	Unknown, but likely to have been around 230 tons
Crew	Frank Matthews Nine Elms MPD
Recorder	Les Kent

	miles	sched	mins	secs	speed	
Basingstoke	0.00	0.00	00	00		
Worting Jct	2.51	7.00	05	33	49	
Wootton Box	4.75		08	34	56	
Roundwood Box	8.45		12	15	71	
Micheldever	10.30		13	44	88	
Weston Box	12.45		15	12	97/100	
Wallers Ash Box	13.95		16	43	51*/43*	tsr
Winchester Jct Box	16.70	23.30	20	01	48/51	
Winchester City	18.80	26.30	23	05		

Table 46

EVEN TIME RUNS ON THE 6.35/6.38 PM SALISBURY TO WATERLOO 1966
BASINGSTOKE TO WOKING 23.46 MILES

Date	Engine	Driver	Load	Time	Maximum	Average	Notes
		70A MPD			Speed	mph	
18.05.1966	34032 Camelford	Gale	11 for 285 tons	21 mins 38 secs	87	65.07	
14.06.1966	73171	Cummings	11 for 325 tons	23 mins 20 secs	74½	60.33	
16.06.1966	34009 Lyme Regis	Cummings	9 for 260 tons	19 mins 48 secs	93	71.09	19 mins net
07.07.1966	34093 Saunton	Matthews	11 for 315 tons	22 mins 53 secs	86	61.51	20 mins net
10.08.1966	73088	Ball	12 for 325 tons	22 mins 48 secs	79	61.74	22 mins net
15.08.1966	34047 Callington	Bennett	12 for 305 tons	23 mins 00 secs	73	61.2	
22.08.1966	73087	Porter	9 for 285 tons	21 mins 50 secs	83	64.47	
21.09.1966	34013 Okehampton	Payne	10 for 305 tons	23 mins 08 secs	90	60.85	20 mins net
29.12.1966	34057 Biggin Hill	Evans	6 for 185 tons	19 mins 14 secs	93	73.19	

CHAPTER SIX
1967

The year started with new engine diagrams and duty rosters bringing with them a further decline in steam operation. Chapter Two sets out the detail but 122 steam locomotives remained, including ten Merchant Navy pacifics, to cover just 53 diagrams on Mondays to Fridays. The number of steam hauled departures from Waterloo was now down to just twelve on Mondays to Fridays and less at weekends. My year started with a run down to Basingstoke on Monday 2nd January on the first electric worked 5.41 pm to Basingstoke, and I returned behind an overloaded BR Standard class 4 2-6-0 No. 76066 on 345 tons working the 6.38 pm Salisbury up, which J J

Smith of Nine Elms did his best with. The log of this run as far as Woking appears in my book is in Table 14 – *See page 63*. The choice of steam hauled trains after work was now much more limited to the 5.09 pm which I could not always catch and the 6.30 pm, except on Fridays and diesel failures. The detail is set out in Chapter Two, but inevitably I found myself on the 6.30 pm down with Bournemouth crews for many dreary runs, returning to Woking on the Mogul train. An example was on 4th January when driver Boston took no less than 83 minutes 14 seconds to Winchester, net about 77 minutes, with nothing higher than 64 mph down Roundwood and speed languishing in the 50s

Unconverted Battle of Britain class pacific No. 34057 *Biggin Hill* **at Nine Elms on 29th May 1967.** *Mike Hodges*

for many miles. This was with No. 34057 on 10 for 375 tons. The return on the 'Mogul Train' behind No. 76063 was much better, the highlight being a time of 6 minutes 58 seconds start to stop Basingstoke to Hook for the 5.59 miles, max 70½ mph. To catch the 'Club Train' meant being on the 1.30 pm also with Bournemouth men, or the 3.30 pm, but at least getting the 1.30 pm got me right through to Bournemouth and back with steam. An alternative was the 6.54 pm down with Salisbury men as far as Woking, returning on the 6.38 pm Salisbury. It was not all doom and gloom though as the last Weymouth fortunately reverted to steam at the beginning of March and the final three months in particular saw some quite astonishing loco performances including another six runs which gave 100 mph or more, one of which produced no less than three separate 'tons' !

Tuesday 17th January saw three good runs starting with No. 35023 on the 11.07 am Bournemouth to Waterloo which with 11 for 390 tons and driver Mick Dominey from Nine Elms in charge ran Basingstoke to Woking in 20 minutes 26 seconds with a maximum of 89 at Pirbright and slight adverse signals outside Woking. This was timed by Bob Thompson. My day started on the 1.30 pm with driver Cooper of Bournemouth having to cope with 14 bogies for 475 tons which No. 35003 struggled with in the heavy rain and with dragging brakes so I abandoned this at Brockenhurst 29 minutes late and returned to Southampton to pick up the 3.30 pm with No. 35007 with driver Lovell of Bournemouth who ran Southampton to Brockenhurst in 16 minutes 34 seconds, maximum 76 mph and under 20 minutes on to Bournemouth with 83 mph down the bank after Hinton Admiral, arriving over five minutes early. All this was a prelude to the much anticipated 5.30 pm from Weymouth 'Club' Train as that top Nine Elms team of Gordon Porter and Tom Moult were booked to take the train from Southampton. From Bournemouth we had driver Phillips of Weymouth with light pacific No. 34098 on 11 bogies for 365 tons and after leaving two minutes late ran well

enough to the changeover, from where we left five minutes late. The detail of this run and that of 19th January, with No. 34036, is shown in **67.01 and 67.02**. The net times of 72 minutes were amongst the best recorded with light pacifics for the 79.24 miles and they were similar in most respects with some very hard work up Roundwood resulting in 67½ and 71 mph before checks and wonderful dashes from Hook to Brookwood, averaging 84.46 and 85.88 mph respectively. On the first night the headlong flight continued fearlessly and unchecked down past Woking at 95 mph, possibly the highest speed with steam ever seen at that point, an unforgettable experience for all of us present. The average speed over the 26.49 miles from Winchfield to Hampton Court Junction was 87.01 mph. My notes state the engine was steaming well and that it was being worked generally with full regulator (of course!) and 15-20% cut off. On the 19th the start was faster and speed up the 1-in-252 was higher before checks and we were running faster along the racing stretch but there were hints of a little less steam being available before checks intervened to prevent another 90 mph plus sprint past Woking. These were two excellent runs to lift my spirits as was a very similar performance on the 18th January timed by Terry Jackson when Porter had No. 35013 on 385 tons, producing 71 mph up the bank and a sustained 90-91 mph from Fleet to Farnborough, averaging 87.06 mph from Hook to Brookwood before checks intervened. Net time was again 72 minutes though this time with a big pacific.

Terry also timed a good run with No. 35030 on the 10.30 am down on 25th January when with 11 for 395 tons Gordon Hooper got past Woking in 24 minutes 55 seconds and with a good start and nothing more than 78 in the Byfleet dip and then after being checked most of the way from Sturt Lane to Micheldever produced 96 mph after Shawford to lose just two minutes on the 93 minute booking to Southampton. Terry had a good day on Saturday 4th February when he caught the 8.35 am down behind No. 35023 on a light load of 290 tons. Fred Burridge was in

Basingstoke 8th May 1967. No. 35023 on the up Channel Islands Express. *Author*

good form running from Surbiton to Woking in just 13 minutes 3 seconds, with 81 in the Byfleet dip and later taking just 8 minutes 41 seconds for the 8.35 miles from Winchester to Southampton Airport, maximum speed 84 mph after Shawford. The continuation on to Bournemouth was equally good with 80s before and after the Brockenhurst stop. He returned on the 'Club Train' with No. 35030 being driven by Eastleigh's Roy Sloper and the detail of this fine run is shown in 67.03 . 72 mph up the bank and 97 mph after Winchfield plus a good spell of running in the 80s produced another 72 minutes net time up from Southampton. As far as I know the 97 mph was Roy Sloper's highest with steam and no doubt the speedometer needle was right on the 100 mph line. Just look at the gain of time over the schedule and with only the slightest of signal checks but with no less than four temporary speed restrictions for track work. This run is in the top drawer of the fastest net times up from Southampton.

Elder Dempster Lines was in fine fettle at that time, lasting right to the very end of steam as it worked the last up train into Waterloo on Sunday 9th July. I was not out that day but was on the following day, Sunday 5th February as Gordon Porter and Tom Moult were known to be on the up excursion. I went down to Winchester on the 1.30 pm behind *Clan Line*, from memory accompanied by my future wife and we apparently managed to happily while away the four and a half hours prior to catching the up train at 7.24 pm!. Gordon Porter had No. 34021 on 9 coaches for 325 tons and produced his usual high standard of running between checks, 66 mph at Roundwood after being put through the Wallers Ash loop and 90 after Winchfield, plus an even time run from Woking to Surbiton, maximum 83 mph.

Then followed a quiet spell until 16th February when I had a 73 minute net time up from Southampton behind No. 35013 on 360 tons with Dave Parsons and Bob Lee doing the honours. We left Southampton 23 minutes late on a cold wet night and after running well enough up the bank enjoyed a fine spell of fast running from Worting Junction to a signal check at Weybridge averaging 83.20 mph from Basingstoke to Byfleet, maximum 94 mph after Winchfield before the engine slipped violently and was eased to avoid any damage. Dave was working *Blue Funnel* in full regulator and 25% cut off but told me that the engine was rough riding and with poor acceleration above 80 mph. Nevertheless she was steaming well and was only fired once between Micheldever and Vauxhall, at Farnborough. I think Dave was disappointed that night as he wanted to join the '100 Club' and probably would have done with the right engine. With all the checks we were still 17 late at Waterloo. The month continued with runs on the 6.30 pm down, returning on the Mogul train with nothing out of the ordinary

though Standard class 4 4-6-0 No. 75074 ran Basingstoke to Hook in 6 minutes 26 seconds for the 5.59 miles on 22nd February working the 'Mogul Train', maximum 74 mph. Finally in February Terry Jackson timed a couple of good runs on the 28th, down on the 10.30 am again, this time with No. 35014 and Gordon Hooper doing his stuff producing a good solid performance, especially between Southampton and Bournemouth, minimum 59 mph after Lymington Junction from 66 mph through Brockenhurst and 88 mph down Hinton Admiral bank. He returned with Gordon Hooper driving No. 34044 on the 11.25 am Weymouth which ran well throughout with 400 tons. 60-65 up the bank was followed by a very fast spell, maximum 94 after Winchfield.

And so to March and from Monday 6th the last up Weymouth reverted to steam haulage which greatly enhanced the evening opportunities

BR Standard 4-6-0s Nos. 73065 and 75074 on a boat train from Waterloo to Southampton Docks seen soon after passing Southampton Central on 8th February 1967. *Bob Randall*

especially as the train was worked by Nine Elms men. It would produce some quite fantastic runs over those last few weeks, including the highest known speed with Southern steam, the highest speed at Roundwood with steam and the fastest time ever with steam from Basingstoke to Woking start to stop, resulting in the best actual and net start to stop average speed. I did not have to wait long for the first of these records as this was on Thursday 9th March when Bill Anderson and Les Greer had charge of No.34087 on just 195 tons on the last Weymouth. The log is shown in **67.04** . I had gone down on the 6.30 pm behind No. 34008 which with driver Lovell of Bournemouth was par for the course on this train, arriving at Southampton 16 late. The up train was on time but it was a wet night and 34087 slipped in the early stages and also at a crucial point at top of the climb. The fireman produced plenty of steam and so we topped Roundwood at 83 mph, a record for steam. Bill was using about two thirds regulator and 30% cut off using about 190 of the 230 lbs of steam available and with half a glass of water, so not really pushing the engine, which was clearly in top nick. There was a blow back in Litchfield tunnel which caused some problems on the footplate and Bill braked after the tunnel but carried on after that as usual. The net time Winchester to Basingstoke was just 18 minutes and 19½ on to Woking, with 92 mph after Winchfield and again at Brookwood. My notebook records nothing of note after that for a while although the 6.38 pm up Salisbury with No. 34037 had to be diverted via Virginia Water, Twickenham and Putney on 13th March due to a derailment at Hampton Court Junction. Just as well Bert Fordrey knew the route! On 25th March Terry Jackson had a very good run on the 11.25 am from Weymouth with No. 34089 on 325 tons. Mick Dominey and J Martin from Nine Elms produced some fast running up from Basingstoke, reaching 92 after Fleet and kept time despite many checks. On 29th David Foale had an even better run with the same engine on the 9.16 am from Weymouth with Reuben Hendicott and Ray McQuade

driving and Bill Stanley firing. After being checked up the bank *602 Squadron* averaged 91.42 mph from Hook to Brookwood with a maximum speed of 96 mph. The log is shown in **67.05** . I had no such luck with my days off as on 28th March for instance I went down on the 10.30 am behind No. 34104 with Ron Hamlin of Nine Elms and with 12 on for 440 tons we were badly checked and short of steam and so arrived in Bournemouth no less than 69 minutes late. The return run on the 1.25 pm Weymouth was better with No. 34090 also on 12 for 440 tons as we managed a minimum of 54 before New Milton, but struggled on Roundwood with speed in the 44-51 range though touched 80 mph after Winchfield. Waterloo was reached 18 late after two signal stops and a relaying check. This would be my last chance for a run on the 10.30 down with steam as the rosters changed on 3rd April bringing a further reduction in steam hauled trains as the route was now electrified through to Bournemouth. **Table 48** – *See page 202.* Of the thirty seven down trains booked for steam on weekdays, nineteen were west of Eastleigh and just ten out of Waterloo. There was now no booked steam departure from Waterloo between the 8.35 am to Weymouth and 5.09 pm to Basingstoke. Fortunately the new electric units were not yet available and there were still many diesel locomotive failures and so although there were for instance only three diagrams for Merchant Navy pacifics, there were enough spare to cover for diesel failures which continued apace. There were fewer steam hauled trains at weekends with just five out of Waterloo and eight into Waterloo on Saturdays and only the 11.30 am down on Sundays plus the 7.36 pm up from Bournemouth.

On 7th April David Foale timed a very good run on the 8.35 am down which was headed by No. 35012 and had 10 on for 330 tons. Dave Parsons was driving and the highlights were 85 mph at Newnham Siding before the Basingstoke stop and 94 mph at Winchester Junction. This engine, veteran of the record breaking up *Belle* run was withdrawn soon after

No. 35012 *United States Line* **at Southampton Central in 1967.** *Bob Randall*

this run but was stored out of use until the end of steam. On 9th April Terry Jackson was on the LCGB Hamphire Branch Lines Railtour which started with a nonstop booking to Salisbury in 89 minutes though checks ensured that the actual time was 96 minutes 38 seconds. No. 35023 had just 9 coaches for 325 tons but any thoughts of emulating the same engine's 100 mph feat of 15th October the previous year were dispelled by much more sedate running perhaps due to the presence of Inspector Tim Crowley on the footplate with driver Ernie Doust of Nine Elms. Nevertheless they ran from Worting Junction to Salisbury in 27 minutes 53 seconds, over two minutes inside the old ACE schedule. Speeds were 89 at Hurstbourne, and 87 at Andover, followed by a minimum of 66½ mph over Grateley and 93 after Porton, not bad so late in the day for steam. On 12th April the same engine deputised for a Brush Type 4 on the Poole to Newcastle train in both directions Poole and Reading though the running with only 8 coaches was not spectacular. However David Foale's commentary is interesting:

'No record outputs, but a run to Reading late in the day. The running was just what was needed from the point of view of BR, arriving at Reading on time after delays before Winchester, and timekeeping running on the way back as well (and with a Bournemouth driver). The through workings to Oxford had gone some time before this, with the trains altered to run into Reading General (instead of stopping at Reading West), and rostered for a Brush Type 4 to run round (I think a WR loco). I had seen the train on its way to Poole the previous afternoon with steam, which meant that the Poole to Newcastle the following morning was also likely to be steam, as it proved. The WR was supposedly steam free by then, so steam was probably banned officially at

Reading given the obsessive attitudes that prevailed at the time. Certainly 35023 disappeared immediately we arrived and was not seen again until the very last minute when it had to couple on the train !! '

Meanwhile I had been clocking up the miles and even time runs on the 6.38 pm Salisbury up, the best of which was on Tuesday 18th April when Reuben Hendicott and Ray McQuade had No. 34008 and ran Basingstoke to Woking in 22 minutes 12 seconds, maximum speed 83 with a load of 310 tons and arrived at Waterloo, unchecked, seven minutes early. The 19th April proved to be a very good day for steam as David Foale timed an above par run with unconverted No. 34023 *Blackmore Vale* on the 5.30 pm Weymouth 'Club Train'. With 380 tons, driver Allen ran Bournemouth to Southampton in two seconds over 30 minutes, the fastest time I can find with steam. 67.07 The minimum before New Milton was 62½ mph and the maximum overall only 74 mph. The time was all the more remarkable as there was a slight signal check to 50 mph before Brockenhurst. Even better on that day the 6.38 pm Salisbury up was hauled by No. 35003 *Royal Mail* and with George Enticknapp and John Gaffney on the footplate with a load of just 215 tons it produced the first of its total of six 100 mph speeds in 1967 after Winchfield, timed by Les Kent and shown in 67.06. I was out on both the 18th and 20th April and so missed the run on the 6.38pm. I made a bit of a habit of this as I also missed the triple 100 mph run on the 27th shown in 67.09. On that evening I had gone down on the 6.54 pm but got off at Woking and went home feeling unwell. I felt even sicker that evening when my brother came home with the news that driver Chapman had broken two records, one for the most 100 mph speeds on one train and the second for the fastest start to stop average speed with Southern steam, 76.64 mph for the time of 18 minutes 22 seconds from Basingstoke to Woking.This would keep the electric schedule to be introduced three months later. No. 35003 was beginning to get

a reputation despite the way you could identify it due to the clanking of connecting rods as it approached and its general run down condition. On 23rd April, a Sunday, it worked the 11.30 am down and produced a quite extraordinary performance between New Milton and Christchurch, 5.80 miles, ran in six minute dead. Even time was reached in exactly five minutes, at the time probably a record for British steam, but eclipsed later; see the run with No. 35007 on 11th May later in the chapter. Even with 215 tons, Dave Pawson calculated that the Indicated Horsepower (IHP) reached 2,870 at 67 mph. Maximum speed was an amazing 86½ mph and full detail is shown in the table. Table 49 – *See page 203*. The running earlier had also been very good, with 85 mph before Woking, 87 mph after Fleet and at Newnham Siding plus 95 mph down Roundwood bank.

Brother Bryan also timed a high speed effort with unconverted No. 34102 on the 6.38 pm Salisbury on 21st April as shown in 67.08. Average speed over the seven miles between mileposts 38 and 31 was 94.38 mph and 98 mph was reached twice, so near to that magic 'ton'. Clive Groome had obviously entered into the spirit of things and was trying to join the '100 Club'. *Lapford* did though join this exclusive club two months later. Back in the more normal world, I had a very good evening on 20th April as the 6.30 pm down was steam worked and Bill Sanson showed the other Bournemouth men how it should be done when he took No.34071 down to Winchester in 71 minutes 34 seconds, a gain of seven minutes on schedule with 11 for 395 tons. Maximum speed was 79 mph and net time was 66½ minutes. I returned on the last Weymouth, 6.15 pm up with Reuben Hendicott and Ray McQuade who with No.34025 on 305 tons ran Basingstoke to Woking in 20 minutes 13 seconds, maximum speed 90 mph and ran into Waterloo five minutes early. This despite Reuben telling me that the engine was in 'foul condition' and had 'no go in it' with steam pressure dropping back quickly. In fact there was 160 lb of steam at Winchfield and 130 lbs from there to Woking, just enough to keep the

No. 35003 *Royal Mail* at Winchester on 23rd April whilst working the 11.30 am Waterloo to Bournemouth, having touched 95 mph before the stop. This was the day of the extraordinary effort from New Milton to Christchurch. On the footplate are Reuben Hendicott and Ray McQuade and on the platform, amongst others are Bryan Benn and Les Kent. *Les Kent collection*

brakes off. This was no reflection on Ray who was known to be a very good fireman, as well as being an enthusiast, often being seen with a camera. *Whimple* did however last to the end of steam. As April turned into May, my notebook tells me that the up *Royal Wessex* and 11.57 am arrivals had reverted to steam haulage due to failures of the new REP electric units, keeping No. 35007 in particular very busy. The 4.35 pm and 6.30 pm down were also both regularly steam hauled again. The start of May 1967 was unseasonably cold with heavy snow showers noted on the 1st, though these did not prevent Robin Brown from Nine Elms giving me a good run on the 5.09 pm down with No. 34089 on 385 tons, reaching Woking in 27 minutes 48 seconds, net 27, maximum 76 mph in the Byfleet dip.

At this point, with just over two months to go it might be useful to reflect on my travels for

1967 to the beginning of May, bearing in mind that I had a full time day job and was spending a lot of time organising the purchase of a house which was being built in Ashford, Kent, in preparation for my forthcoming marriage. For 1967 to date I had enjoyed a total of 115 runs behind steam locomotives, the distribution being: 27 with Merchant Navy pacifics, 6 with unconverted light pacifics, 56 with rebuilt light pacifics, 12 with Standard class 5s, 5 with Standard class 4 4-6-0s, 7 with Standard class 4 2-6-0s, and 2 with Standard class 4 2-6-4 tanks. Total steam mileage was 4,910 which was not in the same league as the hardened bashers but not inconsiderable. I had also timed eight even time runs, all between Basingstoke and Woking, three of which were with No. 34008 *Padstow.* As to speed, well I timed runs at 90 mph or more on 10 separate occasions, five with Gordon Porter, two each with Bill Anderson and Reuben Hendicott and one with Dave Parsons. However things were now to step up a gear as the final weeks approached and even the lowly 'Mogul Train' began to enter the high speed stakes, especially in the month of May as we will see. But the evenings of quite normal running continued, such as on 2nd May when I opted to go down on the 6.00 pm Salisbury as far as Basingstoke behind D6526 on an 11 coach TC set, which kept time but was below par compared to what could be expected from a Salisbury man driving a Bulleid light pacific. From Basingstoke I caught the 7.06 pm to Winchester which had No. 76005 on 175 tons and driver Lovell of Bournemouth and did no more than 70 mph to keep time easily. Then super power in the form of No.35028 no less, instead of the booked light pacific on the 7.50 pm to Southampton with another Bournemouth driver, Kiddle who could do nothing in the face of continuous checks to arrive 19 late, but still in time for us to catch the last Weymouth behind No. 34008 and Bill Anderson who, with 265 tons reached 70 mph at Roundwood from the Winchester restart and 88 mph after Winchfield before checks. On 4th May I noted 34108 on the 5.09 pm down, 34057 deputising for a Brush Type 4 on the up *Belle*, 35003 on the 6.38 pm Salisbury up, 34087 on the 'Club Train', 34036 on a down Southampton Docks boat train and 34060 deputising for a diesel on the 10.35 pm down. I travelled behind 35023 on the 6.54 pm Basingstoke and returned behind 34098 on the last Weymouth with Bill Anderson driving. With 215 tons he produced yet another very fast climb to Roundwood, passed at 77 mph in 11 minutes 36 seconds from the Winchester start for the 10.35 miles. The running after that was nothing special but there followed on 22nd, 24th and 25th May a fine series of runs on the last Weymouth with drivers Jim Evans and Bert Fordrey. On each day there was a temporary speed restriction in force at milepost 63 but the speeds at Roundwood recovering from that were 73, 67½ and 71½ mph with No. 34001 twice and with No. 35023. Then followed sub 20 minute actual or net times to Woking with

Exeter twice exceeding 70 mph start to stop and the Merchant only failing to do so due to a signal check outside Woking. The running on to Waterloo was equally impressive. Did steam really have less than two months to live? **67.11**, **67.12 and 67.13** show the detail of this superb series of runs.

The last Weymouth did not have the monopoly of fast running of course as the was just as much if not more on the 6.38 pm from Salisbury. On 5th May Joe Jolliffe timed a 97 mph effort behind No. 34037 and on 7th June a 95 mph run with No. 34100. Both had net times of under 20 minutes which equates to 70 plus mph start to stop. These runs are shown in **67.10 and 67.16**. On Sunday 7th May driver Peyton had No. 34024 instead of a Brush Type 4 on the 8.55 am from Bournemouth. 65½ mph was reached before the Micheldever stop from the Winchester start and 55 at Litchfield tunnel from the restart. The load was 215 tons so no great effort was needed. No.34024 seemed to be in good condition at this time. David Foale was on this train and comments as follow:

'A totally unexpected smart little run on a Sunday morning. My logbook shows that there was a signal failure in the vicinity of Milepost 70, which caused an overrun by 3 coaches (I don't think the term SPAD had been invented then). Now the train would probably be cancelled immediately, the Driver suspended, and the passengers turned out at Shawford. Then it was sorted out quickly, and the 8 minute late departure from Winchester was nearly all made up by Basingstoke with a combination of good running and an easy schedule. I didn't record many runs which stopped at Micheldever, but as you see it was an excellent start uphill. So some Bournemouth drivers did know what was needed !!'

On 9th May Bob Thompson had a good run on the 5.09 pm down behind No. 34052 on 10 for 365 tons. Jim Evans was nominally in charge but I am not sure how much he actually drove

No. 34052 *Lord Dowding* before leaving Waterloo on 8th May 1967 with the 5.09 pm
Waterloo to Basingstoke. Les Kent on the platform. *Author*

after Woking as Les Kent had taken charge
the previous evening. Anyway with 81 mph at
Byfleet Junction and 66 before milepost 31 the
running was very good. Bob returned with Jim
Evans on the 6.38 Salisbury when No. 34037
produced another fine run, particularly up from
Woking with Hampton Court Junction passed
in only 10 minutes 14 seconds after 87 mph at
Hersham. The load was a respectable 315 tons.
On the 10th I timed a very good run on the up
Salisbury with the same crew of Jim Evans

and Graham Pack driving No. 73037 with an
unusually heavy load of 380 tons. 76 mph at
Hersham and 10 minutes 58 seconds to pass
Hampton Court Junction was good going with
this load. On 11th and 13th May the 6.51 pm
Bournemouth to Waterloo Mogul train had no
less than No. 35007 in charge and it produced
some electric accelerations with Ken Parker of
Basingstoke shed in charge from that station.
On the 11th the time for the 5.59 miles to the
Hook stop was 5 minutes 48 seconds with

bad breaking for the stop, maximum speed 89 mph and on the 13th the time was 6 minutes 3 seconds, maximum 80 mph. The start to stop average on the 11th was 57.83 mph and milepost 43, 4.75 miles from the start passed in 4 minutes 30 seconds, even time having been reached just before Newnham Siding in less than four minutes from the start, probably after exactly four miles which would have been passed in 3 minutes 58 seconds. This was probably a record for British steam, surpassing even the run with No. 35003 on 23rd April shown above. The table shows the detail that I recorded. Table 50 – *See page 204.* My notes make interesting reading as they suggest that with a normal finish the start to stop time would have been about 5 minutes 30s seconds but I think Ken Parker was concerned about lack of braking power with a vacuum braked train of

only 105 tons. (That issue has come back to haunt the current operation of main line steam!). Ken was working No. 35007 at full regulator and 40% cut off at the start but eased back to 20-25% after about a mile. 60 mph was reached in exactly one mile. No. 35007 also worked this train on 13th and John Clifford timed the train all the way from Bournemouth to Woking. The running from Basingstoke to Hook was more subdued with only 80 mph before the stop. The BR Standard class 5s did well on this train due to their superior starts compared to the pacifics. The table shows a summary of the best Basingstoke to Hook times that I could find in May and June 1967. Table 51 – *See page 204.*

On 24th May No. 34100 deputised for a failed Warship diesel on the 7.00 pm down but was just short of being right time at Basingstoke due to shortage of steam and No. 34089 worked

10th May 1967. BR Standard Class 5 No. 73037 arriving at Woking with the 6.38 pm from Salisbury to Waterloo. *Author*

the 5.09 pm down on 23rd and 24th May. Due to unavailable diesels (Cromptons) the 6.09 pm down was worked by 34024 on the 23rd and 34036 on the 24th May and on 25th the 10.35 pm down Mail was steam worked again. I had a day off on Tuesday 30th May and went down on the 8.35 am behind No. 35030 on 10 coaches and a van for 395 tons gross. Driver Alfie Sutton did OK in the rain and inevitable checks including from No. 34060 on the 8.24 am Waterloo to Southampton Docks which had failed in front of us at Waltham and caused us 43 minutes delay, of which five minutes were pulled back by Bournemouth. So it was not only the diesels which were failing! I came back with Alfie Sutton on the 11.25 am Weymouth up which had No. 34087 on 12 for 435 tons. This was a good run throughout with the usual foul operating. We left Bournemouth just over 15 late and ran to Southampton in 31½ minutes net, with 53½ mph minimum before New Milton and 74 after Brockenhurst. Speed up Roundwood bank was in the 56-60 mph range and we were running at 78 to 83 mph after Basingstoke before a severe temporary speed restriction to 10 mph at Sturt Lane and then a series of signal checks from before Woking until Weybridge cost us an on time arrival at Waterloo, which however was under four minutes late. Actual time was 88 minutes 38 seconds and net about 75 minutes, good with this load and a light pacific. It rained heavily throughout this run.

On 30th May I noted steam locos as shown here:

35030 on the 8.35 am down and 5.30 pm
    Weymouth up

75068 light engine at Wimbledon at 8.50 am

35008 on the 8.10 Channel Islands down

34060 on the 8.24 am to Southampton Docks

34037 on the 8.43 am to Southampton Docks

34087 on the 11.25 am from Weymouth and
    6.54 pm down

34034 on an up freight at Pokesdown

34024 on an up Southampton Docks boat
    train

80134 at Eastleigh

34001 at Nine Elms, Loco Junction

35008 on the up Channel Islands Express

35007 up Bournemouth relief at Woking
    8.14 pm

73043 on the 6.38 pm up Salisbury

So into June and the final full month. Just 85 steam locos were left and from 12th June we were living on borrowed time as the new steam-free timetable should have applied, but we had a stay of execution as insufficient stock was ready. So a final set of diagrams was issued which gave steam a continued life and even on Sundays there were seven diagrams involving some work though the only booked passenger turns were for an Eastleigh Standard class 4 4-6-0 on the 11.25 pm Portsmouth and Southsea to Eastleigh and a Bournemouth light pacific on the 7.36 pm Bournemouth to Waterloo due at 10.10 pm plus another light pacific on the 10.35 pm (Saturdays) Waterloo to Weymouth, from Eastleigh at 12.54 am and 10.13 pm Weymouth to Bournemouth.

On 2nd June No. 35003 worked the 5.30 pm Weymouth to Waterloo 'Club Train' with Gordon Porter and Eddie Presland doing the honours. After a steady run up the bank with 395 tons Gordon had yet another go at 100 mph after Winchfield, but just failed as speed reached 98 mph. After the temporary speed restriction at Sturt Lane and a signal check before Woking speed was up to 92 mph again before Hersham but checks spoiled the rest of the run, as was so often the case. This run is shown in 67.14 and the net time was a very good 74 minutes. The next day the very busy *Aberdeen Commonwealth* worked a special from Waterloo to Bournemouth, the *Dorset Ltd* and on Sunday 4th June there was an interloper in the form of Gresley A4 pacific No. 4498 which worked a special from Waterloo to Weymouth, which I photographed at Waterloo and Wimbledon. On 6th June Ted Dente and Ray McQuade produced a good effort with No. 34023 on the 6.38 pm from Salisbury, the run up from Woking being quite exceptional with a reasonable 290 ton

A4 pacific No.4498 *Sir Nigel Gresley* **at Waterloo on 4th June 1967 after arriving with a special train.** *Author*

load for this train, as shown in ▮67.15▮. Even time Woking to Waterloo was very unusual and the time to pass Hampton Court Junction one of the fastest recorded. The next day the same engine worked the 'Club Train' and with Peter Giles driving and Tom Moult firing produced a fine overall effort. On 11 for 385 tons speed up the bank from Eastleigh was in the 55-64 mph range in between checks and in the eighties where possible after Basingstoke. An actual time of just over 85 minutes was noted, giving a

12 minute early arrival at Waterloo at 8.39 pm, which would have been a minute early on the old two hour train timetable. No. 34023 was in good condition at that time. David Foale had a particular fondness for No.34023 *Blackmore Vale* which was destined for preservation and kept a record of its movements in the week leading to its withdrawal on 25th June. This is in Appendix I.

On the same day Joe Jolliffe timed No. 34100 at 95 mph on the 6.38 pm from Salisbury with

10th May 1967. No. 34013 *Okehampton* at Woking on the 6.54 pm Waterloo to Salisbury. *Author*

driver Taylor as shown in 67.16. That evening I had gone down with driver Taylor on the 5.09 pm (that train and the 6.38 pm Salisbury up now being worked by Guildford and not Nine Elms men) and as he produced nothing of note with No.34013, I carried on down to Southampton behind No. 34093 on the 7.06 pm from Basingstoke and 76066 on the 7.50 pm from Winchester in order to return behind No. 34037 with Dickie Budd on the last Weymouth, which was quite ordinary. Wrong choice again! Never mind you could not win them all and second guessing what a fairly unknown driver might do was not easy. At least I made the right choices on

Monday 12th June as, having chosen to ride in a REP+ TC formation to Basingstoke on the 5.30 pm down, I returned on the 6.38 pm Salisbury behind 76026 on 245 tons which even John Gaffney couldn't do anything with so I bailed out at Woking and returned to Basingstoke in a Western Region DMU for the last Weymouth. This had No. 35023 on 230 tons and the Nine Elms pair of drivers Albert Wright and Fred Burridge turned in a good performance, running to Woking in 21 minutes 40 seconds including the temporary slack to 45 mph at Sturt Lane, maximum 90 mph after Fleet and then ran the 17.10 miles to a special stop at Wimbledon in

16 minutes 21 seconds, maximum 85 mph at Walton-on-Thames. Arrival at Waterloo was nearly seven minutes early at 10.49 pm. The crew shared the driving and firing.

Monday 12th June was the first day of the final timetable for steam and I kept a record of every steam locomotive that I saw from then to the end of steam, and with help from others built up what I believe to be the most comprehensive record of which diagram was worked by which engine over that period. This is shown in Appendices A, B and C. Of course other non diagrammed workings such as cover for diesel failures and boat trains to Southampton Docks were also steam worked from time to time. Wednesday 14th June proved to be a good day to be out timing steam and it started early for David Foale who was on the 6.30 am Fareham to Eastleigh, hauled by Standard tank No. 80039 which with just 2 coaches for 70 tons went like a rocket, the incentive being a 10 minute late start. 44 mph was reached at the top of the 1-in-100 out of Fareham and 72 before the Botley stop reached over two minutes inside schedule. The tank then just failed to reach 80 mph before a signal check outside Eastleigh reached with an overall gain of over five minutes on the schedule. Later that day David was on the 6.38 pm from Salisbury behind unconverted No. 34102 and with 235 tons this managed just over 60 mph on Porton bank reaching Andover in under 20 minutes. Driver Porter of Basingstoke was the driver. At Basingstoke Nine Elms driver John (Boy) Gaffney and fireman Bob Lee took over and I joined the train having gone down on the 6.09 pm with VEP electric units. Then followed the only known 100 mph speed with an unconverted light pacific, fully supported by the milepost times. My notebook is littered with comments such as 'utterly thrashed to hell' and 'sounds like it might be priming' plus 'engine in terrible condition but steaming well'. Later after talking to 'Gaff' I wrote 'Engine priming badly at the start with the lever slipping. After MP 45 Gaff put the lever into 40% and the engine roared along throwing out fire and making a fantastic noise. Engine in terrible

mechanical condition'. The average speed between mileposts 39 and 35 was 97.33 mph and 98.18 mph from milepost 38 to 35. Speed variations followed the gradient profile almost exactly. This effort would have required about 1,100 EDBH or 2,400 IHP. Net time was under 19 minutes despite the relatively slow start. Stormy *Lapford* indeed. **67.17** Not content with that I returned to Basingstoke to pick up the last Weymouth behind No. 35023 which again ran well with Nine Elms man Peter Gyles at the regulator, but without being exceptional, giving another early arrival in Waterloo. The next day on 15th June BR Standard class 5 worked the same train and although Gaffney realised he would not get the 4-6-0 up to 100 mph he produced one of the best runs I had with one of these good all round engines as shown in **67.18**. Even with two checks the actual start to stop average from Basingstoke to Woking was over 65 mph and the net time 20 minutes. On the 16th the same engine produced 83½ mph down the bank from Grateley on the same train, with Porter of Basingstoke driving. Also on that day No. 34037 worked the 2.45 am down, 34036 was on the 8.35 am, 34013 on the 5.23 pm, 34021 on the 11.25 am from Weymouth and 35023 on the last Weymouth. On Saturday the 17th No. 34037 worked the 2.30 am down and 35007 deputised for a diesel on the 8.30 am. On Monday 19th David Foale timed a very good run behind No. 35007 on the 8.35 am with driver Clive Groome in charge. The best section was Basingstoke to Winchester which was run in just over 20 minutes, maximum 94 mph. That evening I came up on the last Weymouth when that ace Nine Elms pairing of Hendicott and McQuade produced another stunning climb of Roundwood, reaching 73 mph with No. 34093 on 210 tons after a tsr at Winchester Junction and yet another sub 20 minute net time from Basingstoke to Woking, maximum speed 95. On Wednesday 21st the same pairing did even better up Roundwood with 76 mph and net sub 20 minutes over the racing stretch. This is shown in **67.19**. Terry Jackson timed them again on the 23rd when with No. 34060 they

No.34034 *Honiton* at Nine Elms in 1967. On the footplate are Les Kent, Tony Leaver and Alan Heyes. *Les Kent collection*

were doing 77 mph after Micheldever before getting adverse signals and were past Hampton Court Junction from Woking in 9 minutes 24 seconds, the second fastest time with steam. In fact the time of 3 minutes 25 seconds to pass West Byfleet is the fastest I have been able to

discover, even beating by five seconds the run with 34077 on 10th December 1966 shown in 66.24 . This run is shown in 67.20 . There was admirable consistency of running with these three runs, which was to be repeated during the next week with different crews. Also that week No. 35028 was reported to have reached 91 mph at Fleet with driver Ted Dente on the 'Club Train' on the 19th, 34034 touched 95 mph at Fleet on the 6.38 pm up Salisbury with driver Bennett also on the 19th and No. 35007 reached 97 at Fleet on the 11.25 am from Weymouth with driver Peter Gyles on 20th. The 90 mph plus runs were now coming thick and fast, although I have not been able to obtain full details of all of them those for 1967 that have been reported or are referred to in this book and which are authenticated are shown in Appendix K. No less than 100 occasions when 90 mph or more was recorded in that last year of steam!

The next week beginning 26th June was the penultimate week of steam and it saw some quite remarkable performances, not for hauling power but for sheer speed. These exploits have been discounted in some quarters, even by a few of the more respected observers as being exaggerated or timed from misplaced mileposts but all I can say is that I can fully vouch for those which I timed, all having detailed support of pass to pass averages and most of which were timed by a number of other experienced enthusiasts. In most cases also the maximum speeds were agreed on exactly. Three of the best runs were on the last Weymouth, all with light loads and two of them produced speeds in excess of 100 mph. On Monday 26th June I went down with a REP and TC combination on the 5.30 pm to return as far as Woking behind No. 34060 on the up Channel Islands express. With 12 for 425 tons the Eastleigh crew did no more than keep time to Woking where I transferred to the down side to pick up the 6.54 pm down which had No. 35013 on 345 tons and ran well enough to keep time to Basingstoke. Here I caught Hants unit 1104 to Winchester in order to join the last Weymouth. This had a light load of only three coaches and two vans

Salisbury shed Saturday 1st July 1967. No. 34060 *25 Squadron* awaits it's next duty. *Mike Hodges*

for 180 tons and was headed by that wheezing, clanking run down Merchant No.35003 *Royal Mail.* In charge were Fred Burridge and Robert Symon. With such a light load we were not all that surprised at the 76 mph at Roundwood summit. It was from Basingstoke that the fireworks were experienced. Nobody had expected what followed as Burridge was known to be a 'limit' man and so the debate as to who should have the footplate ride was easily resolved and it was given to my younger brother, Bryan, one of the juniors of our group, to the regret of others with the benefit of hindsight. For that evening we were to record the highest known speed with Southern steam, 106 mph just after the foot of Winchfield bank,

and average 102.28 mph over the five miles between mileposts 39 and 35. Proceedings were interrupted by the long standing tsr after Sturt Lane, but 95 mph after Pirbright ensured an actual start to stop average of just under 75 mph from Basingstoke to Woking. I have calculated that the net time would have been 17 minutes 24 seconds or 80.9 mph, never before achieved on the Southern and not often done with trains today. On the Wednesday evening the running was similar with a maximum speed of 105 mph and exactly the same average speed between mileposts 39 and 35 and another 80 mph net average start to stop speed. These two runs are shown in **67.21 and 67.22**. Details of the times and engine working for the 26th June are shown

No 35003 *Royal Mail* at Basingstoke on 10th July 1965. *Author*

in the next chapter. On Tuesday 27th Burridge had No. 35028 *Clan Line* with a slightly heavier load of 220 tons and on a wet evening 'only' managed 95 mph before Fleet, though the engine was slipping at high speed and there was some concern amongst the group of people who were leading the bid to take the engine into preservation that 'their' engine should not be damaged. The time from Basingstoke to Woking was however only 19 minutes 24 seconds, or about 18 minutes net. David Foale rode this all the way from Bournemouth and his commentary is very interesting. The full log of this run is contained in my book *Southern Steam Twilight-Supplement* to complement this book.

'Attention has usually focussed on the failure to reach 100 after the previous evening with 35003. I have always considered the best part of the run to be from Bournemouth to Winchester. I am not sure that all those present at the time realised just how smart the running was, as Burridge was a good engineman who did it without appearing to push the

engine too hard, coupled with some good braking. I believe they had trouble with one injector after Winchester. It is also worth noting that we left Bournemouth 30 mins late, but were slightly ahead of time into Waterloo. Whilst the timings were not tight, an analysis of the run shows that the schedule from Bournemouth was 199 mins with 10 intermediate stops, split 164 mins running and 35 mins stopping time. The actual time was 166min 04 secs, which splits down into 139m 13s running and 26m 51s standing. The sections from Brockenhurst to Southampton and Winchester to Basingstoke must have about 15 mins of checks between them. With the other less severe checks at St Cross and Farnborough the net running time is probably of the order of 122 to 123 mins (with 10 stops !!). If a faster steam service to Bournemouth was wanted think what might have been done with a MN and say 8 coaches with one stop at Southampton. The Burridge run on Friday

Nine Elms driver Reuben Hendicott. *Les Kent collection*

30/06/67 with 34021 was a superior run from Winchester to Waterloo compared with 35028.'

Fred Burridge had a rest day on the 29th and driver Walker and fireman Pack had No.34001 that evening, putting up a good show with 245 tons and a seven minute early arrival at Waterloo. On Friday 30th Fred Burridge had No. 34021 and achieved no less than 80 mph at Roundwood with 205 tons and the 98 mph after Winchfield as shown in 67.25. This was in fact one of the best Basingstoke to Woking sprints and possibly the fastest actual and net by a light pacific. Meanwhile the Channel Islands boat train had been providing some entertainment as shown in 67.23 and 67.24. On 29th the Nine Elms pairing of Hendicott and McQuade gave a virtuoso performance on the down train with 34087 on 420 tons reaching 96 mph down the bank during the course of a 31 minute net run from Basingstoke to Southampton and on the

return run with Eastleigh driver Shepherd of Eastleigh ran Basingstoke to Woking in a net time of just over 20 minutes, maximum speed 92 mph at Bramshott. There were two end of steam specials on Sunday 2nd July, one with No. 35028 and the second with No. 35007 and 35008. Also on Sunday 2nd July David Foale timed a very fine run on the 7.36 pm up from Bournemouth which with driver Miles of Eastleigh on No. 34037 and 330 tons ran up from Winchester in a net time of 60 minutes, one of the fastest on record and included an even time run from Winchester to a signal stop at Vauxhall. Even the many delays couldn't prevent a 15 minute early arrival at Waterloo. This superb run is shown in 67.26 . David comments:

> 'This is possibly the fastest known with this engine. An excellent run with an Eastleigh driver I had not come across before. The schedule was so easy that we passed Clapham Jct 26 mins early !! He also proved to be very pleasant company the following day (Monday evening 3rd) when he gave me a footplate ride from Woking to Eastleigh on the 22.35 down Mails. This was on 34025, which had worked the *Belle* in both directions that day, and then the 22.35. I think it may have been the last steam on the *Belle* and the Mails.'

And so to the last week of steam. After two years of ever frantic efforts by the fraternity to capture the performances of their beloved engines it had come down to this with very few steam hauled trains left and just 72 locomotives still on the books. Table 9 – *See page 58.* I was content to be on some of the trains with known 'thrash' men and to say farewell to my favourite drivers rather than to rush about trying to maximise my steam haulage as others did and I also called it a day on the last Saturday even though this meant I would miss the last steam hauled train into Waterloo on the Sunday. On Monday 3rd July a number of the group were on the 'Club Train' which had No. 35007 on 370

Sunday 2nd July 1967. No. 35008 *Orient Line* near West Byfleet with the 3 pm special from Weymouth to Waterloo which ran from Basingstoke to Waterloo in 44 minutes for the 47.75 miles start to stop. *Mike Hodges*

tons with Bennett and Deadman in charge. They produced a net time of 72 minutes with nothing special up the bank but 95 mph after Fleet. This is shown in `67.27`. Arrival at Waterloo was no less than 16 minutes early. I really should have been on this as I would not get another chance to be on the 'Club Train' but on that day I went down on the 5.30 pm to Basingstoke with REPS and TCs and returned to Woking on the up Channel Islands boat train which had No. 34001 on 12 for 435. Wickens of Eastleigh did well with this big load and ran to Woking inside even time, despite the tsr at Sturt Lane and a signal check outside Woking, maximum speed 82 mph. I went back to Basingstoke on the 6.54 pm behind No. 35023 and then down to Winchester for the last Weymouth behind No. 73020 and driver Lloyd, Nine Elms top link. This kept time easily with no higher speed than 68. On the night of 3rd/4th July after arriving at Waterloo on the last Weymouth with No. 73020, I visited Nine Elms shed between 11.30 pm and 1.20 am to get some tape recordings of

the engine movements and to record details of the locomotives present as shown here.

34047, 41284, 34002, 34019, 34023, 34102 (for 2.30 am down) , 34024, 35007 (for exams) 35028 (for the 8.35 am down), 34100, 34089, 35008, 73065, 34001 (for 2.45 am down)

I walked back to Waterloo and joined the 2.45 am down which had No. 34001 *Exeter* on three coaches and five vans from Waterloo, 215 tons. I had chosen this train as Gordon Porter was in charge and aided by fireman Randall it was worth losing a night's sleep for. Gordon told me that he had been allocated No. 73020 but had swapped this for No. 34001 which was known to be in good condition and which had given me the good run the previous evening. He also said that he was out 'to get a few records Don', which he did. We were over nine minutes late away and then started with a signal check across to the down slow line and so took over four minutes to pass Vauxhall. It wasn't until Hampton Court Junction that we crossed to the fast line but then flew along reaching 88 mph in the Byfleet dip before getting checked to cross to the slow line again outside Woking, reached on time in a record net time of 23 minutes from Waterloo. Away again seven minutes late and with the load reduced to 180 tons we crossed to the fast line and with full regulator and 40% cut off proceeded to reach 83 mph at milepost 31, a record for steam and were inside even time by Farnborough. After 90 mph at Sturt Lane and an easing to 85 mph for the curve at Farnborough we then averaged exactly 90 mph from mileposts 35 to 43, a record for steam and after getting a signal check to the slow line ran into Basingstoke in 20 minutes 43 seconds from Woking another record for steam. Net time was under 20 minutes. With the load further reduced to 170 tons we had high hopes of another record time to Winchester aided by a 'ton' down the bank but the Basingstoke signalman had other

ideas as a freight train had been let out in front of us which we caught soon after leaving and again all the way from Waltham to before Weston. We passed it in the Wallers Ash loop as we accelerated rapidly from 62 at Weston to 80 mph past Wallers Ash box, to 90 just after the tunnel and no less than 98 mph past Winchester Junction. Some recorders claimed 100 mph at this point and I would not discount this although I didn't get anything less than 9.2 seconds for the best quarter mile. Oh for the benefits of modern GPS which would have settled the matter for certain. I was standing in the corridor when at Wallers Ash something broke the window near me and crashed to the floor at the end of the coach, narrowly missing a number of us. This was piece of metal about four square inches in size and was later identified as part of a mechanical lubricator. A narrow escape indeed. Details of this, my best run of the week and one

Early morning at Bournemouth after arrival of the 2.45 am from Waterloo on 4th July 1967. From left to right David Foale, Les Kent, Paul Howard, Andrew Clark and Alan Heyes. In the left background are driver Gordon Porter and fireman Randall from Nine Elms MPD who had brought the train down from Waterloo. The driver in the middle of the shot is thought to be Sid Fagg. *Les Kent collection*

John Tiley and Squire Huntley on the footplate of No.35007 *Aberdeen Commonwealth* at Nine Elms in July 1967. *Les Kent*

No. 35023 *Holland Afrika Line* on the turntable at Nine Elms in July 1967 with Les Kent on the footplate. *Les Kent collection*

No. 35023 again this time with Les Kent and Paul Howard on the footplate. Nine Elms July 1967. *Les Kent collection*

No.34057 *Biggin Hill* **at Nine Elms with Les Kent and John Braybook on the footplate.** *Les Kent collection*

of the best ever, though with a light load are shown in **67.28**. I continued to Southampton and then returned to Basingstoke in a Hants unit No. 1101 to catch the 7.14 am which would have got me to Waterloo at 8.22 am in time to catch the 8.35 am down behind No. 35028 but for some reason I caught the 9.00 am down west of England train back to Basingstoke behind Warship D822, followed by E6038 on the 9.30 am down to Southampton. I can only assume that the 7.14 am was late enough at Waterloo to have missed the 8.35 am. Or maybe it was rover rot!

During that week there were many visits

by the fraternity to Nine Elms shed and many photographs taken of some on the engines on shed. No such thing as Health and Safety in those days of course; we just took care of ourselves without the nanny State! At that time failures of Brush Type 4 diesels were still common and No. 34025 covered all or part of one diagram for a while being seen on the 9.24 am Bournemouth to Waterloo on Saturday 1st July, the 9.33 am Waterloo to Bournemouth and 7.59 pm return on Sunday 2nd, the 2.15 am Waterloo to Bournemouth, 6.22 am Bournemouth to Waterloo, 12.30 pm down *Belle* and 4.33 pm up *Belle* and 10.35 pm down mails on Monday 3rd July. Who needed the Type 4s anyway! On Tuesday 4th I knew that No. 34024 was also standing in for a Brush and was on the 11.07 am from Bournemouth to Waterloo which I caught from Southampton. We had seven and a van for 285 tons and Billy Hughes and Alan Newman made mincemeat of the schedule though with no exceptional running apart from at the end. After passing Clapham Junction seven minutes early there was an almighty roar from up front as Billy Hughes put *Tamar Valley* into 50% cut off and with full regulator stormed past Loco Junction and Nine Elms shed at 67½ mph, his final tribute to steam on an up train, though he had another turn to work down on the last Saturday. We were eight minutes early at Waterloo and the 11.25 am from Weymouth behind No. 34021 with Ted Dente at the regulator followed us in at 2.40 pm, 12 minutes early. The Nine Elms men were now clearly enjoying the swan song of steam. Copious notes now filled my notebook covering the next and therefore final few days of steam and in truth I was a bystander to most of it until the last Saturday morning. Many of the group visited Nine Elms MPD and could be seen on the footplates of steam locomotives, though I

did not join them. The next day, Wednesday 5th July I went down on the 6.54 pm behind No.34013, but only as far as Woking where I caught the 6.38 pm Salisbury back to Waterloo behind No. 35008 with Ainsley and Phil Bassett in charge. Unfortunately I had missed one of the 100 mph runs as De'Ath of Basingstoke had coaxed *Orient Line* up to 102 down Grateley bank before the Andover stop. This is shown in **67.29** Not only that but Ainsley had got close to another ton with 98 mph at Fleet! On that day No. 34024 worked the *Bournemouth Belle* in both directions standing in for a Brush Type 4. No. 76011 worked the 4.51 pm Basingstoke to Salisbury and reached 82 mph before the Andover stop but unfortunately I have not been able to unearth the full details of this run. The best I could do the next day was the 6.54 pm down right through to Basingstoke which had No. 34087. My notes tell me that there were many hundreds of enthusiasts on the train and at the lineside and that 'an old boy of about 90 years of age was helped onto the train at Waterloo for his last steam run'. At Fleet we were passed by No. 35007 travelling at 98 mph on the up 'Club' Train and fortunately a

Nine Elms MPD from the train passing Loco Junction in May 1967. *Peter Austin*

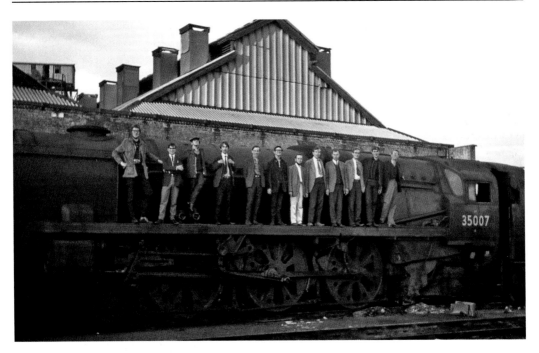

A motley gang on the running plate of No. 35007 at Nine Elms after it had been
withdrawn following its problem on the Club Train. 8th July 1967. *John Tiley*

number of the group were on it. **67.30** shows
the detail recorded by John Clifford. This run
marked the end for No. 35007 after a sparkling
last few weeks, the reason being that *Aberdeen
Commonweath* had blown a cylinder gland
whilst travelling at 98 mph just as it passed us
on the 6.54 pm down. It can be seen from the log
that there was a stop to examine at Brookwood
and John Tiley tells the story of this run and this
unfortunate episode:

'A number of us were on it. It was the Club
Train on 6th July 1967 with Fred Domm
and Fireman Deadman. Deadman stirred
up Fred suggesting they went for the ton
on their last trip. Given that it was Fred
none of us took much notice, I did not
tape record and settled in the 7th coach.
As we came through Swaythling we were
doing 56 and a rattling on the coach roof
gathered intensity as cinders rained down.
72 before Winchester and then a pw
before Wallers Ash to 46. Away again we
topped Roundwood at 70.5. Load 10 cars.

Then Fred went for it getting a max
of 98 below Fleet. However 35007 was
wounded blowing a left cylinder gland
at mp 39. We stopped at Brookwood for
assessment before continuing to Waterloo
in 84.17 from Soton. My notebook
records. '35007 arrived at Waterloo her
left big end red hot and left gland blown.
As a final challenge she blew off steam
and the roar echoed round Waterloo as a
faithful MN retired after a great career.'

Only a steam locomotive could have continued
almost as normal after such an event. I have
done a timeline of the last few weeks of No
35007's life and this is shown in Appendix J.

On the same evening my notebook tells me
that No. 73043 achieved 90 mph before Andover
on the 4.51 pm Basingstoke to Salisbury and
this is shown in **67.31**. I did nothing more
exciting than to catch Unit 1121 to Winchester
for the last Weymouth which had No. 34004 on
295 tons and returned me to London over eight
minutes late after some mediocre running. Not

a good day for me then. No. 34021 worked an 8.20 am boat train to Southampton Docks and No. 73092 worked one at 8.54 am. No. 34024 was covering for a Type 4 again. Would it really all be gone the next week? Somehow it did not seem possible, but it was. I didn't go out on Friday 7th July but Joe Jolliffe was on the 11.25 Weymouth and recorded the fine run shown in **67.32** The net time was as low as 71 minutes due to the very fast start to Winchester, probably a record for steam. This needed 40% cut off and it was wonderful to record an actual time of 76 minutes 34 seconds so close to the end of steam. A 16 minutes late start was converted into an arrival eight minutes early. At 2 pm the GM, David McKenna decreed that the last *Bournemouth Belle* must not be steam hauled. Such was the paranoid feelings at management level about getting rid of the old order.

And so to the last weekend. The known actual last workings for steam on Saturday 8th July are shown here.

SATURDAY 8TH JULY
2.30 am Waterloo to Portsmouth. 34037
2.45 am Waterloo to Bournemouth. 34095
4.40 am Waterloo to Woking. 76066
6.30 am Woking to Salisbury. 76066
7.18 am Waterloo to Salisbury. 82029
8.30 am Waterloo to Weymouth. 35023
10.43 am Southampton to Bournemouth. 77014
6.20 pm Waterloo to Southampton Docks. 34037
9.00 pm Bournemouth to Weymouth. 34095
11.26 am Portsmouth to Willesden. 34037
10.13 am Weymouth to Bournemouth. 34095
Southampton Central to Eastern Docks. 80152
12.12 pm Weymouth to Bournemouth. 73092
4.00 pm Weymouth Quay to Waterloo. 35023
9.20 pm Bournemouth to Eastleigh. 73092
Waterloo empty stock workings:
41298, 41319, 80015, 82019

I started the day by being at Waterloo in time to see the last Weymouth arrive behind No.34095,

The gang mingle freely and discuss the prospects for the last Saturday of steam after the arrival of No.34095 on the last Weymouth 7th July 1967. *Author*

Fireman Graham Pack at Waterloo on the footplate of No.34095 *Brentor* **after arrival of the last 6.15 pm from Weymouth on Friday 7th July 1967.** *Copyright John McIvor, SVS Films*

which was to be our engine for the 2.45 am down. The last 'Club Train' had been No. 34013, a fine engine, one of the 100 mph light pacifics and still going strong and the last 6.38 pm from Salisbury was 73029. No. 41319 and 82019 were on empty stock and the three coaches and six vans for our train were in the platform soon after midnight. By the time we left I counted 129 passengers, mostly enthusiasts, all hoping for a good run as Gordon Porter was driving. It was raining and we were not banked out of Waterloo so the start was very slow and nothing special was noted to Woking, except for a lively 75 after Raynes Park. From Woking though, still in the rain, we ran very well to Basingstoke, reaching 75 mph at milepost 31 and 90 mph after Fleet, where steam pressure was down to 130 lbs. Even so we ran from Woking inside even time and then gave me my fastest actual

time to Winchester of 18 minutes 13 seconds, with a nice spell in the 90s down the bank. **67.33** shows the detail of this run. We were eight minutes early at Winchester and during that time word came back that Gordon Porter had requested my presence up front and so for the last time on that damp and misty morning I rode on the footplate of an engine on the main line, and with my favourite driver as well. It could hardly have been any better. Details are shown in the next chapter. Quite a few of us got off at Southampton in order to return to Waterloo for No.35023 on the 8.30 am down which was booked fast to Winchester and on which I had arranged to meet my wife to be. But then disaster as the Hants unit taking us to Basingstoke expired at Winchester and we had to wait there for the next train, which we knew would not get us back to Waterloo in time to

Just after midnight on Saturday 8th July 1967, No. 82019 on the stock of the 2.45 am to Bournemouth. *Author*

On what was now a hot day, Billy Hughes and Alan Newman lean out of the cab of No. 35023 at Winchester after bringing the 8.30 am from Waterloo down from Woking at better than even time. *Les Kent*

catch the 8.30. Panic set in but we went to see the station supervisor and after explaining the problem, he promised to speak to train control to see if the 8.30 down could be stopped at Woking to collect us. I also asked him if an announcement could be made at Waterloo telling my fiancé what was happening so she should board the 8.30 and be at the front of the train. All this of course was in the days before mobile phones or internet. At Woking we went to the station office and much to our relief were assured that everything had been arranged.

8th July 1967. 35023 stands at the buffer stops at Weymouth after arrival with the 8.30 am from Waterloo. On the right are Bryan Benn, John Clifford and David Sprackland. *John Tiley*

Imagine trying to get something like that done today on our fragmented and inflexible railway.

On what was now a fine hot day, *Holland Afrika Line* rolled in on 11 coaches, very full for 405 tons and I duly found my girlfriend standing in the corridor of the front coach, not much amused by the situation! The engine was filthy and had the words 'The End' and 'The Last One' chalked on the smoke box but was obviously still in good nick. What a fine run down to Bournemouth that was though, fitting for the occasion. Billy Hughes and Alan Newman took No. 35023 along in fine style,

whistling at the many linesiders and storming along after an initial signal stop before Woking Junction. Speed was kept in the eighties along the racing stretch and reached 95 mph down the bank, enough to produce a final even time run. The start to stop average from the signal stop was 65.48 mph and we had averaged 76.48 mph over the 31.09 miles from Farnborough to Winchester Junction including slowing for the Basingstoke restriction. The running on to Southampton and Bournemouth was equally good and in fact the time of one second under 30 minutes to Bournemouth was one of the fastest

Bournemouth Saturday 8th July 1967. Some of the gang plus my fiancé in an engineman's cap waiting for a local train to Southampton in order to join the up Channel Islands Express. *Author*

recorded and my best. It was good enough to get us in over seven minutes early. What a splendid final down run to end with. **67.34** Many of the group carried on to Weymouth behind *Holland Afrika Line* but we spent the day on the beach before returning to the station to board a local train to Southampton in order to catch the up Channel Islands Express on which No. 35023 was returning to London. Noted on shed at Bournemouth at 3 pm were 73020, 73018, 80134, 76026, 34093 and 34095. As we waited on the up platform at Southampton there was time to reflect on the many other occasions that we had waited there to board an up train and to time yet another superlative performance with steam. On time No 35023 rolled in with 12 for 425 tons to give us our last run with steam. The Eastleigh driver, Pearce gave a good steady

display of pacific power without any fireworks but just solid timekeeping to get us back to Waterloo over three minutes early. **67.35** Thus ended the story which had started for me seven summers before on a semi-fast train from Waterloo, as I did not go out the next and final day when No. 35030 worked the 2.07 pm Weymouth to Waterloo, the last steam arrival. The thirty months since the start of 1965 when the writing was on the wall for steam had been a fantastic journey for myself and all those who timed the most incredible set of performances ever to have been achieved anywhere on the British rail system. The final chapter sets out the perspective from a Nine Elms fireman who is around today and stays in touch with many of us, together with some runs timed from the footplate.

Southampton on 8th July 1967. No. 35023 arrives with the 4 pm from Weymouth Quay to Waterloo. *Author*

The very last one. Some of the gang including Les Kent stand next to No. 35030 before it worked the 2.07 pm to Waterloo on Sunday 9th July 1967. *Les Kent collection*

Table

Table 48

DOWN STEAM HAULED TRAINS ON WEEKDAYS FROM 3RD APRIL 1967	
1.57 am Eastleigh to Portsmouth Harbour	BR Standard class 4 2-6-4 tank
2.30 am Waterloo to Portsmouth Harbour	Bulleid light pacific
2.45 am Waterloo to Bournemouth	Bulleid light pacific
3.40 am Waterloo to Basingstoke (from Woking)	BR Standard class 5
4.40 am Waterloo to Woking	BR Standard class 5
7.08 am Bournemouth to Weymouth	BR Standard class 4 2-6-4 tank
5.30 am Waterloo to Weymouth (from Bournemouth)	BR Standard class 4 2-6-4 tank
6.30 am Woking to Salisbury	BR Standard class 5
7.56 am Brockenhurst to Bournemouth	BR Standard class 4 2-6-4 tank
8.29 am Eastleigh to Bournemouth	BR Standard class 4 2-6-0
7.18 am Waterloo to Salisbury	BR Standard class 4 4-6-0
8.10 am Waterloo to Weymouth Quay	Bulleid light pacific
8.16 am Clapham Junction to Kensington Olympia	BR Standard class 4 2-6-4 tank
8.30 am Waterloo to Weymouth (from Bournemouth)	BR Standard class 4 2-6-0
8.35 am Waterloo to Weymouth	Merchant Navy
8.46 am Clapham Junction to Kensington Olympia	BR Standard class 4 2-6-4 tank
10.43 am Southampton to Bournemouth	BR Standard class 4 2-6-0
1.08 pm Bournemouth to Weymouth	BR Standard class 4 2-6-0
3.01 pm Bournemouth to Weymouth	Bulleid light pacific
2.02 pm Eastleigh to Bournemouth	BR Standard class 4 2-6-4 tank
4.03 pm Brockenhurst to Christchurch	Bulleid light pacific
5.02 pm Bournemouth to Dorchester	BR Standard class 4 2-6-4 tank
4.20 pm Southampton to Bournemouth	BR Standard class 4 4-6-0
4.22 pm Eastleigh to Bournemouth	BR Standard class 4 2-6-4 tank
5.16 pm Southampton to Bournemouth	BR Standard class 4 2-6-4 tank
5.20 pm Eastleigh to Fratton	BR Standard class 4 2-6-4 tank
4.51 pm Basingstoke to Salisbury	BR Standard class 4 2-6-0
6.30 pm Southampton to Bournemouth	BR Standard class 4 2-6-4 tank
5.09 pm Waterloo to Basingstoke	Bulleid light pacific
5.23 pm Waterloo to Bournemouth (FO)	Bulleid light pacific
7.06 pm Basingstoke to Southampton	Merchant Navy
7.11 pm Basingstoke to Salisbury	Bulleid light pacific
6.22 pm Waterloo to Bournemouth (FO)	Bulleid light pacific
6.30 pm Waterloo to Weymouth (from Bournemouth)	Merchant Navy
6.54 pm Waterloo to Basingstoke	Merchant Navy
7.50 pm Eastleigh to Bournemouth	Bulleid light pacific
10.35 pm Waterloo to Weymouth (from Eastleigh)	Bulleid light pacific

Table 49

EXTRACT OF RUN WITH NO. 35003 ROYAL MAIL

Date	23rd April 1967.
	11.30 Waterloo - Bournemouth
MN	class pacific 35003, "Royal Mail". Load 6 200/215 tons.
Driver:	Reuben Hendicott and fireman Ray McQuade, Nine Elms MPD
Recorder:	Bryan Benn.

Dist. miles	Location	Sched	Min	Sec	Speed Mph	Av speed calc Secs	IHP		
0.00	New Milton		0	0					Y
0.19	MP 98.75		0	48		48			Y
0.44	MP 99		1	15	33	75	1944		Y
0.69	MP 99.25		1	35		95	2307		
0.94	MP 99.5		1	52	54	112	2519		Y
1.19	MP 99.75		2	7	59	127	2651		
1.44	MP 100		2	21	63	141	2757		Y
1.69	MP 100.25		2	35	67	155	2870		Y
1.94	MP 100.5		2	47	72	167	2513		Y
2.19	MP 100.75		2	59	77	179	1974		Y
2.44	MP 101		3	10	80	190	2005		
2.49	Hinton Admiral		3	12	82	192	2017		Y
2.69	MP 101.25		3	21	82	201	2023		
2.94	MP 101.5		3	31	84	211	2038		
3.19	MP 101.75		3	42	86	222	2050		
3.44	MP 102		3	52	86½	232			Y
3.69	MP 102.25		4	2	85	242			
3.94	MP 102.5		4	13	84	253			
4.19	MP 102.75		4	24	84	264			
4.44	MP 103		4	35	83	275			Y
4.69	MP 103.25		4	46	82	286			
4.94	MP 103.5		4	57	83	297			Y
5.00			4	59.7		300	Estimated even time point, i.e 5 mins 00 secs		
5.19	MP 103.75		5	8	74	308			Y
5.44	MP 104		5	21	70	321			
5.69	MP 104.25		5	36	50	336			
5.80	Christchurch		6	0		360			Y

98.56 miles used as New Milton station distance
"Y" equals data from log book. Other data was in the back of my log book and was probably drawn from logs of others on the train and/or a detailed estimate from stop watch times etc.
Overall distance may be in excess of 5.8 miles as I think we overshot Christchurch station by maybe a coach or two.
Dave Pawson estimated the distance travelled as 5.90 miles
IHP calculations are by Dave Pawson. The figure of 2870 is very high for a 6 coach load
Average speed over the 4 miles from MP 100 to MP 104 was 80 mph. With a max of 86½ mph on a 5.8 mile section.
It looks like Reubens eased back when close to 80 mph. Shutting off at the bottom of the short stretch of 1/137 near MP 103.5

Table 50

BASINGSTOKE TO HOOK

Date	Thursday 11th May 1967				
Train	651 pm Bournemouth to Woking				
Loco	Rebuilt Merchant Navy class 4-6-2 No.35007 *Aberdeen Commonwealth*				
Load	3 coaches, 101 tons tare, 105 tons gross				
Driver	Ken Parker, Guildford MPD				
Recorder	DB				

	miles	sched	mins	secs	speed	
Basingstoke	0.00	0.00	00	00	slow line	1 minute late
MP 47	0.75		01	28	50½	
MP 46	1.75		02	22	73	
MP 45	2.75		03	07	84	
MP 44	3.75		03	49	87	
Newnham Siding	4.05		04	02	89	
MP 43	4.75		04	30	83*	
Hook	5.59	8.00	05	48		
	even time point 3 minutes 58 seconds					

Table 51

THE MOGUL TRAIN-6.51 PM BOURNEMOUTH TO WOKING
BASINGSTOKE TO HOOK 5.59 MILES

DATE	ENGINE	TIME	MAX SPEED	DRIVER
Monday 8th May	75076	6 mins 00 secs	80	Ken Parker
Wednesday 10th May	73030	5 mins 45 secs	82	Ken Parker
Thursday 11th May	35007	5 mins 48 secs	89	Ken Parker
Saturday 13th May	35007	6 mins 03 secs	80	Reeves
Monday 15th May	34098	5 mins 58 secs	82	Earl
Tuesday 16th May	80133	6 mins 02 secs	80	B L Ward
Wedesday 17th May	34098	5 mins 49 secs	86	W Ward
Friday 2nd June	73085	5 mins 47 secs	88	
Thursday 15th June	73043	5 mins 57 secs	79	

CHAPTER SEVEN
ON THE FOOTPLATE

None of the runs in the preceding chapters would have been possible without the hard work of the footplate crews, especially the firemen and so I start this chapter with a piece written by Dave (Dropgrate) Wilson who was a fireman at Nine Elms and who features in some of the runs described. Dave has also written books on railways and other subjects and stays in touch through my email group. After this insight of life on the footplate I will go on to describe some loco performance as seen from the perspective of footplate observers. So over to Dave:

'50 years on from the days of steam, it is very hard trying to peel off the rose tinted views of London, and Nine Elms Engine Shed in particular where I worked as a fireman initially in No 4 Link, then moving to No 3 Link, in the swinging 60s. However, in my case, the swinging was mostly of a shovel, filled with coal, being heaved into the firebox of some fire breathing behemoth, at the rate of one every 20 seconds or so, when we were 'flying along' in the final days of steam!

Before we get to 'flying along' there's a great deal more to be said and done. When I walked into 70A shed (Nine Elms), early in 1963, I was 16, had spent the best part of a year as a cleaner/passed cleaner at 55C Farnley Junction and my experience on the footplate amounted to a couple of dozen trips over the Pennines with goods trains, some local trip workings and station pilot duties – I had read a lot of O. S. Nock though! A pretty accurate description of the situation would be, 'green as grass' but, 'keen as mustard'. At 16 you were not only learning the practicalities of footplate work but, those of how to deal with one's fellow human beings. I was from 'up North' – this, naturally, became a source for wind-up – there was a lot

of that on the railway, at the blue collar level, anyway.

The first thing I noticed was the difference in ages between the drivers at 55C and those at 70A – at Farnley Junction drivers were 40+, passed firemen, 30 somethings. The situation at 70A was very different; young hand drivers were in their mid / late 20s, top link firemen all early 20s; and this was why I was there. If I was to have any chance at all of being a 'main line' fireman before the steam was gone, it was at a depot like Nine Elms – and so it turned out to be. To be perfectly honest, it turned out beyond my wildest expectations; and the period I spent in No.3 Link during 1964 and 65 really was the icing on the cake.

When you walked into 70A, there was a kind of bustling, dilapidation, everything had a layer of coal dust, odd lumps of coal and bent fire irons lying around, half the shed had a roof, half did not, a huge coaling plant dominated the scene; there were veritable mountains of clinker alongside the ash pit road. In a corner, near the Booking On / Shed Master's office, was the turntable, a short run off gave little room for error, inevitably the day came when it wasn't long enough and an engine ended up 'off-shed' in the green space around a block of flats – retrieval was quite a business. I did not see the 'incident' myself, but the legend grew with each retelling of the tale; embellishment of pitfall and pratfalls became part of the daily banter in every engine shed. Every shift began with booking / signing on, usually followed by visiting the mess room, how long you spent in there depended on what duty you were rostered to. In the mess room would be the 'spare' crew, they sat around playing cards, reading, passing the time until the crews they were there to cover had turned up, or not. Men on P&D, (preparing and disposal duties), would be in and out of the mess room, frequently, during their shift. Crews on 'running turns', whether they were on ECS (empty coaching stock) workings or the *Royal Wessex*, would come to the mess room for five minutes to make a brew before going off shed. Sometimes there would be crew from Feltham, Guildford, Eastleigh, or wherever having their 'bait' before working home. These were all male domains, 'Political Correctness' had not been invented in 1964; swearing, and tasteless jokes were common parlance – some chaps were as rough as the proverbial bear's posterior. However, there was a very definite 'gentleman' element too, especially with some of the old drivers, men whose own railway work had started in World War I. Like any large body of men there were time servers, the 'it's a job' types who turned up and did what had to be done to get by, but no more. In the enginemanship category, one school took the view you ran, as near as you could, to time, attempting to do so using as little coal and water as possible. Another was, 'this is all going to end very soon, within reasonable margins of safety let's see how much we can get out of these machines' – 'we're not paying for the coal'! As you might expect there were many shades in between.

All the firemen in No 3 Link at Nine Elms were under 20 and the drivers were just in their 30s. No.3 Link's work consisted of turns like the 8.35 am Waterloo – Weymouth which they worked to Bournemouth, the 4.40 am Waterloo – Salisbury, and perhaps, most notably of all, the 5.30 pm Waterloo – Weymouth turn, which was worked as far as Southampton. However, as well as these duties there were ECS workings, between Clapham carriage sidings and Waterloo, which could be fun – quite a few drivers would let the fireman drive on these turns.

Three Link also had its share of P&D turns and 'cover duties'. These latter duties could see you on a different turn, with a different mate every day, or you could draw a whole week on the same turn. The real problem at Nine Elms was an almost chronic shortage of staff, especially

firemen; rest day and overtime working were the norm. The shortages of firemen could, and on occasions did, lead to tensions, especially with the habit of 'borrowing' crew from other depots, which sometimes meant young lads, with almost no experience of the footplate, being asked to work passenger trains from Waterloo to points south and west – very unfair on them and the driver. Not all the young firemen were there because they 'wanted to be engine drivers', for some it was, 'just a job', and being there for as little time as you could get away with, and for as much money as you could grab, was all that mattered. If these lads had girlfriends, dropping shifts at weekends or looking to swap 'unsocial turns' like 4.40 am or 5.30 pm had its benefits for someone like myself – more than once I found myself working to Bournemouth and back, because bed and the girlfriend were much more important than turning up for work on time, or at all!

The P&D shifts were damned hard work, preparing wasn't too bad, but the disposal part could be awful, resulting in burned flesh, skinned knuckles, eyes full of grit, and they were the good bits. There was often overtime on the P&D work, 12 hours was the norm. However, 12 hours did not mean 12 hours actually in the depot. Each set of duties had a 'booked' time – if you did it in less, then, that was your good fortune. In practice the P&D shift would last 6 or 7 hours and you would be paid for 12, it could be better paid than main line work and some would swap main line work for P&D to get home sooner and have more money. Once again, this was often to my benefit, I would regularly swap P&D work for a running turn. The benefits may not have been financial, but they did give me what I was there for – working out on the main line. It also meant I worked with a lot of the drivers from links 1,2, and 3, my regular driver was Eric 'Sooty' Saunders, but I fired for many of the other names which appear in this work, not least the two Gordons, Porter and Hooper, both of whom were a joy to work with, as was 'Sooty'.

I did some turn, or other, on every one of the

Merchant Navies, my first, whilst I was in 4 Link, was 35014 *Nederland Line*, not my favourite. I have however, some very enjoyable memories of 35001 *Channel Packet*, 35004 *Cunard White Star*, 35023 *Holland Afrika Line*, 35024 *East Asiatic Company* and 35029 *Ellerman Lines*. However, the real stand out engines, for me, were 35013 *Blue Funnel* and 35005 *Canadian Pacific*. From the 'light' Pacifics, 34001 *Exeter*, 34007 *Wadebridge*, and quite a few of the others too, have a place, if for no more than they were 'regulars', like Nos. 34008, 34010, 34087, 34089. The Standard Arthurs and their little sisters the BR4s were generally pretty good, though one or two of the 5s did have a reputation for being 'steam shy'. One of the oddities of footplate work was that although all the engines in a class were built to the same design, they all had their little idiosyncrasies. I mentioned earlier No.35004 *Cunard White Star* her little peculiarity, amongst all the Merchants, was that she would only steam really well if

fired in 'copy book' light and bright style – though when she was fired this way she did steam very well. If I explain my soft spot for 35004 it will also give you some idea of what happened, on the footplate, on a journey I had with this engine. We had worked down to Bournemouth overnight with the 2.45 am paper train and waiting on Bournemouth MPD for our return working was No.35004 *Cunard White Star*. We ran light engine to Bournemouth West to collect our train, then to Bournemouth Central, calling at Brockenhurst, Southampton, Winchester, and Waterloo. On this day we were to have a footplate visitor from Southampton to Waterloo – he was from Swindon works! Red rag and bull doesn't even come close.

When we rolled into Southampton the drill was to 'put the bag in', (take water), and pull coal down, the footplate had been given a good swill down with the slacker pipe to keep the dust from flying. The atmosphere in the cab was 'humid', the fire door on the first notch,

Disaster! No 35004 stands at Hook on 28th October 1965 whilst working the 7.24 am Bournemouth to Waterloo. It had broken and bucked coupling rods caused by slipping at high speed. This incident lead to its withdrawal. *Les Kent collection*

back damper open, the blower on, just a touch, the firebed around 6 to 9 inches thick, a little more in the back corners and under the door – we were ready for the guard to give us the tip. Pulling away from the platform I shut the doors and left them that way until we cleared the tunnel, then fired six or seven shovels full to the bright spots, trying to keep the fire level across the grate. The injector would go on and stay on, maybe it would be shut it off before we ran into Winchester, but once we set off from there on it would go on again. After putting the few rounds on there was little time to sit down, and by this time the man from Swindon was on my seat – well out of the way! The pattern of firing six, seven or eight shovels full at a time and then waiting for the exhaust to turn light grey again would take around two minutes, at the same time, you were watching the gauge glass, the pressure gauge, checking, occasionally, that the injector wasn't wasting water, possibly having a flick round with the sweeping brush to keep the footplate clear and the dust down. When you write it all down it just sounds like a piece of cake. Imagine standing in the vestibule, keeping your balance, not with a can of lager, but with a shovel, filled with about eight to ten bags of sugar, held in your hands, your posture is a stoop and you're standing at right angles to the tender shovelling plate and the fire door. Having swung the eight bags of sugar from the tender through the firehole you then need to land them onto a fairly precise area of the firebed, little less cakey now!

Having said all that, 'copy book' firing wasn't the 'common' method of firing on a Bulleid. The regular method was to 'box them up'. This meant slowly building a big fire, up to the level of the lip plate, under the door, above this level in the back corners, sloping gently towards the tube plate. Once you had built the fire up like this you then got the chance to sit down for a mile or two, enjoy the scenery and probably have a swig of tea from the can and a fag, if you were a smoker – many were in the 1960s. The levels of coal consumed differed little, only the method of delivery changed.

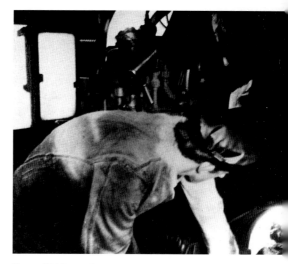

Dave Wilson firing No. 35025. *Dave Wilson collection*

When you were hammering along, on a big engine, like the Bulleid Pacifics, the footplate was quite a noisy environment, conversation was either close to shouting or you stood by the driver and talked at a more reasonable level. Some signals were visible first from the fireman's side of the footplate and you would watch for them, once you knew the road a little, or the driver would call you to look for them, if you didn't. The ride was not uncomfortable but it was 'hard', rail joints, especially those with a dip, junctions and crossovers were definitely 'felt'. The Standard 5s had a ringing sound from the motion at speed, injectors would sing too; when you put the whole lot together it added up to 'decibels'!

The footplate on the Bulleids was quite an enclosed space, in the shed on a hot day the temperature in the cab would be 80 / 90F, and then you opened the fire doors and got to work. Roughly a ton of coal would be needed to get a nice thick fire over the entire grate. The steam riser would have left a fire under the door which you could begin by spreading until it was 'thin' then add choice coals, slowly getting the whole lot burning before adding more. This was how my day began when working the 5.30 down. During the process of building up the fire, you would check the injectors worked, make sure you had a full complement of fire irons, coal pick, detonators, bucket and brush, the latter items being vital equipment and check the smoke box door was properly tightened; it was your own eyebrows that would go missing in any blow back! As if this wasn't enough there were lamps / discs to put on, taking on coal and water, brewing a can of tea and swilling the coal with the slacker pipe before running tender first to Waterloo. On the run up to Waterloo, from the shed, more coal was added to the fire, so that come start time, 5.30, a nice, thick, well burned through fire, and ¾ of a glass of water were all in place. Green ML, a whistle and a wave and game on. The next 40 odd minutes began with sitting down until we passed through Vauxhall then it would be get the injector on and do a spot of shovelling before the PWR through Clapham. The injector did not go off again until we ran into the platform at Basingstoke. Firing was not constant, because a good thick fire had been built up before we set off. However, the spells when not shovelling were 2 or 3 minutes tops – you certainly did not get long enough to smoke a whole cigarette. On a racing 5.30 down you spent 35 of the 43 to 45 minutes that the journey took shovelling – when you stopped at Basingstoke it was necessary to pull coal down, a task normally done at Southampton!

I hope I have managed to convey some of the flavour of what it was like for a teenage lad, 'train daft' to be let loose at the fag end of steam, and what the working environment in those final days was like for the people for whom it was more than 'just a day's work' My thanks go to Don for having given me this space to relive the highlights of my seven years on the footplate at the death knell of the steam driven railway. Finally, may I say that behind every one of the top runs in this book is a top fireman – no steam no show!'

You can only admire the skills of someone so young and the footplate runs described in this chapter need to be read and admired not just for the loco performance but the brilliance and hard work of those young firemen who made it all

possible. I had my first ride in 1964, courtesy of Roy Sloper of Eastleigh MPD who gave me two rides on the 'Club Train' from Southampton to Waterloo. One of these is described in my book *'Biography of British train travel'*, published by Pen and Sword. These runs gave me an insight to the world up front and prepared me for the noise, rough ride (in comparison to being in the train) and dirt to be expected on the footplate. My next series of runs was in a cold and snowy week in January 1966 when Dave Parsons, a friendly Nine Elms 4 link driver, worked the 5.30 pm down for most of a week. He had wanted me to ride from Waterloo but at that time of day there were still too many people in authority around and it would have been easy to spot a 'civvi' on the footplate even in the dark, so that did not happen and I had to be content with riding from Basingstoke. Throughout the week we had the standard 11 coach load of around 410 tons full and a different loco each evening, each with its own characteristics. I did not go out on the Monday but on Tuesday 11th January we had No. 34036 *Westward Ho!* And after leaving just over a minute late got checked at the start and again at Surbiton, the recovery from which prompted Dave to use full regulator and 40% cut off which produced 78 mph in the Byfleet dip before the engine was eased at Woking. This was during the period of slow line running between Farnborough and Hook so the time to the Basingstoke was over 60 minutes though we were slightly early on arrival. There I joined the crew up front and we were away just over three minutes late in the snow. It was soon clear that the engine was steaming well but was heavy on coal but quite clean, unlike some Bulleids. It was however very rough riding and this was probably why Dave eased her after regaining speed following the severe signal check at Micheldever, cause unknown. The 15-20 lb difference between boiler and steam chest pressure was maybe a little on the high side for a Bulleid. **RUN 1** – *See page 214.* On the Tuesday Dave had a rest day and the 5.30 pm down was worked by No.35017 with driver Jack Aplin, Nine Elms number three link in charge. On Wednesday 13th our loco was No. 34012 *Launceston* and after leaving over four minutes late we reached Basingstoke on time after 77 pm at Byfleet and the usual checks after Woking. This was not helped by a boat train in front at 5.23 pm. Once again I joined the crew at Basingstoke and soon realised that this was a very different engine to No.34036. She was very smooth riding and clean plus firing was light but had a tendency to be light footed and slipped a couple of times. No. 34012 was though a bit sluggish. She was also inclined to shake the fire about and towards the front of the firebox. The difference between boiler and steam chest pressure was only 10-15 lb and despite the light firing the engine blew off steam twice. We were just getting going off the long track relaying slack past Waltham when Dave spotted adverse signals through the other side of Wallers Ash tunnel and so the brakes came on. **RUN 2** – *See page 215.* My final run with Dave Parsons that week was on Friday 14th January and it proved to be the best with an engine in tip top condition No. 34026 *Yes Tor.* The prelude was just under 80 mph in the Byfeet dip which took us past Woking in 26 minutes 53 seconds despite a very slow Windsor lines start and 8 minutes 35 seconds to Clapham Junction. We topped milepost 31 at 65 but checks ensured that we took over an hour to the Basingstoke stop. Up front again and this time with my tape recorder I made sure that the rough and tumble of the footplate was recorded for my archives with the initial section to Wootton consigned to tape. No. 34026 was rough riding but free steaming and strong with little difference between boiler and steam chest pressure, truly a tribute to the design of Bulleid's boiler. **RUN 5** – *See page 218* We made the fastest start of the week to Worting and then took the long trs a little less slowly than on the two previous nights and recovered well to be doing just over 70 mph at Micheldever. I was hanging on grimly and praying for a clear road as Dave had kept the regulator 'in the roof' and so despite only 22% reducing to 20% cut off speed was up to 86 at Wallers Ash. As we

approached the tunnel the fireman made sure the blower was on and Dave eased *Yes Tor* and told me to stand behind him for we had a slight blow back through the closed firehole doors as we entered the tunnel. Out in the open and back to 22% cut off speed soon lifted to 90 mph and with clear signals and still on full regulator speed was allowed to reach 95 past Winchester Junction to give us a net time from Basingstoke of 19½ minutes, the fastest of the week. No words can adequately describe the thrill of this never to be forgotten total steam experience on a dark and snowy night. As we went past Winchester Junction the fireman came across the footplate to look at the speedometer which was just touching the 100 mph mark, probably something that he too would never forget. At Winchester after I had got down from the footplate a 'city gent' came up to the front of the train and asked what our speed had been and Reg Elliot, who had been timing from the train, told him with a straight face '85 mph guv'! We got 78 mph before the Eastleigh stop and then made the minus 12 minute connection onto the 'Club Train' back to London, which was driven by Pearce of Eastleigh MPD who was the driver who gave me my last ever run before the end of steam.

Next is **RUN 3** – *See page 216.* on the night of Friday 18th February 1966 on the 10.35 pm down Mails. This was my favourite of all my footplate runs as firstly the crew were Gordon Porter and Tom Moult, secondly it was out of Waterloo and last but not least it was on one of my favourite locos, No. 34037 *Clovelly.* The fact that the engine was in poor condition and struggling for steam only served to heighten another total steam experience though those on the train could not possibly have guessed at the struggle going on up front such was the train running that night. As *Clovelly* backed down onto the train at Waterloo the safety valves were lifting but it was clear once I was on board that all was not well. For a start the coal seemed to be comprised mainly of dust with a few large lumps scattered about and secondly, although less of worry the steam chest pressure gauge was not working. That would not be of much concern to our driver though since he normally drove with the regulator in one position, fully open! Prompt to time and in the rain Gordon Porter got the 12 vehicle 375 ton train on the move although not without a fair amount of slipping on the wet rails. Full regulator and cut off gradually reduced to 22% saw us up to 56 mph by Queens Road and a liberal interpretation of the 40 mph limit through Clapham Junction took us past my timing point on the platform in just 6 minutes 35 seconds from the start. The bad news was that the boiler pressure, nearly up to the red line at the start, had already fallen to 205 lbs though the engine was blowing off at 240 lbs rather than the rated 250. Our fireman was doing his best to keep the pressure up and in the process seemed to be in danger of using up the coal supply by Basingstoke. The brief spell with the regulator shut had lifted the pressure slightly to 215 lbs and so once clear of the curves the handle went up into the roof and cut off was advanced to 35%. I had to

hold on tight as we rocked past Wimbledon at 65 mph and were up to 75 mph just after New Malden before adverse signals intervened. 60 mph limit. What 60 mph limit? Before the check pressure had fallen to 190 lbs and only rose slightly while the regulator was shut so it was no surprise that once we had green signals again the use of full regulator and 35% dragged pressure back again and with the engine eased somewhat both enginemen busied themselves with the fire. It was just as well we were stopping at Woking as that gave time for more work on the fire. With the load increased to 400 tons we left Woking on the slow line in the rain with the safety valves lifting and with 40% cut off No.34037 produced superb pyrotechnics as we reached 50 mph on the 1-in-334 gradient before catching adverse signal from an Alton train stopping at Brookwood in front of us, which could be a problem on this train. Careful handling away from the check coped well albeit with another bout of slipping as full regulator was the order of the day again, apart for a

No 34037 passing Weybridge with an up Bournemouth express on 30th April 1966. *Author*

slight easing in deference to the curves through Farnborough. The 65 mph at milepost 31 was probably the best piece of work of the night and showed what could be done with a reasonable amount of steam in the boiler. But as a result of the reduction in pull on the fire caused by the easing through Farnborough the pressure needle resumed its downward path. This time however the regulator was left fully open and I watched fascinated to see what would happen as pressure fell steadily. Speed rose to 77½ after Fleet and was still 74 mph at Winchfield when with only 140 lbs of steam discretion seemed the better part of valour and the lever was wound back a little to 27%. After getting adverse signals at Basing village we limped over the crossovers and stopped on the down main at Basingstoke in just under 25 minutes from Woking, with pressure down to a desperate 120 lbs and the brakes dragging.

After just over 20 minutes standing, whilst the Post Office men did their job and Tom Moult his, we were away again four minutes late and with pressure up to 230 lbs. The climb to Wootton was nearly as good as that out of Woking with 57 mph reached on the 1-in-249 after just over three miles. The worst was now over since a long permanent way slack followed all the way to beyond Steventon. I was looking forward to a fast run down the bank and I was not to be disappointed. With the regulator in its normal position – hard against the upper stop block- and cut off progressively reduced from 35 to 22%, speed rose from 55 mph at Roundwood to 80 mph at Weston. Pressure was still around 200 lb so cut off was advanced to 27%% in an effort to coax *Clovelly* up to the 90 mph mark. The quarter mile before Wallers Ash tunnel was timed at 88 mph but immediately inside the tunnel the engine slipped and speed fell slightly as steam was shut off. I also got a singeing as the sudden cessation of pull caused a minor blow back. Out in the open again and the application of 35% cut off lifted speed to 90 mph past Winchester Junction, with a fine display of fireworks in the rain and the engine riding quite superbly. A steady run down to

Eastleigh saw me alight with my friendly crew into the quiet stillness of a cold wet night to await the up Mail back to Waterloo an hour later. I was in the train for the return run behind No. 34101 *Hartland* but brother Bryan was on the footplate from Basingstoke to Woking and his log is shown here **RUN 7** – *See page 219.* Bryan's comments on the run were:

At that time there was generally felt to be a 65 mph speed limit through Farnborough on the local line. Gordon respected that speed limit by taking his tea urn off the "shelf" above the fire box and holding on to it as we rocked and rolled through the station.
Taking my lead from Gordon I hung onto part of the driver's side door like grim death.
Tom just kept working on the fire!

On 8th May 1966 I had a ride on the 5.41 pm down between Fleet and Basingstoke on the footplate of No. 34032 *Camelford.* This run is described in Chapter Five. The crew were Dave Parsons and fireman Ray McQuade who returned to London on the 6.35 pm Salisbury up and Dave asked me if wanted to rIde with them as far as Woking, which of course I did. The engine was unconverted light pacific No. 34006 *Bude* and the load 255 tons. Once we were rolling Dave only had to use about 20% cut off to get the free running pacific up to 95 mph after Fleet before adverse signals intervened. I say about 20% as it was difficult to be certain on one of the original locos and when I asked about the setting Dave said the engine sounded right and he just left the lever where it was after the engine had settled down from the start. The net time of this excellent run was under 19 minutes for the 23.46 miles. **RUN 8** – *See page 220.* I had another short run with the same engine on the 5.41 pm down on 5th October 1966 when Les Cummings and Dave Davis were the footplate crew. This is shown as **RUN 6** – *See page 218.* In complete contrast to the two efforts with a Bulleid in good condition was the run on 24th October 1966 when Roy Sloper had rebuilt pacific No. 34034 *Honiton* on the heavy 13 vehicle 445 ton 3.50 pm Weymouth to Waterloo. Each time

Roy opened up the pacific the boiler pressure dropped so he was content to let the engine find its own speed and although time was being lost unchecked we would still have only taken 25 minutes from Basingstoke to Woking. **RUN 9** – *See page 221.* Footplate riding for me then ceased until the last Saturday morning of steam but brother Bryan was the lucky one who managed to be riding on No. 35003 *Royal Mail* the evening it produced the highest known speed with Southern steam, 26th June 1967. My log of this run is shown in **67.21** in the previous chapter and Bryan's log taken from the footplate is shown here **RUN 10** – *See page 222.* We had been offered a ride by Fred Burridge and as he was not known to be a high speed man, in fact had said before the run that he would stick to the 85 mph limit, we decided that the junior in our group could have the ride. How lucky he was! He wrote recently: 'There won't ever be a better run for me than that night on the footplate of No.35003. I can still remember so much of it very clearly, especially the fireman coming across the footplate and taking a long hard

look at the speedo as we reached the 106 mph max. Then he went back and sat down again; he didn't need to do much work. Such a shame No. 35003 wasn't one preserved for main lime use. She seemed to have something over the other Merchant Navies for sheer speed, and that was over the five years that I timed runs with her.' The ease with which *Royal Mail* exceeded 100 mph that night and again two nights later even if with light loads confirms Bryan's point. My final footplate ride, appropriately, was with Gordon Porter on the 2.45 am down on the last Saturday of steam, 8th July 1967. **RUN 4** – *See page 217.* The full run is shown in the previous chapter and while the train was sitting at Winchester word came back from up front that Gordon Porter had requested my presence on the footplate. And so I had that final ride in the cool damp dawn at the end of steam. Another virtuoso performance from a great steam driver. Gordon Porter and Fred Burridge died within a few weeks of each other in the autumn of 1999, but what memories they left behind.

On 14th September 1966 Dave Parsons is ready to leave Southampton Central on the 8.35 am Waterloo to Bournemouth with West Country class pacific No.34015 *Exmouth*. *Terry Jackson*

Footplate Logs

Date	11th January 1966
Train	530 pm Waterloo to Weymouth
Loco	Rebuilt West Country class 4-6-2 No. 34036 *Westward Ho!*
Load	11 coaches, 374 tons tare, 410 tons gross
Driver	Dave Parsons, Nine Elms
Fireman	Harrington, Nine Elms
Weather	Snow
Position	DB from the footplate

	miles	sched	mins	secs	speed	regulator	cut off %	boiler lb	steam chest lb	
Basingstoke	0.00	0.00	00	00		full	70	215	200	3¼ mins late
Worting Jct	2.51	5.30	05	54	44	¾	25	225	200	
Wootton	4.75		08	45	50	½	25	215	160	
Steventon	6.20		12	13	trs 16*	shut	25	230	0	
Waltham	7.35		15	40	trs 14*	¼	25	215	60	
Roundwood	8.45		17	37	53/61	¾	30	220	190	
Micheldever	10.31		21	20	sigs 11*	shut	25	240	0	
Weston	12.45		24	54	59	full	25	240	220	
Wallers Ash	13.95		26	20	70	½	15	210	170	
MP 63	15.20		27	22	74½	½	15	215	170	
Winchester Jct	16.70	21.30	28	32	78	¾	15	215	180	
Winchester City	18.80	25.00	30	52						9¼ mins late
			net time 21¼ minutes							

Run 2

Date					13th January 1966					
Train					530 pm Waterloo to Weymouth					
Loco					Rebuilt West Country Class 4-6-2 No. 34012 *Launceston*					
Load					11 coaches, 374 tons tare, 410 tons gross					
Driver					Dave Parsons, Nine Elms					
Fireman					Harrington, Nine Elms					
Weather					Snow					
Position					DB from the footplate					

	miles	sched	mins	secs	speed	regulator	cut off %	boiler lb	steam chest lb	
Basingstoke	0.00	0.00	00	00		¾	55	240	195	right time
Worting Jct	2.51	5.30	05	52	42	¾	35	230	180	
MP 51	3.20		06	53	47½	full	25	220	210	
Wootton	4.75		08	43	50	full	25	220	210	
Steventon	6.20		13	23	trs *27	shut	20	215	0	
Waltham	7.35		15	51	trs *19	¼	22	240	60	svo
Roundwood	8.45		17	52	47½	½	27	230	190	slipping
Micheldever	10.31		19	55	63	full	20	215	200	
Weston	12.45		21	49	72½	full	15	210	200	
Wallers Ash	13.95		23	01	78	full	15	210	200	
MP 63	15.20		24	02	81	½	15	240	150	svo
Winchester Jct	16.70	21.30	26	58	sigs *12	shut	15	235	0	
MP 65	17.20		27	50	50	½	35	215	90	
Winchester City	18.80	25.00	30	49						
								svo=Safety Valves open		
		net time 20½ minutes								

Run 3

Date				18th February 1966				
Train				1035 pm Waterloo to Weymouth				
Loco				Rebuilt West Country Class 4-6-2 No. 34037 *Clovelly*				
Load to Woking				3 coaches and 9 vans, 342 tons tare, 375 tons gross				
Load from Woking				3 coaches and 10 vans, 368 tons tare, 400 tons gross				
Driver				Gordon Porter				
Fireman				Tom Moult				
Weather				Rain				
Position				DB from the footplate				

	miles	sched	mins	secs	speed	regulator	cut off %	boiler lbs	
Waterloo	0.00	0.00	00	00		¼	70	230	right time
Vauxhall	1.29		03	24	36	full/shut	35	220	slipping
Queens Road	2.81		05	06	52½/56	full	22	205	
Clapham Junction	3.93	7.00	06	35	47*	shut	27	210	
MP 5	5.00		07	53	53	full	35	215	
Earlsfield	5.58		08	32	59	full	35	215	
Wimbledon	7.24		10	08	65½	¾	25	210	
Raynes Park	8.64		11	24	70	¾	30	215	
New Malden	9.78		12	19	73/75	¾	30	190	
Berrylands	10.98		13	18	74	¼	30	190	
Surbiton	12.04		14	43	sigs*25	shut	30	205	
Hampton Court Jct	13.34	18.30	16	22	56	full	35	200	
Esher	14.39		17	24	64	full	30	190	
Hersham	15.91		18	47	66	full	27	180	
Walton	17.08		19	48	67½	¾	27	160	
Oatlands Box	18.12		20	45	64	¾	27	150	
Weybridge	19.15		21	42	66	¾	27	145	
Byfleet	20.40		22	49	73	½	27	145	
West Byfleet	21.68		23	53	68	½	27	140	
Woking	24.29	31.00	27	14					to local line
	0.00	0.00	00	00		¼	70	240	2 mins late
Woking Jct	0.46		01	49	26½	½	30	240	svo/slipping
MP 27	2.71		05	20	50/sigs*47	full/shut	40	220	
Brookwood	3.70		06	34	50½	full	40	220	slipping
Pirbright Jct	5.40		08	18	61	full	35	230	
MP 31	6.71		09	39	65	full	35	220	
Sturt Lane Jct	7.86		10	45	68	½	20	205	
Farnborough	8.91		11	38	67	shut	20	210	
Fleet	12.19		14	23	75/77½	full	27	180	
MP 38	13.71		15	38	76	full	35	170	
Winchfield	15.54		17	06	74	full	35	160	
Hook	17.87		18	58	73/71	full	27	140	

	miles	sched	mins	secs	speed	regulator	cut off %	boiler lbs	
Newnham Siding	19.41		20	15	72/74	full	27	130	
MP 47	22.71		23	10	sigs *30	shut/½	27	125	to main line
Basingstoke	23.46	38.00	24	48				120	
	0.00	0.00	00	00		¼	70	230	3½ mins late
Worting Jct	2.51	5.30	04	50	54½	full	40	210	
MP 51	3.20		05	40	57	full	22	205	
Wootton	4.75		07	36	trs *18	shut	22	200	
Steventon	6.20		11	33	trs *23	¼	22	240	svo
Waltham	7.35		13	27	41	full	35	215	
Roundwood	8.45		15	00	55	full	30	210	
Micheldever	10.31		16	45	68	full	22	215	
Weston	12.45		18	27	80	full	22	200	
Wallers Ash	13.95		19	32	86/88	full	27	180	slipping
MP 63	15.20		20	24	86½	shut	27	175	
Winchester Jct	16.70	23.30	21	23	90	full	35	160	
Winchester City	18.80	26.30	23	34					
	svo=safety valves open								
net times:	Waterloo to Woking: 25¼ mins, Woking to Basingstoke: 23½ mins, Basingstoke to Winchester: 19 mins								

Run 4

Date	Saturday 8th July 1967
Train	245 am Waterloo to Bournemouth
Loco	Rebuilt West Country class 4-6-2 No. 34095 *Brentor*
Load	3 coaches and 4 vans, 178 tons tare 190 tons gross
Crewe	Driver Gordon Porter and fireman Randall, Nine Elms MPD
Weather	Damp and misty
Recorder	DB from footplate

	miles	sched	mins	secs	speed	regulator	cut off %	boiler lbs	steam chest
Winchester	0.00	0.00	00	00		¼	50	230	50
St Cross Box	1.23		02	14	59/60	full	40	200	190
			trs		46*	shut	22	210	0
Shawford Jct	2.47		03	30	44*	½	25	200	160
Shawford	3.12		04	21	60½	¾	25	200	180
MP 70	3.55		04	42	68	¾	25	205	190
MP 71	4.55		05	32	78	full	25	210	200
			sigs		35*	shut	25	230	0
Allbrook Box	6.06		07	26	40		25	215	140
Eastleigh	6.96	11.00	09	08					
net time 8 minutes									

Run 5

Date	14th January 1966
Train	530 pm Waterloo to Weymouth
Loco	Rebuilt West Country class 4-6-2 No. 34026 *Yes Tor*
Load	11 coaches, 374 tons tare, 410 tons gross
Driver	Dave Parsons, Nine Elms
Fireman	Harrington, Nine Elms
Weather	Snow
Position	DB from the footplate

	miles	sched	mins	secs	speed	regulator	cut off %	boiler lb	steam chest lb	
Basingstoke	0.00	0.00	00	00		¾	55	225	200	3 mins late
Worting Jct	2.51	5.30	05	07	46	full	20	220	215	
Wootton	4.75		07	54	54½	¾	27	215	200	
Steventon	6.20		11	37	trs 19*	shut	30	220	0	
Waltham	7.35		14	18	trs 23*	¼	30	220	80	
Roundwood	8.45		16	14	53	full	30	220	215	
Micheldever	10.31		18	10	70½	full	22	225	220	
Weston	12.45		19	55	81	full	20	220	210	
Wallers Ash	13.95		21	00	86	full	20/15	225	210	
MP 63	15.20		21	50	90	full	22	220	215	
Winchester Jct	16.70	21.30	22	48	95	full	22	210	200	
Winchester City	18.80	25.00	25	42						
	net time 19½ mins									

Run 6

Date	5th October 1966
Train	541 pm Waterloo to Salisbury
Loco	Unrebuilt West Country Class 4-6-2 No. 34006 *Bude*
Load	11 coaches, 350 tons tare, 380 tons gross
Driver	Les Cummings
Fireman	Dave Davis
Weather	sunny periods
Position	DB from the footplate

	miles	sched	mins	secs	speed	regulator	cut off %	boiler lb	steam chest lb
Fleet	0.00	0.00	00	00		¼	75	220	60
MP 37	0.52		01	43	25	full	60	220	190
MP 38	1.52		03	20	43½	¾	30	210	170
MP 39	2.52		04	38	49	¾	25	210	170
			trs		33*	shut	25	220	0
Winchfield	3.35	6.30	06	38					

Run 7

Date				Saturday 19th February 1966					
Train				1013 pm (Friday) Weymouth to Waterloo					
Loco				Rebuilt West Country class 4-6-2 No. 34101 *Hartland*					
Load				3 coaches and 7 vans, 302 tons tare, 325 tons gross					
Crew				Gordon Porter and Tom Moult, Nine Elms MPD					
Also on the footplate				Bryan Benn					
Recorder				Bryan Benn					

	miles	sched	mins	secs		speed	regulator	cut off %	boiler lbs	steam chest lbs
Basingstoke	0.00	0.00	00	00			½/F	60/35	220	180
Newnham Siding	4.10		04	55		78	F	30	200	160
Hook	5.59		06	01		83	F	25	200	160
Winchfield	7.92		07	40		88	F	25	160	120
Fleet	11.27		09	56		90	F	25	145	105
Bramshot Halt	12.20		10	31		88	F	25	140	100
Farnborough	14.55		12	13		82	S/F	25	140	100
Sturt Lane Junction	15.60		13	00		82	F	25	140	100
MP 31	16.75		13	53		79	F	25	140	100
Pirbright Junction	18.26		14	53		84	F	25	160	120
Brookwood	19.76		16	01		88	F	25	160	120
Woking Jct	23.00		20	05		32*	S/¼	25	190	80
Woking	23.46	36.00	21	14			S	60	210	0
	0.00	0.00	00	00			¼/F	60	225	80
West Byfleet	2.61		04	10		66½	F	20	205	180
Byfleet	3.89		05	17		69	½/S	20	200	150
Weybridge	5.14	11.00	07	00			S		220	0
	0.00	0.00	00	00			¼	60	220	80
Oatlands Box	1.03		03	17		41	¾	20	200	145
Walton	2.07		04	28		58	½	20	210	150
Hersham	3.24		05	35		61	½	20	210	150
Esher	4.76		07	01		64½	¼	20	200	100
Hampton Court Jct	5.81	9.00	08	37		30*	S/¾	20	220	130
Surbiton	7.11	12.00	11	02			S	20	220	0
	Slow line all the way									
	Basingstoke to Woking start to stop average: 63.31 mph									
net time	Basingstoke to Woking 21 minutes									

Run 8

Date			9th May 1966							
Train			635 pm Salisbury to Waterloo							
Engine			Unconverted West Country class 4-6-2 No.34006 *Bude*							
Load			5 coaches and 3 vans, 239 tons tare, 255 tons gross							
Crew			Dave Parsons and Ray McQuade , Nine Elms MPD							
Position			Footplate							
Recorder			Don Benn							
Weather			Damp							

	miles	sched	mins	secs	speed	regulator	cut off %	boiler	steam chest	
Basingstoke	0.00	0.00	00	00		¼	50	230	70	11 late
MP 46	1.75		03	27	28*/62	S/F	50/40	210	0/200	tsr
Newnham Siding	4.10		05	24	77½	F	30	215	205	
Hook	5.59		06	31	82	F	20	220	210	
MP 41	6.75		07	23	84½	F	20	215	205	
Winchfield	7.92		08	13	87	F	20	210	200	
MP 38	9.75		09	25	94	F	20	210	200	
Fleet	11.27		10	23	93	F	20	200	190	
MP 35	12.75		11	21	95	F	20	200	190	
Farnborough	14.55		13	25	23*	S	20	205	0	sigs
Sturt Lane	15.60		15	35	36*	¼	20	200	80	sigs
MP 31	16.75		17	19	48	¾	30	210	190	
Pirbright Jct	18.26		18	40	70	F	20	200	190	
Brookwood	19.76		20	05	81	F	25	195	180	
MP 27	20.75		20	47	87	F	25	180	170	
Woking Jct	23.00		23	06	23*	S	15	200	0	sigs stop
			sigs stop		0*			210	0	75 secs
Woking	23.46	28.00	27	58						
	net time 18¾ mins									

Run 9

Date	24th October 1966
Train	350 pm Weymouth to Waterloo
Engine	Rebuilt West Country Class 4-6-2 No. 34034 *Honiton*
Load	11 coaches and 2 vans, 412 tons tare, 445 tons gross
Driver	Roy Sloper, Eastleigh
Position	DB from the footplate

	miles	sched	mins	secs	speed	regulator	cut off %	boiler lb	steam chest lb	
Basingstoke	0.00	0.00	00	00		¼	45	210	80	12 late
MP 46	1.75		03	44	50	¾	30	210	180	local line
Newnham Siding	4.10		06	07	60	½	20	200	145	
Hook	5.59		08	27	trs *24	shut	35	225	0	
MP 41	6.75		10	26	42	¾	35	195	150	
Winchfield	7.92		12	03	51	full	22	170	160	
MP 38	9.75		13	49	63	½	22	160	100	
Fleet	11.27		15	17	62½	½	22	190	120	
MP 35	12.75		16	48	56½	shut	22	175	0	
Farnborough	14.55		18	35	61	¾	22	205	175	
Sturt Lane	15.60		19	34	62½	¾	22	190	160	
MP 31	16.75		20	44	62	½	30	180	140	
Pirbright Jct	18.26		22	06	67	½	30	170	90	
Brookwood	19.76		24	04	39*	shut	22	180	0	sigs
MP 27	20.75		-	-	45	¼	22	180	30	sigs
Woking Jct	23.00		28	39	23*	shut	50	200	0	sigs
Woking	23.46	28.00	29	56						13 late
	Net time 25 minutes									

Date	Monday 26th June 1967						
Train	615 pm Weymouth to Waterloo						
Loco	Rebuilt Merchant Navy class 4-6-2 No. 35003 *Royal Mail*						
Load	3 coaches and 2 vans, 164 tons tare 180 tons gross						
Crew	Fred Burridge and R Symon, Nine Elms MPD						
Also on Footplate	Bryan Benn						
Weather	Damp						
Recorder	Bryan Benn						

	miles	sched	mins	secs	speed	regulator	cut off %	boiler lbs
Basingstoke	0.00	0.00	00	00		2/3	50	240
MP 47	0.75		01	44	42½	2/3	30	240
MP 46	1.75		02	45	68	2/3	25	240
MP 45	2.75		03	34	79½	2/3	20	240
MP 44	3.75		04	19	82	2/3	20	240
Newnham Siding	4.05		04	33	84	2/3	20	220
MP 43	4.75		05	03	86	2/3	20	220
Hook	5.59		05	35	90	2/3	20	210
MP 41	6.75		06	23	94	2/3	20	210
Winchfield	7.92		07	07	98	2/3	20	240
MP 39	8.75		07	36	100	3/4	20	240
MP 38	9.75		08	11	103/106	3/4	20	240
MP 37	10.75		08	45	105	3/4-1/4	20	240
Fleet	11.27		09	02	100	3/4	20	240
MP 35	12.75		09	56	100	3/4	20	240
MP 34	13.75		10	32	97	3/4-shut	20	240
Farnborough	14.55		11	02	71½*	shut	20	240
Sturt Lane Jct	15.60		12	00	68* tsr	shut	20	240
MP 31	16.75		13	01	74½	3/4	20	240
Pirbright Jct	18.26		14	01	90/95	3/4	20	230
Brookwood	19.76		15	04	91	shut	20	240
Woking Jct	23.00		17	50	51* sigs	shut	20	220
Woking	23.46	26.00	18	48				

start to stop average: 74.87 mph

average speed MP 39 to MP 34: 102.28 mph

net time 17 minutes 24 seconds: 80.9 mph

ACKNOWLEDGEMENTS

Whilst my notes from the period covered by this book are very comprehensive, it would not have been possible for coverage to have been so complete without the input from many friends from those days, most of whom stay in touch via an email group. Those whose train running logs and/or photos appear in this book for which I am very grateful are Bob Randall, Richard (Joe) Jolliffe, John Clifford, John Tiley, David Sprackland (aka Andover), Bob Thompson, Peter Austin, Terry Jackson, Les Kent, Dave Wilson, Brian Smith, David Foale, Peter Trapp, Mike Hodges, Bryan (Wedgie) Benn and to anybody else I may have forgotten. In particular I must thank Terry Jackson and David Maidment for the hours they spent painstakingly going through the manuscript and train running logs, correcting and adding detail and Les Kent for supplying the actual Nine Elms duty boards and rosters, copies of which are shown in the Appendices and for his enlightening and at times amusing anecdotes. Dave Wilson's significant contribution about life as a young fireman in Chapter Seven is priceless. I hope they all find this book a fitting record of those exciting days at the end of Southern Steam.

Train Running Logs

Date	28th February 1965
Train	East Devon Railtour-9 am from Waterloo
Loco	Merchant Navy Class 4-6-2 No. 35022 *Holland America Line*
Load	10 Coaches, 339 tons tare, 365 tons gross
Crew	Spot' King and Dave Wilson, Nine Elms MPD
Inspector	Arthur Jupp
Recorder	DB

	miles	sched	mins	secs	speed	
Waterloo	0.00	0.00	00	00		1½ mins early
Vauxhall	1.29		03	58	32	
Queens Road	2.81		05	55	49	
Clapham Junction	3.93	7.00	07	38	43*	
Earlsfield	5.58		09	51	52	
Wimbledon	7.24		11	43	55½	
Raynes Park	8.64		13	05	62½	
New Malden	9.78		14	08	66	
Berrylands	10.98		15	11	68	
Surbiton	12.04		16	09	69	
Hampton Court Jct	13.34	17.00	17	17	71	
Esher	14.39		18	10	72	
Hersham	15.91		19	30	71	
Walton	17.08		20	27	70	
Oatlands Box	18.10		21	22	66	
Weybridge	19.15		22	15	69	
	20.40		23	23	73	
Byfleet & New Haw	21.68		24	27	72	
			sigs stop			
MP 23	23.00		27	22	0*	
			30	42		
Woking	24.29		34	45		
Woking Jct	24.75	27.00	35	27	38	
Brookwood	27.99		39	42	52	
Pirbright Jct	29.65		41	33	55	
MP 31	31.00		43	00	56½	
Sturt Lane Jct	32.20		44	15	62	
Farnborough	33.20		45	15	64½/70	

	miles	sched	mins	secs	speed	
Fleet	36.48		48	09	69/72	
Winchfield	39.83		51	00	70/69	
Hook	42.16		53	01	73/72	
Newnham Siding	43.70		55	11	75/77	
Basingstoke	47.75		58	38	34*	sigs
Worting Jct	50.30	50.00	61	36	54	
MP 51	51.00		62	35	56½	
Oakley	52.38		63	54	65½	
Overton	55.55		66	44	75	
Whitchurch	59.10		69	37	79	
Hurstbourne	61.14		71	05	82	
MP 62½	62.50		72	12	76	
Andover	66.35		74	53	90	
Red Post Jct	67.65		75	52	79½	
MP 68¾	68.75		76	44	82	
Grateley	72.70		80	05	59	
Allington Box	75.60		82	50	70	
Porton	78.29		84	56	82/86	
Tunnel Junction	82.56		88	35	39*	
Salisbury	83.66	78.00	90	55	*	
Wilton South	86.16	83.00	95	43	49	
Dinton	91.96		102	02	65½/62	
Tisbury	96.26		106	07	65	
Semley	101.26		111	01	54/30*	tsr
Gillingham	105.36		116	00	73/75	
MP 107½	107.61		117	59	63	
MP 109½	109.61		119	38	82	
Templecombe	112.16		121	33	72	
MP 113½	113.61		123	03	55½	
Milbourne Port	114.56		123	58	65	
Sherborne	118.05		126	49	90	
MP 121	121.11		sigs		39*	
Yeovil Junction	122.65	123.00	132	49		8 mins late
			net time 117½ mins			

65.02

Date	Saturday 13th March 1965
Train	835 am Waterloo to Weymouth
Loco	Battle of Britain clas 4-6-2 No. 34064 *Fighter Command*
Load	9 coaches and 2 vans, 368 tons tare, 395 tons gross
Driver	Gordon Hooper, Nine Elms MPD
Recorder	DB

	miles	sched	mins	secs	speed	
Waterloo	0.00	0.00	00	00		right time
Vauxhall	1.29		04	24	25*	sigs
Queens Road	2.81		06	40	32*/49	tsr
Clapham Junction	3.93	7.00	08	26	36*	
Earlsfield	5.58		11	00	49	
Wimbledon	7.24		12	56	54	
Raynes Park	8.64		14	21	61	
New Malden	9.78		15	27	66	
Berrylands	10.98		16	29	68½	
Surbiton	12.04	17.30	18	01		
	0.00	0.00	00	00		right time
Hampton Court Jct	1.30	3.00	03	23	42	
Esher	2.35		04	44	54½	
Hersham	3.87		06	23	60½	
Walton	5.04		07	29	64	
Oatlands Box	6.08		08	27	65	
Weybridge	7.11		09	21	69	
Byfleet & New Haw	8.36		10	27	74½	
West Byfleet	9.68		11	21	73	
Woking	12.25	15.30	14	21		
	0.00	0.00	00	00		right time
Woking Jct	0.46		01	58	25	
Brookwood	3.70		07	18	45	
Pirbright Jct	5.20		09	18	50	
MP 31	6.71		10	55	53½	
Sturt Lane Jct	7.86		12	10	61	
Farnborough	8.91		13	08	65	
Fleet	12.19		16	00	72½/75	
Winchfield	15.54		18	42	73/71	
Hook	17.87		20	42	73/71	
Newnham Siding	19.41		21	59	75	
			sigs stop		0*	
MP 47¼	22.96		26	21		
			26	51		
Basingstoke	24.29	29.00	29	57		
	0.00	0.00	00	00		1¼ mins late

	miles	sched	mins	secs	speed	
Worting Jct	2.51	5.30	05	57	37/41	
MP 51	3.20		07	04	32*	tsr half mile
Wootton Box	4.75		09	11	46	
Steventon Box	6.20		10	53	57	
Waltham Box	7.35		12	04	59	
Roundwood Box	8.45		13	12	63	
Micheldever	10.30		14	50	75	
Weston Box	12.45		16	27	82	
Wallers Ash Box	13.95		17	31	87	
MP 63	15.35		18	28	90	
Winchester Jct	16.70	21.00	19	23	93	
Winchester City	18.80	24.00	21	54		2 mins early
	0.00	0.00	00	00		right time
St Cross Box	1.23		03	11	47½	
Shawford Jct	2.47		04	23	60	
Shawford	3.12		05	08	64½	
Allbrook Box	6.06		07	36	75	
Eastleigh	6.96	9.00	08	16	77	
Swaythling	9.22		10	03	78	
			sigs stop			
St Denys	10.63		11	41	0*	
			13	10		
Northam Jct	11.61	14.00	17	20	5*/12*	sigs/tsr
Southampton Central	12.60	17.00	21	53		5 mins late
Net times: Waterloo to Surbiton 16¾ mins, Woking to Basingstoke 26¼ mins						
Basingstoke to Winchester 20½ mins, Winchester to Southampton 15 mins						

65.03

Date	Tuesday 6th April 1965
Train	630 pm Waterloo to Weymouth
Loco	Rebuilt Merchant Navy class 4-6-2 No. 35007 *Aberdeen Commonwealth*
Load	12 coaches, 403 tons tare, 435 tons gross
Crew	Jack Varney and Condon, Bournemouth MPD
Recorder	DB

	miles	sched	mins	secs	speed	
Waterloo	0.00	0.00	00	00		right time
Vauxhall	1.29		03	46	32/30*	tsr
Queens Road	2.81		06	07	39*	sigs
Clapham Junction	3.93	7.00	08	02	42	
Earlsfield	5.58		10	16	53½	
Wimbledon	7.24		12	04	57	
Raynes Park	8.64		13	29	60	
New Malden	9.78		14	39	61	

	miles	sched	mins	secs	speed	
Berrylands	10.98		15	46	62	
Surbiton	12.04		16	50	63½	
Hampton Court Jct	13.34	18.00	18	01	68½	
Esher	14.39		18	55	71	
Hersham	15.91		20	16	70	
Walton	17.08		21	16	68	
Oatlands Box	18.12		22	12	66	
Weybridge	19.15		23	05	70	
Byfleet & New Haw	20.40		24	11	73	
West Byfleet	21.68		25	17	71½	
Woking	24.29		27	39	66½	
Woking Jct	24.75	28.00	27	57	67	
Brookwood	27.99		30	56	69	
Pirbright Jct	29.49		32	20	70½	
MP 31	31.00		33	32	70	
Sturt Lane Jct	32.15		34	32	74	
Farnborough	33.20		35	23	76	
Fleet	36.48		37	51	82/85	
Winchfield	39.83		40	16	83/81	
Hook	42.16		42	01	84/80	
Newnham Siding	43.70		43	10	81/82	
Basingstoke	47.75		46	42	62*	
Worting Jct	50.26	52.00	49	16	57	
Wootton Box	52.50		51	35	57	
Steventon Box	53.95		53	00	65½	
Waltham Box	55.10		54	01	66½	
Roundwood Box	56.20		55	03	68½	
Micheldever	58.05		56	39	74	
Weston Box	60.20		58	19	79	
Wallers Ash Box	61.70		59	26	82	
MP 63	63.10		60	25	83	eased
Winchester Jct	64.45	66.00	61	26	77½	
Winchester City	66.55	69.00	64	24		4½ mins early
	average speed Brookwood to Newnham: 77.05 mph					
	net time 63 minutes					
	actual start to stop average : 62.00 mph					

Date	Wednesday 21st April 1965
Train	630 pm Waterloo to Weymouth
Loco	Rebuilt Merchant Navy class 4-6-2 No. 35007 *Aberdeen Commonwealth*
Load	12 coaches, 401 tons tare, 435 tons gross
Crew	Jack Varney and Condon, Bournemouth MPD
Recorder	DB

	sched	mins	secs	speed	
Waterloo	0.00	00	00		1¼ mins late
Vauxhall		03	53	32	
Queens Road		05	44	46	
Clapham Junction	7.00	07	36	45/44	
Earlsfield		09	41	49½	
Wimbledon		12	09	26*	tsr quarter mile
Raynes Park		14	28	47½	
New Malden		15	48	57	
Berrylands		17	01	62	
Surbiton		18	02	67	
Hampton Court Jct	18.00	19	10	72½	
Esher		20	01	75	
Hersham		21	16	75½	
Walton		22	11	75	
Oatlands Box		23	00	74	
Weybridge		23	47	77½	
Byfleet & New Haw		24	47	81	
West Byfleet		25	44	79	
Woking		27	54	73	
Woking Jct	28.00	28	13	71/70	
Brookwood		30	59	71	
Pirbright Jct		32	23	70/70½	
MP 31		33	36	70	
Sturt Lane Jct		34	36	73	
Farnborough		35	27	75	
Fleet		37	59	81/83½	
Winchfield		40	22	82/79	
Hook		42	07	82/80	
Newnham Siding		43	15	83/85	
Basingstoke		47	26	25*	sigs
Worting Jct	52.00	52	24	38	
Wootton Box		55	21	49	
Steventon Box		56	50	62½	
Waltham Box		57	54	66	
Roundwood Box		58	58	67½	
Micheldever		60	27	77	

	sched	mins	secs	speed	
Weston Box		62	04	80/82½	
Wallers Ash Box		63	43	30*	sigs
MP 63		sigs		8*	
Winchester Jct	66.00	67	17	54½	
Winchester City	69.00	70	34		2¾ mins late
	average speed Brookwood to Newnham: 76.85 mph				
	net time 61½ mins				

65.05

Date	Sunday 4th April 1965
Train	434 pm Bournemouth West to Waterloo 'Bournemouth Belle'
Loco	Rebuilt Merchant Navy class 4-6-2 No. 35012 *United States Line*
Load	10 Pullmans + 1 bogie van, 428½ tons tare, 455 tons gross
Crew	Gordon Hooper and Paul Daley, Nine Elms MPD
Also on footplate	Brian Smith
Timed by	DB
Weather	Fine and sunny light SW wind

	miles	sched	mins	secs	speed	
Southampton	0.00	0.00	00	00		½ min late
Northam Jct	1.05	3.30	03	23	30/14*	
St Denys	2.11		05	17	41	
Swaythling	3.45		07	04	54½	
Eastleigh	5.80	10.00	09	24	63	22% cut off
Allbrook Box	6.66		10	17	64½	
Shawford	9.61		13	02	65½	
Shawford Jct	10.46		13	45	67	
St Cross Box	11.50		14	43	68	
Winchester City	12.70		15	51	69½	
Winchester Jct	14.80		17	43	71	27% cut off
Wallers Ash Box	17.55		20	02	72	
Weston Box	19.05		21	14	73	
Micheldever	21.20		22	59	75	
Roundwood Box	23.05		24	28	76	
Waltham Box	24.15		25	22	80	
Steventon Box	25.30		26	12	83	
Wootton Box	26.75		27	17	77½	
Worting Jct	28.98	37.00	30	53	7*/23	sigs severe
Basingstoke	31.50		34	06	65½	
Newnham Siding	35.55		37	13	78	
Hook	37.08		38	21	84	
Winchfield	39.41		40	00	90/93	
Fleet	42.76		42	13	90/92½	
Farnborough	46.05		44	24	88	

	miles	sched	mins	secs	speed	
Start Lane Jct	47.05		45	07	89	
MP 31	48.25		45	56	87	
Pirbright Jct	49.60		46	54	92	
Brookwood	51.25		47	56	94	eased
Woking Jct	54.50	58.00	50	12	85	SVO
Woking	54.95		50	28	86	
West Byfleet	57.56		52	19	86½	
Byfleet and New Haw	58.84		53	13	87	
Weybridge	60.09		54	10	81	
Oatlands Box	61.15		55	54	83	
Walton	62.16		56	38	85	
Hersham	63.33		56	27	87	
Esher	64.85		57	33	86½	
Hampton Court Jct.	65.90	67.30	58	17	88	
Surbiton	67.20		59	10	85	
Berrylands	68.26		59	59	83	
New Malden	69.46		60	53	70*	
Raynes Park	70.60		61	57	65½	
Wimbledon	72.05		63	13	67	
Earlsfield	73.66		64	43	71	
Clapham Junction	75.31	77.00	66	38	41*	
Queens Road	76.43		68	38	38*/33*	sigs/tsr
Vauxhall	77.93		70	36	45	
Waterloo	79.24	84.00	74	13		9¼ mins early
net time	69½ mins actual start to stop average: 64.06 mph average speed Hook to Surbiton 86.82 mph full regulator 22% to Winchester increased to 27% to Roundwood					

65.06

Date	Wednesday 14th April 1965
Train	245 am Waterloo to Bournemouth
Loco	Rebuilt West Country Class 4-6-2 No. 34042 *Dorchester*
Load to Woking	3 coaches and 10 vans, 288 tons tare, 335 tons gross
Load from Woking	3 coaches and 8 vans, 254 tons tare 290 tons gross
Load from Basingstoke	3 coaches and 7 vans, 237 tons tare 270 tons gross
Load from Eastleigh	3 coaches and 4 vans, 186 tons tare 205 tons gross
Crew	Gordon Hooper and Paul Daley, Nine Elms MPD
Recorder	Brian Smith

	miles	sched	mins	secs	speed	
Waterloo	0.00	0.00	00	00		2½ mins late
Vauxhall	1.29		04	36	36	sigs to slow line
Queens Road	2.81		06	27	51	
Clapham Junction	3.93	7.00	07	52	55	

	miles	sched	mins	secs	speed	
Earlsfield	5.58		09	38	59	
Wimbledon	7.24		11	18	63½	
Raynes Park	8.64		12	40	64	
New Malden	9.78		13	42	65½	
Berrylands	10.98		14	47	68	
Surbiton	12.04		15	45	70	
Hampton Court Jct	13.34	18.00	16	51	74	
Esher	14.39		17	42	75	
Hersham	15.91		18	55	78	
Walton	17.08		19	49	76/71	
Weybridge	19.15		21	27	75	
Byfleet and New Haw	20.40		22	27	81	
West Byfleet	21.68		23	24	78	
Woking	24.29	32.00	26	33		
	0.00	00.00	00	00		right time
Woking Jct	0.46		01	33	26	
Brookwood	3.70		05	50	60	
MP 31	6.71		08	41	66	
Sturt Lane Jct	7.86		09	37	73	
Farnborough	8.91		10	34	77	
Fleet	12.19		13	03	79/84	
Winchfield	15.54		15	31	82/80	
Hook	17.87		17	14	84	
Newnham Siding	19.41		18	19	87/88½	
			2 sigs stops		0*	
Basingstoke	23.46	26.00	30	32		
	0.00	0.00	00	00		3½ mins late
Worting Jct	2.51	5.30	04	45	53	
Wootton Box	4.75		07	05	65/81½	
Roundwood Box	8.45		10	10	77	
Micheldever	10.30		11	33	79	
Wallers Ash Box	13.95		14	08	94	
Winchester Jct	16.70	22.00	15	49	102	
Winchester City	18.80	25.00	18	00		
	0.00	0.00	00	00		right time
Shawford Jct	2.47		03	43	64	
Shawford	3.12		04	21	69/82	
			sigs		*	
Allbrook Box	6.06		07	05	22*/36	
Eastleigh	6.96	10.00	09	13		
Eastleigh	0.00	0.00	00	00		right time
Swaythling	2.22		04	07	60/68	

	miles	sched	mins	secs	speed	
St Denys	3.70		05	27	62	
Northam Jct	11.71	7.00	06	54	16*/32	
Southampton Central	12.75	10.00	10	04		
	0.00	0.00	00	00		right time
Millbrook	0.95		02	43	36½/54	
Redbridge	2.70		04	41	46*	
Totton	3.26		05	28	50	
Lyndhurst Road	6.18		08	30	65	
Beaulieu Road	8.80		10	44	74/78	
			tsr		14*/58	
Brockenhurst	13.56	19.00	17	41		
	0.00	0.00	00	00		2¼ mins late
Lymington Jct	0.95	2.30	02	43	38	
Sway	2.75		04	58	60/73	
New Milton	5.75	10.00	08	11		
	0.00	0.00	00	00		1¾ mins late
Hinton Admiral	2.50		03	27	81/90	
Christchurch	5.80	8.00	06	16		
	0.00	0.00	00	00		right time
Pokesdown	2.00		03	28	52	
Boscombe	2.50		04	04	57/60	
			sigs stop		0*	
Bournemouth Central	3.70	7.00	13	14		6¼ mins late
net times		Waterloo to Woking			26 minutes	
		Woking to Basingstoke			22 minutes	
		Basingstoke to Winchester			18 minutes	
		Winchester to Eastleigh			9½ minutes	
		Eastleigh to Southampton			10 minutes	
		Southampton to Brockenhurst			15¾ minutes	
		Brockenhurst to New Milton			8¼ minutes	
		New Milton to Christchurch			6¼ minutes	
		Christchurch to Bournemouth			6 minutes	
		start to stop average Basingstoke to Winchester 62.67 mph				

65.07

Date		Saturday 17th April 1965				
Train		1130 am Weymouth to Waterloo				
Loco		Rebuilt Merchant Navy class 4-6-2 No. 35019 *French Line CGT*				
Load		12 coaches, 403 tons tare, 440 tons gross				
Crew		Hutton, Bournemouth MPD				
Weather		Not recorded				
Recorder		DB				

	miles	sched	mins	secs	speed	
Bournemouth Central	0.00	0.00	00	00		2½ mins late
Boscombe	1.20		03	26	33	
Pokesdown	1.75		04	22	44	
Christchurch	3.70		06	20	63/60	
Hinton Admiral	7.00		09	35	62½	
MP 100	8.05		10	41	56	
New Milton	9.50		12	07	63	
Sway	12.50		14	51	70½	
Lymington Jct	14.30		16	31	64½*	
Brockenhurst	15.25		17	23	66½	
MP 92	16.05		18	10	72/66½	
Woodfidley Box	18.35		20	06	73	
Beaulieu Road	19.95		21	33	66/69	
Lyndhurst Road	22.65		23	58	63	
MP 84	24.05		25	20	64	
Totton	25.50		26	52	51*	
Redbridge	26.15		27	41	46*	
Millbrook	27.90		29	49	51	
Southampton Central	28.80	32.00	31	54		2½ mins late

65.08

Date		Sunday 2nd May 1965
Train		434 pm Bournemouth West to Waterloo 'Bournemouth Belle'
Loco		Rebuilt Merchant Navy class 4-6-2 No. 35011 *General Steam Navigation*
Load		10 Pullmans and one bogie van, 428½ tons tare, 455 tons gross
Crew		Reuben Hendicott and Bill Stanley, Nine Elms MPD
Also on footplate		Brian Smith
Weather		Hot and sunny
Recorder		DB

	sched	mins	secs	speed	
Bournemouth Central	0.00	00	00		½ min early
Boscombe		03	21	37½	
Pokesdown		04	11	52	
Christchurch		06	01	63½/61	
Hinton Admiral		09	12	63½	

	sched	mins	secs	speed	
MP 100		10	16	59	
New Milton		11	39	67½	
Sway		14	14	73	
Lymington Jct		15	49	54*	sigs
Brockenhurst		16	51	51*	sigs
MP 92		17	42	64½	
Woodfidley Box		19	44	72½/75	
Beaulieu Road		21	05	71½/76½	
Lyndhurst Road		23	15	66*	
MP 84		24	32	70½	
Totton		25	56	50*	
Redbridge		26	45	46*	
Millbrook		28	51	51	
Southampton Central	32.00	30	42		1¾ mins early
	net time 30¼ minutes				

65.09

Date	Sunday 2nd May 1965
Train	434 pm Bournemouth West to Waterloo 'Bournemouth Belle'
Loco	Rebuilt Merchant Navy class 4-6-2 No. 35011 *General Steam Navigation*
Load	10 Pullmans + 1 bogie van, 428½ tons tare, 455 tons gross
Crew	Reuben Hendicott and Bill Stanley. Nine Elms MPD
Also on footplate	Brian Smith
Recorder	DB
Weather	Hot and sunny

	miles	sched	mins	secs	speed	
Southampton	0.00	0.00	00	00		¾ min early
Northam Jct	1.05	3.30	03	18	22*	
St Denys	2.11		05	03	21*	tsr for ¾ mile
Swaythling	3.45		08	35	34*/41	sigs
Eastleigh	5.80	10.00	12	05	37*	sigs
Allbrook Box	6.66		13	12	49	
Shawford	9.61		16	27	61	
Shawford Jct	10.46		17	09	62½	
St Cross	11.50		18	11	64½	
Winchester City	12.70		19	20	67	22% cut off
Winchester Jct	14.80		21	16	68	
Wallers Ash Box	17.55		23	40	67	30% cut off
Weston Box	19.05		24	58	69	
Micheldever	21.20		26	47	71	
Roundwood Box	23.05		28	22	72½	
Waltham Box	24.15		29	19	76	
Steventon Box	25.30		30	11	78	

	miles	sched	mins	secs	speed	
Wootton Box	26.75		31	17	79	
Worting Jct	28.98	37.00	33	16	60*	
Basingstoke	31.50		35	26	74	
Newnham Siding	35.55		38	30	84	SVO
Hook	37.08		39	37	81/84	
Winchfield	39.41		41	19	83/86	
Fleet	42.76		43	42	83	
Farnborough	46.05		46	05	82	
Sturt Lane Jct	47.05		46	53	80	
MP 31	48.25		47	48	78	
Pirbright Jct	49.60		48	50	84	
Brookwood	51.25		49	58	86	eased
Woking Jct	54.50	58.00	52	24	78*	
Woking	54.95		52	43	81	
West Byfleet	57.56		54	38	85	
Byfleet & New Haw	58.84		55	31	86½	
Weybridge	60.09		56	29	82	
Oatlands Box	61.15		57	13	80½	SVO
Walton	62.16		57	59	83	
Hersham	63.33		58	49	83½	
Esher	64.85		60	00	80	
Hampton Court Jct.	65.90	67.30	60	47	77½	
Surbiton	67.20		61	49	75½	
Berrylands	68.26		62	40	75	
New Malden	69.46		63	38	68*	SVO
Raynes Park	70.60		64	42	63	
Wimbledon	72.05		66	03	58	
Earlsfield	73.66		67	45	60	
Clapham Junction	75.31	77.00	69	45	41*	
Queens Road	76.43		71	21	52	
Vauxhall	77.93		73	08	33/*	sigs
Waterloo	79.24	84.00	76	48		8 mins early
	net time 73 minutes actual start to stop average 61.90 mph average speed Hook to Surbiton: 81.41 mph					

65.10

Date	Friday 7th May 1965				
Train	830 am Waterloo to Weymouth				
Loco	Rebuilt Merchant Navy class 4-6-2 No. 35028 *Clan Line*				
Load to Southampton	13 coaches, 438 tons tare 475 tons gross				
Load from Southampton	11 coaches, 370 tons tare 400 tons gross				
Crew	Gordon Hooper and Paul Daley, Nine Elms MOD				
Also on footplate	Brian Smith				
Recorder	Terry Jackson				

	miles	sched	mins	secs	speed	
Waterloo	0.00	0.00	00	00		18½ mins late
Vauxhall	1.29		03	30	38	
Queens Road	2.81		05	08	53½	
Clapham Junction	3.93	7.00	06	47	39*	
Earlsfield	5.58		09	00	52	
Wimbledon	7.24		10	45	60/61	
Raynes Park	8.64		12	12	58/58½	
New Malden	9.78		13	22	60	
Berrylands	10.98		14	28	65	
Surbiton	12.04		15	27	70½	
Hampton Court Jct	13.34	18.00	16	33	73½	
Esher	14.39		17	24	76/34½*	sigs
Hersham	15.91		19	27	40½	
Walton	17.08		20	52	52½	
Weybridge	19.15		23	01	63	
Byfleet & New Haw	20.40		24	09	72	
West Byfleet	21.68		25	12	74	
Woking	24.29		27	23	73	
Woking Jct	24.75	28.00	27	46	72	
Brookwood	27.99		32	33	5*	sigs
MP 31	31.00		37	36	58	
Sturt Lane Jct	32.15		38	47	66	
Farnborough	33.20		39	41	71	
Bramshot Halt	35.70		41	36	77	
Fleet	36.48		42	17	79/78/80	
Winchfield	39.83		44	49	71/65½*	sigs
Hook	42.16		46	56	69/68/76	
			sigs stop		0*	
Basingstoke	47.75		55	11	30*	to slow line
Worting Jct	50.26	52.00	59	52	55	
Wootton Box	52.50		61	09	61	
Waltham Box	55.15		63	24	72	
Roundwood Box	56.20		64	20	73	
Micheldever	58.05		65	45	83	
Weston Box	60.20		67	15	87	

	miles	sched	mins	secs	speed	
Wallers Ash Box	61.70		68	15	91	
Winchester Jct Box	64.45	66.30	70	00	92/93	
Winchester	66.55		71	24	92/86	
Shawford Jct	68.96		73	04	87	
Shawford	69.61		73	37	88/90	
Allbrook Box	72.55		75	38	54½*	sigs
Eastleigh	73.45	74.00	76	55	20½*	sigs
Swaythling	75.71		80	23	58/10*	sigs
St Denys	77.12		84	18	25/35	
Northam Jct	78.20	79.00	86	18	14*	
Southampton Central	79.24	82.00	89	42		
				net time 72 minutes		
Southampton Central	0.00	0.00	00	00		27½ mins late
Millbrook	0.90		02	29	40	
Redbridge	2.65		04	46	48	
Totton	3.30		05	32	50½	
Lyndhurst Road	6.15		08	28	63/72½	
Beaulieu Road	8.85		10	43	71/74	
Woodfidley Box	10.45		12	03	69/16*	tsr
Brockenhurst	13.55		16	47	61	
Lymington Junction	14.50	17.00	17	43	61½	
Sway	16.30		19	25	68/79	
New Milton	19.30		21	47	71	
Hinton Admiral	21.80		23	35	90/94	
Christchurch	25.10		26	00	58*/63	
Pokesdown	27.05		27	57	58	
Boscombe	27.60		28	30	60	
Bournemouth Central	28.80	34.00	30	39		24 mins late
				net time 28 minutes		

65.11

Date	Tuesday 11th May 1965
Train	630 pm Waterloo to Weymouth
Loco	BR Standard class 5 4-6-0 No. 73117
Load	12 coaches, 403 tons tare, 435 tons gross
Driver	Hutton, Bournemouth MPD
Recorder	DB

	miles	sched	mins	secs	speed	
Waterloo	0.00	0.00	00	00		5 mins late
Vauxhall	1.29		03	36	33/23*	sigs
Queens Road	2.81		06	21	36	
Clapham Junction	3.93	7.00	09	24	14*	sigs
Earlsfield	5.58		13	19	37½	

	miles	sched	mins	secs	speed	
Wimbledon	7.24		15	46	45	
Raynes Park	8.64		17	30	51	
New Malden	9.78		18	49	54	
Berrylands	10.98		20	06	55	
Surbiton	12.04		21	16	56	
Hampton Court Jct	13.34	18.00	22	36	60½	
Esher	14.39		23	37	61½	
Hersham	15.91		25	08	62½	
Walton	17.08		26	16	61	
Oatlands Box	18.12		27	18	58½	
Weybridge	19.15		28	19	60	
Byfleet & New Haw	20.40		29	35	65	
West Byfleet	21.68		30	47	63½	
Woking	24.29		33	28	59	
Woking Jct	24.75	28.00	33	54	57½	
Brookwood	27.99		37	27	53½	
Pirbright Jct	29.49		39	17	53	
MP 31	31.00		40	53	52½	
Sturt Lane Jct	32.15		42	13	57½	
Farnborough	33.20		43	17	59½	
Fleet	36.48		46	27	63/67½	SVO
Winchfield	39.83		49	29	64/63	
Hook	42.16		51	44	64½/63	
Newnham Siding	43.70		53	11	65½/68½	
Basingstoke	47.75		56	56	63	SVO
Worting Jct	50.26	52.00	59	31	56	
Wootton Box	52.50		61	59	54	
Steventon Box	53.95		63	30	61	SVO
Waltham Box	55.10		64	36	62½	
Roundwood Box	56.20		65	42	65½	
Micheldever	58.05		67	22	71½	
Weston Box	60.20		69	04	77½	
Wallers Ash Box	61.70		70	15	81	
MP 63	63.10		71	13	83	
Winchester Jct	64.45	66.00	72	12	84	
Winchester City	66.55	69.00	74	39		10½ mins late
	net time 69 minutes services disrupted by Clapham Junction signal box collapse					

65.12

Date		15th May 1965				
Train		920 pm Waterloo to Bournemouth				
Loco		Rebuilt Merchant Navy class 4-6-2 No. 35005 *Canadian Pacific*				
Load		9 coaches and 1 van, 336 tons tare, 355 tons gross				
Crew		Gordon Hooper and Dave Wilson, Nine Elms MPD				
Also on the Footplate		Brian Smith				
Weather		Fine				
Recorder		DB				

	miles	sched	mins	secs	speed	
Waterloo	0.00	0.00	00	00		right time
Vauxhall	1.29		03	36	40	no banker
Queens Road	2.81		05	19	54½	
Clapham Junction	3.93	7.00	06	49	40*	
Earlsfield	5.58		09	00	54/59	
Wimbledon	7.24		10	43	19*	tsr quarter mile
Raynes Park	8.64		13	33	45½	
New Malden	9.78		14	53	60	
Berrylands	10.98		16	03	64½	
Surbiton	12.04		17	00	69	
Hampton Court Jct	13.34	18.00	18	05	75½	
Esher	14.39		18	52	80	
Hersham	15.91		20	03	82½	
Walton	17.08		20	53	82	
Oatlands Box	18.12		21	39	80½	
Weybridge	19.15		22	22	84	
Byfleet & New Haw	20.40		23	16	89	
West Byfleet	21.68		24	10	88	
Woking	24.29		26	04	84	
Woking Jct	24.75	28.00	26	23	83	
Brookwood	27.99		28	48	82	
Pirbright Jct	29.49		30	00	80	
MP 31	31.00		31	06	77½	
Sturt Lane Jct	32.15		31	59	82	
Farnborough	33.20		32	44	83	
Fleet	36.48		35	04	86/89	
Winchfield	39.83		37	22	87/84½	
Hook	42.16		39	03	87/85	
Newnham Siding	43.70		40	05	90	
Basingstoke	47.75	55.00	43	48		11¼ mins early
	0.00	0.00	00	00		right time
Worting Jct	2.51	5.30	05	09	48½	¾ regulator and
Wootton Box	4.75		07	38	60	22% cut off
Steventon Box	6.20		08	55	70½	

	miles	sched	mins	secs	speed	
Waltham Box	7.35		09	56	72½	
Roundwood Box	8.45		10	51	76	
Micheldever	10.30		12	16	86½	
MP 59	11.35		13	00	90	
Weston Box	12.45		13	42	94	27% cut off
MP 61	13.35		14	16	97	210 lbs steam
Wallers Ash Box	13.95		14	39	100	
MP 63	15.35		15	28	105	
Winchester Jct	16.70	21.00	16	16	102	eased/brakes
Winchester City	18.80	24.00	18	50		
	0.00	0.00	00	00		right time
St Cross Box	1.23		02	53	49	
Shawford Jct	2.47		04	01	63	
Shawford	3.12		04	45	68/83	
Allbrook Box	6.06		07	05	*	
			sigs stop			
MP 73	6.55		07	49	0*	sigs stop
			08	7		
Eastleigh	6.96	9.00	09	38		
Swaythling	9.22		12	45	62/70	
St Denys	10.63		14	05	68	
Northam Jct	11.71	14.00	15	41	15*/30	
Southampton Central	12.75	17.00	19	20		2¼ mins late
	average speed Farnborough to Newnham Siding=85.71 mph					
	Waterloo to Basingstoke	start to stop average 65.41 mph				
		net time 41¼ minutes				
	net time Winchester to Southampton: 14½ minutes					

65.13

Date	Saturday 22nd May 1965
Train	720 am Bournemouth to Waterloo
Loco	Rebuilt Merchant Navy class 4-6-2 No. 35023 *Holland Afrika Line*
Load	11 coaches, 372 tons tare, 400 tons gross
Crew	Gordon Porter and fireman Ibbs, Nine Elms MPD
Weather	Cold
Recorder	David Sprackland

	miles	sched	mins	secs	speed	
Winchester City	0.00	0.00	00	00		
Winchester Jct	2.10	5.30	04	25	52	
Wallers Ash Box	4.85		07	16	62	
Weston Box	6.35		08	36	68	
Micheldever	8.50		10	25	72	
Roundwood Box	10.35		11	58	74	

Waltham Box	11.45		-	-	75	
Wootton Box	14.05		14	56	74½	
Worting Jct	16.28	23.00	17	33	39*	sigs
Basingstoke	18.80		20	05	71½/80	
Hook	24.38		24	59	55*	sigs
Winchfield	26.71		27	07	76	
Fleet	30.06		29	41	84	
Farnborough	33.35		32	00	86	
MP 31	35.55		33	36	83/90	
Brookwood	38.55		35	39	86/40*	sigs
Woking	42.25		39	34	62	
West Byfleet	44.86		41	53	76	
Byfleet & New Haw	46.14		42	51	81	
Weybridge	47.39		43	48	78	
Walton	49.46		45	17	83	
Hersham	50.63		-	-	86½	
Esher	52.15		47	09	85	
Hampton Court Jct.	53.20	55.30	47	55	*	
			sigs stop		0*	
MP 13¼	53.30		48	25		
			49	09		
Surbiton	54.50		52	50	*	
New Malden	56.76		56	24	*	
Wimbledon	59.35		61	13	19*	tsr half mile
Earlsfield	60.96		64	07	45	
Clapham Junction	62.61	65.00	66	16		
Vauxhall	65.23		69	47		
Waterloo	66.55	72.00	73	22		
	net time 59½ minutes					
	start to stop average to signal stop: 66.05 mph					

65.14

Date	Friday 4th June 1965
Train	830 am Waterloo to Bournemouth
Loco	Rebuilt Merchant Navy class 4-6-2 No. 35005 *Canadian Pacific*
Load	11 coaches, 369½ tons tare 400 tons gross
Driver	Reuben Hendicott and Bill Stanley, Nine Elms MPD
Recorder	Terry Jackson

	miles	sched	mins	secs	speed	
Waterloo	0.00	0.00	00	00		
Vauxhall	1.29		03	20	41	
Queens Road	2.81		04	58	54½	
Clapham Junction	3.93	7.00	06	30	41½*	
Earlsfield	5.58		08	37	55½	

	miles	sched	mins	secs	speed	
Wimbledon	7.24		10	18	63	
Raynes Park	8.64		11	39	64	
New Malden	9.78		12	42	67	
Berrylands	10.98		13	42	70	
Surbiton	12.04		14	37	75	
Hampton Court Jct	13.34	18.00	15	39	77	
Esher	14.39		16	28	80	
Hersham	15.91		17	36	83	
Walton	17.08		18	26	81/79	
Weybridge	19.15		19	58	80	
Byfleet & New Haw	20.40		20	54	84	
West Byfleet	21.68		21	49	83	
Woking	24.29		23	47	80	
Woking Jct	24.75	28.00	24	08	79	
Brookwood	27.99		26	36	77	
MP 31	31.00		28	57	75½	
Sturt Lane Jct	32.15		29	53	79	
Farnborough	33.20		30	37	81/84	
Fleet	36.48		32	59	83	
Winchfield	39.83		35	20	83/86/85	
Hook	42.16		37	02	84/83/86	
Basingstoke	47.75		41	57	32½*/37	sigs
Worting Jct	50.26	52.00	47	18	22½*	sigs
Wootton Box	52.50		51	00	47	
Roundwood Box	56.20		54	37	68½	
Micheldever	58.05		56	08	75½	
Weston Box	60.20		57	58	54½*/15*	tsr
Wallers Ash Box	61.70		61	43	17½	
Winchester Jct Box	64.45	66.30	65	34	63	
Winchester	66.55		67	23	75	
Shawford Jct	68.96		69	17	76½	
Shawford	69.61		69	53	75½/76½	
Allbrook Box	72.55		71	12	72	
Eastleigh	73.45	74.00	72	54	71	
Swaythling	75.71		75	41	22½	sigs
St Denys	77.12		77	55	45½	
Northam Jct	78.20	79.00	81	23	10*/12½	
			sigs stop		0*	
Southampton Central	79.24	82.00	90	47		
	0.00	0.00	00	00		
Millbrook	0.90		02	28	37½	
Redbridge	2.65		04	49	50	
Totton	3.30		05	34	50	

	miles	sched	mins	secs	speed	
Lyndhurst Road	6.15		08	39	58½/69	
Beaulieu Road	8.85		11	04	65½	
Woodfidley Box	10.45		12	27	73/70½/76	
Brockenhurst	13.55		15	02	66	
Lymington Junction	14.50	17.00	15	58	63/60½	
Sway	16.30		17	42	65/76	
New Milton	19.30		20	10	73½/77/76	
Hinton Admiral	21.80		22	07	83/86	
Christchurch	25.10		24	35	70½/72½	
Pokesdown	27.05		26	18	63	
Boscombe	27.60		26	53	57	
Bournemouth Central	28.80	34.00	29	12		
	net time 71½ minutes					

65.15

Date	Monday 7th June 1965
Train	10 am Salisbury to Waterloo
Loco	Rebuilt West Country class 4-6-2 No. 34032 *Camelford*
Load	6 coaches, 199 tons tare 210 tons gross
Driver	Gordon Hooper and R Bell, Nine Elms MPD
Also on the footplate	Brian Smith
Recorder	Terry Jackson

	miles	sched	mins	secs	speed	
Basingstoke	0.00	0.00	00	00		
MP 47	0.80		01	40	43	
MP 46	1.80		02	41	65½	
MP 45	2.80		03	31	79	
MP 44	3.80		04	15	84/85	
Hook	5.60	8.00	06	02		
	0.00	0.00	00	00		
MP 41	1.20		02	10	55½/60	
Winchfield	2.35	5.00	03	44		
	0.00	0.00	00	00	71	
Fleet	3.35	5.00	03	44		
	0.00	0.00	00	00		
Bramshot Halt	0.80		01	57	51/72	
Farnborough	3.25	6.00	04	33		
	0.00	0.00	00	00		
Sturt Lane Jct	1.20		02	03	53½	
MP 32	1.25		02	15	59	
MP 31	2.25		03	13	65	
MP 30	3.25		04	03	75	
MP 29	4.25		04	48	82	

	miles	sched	mins	secs	speed	
Brookwood	5.25	8.00	06	02		
	0.00	0.00	00	00		
Woking Jct	3.25		04	06	73/44½*	
Woking	3.65	6.00	05	03		
	0.00	0.00	00	00		
West Byfleet	2.61		03	38	71	
Byfleet	3.89		04	36	81	
Weybridge	5.14		05	34	80	
Oatlands Box	6.17		06	19	82	
Walton	7.21		07	03	81	
Hersham	8.38		07	54	80	
Esher	9.90		09	05	78	
Hampton Court Jct	10.95	12.00	09	54	79	
Surbiton	12.25		10	53	78	
Berrylands	13.31		11	42	75½	
New Malden	14.51		12	48	60*	
Raynes Park	15.65		14	02	46½*/18½*	tsr
Wimbledon	17.10		17	33	36	
Earlsfield	18.71		19	35	61	
Clapham Junction	20.36	22.00	21	39	37½*	
Queens Road	21.48		23	15	58/60	
Vauxhall	22.98		24	58	36*	
Waterloo	24.29	29.00	27	56		
net times	Woking to Waterloo 25½ minutes					

65.16

Date	Monday 7th June 1965
Train	530 pm Waterloo to Bournemouth West
Loco	Rebuilt Merchant Navy class 4-6-2 No. 35005 *Canadian Pacific*
Load	12 coaches, 406 tons tare, 435 tons gross
Crew	Eric Saunders and Dave Wilson, Nine Elms MPD
Weather	Hot and sunny
Recorder	DB

	miles	sched	mins	secs	speed	
Waterloo	0.00	0.00	00	00		¾ min late
Vauxhall	1.29		03	30	40	
Queens Road	2.81		05	06	55/57	
Clapham Junction	3.93	7.00	06	31	45*	
Earlsfield	5.58		08	35	56	
Wimbledon	7.24		10	13	63½	
Raynes Park	8.64		11	28	68½	
New Malden	9.78		12	25	73	
Berrylands	10.98		13	23	75	

	miles	sched	mins	secs	speed	
Surbiton	12.04		14	16	77½	
Hampton Court Jct	13.34	18.00	15	14	80	
Esher	14.39		15	59	83	
			sigs stop			
MP 15½	15.50		18	39	0*	
			19	21		
Hersham	15.91		21	12	36½	
Walton	17.08		22	48	53	
Oatlands Box	18.12		23	56	59½	
Weybridge	19.15		24	54	67½	
Byleet & New Haw	20.40		26	00	74	
West Byfleet	21.68		27	01	76/75	
Woking	24.29		29	08	76	
Woking Jct	24.75	28.00	29	28	76½	full regulator and
Brookwood	27.99		30	59	78	40% cut off
Pirbright Jct	29.49		33	15	77	
MP 31	31.00		34	21	75	
Sturt Lane Jct	32.15		35	17	78	
Farnborough	33.20		36	06	79½	
Fleet	36.48		38	32	81/82½	
Winchfield	39.83		40	58	81½/79	
Hook	42.16		42	46	80/78	
Newnham Siding	43.70		43	54	80	
			sigs		45*	sigs
Basingstoke	47.75	55.00	48	48		5½ mins early
	net time 41¼ minutes average speed from the signal stop to Basingstoke: 65.7 start to stop					

65.17

Date	Wednesday 9th June 1965
Train	530 pm Waterloo to Bournemouth West
Loco	Rebuilt Merchant Navy class 4-6-2 No. 35017 *Belgian Marine*
Load	11 coaches, 373 tons tare, 400 tons gross
Crew	Eric Saunders and Dave Wilson, Nine Elms MPD
Also on Footplate	Brian Smith
Weather	Rain
Recorder	DB

	miles	sched	mins	secs	speed	
Waterloo	0.00	0.00	00	00		¼ min late
Vauxhall	1.29		03	30	*/42	WL
Queens Road	2.81		05	06	56½/61	
Clapham Junction	3.93	7.00	06	24	43*	SVO
Earlsfield	5.58		08	25	58	

	miles	sched	mins	secs	speed	
Wimbledon	7.24		10	07	61½	
Raynes Park	8.64		11	26	63½	
New Malden	9.78		12	34	66½	
Berrylands	10.98		13	36	70	
Surbiton	12.04		14	30	74½	
Hampton Court Jct	13.34	18.00	15	32	79	
Esher	14.39		16	19	82	
Hersham	15.91		17	26	83½	
Walton	17.08		18	17	82	SVO
Oatlands Box	18.12		19	04	80	
Weybridge	19.15		19	46	84	
Byfleet & New Haw	20.40		20	41	87	
West Byfleet	21.68		21	35	85	
Woking	24.29		23	41	72*	sigs
Woking Jct	24.75	28.00	24	02	73/74½	
Brookwood	27.99		26	58	56*	sigs
Pirbright Jct	29.49		28	35	61½	
MP 31	31.00		30	24	46*	sigs
Sturt Lane Jct	32.15		31	32	63	
Farnborough	33.20		32	26	70	
Fleet	36.48		35	01	81/85	
Winchfield	39.83		37	27	83/81	
Hook	42.16		39	08	85/82	
Newnham Siding	43.70		40	15	85/87	
			sigs		35*	sigs
Basingstoke	47.75	55.00	44	21		
	net time 41¼ minutes average speed Fleet to Newnham Siding: 82.78 mph start to stop average :64.6 mph					

65.18

Date	Sunday 20th June 1965
Train	949 am Weymouth to Waterloo
Loco	West Country class 4-6-2 No. 34019 *Bideford*
Load	13 coaches and 1 van, 458 tons tare, 500 tons gross
Crew	Jim Sullivan and Alan Roe, Nine Elms MPD
Weather	Fine
Recorder	DB

	miles	sched	mins	secs	speed	
Winchester City	0.00	0.00	00	00		19 mins late
Winchester Jct	2.10	5.30	05	51	37½	
MP 63	3.55		07	49	43½	
Wallers Ash Box	4.85		09	39	46	
Weston Box	6.35		11	29	48½	

	miles	sched	mins	secs	speed	
MP 59	7.55		12	57	50	slipping
Micheldever	8.50		14	01	53½	
Roundwood Box	10.35		16	05	54½	
Waltham Box	11.45		17	19	61	
Steventon Box	12.60		18	25	63	
Wootton Box	14.05		19	46	63½/65	
Worting Jct	16.28	24.30	21	54	61½/64	
MP 49	17.55		23	28	14*	sigs
Basingstoke	18.80	28.30	26	19		
	0.00	0.00	00	00		17½ mins late
Newnham Siding	4.10		05	54	64½	slow line
Hook	5.59		07	14	68½	
Winchfield	7.92		09	17	73	
Fleet	11.27		11	57	76/77	
Farnborough	14.55		14	34	70*	
Sturt Lane Jct	15.60		15	28	68½	
MP 31	16.75		16	32	66½	
Pirbright Jct	18.26		17	44	71½	
Brookwood	19.76		19	03	74½	
Woking Jct	23.00		22	23	*	
			sigs stop			
MP 24½	23.25		22	35	0*	
			23	15		sigs stop
Woking	23.46	35.00	25	05		7½ mins late
	net times. Winchester to Basingstoke: 24¾ mins. Basingstoke to Woking: 22¾ mins start to stop average Basingstoke to the signal stop : 61.8 mph					

65.19

Date	Thursday 22nd July 1965
Train	530 pm Waterloo to Bournemouth
Loco	Rebuilt Mechant Navy class 4-6-2 No. 35016 *Elders Fyffes*
Load	11 coaches, 374 tons tare, 405 tons gross
Driver	Gordon Hooper, Nine Elms MPD
Weather	Rain, heavy at times
Recorder	DB

	miles	sched	mins	secs	speed	
Waterloo	0.00	0.00	00	00		½ min late
Vauxhall	1.29		03	43	*/35	WL
Queens Road	2.81		05	33	53½	
Clapham Junction	3.93	7.00	07	14	42*	
Earlsfield	5.58		09	21	55	
Wimbledon	7.24		11	03	63	
Raynes Park	8.64		12	20	66½	
New Malden	9.78		13	25	59*	sigs/SVO

	miles	sched	mins	secs	speed	
Berrylands	10.98		14	44	54½/37*	sigs
Surbiton	12.04		16	14	52½	
Hampton Court Jct	13.34	18.00	17	38	62	
Esher	14.39		18	35	69	
Hersham	15.91		19	56	74	
Walton	17.08		20	52	73	
Oatlands Box	18.12		21	43	72½	
Weybridge	19.15		22	30	76	
Byfleet & New Haw	20.40		23	31	81	
West Byfleet	21.68		24	27	80	
Woking	24.29		26	30	78	
Woking Jct	24.75	28.00	26	50	77½/76	
Brookwood	27.99		29	57	4*	sigs/slow line
Pirbright Jct	29.49		33	45	44	
MP 31	31.00		35	30	52	
Sturt Lane Jct	32.15		36	45	60	
Farnborough	33.20		38	09	35*	to fast line
Fleet	36.48		42	05	66½	
Winchfield	39.83		44	51	74½	
Hook	42.16		46	43	80	
Newnham Siding	43.70		47	50	83/85	
Basingstoke	47.75	63.00	51	50		10¾ mins early
	0.00	0.00	00	00		right time
Worting Jct	2.51	5.30	06	33	36	slipping
Wootton Box	4.75		09	54	45½	
Steventon Box	6.20		11	31	60	
Waltham Box	7.35		12	37	65	
Roundwood Box	8.45		13	39	70/72½	
Micheldever	10.30		15	33	22*	tsr quarter mile
Weston Box	12.45		19	03	61	slipping
Wallers Ash Box	13.95		20	24	74	
MP 63	15.35		21	30	84	
Winchester Jct	16.70	21.30	22	27	86/87	
Winchester City	18.80	25.00	24	49		
	0.00	0.00	00	00		right time
St Cross Box	1.23		03	02	49	slipping
Shawford Jct	2.47		04	15	61	
Shawford	3.12		04	59	64½	
MP 71½	5.05		06	30	76	
Allbrook Box	6.06		07	46	24*	to slow line
Eastleigh	6.96	11.00	09	51		1¼ mins early
	net time Waterloo to Basingstoke: 43 minutes Basingstoke to Winchester 21½ minutes				WL: Windsor lines start	

65.20

Date	Friday 23rd July 1965
Train	530 pm Waterloo to Bournemouth
Loco	Rebuilt Merchant Navy class 4-6-2 No. 35007 *Aberdeen Commonwealth*
Load	10 coaches 331½ tons tare, 355 tons gross
Driver	Gordon Hooper, Nine Elms MPD
Weather	Rain, heavy at times
Recorder	DB

	miles	sched	mins	secs	speed	
Waterloo	0.00	0.00	00	00		5¼ mins late
Vauxhall	1.29		03	30	39/33*	sigs
Queens Road	2.81		05	36	50/53	
Clapham Junction	3.93	7.00	07	10	37*	
Earlsfield	5.58		09	23	56	
Wimbledon	7.24		11	03	62½	
Raynes Park	8.64		12	23	60*	sigs
New Malden	9.78		13	30	63	
Berrylands	10.98		14	35	67	
Surbiton	12.04		15	32	73	
Hampton Court Jct	13.34	18.00	16	35	77½	
Esher	14.39		17	22	82½	
Hersham	15.91		18	31	84	
Walton	17.08		19	20	83	
Oatlands Box	18.12		20	50	7*	sigs
Weybridge	19.15		23	26	32	slipping
Byfleet & New Haw	20.40		25	14	57	
West Byfleet	21.68		26	32	62	slipping
Woking	24.29		28	57	70	
Woking Jct	24.75	28.00	29	19	71½	
Brookwood	27.99		35	11	0*/37	sigs stop/to slow line
Pirbright Jct	29.49		37	26	47½	
MP 31	31.00		39	02	54½	
Sturt Lane Jct	32.15		40	32	43*	sigs
Farnborough	33.20		42	01	30*	to fast line
Fleet	36.48		46	20	63/72	
Winchfield	39.83		49	15	70	
Hook	42.16		52	13	74½	
Newnham Siding	43.70		53	27	78/83/0*	sigs stop
Basingstoke	47.75	63.00	59	58		2¼ mins late
	0.00	0.00	00	00		8¾ mins late
Worting Jct	2.51	5.30	04	39	51	
Wootton Box	4.75		07	03	61	
Steventon Box	6.20		08	25	68½	
Waltham Box	7.35		09	25	70	

	miles	sched	mins	secs	speed	
Roundwood Box	8.45		10	21	74/79	
Micheldever	10.30		12	10	22*	tsr quarter mile
Weston Box	12.45		15	19	66½	
Wallers Ash Box	13.95		16	35	78	
MP 63	15.35		17	35	84	
Winchester Jct	16.70	21.30	18	31	90/91	
Winchester City	18.80	25.00	20	57		
	0.00	0.00	00	00		5¼ mins late
St Cross Box	1.23		02	36	55	
Shawford Jct	2.47		03	41	68	
Shawford	3.12		04	22	73	
MP 71½	5.05		05	46	85	
Allbrook Box	6.06		06	58	27*/39½	to slow line
Eastleigh	6.96	11.00	08	51		3¼ mins late
	net time Waterloo to Basingstoke: 43 minutes Basingstoke to Winchester: 18 minutes					

65.21

Date	Saturday 24th July 1965
Train	1115 am Exmouth to Waterloo
Loco	Rebuilt West Country class 4-6-2 No. 34013 *Okehampton*
Load	10 coaches, 324 tons tare, 355 tons gross
Crew	Bevan and Jones, Exmouth Junction MPD
Recorder	DB

	miles	sched	mins	secs	speed	
Sidmouth Junction	0.00	0.00	00	00		4¼ mins late
MP 158	1.45		03	35	47	
Honiton	4.75		08	36	34/38	
MP 153½	5.95		10	33	36½	SVO
MP 150½	8.95		13	40	74	
Seaton Junction	11.65	16.00	17	30		
	0.00	0.00	00	00		5½ mins late
MP 146¼	1.65		03	59	55/58	
Axminster	3.25	8.00	05	16		
	0.00	0.00	00	00		1¼ mins late
MP 142	2.65		-	-	53	
			stop			SVO
			08	04	0*	brakes
			14	35		dragging
			stop			
Chard Junction	5.10		15	48	0*	
			16	01		
Hewish Crossing	10.50		25	01	52½	

	miles	sched	mins	secs	speed	
MP 133¼	11.40		25	59	51	
Crewkerne	13.15		27	45	74½	
MP 128	16.65		30	20	83	
MP 126¼	18.40		31	45	72½	
Sutton Bingham	19.70		32	51	77½/80	
Yeovil Junction	21.95		34	35	78/67½	
Sherborne	26.55		38	26	74	
MP 115½	29.15		40	57	51	
Milbourne Port	30.20		42	11	58	
MP 113¼	31.40		43	21	58½	
Templecombe	32.60		44	28	75	
MP 110	34.65		45	56	86	
MP 107½	37.15		47	58	63	
Gillingham	39.40		49	56	79	
Semley	43.50		54	00	47½	
Tisbury	48.50		58	45	70½	
Dinton	52.80		62	23	76/77½	
Wilton South	58.60		67	21	41*	
MP 85¼	59.40		68	37	45/47	SVO
Salisbury	61.10	69.00	71	52		
	0.00	0.00	00	00		right time
Tunnel Lct	1.10		03	42	40	slipping
Porton	5.37		08	23	61½/60	
Allington Box	8.06		10	57	64	
Grateley	10.96		13	32	75	
MP 68¾	14.91		16	20	87	
Red Post Jct	16.01		17	17	73	
Andover	17.31	22.00	19	40		
	0.00	0.00	00	00		right time
MP 65	1.35		03	16	25*	tsr quarter mile
MP 62½	3.85		07	30	50	
Hurstbourne	5.21		09	03	64½	
Whitchurch	7.25		10	49	68½	
Overton	10.80		13	47	76	
Oakley	13.97		16	14	80	
MP 51	15.35		17	28	76	
Worting Jct	16.05	18.30	18	02	74½	SVO
Basingstoke	18.60	22.00	21	20		
	0.00	0.00	00	00		2 mins early
Newnham Siding	4.10		05	27	68½	
Hook	5.59		06	44	75	
Winchfield	7.92		08	35	81	
Fleet	11.27		10	58	86	

	miles	sched	mins	secs	speed	
Farnborough	14.55		14	47	30*	to slow line
Sturt Lane Jct	15.60		16	23	48	
MP 31	16.75		18	00	41*	sigs
Pirbright Jct	18.26		19	50	53	SVO
Brookwood	19.76		21	38	54½	SVO
Woking Jct	23.00		27	48	2*	sigs
Woking	23.46	31.00	30	23		to fast line
	0.00	0.00	00	00		2¾ mins early
West Byfleet	2.61		04	23	62	SVO
Byfleet & New Haw	3.89		05	30	72½	
Weybridge	5.14		06	37	70	
Oatlands Box	6.17		07	27	73	
Walton	7.21		08	16	76	
Hersham	8.38		09	09	79½	
Esher	9.90		10	24	77½	
Hampton Court Jct	10.95		11	13	74	
Surbiton	12.25		12	15	75	
Berrylands	13.31		13	10	70	
New Malden	14.51		14	11	70½	
Raynes Park	15.65		15	13	67½	
Wimbledon	17.10		16	29	69/70	
Earlsfield	18.71		18	00	67	SVO
Clapham Junction	20.36	19.30	20	06	41*	
Queens Road	21.48		21	42	59½	
Vauxhall	22.98		23	09	50*	!!
Waterloo	24.29	26.00	26	56		1¾ mins early
	Axminster to Salisbury: net time 59 minutes start to stop average Chard Junction to Salisbury: 60.16 mph net time Andover to Basingstoke: 19½ minutes Basingstoke to Woking: 22 minutes					

65.22

Date	Saturday 14th August 1965
Train	940 am Birmingham to Portsmouth Harbour
Loco	Maunsell U class 4P 2-6-0 No. 31803
Load	10 coaches, 334 tons tare, 355 tons gross
Crew	Unknown, possibly Basingstoke MPD
Weather	Fine
Recorder	DB

	miles	sched	mins	secs	speed	
Basingstoke	0.00	0.00	00	00		right time
Worting Jct	2.51	6.00	06	31	31½	
Wootton Box	4.75		10	24	38	
Steventon Box	6.20		12	20	48½	

	miles	sched	mins	secs	speed	
Waltham Box	7.35		13	43	50	
Roundwood Box	8.45		15	01	53½	
Micheldever	10.30		16	53	63½	
MP 59	11.20		17	42	65	
Weston Box	12.45		18	46	68	
MP 61	13.20		19	24	70	
Wallers Ash Box	13.95		20	02	72	
MP 63	15.20		22	48	19*	tsr half a mile
Winchester Jct	16.70	27.00	24	51	50	
Winchester City	18.80		27	08	62	
St Cross Box	20.03		28	19	67½	
Shawford Jct	21.27		29	17	68	
Shawford	21.92		29	59	65	
Allbrook Box	24.96		33	22	25*	to slow line
Eastleigh	25.76	38.00	35	30	13*	pass
	net time 32 minutes					

65.23

Date	Sunday 3rd October 1965
Train	9 am Spl Waterloo to Ilfracombe Exeter Flyer
Loco	Rebuilt Merchant Navy class 4-6-2 No. 35022 *Holland America Line*
Load	8 coaches 269 tons tare, 285 tons gross
Crew	Gordon Hooper and Robin Brown, Nine Elms MPD
Inspector	Smith
Recorder	DB
Weather	Cloudy and damp

	miles	sched	mins	secs	speed	
Waterloo	0.00	0.00	00	00		right time
Vauxhall	1.29		03	47	36/33*	sigs
Queens Road	2.81		05	45	56	
Clapham Junction	3.93	7.00	07	12	40*	
Earlsfield	5.58		09	17	57½	
Wimbledon	7.24		11	00	61	
Raynes Park	8.64		12	23	56*	sigs
New Malden	9.78		13	37	57*	sigs
Berrylands	10.98		14	48	54*	sigs SVO
Surbiton	12.04		15	59	63	
Hampton Court Jct	13.34	17.00	17	09	73	SVO
Esher	14.39		17	58	76	
Hersham	15.91		19	08	82	SVO
Walton	17.08		19	57	82	
Oatlands Box	18.10		20	43	81	
Weybridge	19.15		21	26	83	

	miles	sched	mins	secs	speed	
Byfleet & New Haw	20.40		22	22	85	
West Byfleet	21.68		23	16	83	
Woking	24.29		25	12	83	
Woking Jct	24.75	28.00	25	39	82	
Brookwood	27.99		27	53	79	
Pirbright Jct	29.65		29	09	76	
MP 31	31.00		30	14	75	
			sigs stop			
MP 31¾	31.75		31	14	0*	
			32	00		
Sturt Lane Jct	32.20		33	47		
Farnborough	33.20		35	31	36*	to slow line
Fleet	36.48		39	09	66/75½	
Winchfield	39.83		41	53	74	
Hook	42.16		43	45	77½	
Newnham Siding	43.70		44	54	80/23*	sigs
Basingstoke	47.75	58.00	49	31		8½ mins early
	0.00	0.00	00	00		1½ mins early
Worting Jct	2.55	5.00	04	59	42	slipping
MP 51	3.35		05	56	49½	
Oakley	4.63		07	21	64	
Overton	7.80		10	00	79	SVO
Whitchurch	11.35		12	37	84/81	
Hurstbourne	13.39		13	59	84	
MP 62½	14.85		15	04	80	
MP 64	16.35		16	18	84	
MP 65	17.35		17	04	41*	tsr quarter mile
Andover	18.60		18	32	54½	
Red Post Jct	19.50		19	55	64	
MP 68¾	21/10		20	55	67/74	
			sigs stop		0*	
Grateley	24.95		25	23		
			26	52		
Allington Box	27.85		31	28	64	
Porton	30.49		33	36	80/86	
Tunnel Junction	34.81		37	20	49*	
Salisbury	35.91	35.00	40	10	16*	pass
MP 85¼	37.61		43	27	38	
Wilton South	38.41	41.00	44	49	39*	SVO
Dinton	44.21		50	35	73/71½	
Tisbury	48.51		54	08	75	
Semley	53.51		58	10	70	
Gillingham	57.61		61	04	88	SVO

	miles	sched	mins	secs	speed	
MP 107½	59.86		62	42	75½	
MP 110	62.25		64	28	87	
Templecombe	64.41	65.30	65	51	80	
MP 113¼	65.61		66	52	72	
Milbourne Port	66.81		67	48	79	
Sherborne	70.30		70	21	90	SVO
Yeovil Junction	74.50	74.00	73	35	80/83	
Sutton Bingham	77.31		75	18	76	
MP 126¼	78.61		76	25	72½	
MP 130	82.36		79	07	88	
Crewkerne	83.86		80	07	81	
MP 133¼	85.61		81	38	67½	
Hewish Xing	86.51		82	21	76	
Chard Junction	91.91		86	08	86½	
MP 142	94.36		88	00	83	
Axminster	97.01	93.00	89	43	86	
MP 146¼	98.61		90	54	86½	
Seaton Junction	100.16		93	57	4*	sigs
MP 149½	101.86		98	48	38	
MP 150½	102.86		100	19	41½	
MP 151½	103.86		101	40	45	
MP 152½	104.86		102	55	48	
MP153½	105.86		104	09	50	
Honiton	107.06		105	14	74½	
MP 158	110.36		107	34	89	
Sidmouth Junction	111.81	108.00	108	28	86	
MP 161¼	113.81		110	02	65*	
Whimple	115.56		111	24	82½	
Broad Clyst	119.26		113	58	88	
Pinhoe	121.11		115	20	76	
Exmouth Junction	122.91	119.00	116	47	68	
Exeter Central	123.96	122.00	118	54		4½ mins early
	net time Waterloo to Basingstoke : 43½ minutes start to stop average Waterloo to signal stop: 60.99 mph Basingstoke to Exeter: net time 105 minutes actual start to stop average: 62.04 mph net start to stop average: 70.26 mph time from Salisbury to Sidmouth Junction: 68 minutes 18 seconds net time Salisbury to Sidmouth Junction: 61 minutes, equivalent to 63 minutes start to stop					

65.24

Date	Sunday 3rd October 1965
Train	2.55 pm Ilfracombe to Waterloo Exeter Flyer
Loco	Rebuilt Merchant Navy class 4-6-2 No. 35022 *Holland America Line*
Load	8 coaches 269 tons tare, 285 tons gross
Crew	Gordon Hooper and Robin Brown, Nine Elms MPD
Inspector	Smith
Recorder	DB
Weather	Rain

	miles	sched	mins	secs	speed	
Exeter Central	0.00	0.00	00	00		right time
Exmouth Junction	1.05	3.00	03	42	30	
Pinhoe	2.80		05	52	61½	
Broad Clyst	4.70		07	27	75	
Whimple	8.35		10	44	59	
MP 161¼	10.15		12	35	54½	
Sidmouth Junction	12.15		15	30	20*	sigs
MP 158	13.45	21.00	17	13	61/55½	
Honiton	16.75		20	88	59	
MP153½	17.95		21	55	55½	
MP 150	21.45		24	50	87	
Seaton Junction	23.65		26	43	62*	
MP 146¼	25,15		27	52	86	
Axminster	26.90	38.00	29	07	80	
Chard Junction	32.00		33	02	75/79	
Hewish Xing	37.45		37	14	73	
MP 133¼	38.25		37	53	72½	
Crewkerne	40.10		39	18	85/88	
MP 128	43.60		41	42	82	
MP 126¼	45.35		43	02	75	
Sutton Bingham	46.65		44	06	83	
Yeovil Junction	48.90	59.00	45	43	76/81	
Sherborne	53.40		49	08	79	
MP 115½	56.10		51	16	61½	
Milbourne Port	57.15		52	16	70½/69	
MP 113¼	58.35		53	14	70	
Templecombe	59.55	70.00	54	11	83	
MP 110	61.60		55	34	87	
MP 107½	64.10		57	32	70	
Gillingham	66.40		59	14	88½	
Semley	70.45		62	25	69	
Tisbury	75.45		66	14	82	max
Dinton	79.75		69	39	72/81	
Wilton South	85.55	95.00	74	24	43*	

	miles	sched	mins	secs	speed	
MP 85¼	86.35		75	38	48½/56	
Salisbury	88.05	100.00	78	58	5*	sigs, 21 mins early
Tunnel Jct	89.15		82	00	44½	
			sigs stop			
MP 81½	90.25		84	24	0*	
			89	32		
Porton	93.50		95	36	51	
Allington Box	96.15		98	33	60	
Grateley	99.00		101	16	68	
MP 68¾	104.00		104	15	86	
Red Post Jct	103.90		104	58	80	
Andover	105.40		106	08	71*	
MP 65	107.75		107	48	36*	tsr quarter mile
MP 62½	109.25		113	11	14*	sigs
Hurstbourne	110.65		114	53	59½	
Whitchurch	112.55		116	52	62½	
Overton	116.15		120	10	68	
Oakley	119.35		123	03	69/72	
Worting Jct	121.45	132.00	125	12	14*/36	tsr 1½ miles
Basingstoke	123.95	136.00	133	16		2¾ mins early
	0.00	0.00	00	00		right time
Newnham Siding	4.05		05	37	68½	
Hook	5.59		06	53	74	
Winchfield	7.92		10	09	29*	to slow line
Fleet	11.27		14	06	70½	
Farnborough	14.55		16	43	79½	
Sturt Lane Jct	15.60		17	30	80	
MP 31	16.75		18	26	78/79	
Pirbright Jct	18.26		19	34	77½*	
Brookwood	19.76		20	47	79½/81	
Woking Jct	23.00	32.00	24	28	22*	to fast line
Woking	23.46		25	27	36	
West Byfleet	26.07		28	30	69	
Byfleet & New Haw	27.35		29	32	76	
Weybridge	28.60		30	34	76	
Oatlands Box	29.63		31	19	77½	
Walton	30.67		32	07	80	
Hersham	31.84		32	57	82	
Esher	33.36		34	08	83	
Hampton Court Jct	34.41	42.00	34	52	81	
Surbiton	35.71		35	50	83	
Berrylands	36.77		36	38	80	
New Malden	37.97		37	44	61*	

	miles	sched	mins	secs	speed	
Raynes Park	39.12		38	50	58½	
Wimbledon	40.51		40	15	61½	
Earlsfield	42.17		41	54	61	
Clapham Junction	43.82	52.00	43	59	40*	
Queens Road	44.94		45	32	56½	
Vauxhall	46.46		47	38	35*	
Waterloo	47.75	59.00	51	29		7½ mins early
net times:	actual time Sidmouth Junction to Salisbury 63 minutes 28 seconds equivalent start to stop time 61½ minutes Exeter to Basingstoke 110 minutes (67.61 mph) Basingstoke to Waterloo: 44¾ minutes start to stop average Exeter to signal stop :64.16 mph					

65.25

Date	Saturday 9th October 1965
Train	835 am Waterloo to Weymouth
Loco	Rebuilt Battle of Britain class 4-6-2 No. 34071 *601 Squadron*
Load to Southampton	8 coaches and 2 vans, 318 tons tare, 345 tons gross
Load from Southampton	8 coaches and 1 van, 294 tons tare, 320 tons gross
Crew	Gordon Porter and Tom Moult, Nine Elms MPD
Also on Footplate	Brian Smith
Recorder	DB

	miles	sched	mins	secs	speed	
Waterloo	0.00	0.00	00	00		right time
Vauxhall	1.29		03	04	41½	
Queens Road	2.81		04	42	57½	
Clapham Junction	3.93	7.00	06	09	45*	
Earlsfield	5.58		08	11	56	
Wimbledon	7.24		09	53	61	
Raynes Park	8.64		11	11	65½	
New Malden	9.78		12	13	68	
Berrylands	10.98		13	15	70	
Surbiton	12.04	18.00	14	49		record time
	0.00	0.00	00	00		slipping
Hampton Court Jct	1.30	3.00	03	03	47½	
Esher	2.35		04	14	61	
Hersham	3.87		05	44	65	
Walton	5.04		06	46	67½	
Oatlands Box	6.08		07	41	68	
Weybridge	7.11		08	31	72	
Byfleet & New Haw	8.36		09	35	76	
West Byfleet	9.68		10	35	74½	
Woking	12.25	15.30	13	28		
	0.00	0.00	00	00		right time

	miles	sched	mins	secs	speed	
Woking Jct	0.46		01	52	33	
Brookwood	3.70		06	06	62½	
Pirbright Jct	5.20		07	36	66	
MP 31	6.71		08	50	69	
Sturt Lane Jct	7.86		10	12	40*	tsr one mile
Farnborough	8.91		11	54	38*	to slow line
Fleet	12.19		15	40	66/67½	
			sigs stop			
MP 38½	14.21		18	28	0*	
			19	12		
Winchfield	15.54		22	55	27*	to fast line
Hook	17.87		26	13	57	
Newnham Siding	19.41		27	40	70½/74/*	sigs
Basingstoke	24.29	37.00	32	23		
	0.00	0.00	00	00		right time
Worting Jct	2.51	5.30	04	59	51	
Wootton Box	4.75		07	24	56½	
Steventon Box	6.20		10	44	17*	tsr half mile
Waltham Box	7.35		12	17	51	
Roundwood Box	8.45		13	32	61½	
Micheldever	10.30		15	13	74	
MP 59	11.35		16	00	78	
Weston Box	12.45		16	48	83	
MP 61	13.35		17	24	85	
Wallers Ash Box	13.95		17	49	87	
MP 63	15.35		18	44	93	
Winchester Jct	16.70	22.00	19	34	97	
Winchester City	18.80	25.30	22	08		
	0.00	0.00	00	00		right time
St Cross Box	1.23		02	26	58½	
Shawford Jct	2.47		03	27	71½	
Shawford	3.12		04	06	76	
Allbrook Box	6.06		06	17	82	
Eastleigh	6.96	10.00	06	56	80	
Swaythling	9.22		08	39	84	
St Denys	10.63		09	44	71	
Northam Jct	11.61	15.30	10	55	18*/30	
Southampton Central	12.75	19.00	13	48		5¼ mins early
	0.00	0.00	00	00		right time
Millbrook	0.90		03	08	30	
Redbridge	2.65	5.00	06	01	45½	
Totton	3.30		06	49	52	
Lyndhurst Road	6.15		09	58	56½	

	miles	sched	mins	secs	speed	
MP 86	6.75		10	32	63/65½	
			sigs stop			
Beaulieu Road	8.85		13	06	0*	
			23	16		
Woodfidley Box	10.45		27	05	55	
MP 90½	11.25		28	00	56	
MP 92	12.75		29	29	63	
Brockenhurst	13.55	21.30	30	56		
	0.00	0.00	00	00		
Lymington Junction	0.95	2.30	02	48	38	
MP 94½	1.70		03	53	41	
Sway	2.75		05	11	58	
New Milton	5.75		07	49	72/70½	
MP 100	7.20		08	59	77½	
Hinton Admiral	8.25		10	01	53*	sigs
MP 103	10.20		12	04	55*	sigs
Christchurch	11.55		13	24	60	
Pokesdown	13.50		15	27	51	
Boscombe	14.05		16	12	42	
Bournemouth Central	15.25	23.00	18	34		3 minutes late
net times	Woking to Basingstoke 22¾ minutes Basingstoke to Winchester 19 minutes Brockenhurst to Bournemouth 16½ minutes					

65.26

	Wednesday 1st December 1965
Train	6 pm Waterloo to Salisbury
Loco	Rebuilt West Country class 4-6-2 No. 34013 *Okehampton*
Load	6 coaches, 201 tons tare, 215 tons gross
Crew	Frank Matthews and Fireman Davis, Nine Elms MPD
Recorder	DB

	miles	sched	mins	secs	speed	
Basingstoke	0.00	0.00	00	00		9¼ mins late
Worting Jct	2.55	5.30	04	08	58½	
MP 51	3.35		04	52	63	full regulator and 30% cut off all the way to Hurstbourne
Oakley	4.63		06	02	74½	
MP 53½	5.80		06	46	77	
Overton	7.80		08	28	87	
Whitchurch	11.35		10	52	95	
MP 60	12.35		11	21	97	
Hurstbourne	13.39		12	02	100	
MP 62½	14.85		12	54	93/95	eased
MP 64¼	16.60		14	42	19*/36	tsr half mile

	miles	sched	mins	secs	speed	
Andover	18.60	23.00	18	28		
	0.00	0.00	00	00		3¼ mins late
Red Post Jct	1.30		03	15	50	
MP 68¾	2.50		04	28	64/69	
Grateley	6.35		08	01	27*	tsr half mile
Allington Box	9.25		12	39	64	
Porton	11.90		14	42	89	
MP 81	14.75		16	30	95	
Tunnel Jct	16.21	19.30	18	07	52*	
Salisbury	17.31	22.00	20	26		1¾ mins late
net times	Basingstoke to Andover: 16¼ minutes Andover to Salisbury: 17¾ minutes Basingstoke to Andover start to stop average: 60.43 mph					

66.01

Date	Saturday 22nd January 1966
Train	1030 am Waterloo to Weymouth
Loco	Rebuilt Merchant Navy class 4-6-2 No. 35022 *Holland America Line*
Load	4 coaches, 134 tons tare, 145 tons gross
Crew	H. Watts, Weymouth MPD
Recorder	DB

	miles	sched	mins	secs	speed	
Bournemouth Central	0.00	0.00	00	00		15¾ mins late
Gasworks Jct	2.20	5.00	04	35	48/45*	
Branksome	2.65		05	08	39*	
Parkstone	3.96		06	40	61½/68	
Poole	5.76	10.00	09	06		
	0.00	0.00	00	00		14½ mins late
Hamworthy Jct	2.23		04	28	45/43*	
MP 117	3.23		05	39	68½	
MP 118	4.23		06	30	74	
Holton Heath	4.99		07	06	77½	
MP 120	6.23		08	06	73/30*	sigs
Wareham	7.10	10.00	09	38		
	0.00	0.00	00	00		13½ mins late
Worgret Jct	1.09	3.00	02	24	49	
MP 123	2.22		03	26	63½	
MP 124	3.22		04	18	72	
MP 125	4.22		05	08	76	
Wool	4.99		05	48	81	
MP 127	6.22		06	42	80	
MP 128	7.22		07	27	80½	
MP 129	8.22		08	13	77½	

	miles	sched	mins	secs	speed	
Moreton	9.44		09	12	76	
MP 131	10.22		09	43	82	
MP 132	11.22		10	27	83	
MP 133	12.22		11	11	80	
MP 134	13.22		12	00	73	
Dorchester South	15.02	18.00	14	12		9¾ mins late
	start to stop average Wareham to Dorchester: 63.47 mph net time Poole to Wareham 9¼ minutes					

66.02

Date	Wednesday 16th February 1966
Train	1035 pm Waterloo to Weymouth
Loco	Rebuilt West Country class 4-6-2 No. 34008 *Padstow*
Load	3 coaches and 9 vans, 342 tons tare, 375 tons gross to Woking
	3 coaches and 10 vans from Woking, 356 tons tare, 385 tons gross
Crew	Gordon Porter and Tom Moult, Nine Elms MPD
Also on Footplate	Brian Smith
Recorder	DB

	miles	sched	mins	secs	speed	
Waterloo	0.00	0.00	00	00		right time
Vauxhall	1.29		03	24	39	
Queens Road	2.81		05	07	51/41*	sigs
Clapham Junction	3.93	7.00	06	40	52/48*	
Earlsfield	5.58		08	34	59	
Wimbledon	7.24		10	10	64	
Raynes Park	8.64		11	24	69	
New Malden	9.78		12	21	74½	
Berrylands	10.98		13	18	77½	
Surbiton	12.04		14	09	80	
Hampton Court Jct	13.34	18.30	15	06	83½	
Esher	14.39		15	52	85	
Hersham	15.91		17	00	86	
Walton	17.08		17	49	83	
Oatlands Box	18.12		18	34	80	
Weybridge	19.15		19	19	82	
Byfleet & New Haw	20.40		20	17	82½	
West Byfleet	21.68		21	14	78/*30	sigs to slow line
Woking	24.29	31.00	24	38		
	0.00	00.00	00	00		4½ mins late
Woking Jct	0.46		01	50	24½/46	
Brookwood	3.70		07	14	32*	sigs
Pirbright Jct	5.20		09	29	51	
MP 31	6.71		10	58	60	

	miles	sched	mins	secs	speed	
Sturt Lane Jct	7.86		12	07	67½	
Farnborough	8.91		13	02	69	
Fleet	12.19		15	43	76/79	
Winchfield	15.54		18	19	77½/74	
Hook	17.87		20	11	77/75	
Newnham Siding	19.41		21	24	78/27*	sigs to fast line
Basingstoke	23.46	38.00	25	54		
	0.00	0.00	00	00		3 mins early
Worting Jct	2.51	5.30	05	32	42	
MP 51	3.20		06	24	50/55½	SVO
Wootton Box	4.75		08	31	32*	tsr
Steventon Box	6.20		12	41	17*	tsr
Waltham Box	7.35		14	51	40½	
Roundwood Box	8.45		16	24	57	
Micheldever	10.30		18	12	70½	
Weston Box	12.45		19	54	79	
Wallers Ash Box	13.95		21	00	85	
MP 63	15.35		21	57	91	
Winchester Jct	16.70	23.30	22	51	90	
Winchester City	18.80	26.30	25	21		
	0.00	0.00	00	00		1 min late
St Cross Box	1.23		02	41	53	
Shawford Jct	2.47		03	48	64	priming
Shawford	3.12		04	32	69	
MP 71½	5.05		06	00	78	
Allbrook Box	6.06		07	30	23*	to slow line
			sigs stop			
MP 73	6.55		09	00	0*	
			12	56		
Eastleigh	6.96	11.00	14	38		4½ mins late
net times	Waterloo to Woking 24 minutes Woking to Basingstoke 23½ minutes Basingstoke to Winchester 20 minutes Winchester to Eastleigh 9½ minutes					

Date	Friday 4th March 1966
Train	830 am Waterloo to Weymouth
Loco	Rebuilt West Country class 4-6-2 No. 34047 *Callington*
Load	11 coaches, 368½ tons tare, 400 tons gross
Crew	Gordon Hooper and Ray McQuade Nine Elms MPD
Weather	Misty and damp
Recorder	DB

	miles	sched	mins	secs	speed	
Waterloo	0.00	0.00	00	00		right time
Vauxhall	1.29		03	49	33	slipping
Queens Road	2.81		05	42	51	
Clapham Junction	3.93	7.00	07	22	40*	
Earlsfield	5.58		09	36	51	
Wimbledon	7.24		11	25	57	
Raynes Park	8.64		12	46	63	
New Malden	9.78		13	53	59*	sigs
Berrylands	10.98		15	06	61	
Surbiton	12.04		16	08	63½	
Hampton Court Jct	13.34	18.00	17	20	68½	
Esher	14.39		18	14	73	
Hersham	15.91		19	30	74	
Walton	17.08		20	26	73	
Oatlands Box	18.10		21	18	71	
Weybridge	19.15		22	08	74	
Byfleet and New Haw	20.40		23	11	78	
West Byfleet	21.68		24	10	76	
Woking	24.29		26	43	21*	sigs
Woking Jct	24.75	28.00	27	45	27*	sigs
Brookwood	27.99		32	48	47	slipping
Pirbright Jct	29.49		34	46	50	slipping
MP 31	31.00		36	27	51	slipping
Sturt Lane Jct	32.15		37	45	59	
Farnborough	33.20		38	45	64½	slipping
Fleet	36.48		41	39	70/71½	
Winchfield	39.83		44	56	43*	tsr/SVO
Hook	42.16		48	33	23*	to slow line
Newnham Siding	43.70		51	10	49½/57½	
Basingstoke	47.75		56	42	23*/15*	sigs to fast line/tsr
Worting Jct	50.26	60.00	61	25	48/50	
Wootton Box	52.50		64	11	44*	tsr
Steventon Box	53.95		68	15	17*	tsr
Waltham Box	55.10		70	48	37½	
Roundwood Box	56.20		72	23	53	

	miles	sched	mins	secs	speed	
Micheldever	58.05		74	14	67½	
Weston Box	60.20		75	58	79	
Wallers Ash Box	61.70		77	05	84	
MP 63	63.10		78	01	88/90	
Winchester Jct	64.45	76.00	78	56	89	
Winchester	66.55		80	26	86	
St Cross Box	67.72		81	18	89	
Shawford Jct	68.96		82	02	92	
Shawford	69.61		82	33	93	
Allbrook Box	72.55		84	34	54*	sigs
Eastleigh	73.45	84.30	85	45	43*	tsr
Swaythling	75.71		88	32	61	
St Denys	77.12		89	50	66½	
Northam Jct	78.20	90.00	90	58	12*/33	
Southampton Central	79.24	93.30	93	54		½ min late
			net time 74 minutes			

66.04

Date	Tuesday 8th March 1966
Train	530 pm Waterloo to Bournemouth
Loco	Battle of Britain class 4-6-2 No. 34057 *Biggin Hill*
Load	11 coaches 374 tons tare, 410 tons gross
Crew	Gordon Porter and Tom Moult, Nine Elms MPD
Weather	Dry
Recorder	DB

	miles	sched	mins	secs	speed	
Waterloo	0.00	0.00	00	00		½ min late/WL
Vauxhall	1.29		04	08	36	priming
Queens Road	2.81		05	54	49½/51	
Clapham Junction	3.93	7.00	07	26	46*	
Earlsfield	5.58		09	32	53	
Wimbledon	7.24		11	22	56½	
Raynes Park	8.64		12	45	63	
New Malden	9.78		13	49	66	
Berrylands	10.98		14	53	70	
Surbiton	12.04		15	48	73	
Hampton Court Jct	13.34	18.00	16	52	76	
Esher	14.39		17	41	80	
Hersham	15.91		18	53	74*	
Walton	17.08		20	03	13*	tsr half mile
Oatlands Box	18.12		24	04	31½	
Weybridge	19.15		25	30	50	
Byfleet & New Haw	20.40		26	53	66½	

	miles	sched	mins	secs	speed	
West Byfleet	21.68		28	02	67½	
Woking	24.29		30	22	70	
Woking Jct	24.75	28.00	30	44	70½	
Brookwood	27.99		33	30	72½	
Pirbright Jct	29.49		34	52	70	
MP 31	31.00		36	08	68½	160 lb steam
Sturt Lane Jct	32.15		37	06	70	
Farnborough	33.20		38	02	71½	
Fleet	36.48		40	44	74	
Winchfield	39.83		44	09	43*	tsr
			sigs stop			
MP 41	41.00		46	44	0*	
			54	12		
Hook	42.16		57	52	43*	sigs to slow line
Newnham Siding	43.70		60	15	49/58	
Basingstoke	47.75	63.00	65	26		SVO
	0.00	0.00	00	00		5½ mins late
Worting Jct	2.51	5.30	05	25	44½/53	SVO
Wootton Box	4.75		08	12	46*	tsr
Steventon Box	6.20		11	46	11*	tsr
Waltham Box	7.35		13	49	45½	
Roundwood Box	8.45		15	17	58½	
Micheldever	10.30		17	04	71	
Weston Box	12.45		18	46	80	
Wallers Ash Box	13.95		19	50	83	
MP 63	15.35		20	48	87	
WinchesterJct	16.70	21.30	21	43	90	
Winchester City	18.80	25.00	23	57		
	0.00	0.00	00	00		5 mins late
St Cross Box	1.23		03	05	45½	
Shawford Jct	2.47		04	21	56	
Shawford	3.12		05	08	61½	
MP 71½	5.05		06	54	64	
Allbrook Box	6.06		08	22	24*/33	to slow line
Eastleigh	6.96	11.00	10	37		4½ mins late
net times	WL: Windsor line start					
	Waterloo to Basingstoke 45 minutes					
	Basingstoke to Winchester 20 minutes					

66.05

Date	Thursday 10th March 1966
Train	530 pm Waterloo to Bournemouth
Loco	Rebult Battle of Britain class 4-6-2 No. 34071 *601 Squadron*
Load	11 coaches 374 tons tare, 410 tons gross
Crew	Gordon Porter and Tom Moult, Nine Elms MPD
Also on Footplate	Brian Smith to Basingstoke
Weather	Rain
Recorder	DB

	miles	sched	mins	secs	speed	
Waterloo	0.00	0.00	00	00	slipping	¼ min late
Vauxhall	1.29		03	20	41	
Queens Road	2.81		04	56	57	
Clapham Junction	3.93	7.00	06	24	46*	
Earlsfield	5.58		08	24	55½	
Wimbledon	7.24		10	07	60	
Raynes Park	8.64		11	25	64½	
New Malden	9.78		12	26	70	
Berrylands	10.98		13	27	73	
Surbiton	12.04		14	21	76	
Hampton Court Jct	13.34	18.00	15	22	79½	
Esher	14.39		16	09	80/79	
Hersham	15.91		17	21	80	
Walton	17.08		18	19	14*	tsr
Oatlands Box	18.12		20	41	38	
Weybridge	19.15		22	01	54	
Byfleet & New Haw	20.40		23	21	67½	
West Byfleet	21.68		24	29	68½	
Woking	24.29		26	48	70	
Woking Jct	24.75	28.00	27	09	70	
Brookwood	27.99		29	58	70½	
Pirbright Jct	29.49		31	22	67½	160 lb steam
MP 31	31.00		32	39	63	
Sturt Lane Jct	32.15		33	46	64	
Farnborough	33.20		34	44	65	
Fleet	36.48		37	44	65½	
Winchfield	39.83		41	42	35*	tsr
			sigs stop			
MP 41	41.00		44	40	0*	
			49	04		
Hook	42.16		52	28	30*	sigs to slow line
Newnham Siding	43.70		54	45	54/63/3*	sigs
Basingstoke	47.75	63.00	61	47		
	0.00	0.00	00	00		1½ mins late

	miles	sched	mins	secs	speed	
Worting Jct	2.51	5.30	05	14	43/47½	
Wootton Box	4.75		08	19	36*	tsr
Steventon Box	6.20		11	55	17*	tsr
Waltham Box	7.35		13	43	47	
Roundwood Box	8.45		15	05	60/64	
Micheldever	10.30		17	16	37*	sigs
Weston Box	12.45		19	30	65½	
Wallers Ash Box	13.95		20	47	76	
MP 63	15.35		21	49	83	
WinchesterJct	16.70	21.30	22	47	85	
Winchester City	18.80	25.00	24	57		
	0.00	0.00	00	00	slipping	1¼ mins late
St Cross Box	1.23		02	35	53½	
Shawford Jct	2.47		03	40	66	
Shawford	3.12		04	19	74	
MP 71½	5.05		05	47	78	
Allbrook Box	6.06		07	04	30*/41½	to slow line
Eastleigh	6.96	11.00	08	47		1 min early
net times	WL: Windsor line start Waterloo to Basingstoke 45 minutes Basingstoke to Winchester 20 minutes					

66.06

Date	Friday 11th March 1966
Train	530 pm Waterloo to Bournemouth
Loco	Rebuilt Merchant Navy class 4-6-2 No. 35003 *Royal Mail*
Load	11 coaches 374 tons tare, 410 tons gross
Crew	Gordon Porter and Tom Moult, Nine Elms MPD
Recorder	Richard Jolliffe

	miles	sched	mins	secs	speed	
Basingstoke	0.00	0.00	00	00		
Worting Jct	2.51	5.30	04	51	55/59½	
Wootton Box	4.75		07	14	56	
Steventon Box	6.20		10	46	18*	tsr
Waltham Box	7.35		12	16	55	
Roundwood Box	8.45		13	30	61	
Micheldever	10.30		15	06	76	
Weston Box	12.45		16	40	84	
Wallers Ash Box	13.95		17	41	90	
Winchester Jct	16.70	21.30	19	28	96	
Winchester City	18.80	25.00	21	49		
net time	18 minutes					

66.07

Date	Friday 1st April 1966
Train	530 pm Waterloo to Bournemouth
Loco	Rebuilt West Country class 4-6-2 No.34021 *Dartmoor*
Load	11 coaches 374 tons tare, 410 tons gross
Crew	Les Cummings and Tom Moult, Nine Elms MPD
Weather	Moderate SW wind
Recorder	DB

	miles	sched	mins	secs	speed	
Basingstoke	0.00	0.00	00	00		3 mins late
Worting Jct	2.51	5.30	05	28	42	
Wootton Box	4.75		08	24	48/52	
Steventon Box	6.20		10	13	40*	tsr
Waltham Box	7.35		11	58	37*	tsr
Roundwood Box	8.45		13	24	56	
Micheldever	10.30		15	10	72½	30% cut off
MP 59	11.35		15	57	78	
Weston Box	12.45		16	48	83	
MP 61	13.35		17	25	85	
Wallers Ash Box	13.95		17	51	87	
MP 63	15.35		18	45	94/97	22% cut off
Winchester Jct	16.70	21.30	19	35	95	
Winchester City	18.80	25.00	21	54		
	0.00	0.00	00	00		½ min late
St Cross Box	1.23		02	43	52	
Shawford Jct	2.47		03	50	65½	
Shawford	3.12		04	32	70½	SVO
MP 71½	5.05		06	05	76	SVO
Allbrook Box	6.06		07	26	33*/37½	to slow lline
Eastleigh	6.96	11.00	09	20		1¼ mins early
net time	Basingstoke to Winchester: 18½ minutes					

66.08

Date	Saturday 2nd April 1966
Train	855 am Spl Waterloo to Exmouth
Loco	Rebuilt West Country class 4-6-2 No. 34032 *Camelford*
Load	9 coaches, 302 tons tare, 325 tons gross
Crew	Bill Plumb and fireman Mortlock Nine Elms MPD
Inspector	Neill
Weather	Rain
Recorder	DB

	miles	sched	mins	secs	speed	
Waterloo	0.00	0.00	00	00		right time
Vauxhall	1.29		03	28	37	

	miles	sched	mins	secs	speed	
Queens Road	2.81		05	13	52½	
Clapham Junction	3.93	7.00	07	25	20*	sigs to slow line
Earlsfield	5.58		10	11	49	
Wimbledon	7.24		13	16	18*	sigs to fast line
Raynes Park	8.64		15	10	54	
New Malden	9.78		16	22	61½	
Berrylands	10.98		17	35	53*	sigs
Surbiton	12.04		18	44	61	
Hampton Court Jct	13.34	18.00	19	56	67	
Esher	14.39		20	50	71½	
Hersham	15.91		22	08	74	
Walton	17.08		23	04	74½	
Oatlands Box	18.10		23	54	72½	
Weybridge	19.15		24	42	75	
Byfleet & New Haw	20.40		25	45	78	
West Byfleet	21.68		26	45	76	
			sigs stop			
MP 23½	23.50		30	22	0*	
			30	34		
Woking	24.29		32	30	33	
Woking Jct	24.75	28.00	33	12	41	
Brookwood	27.99		37	03	59	
Pirbright Jct	29.65		38	39	61½	
MP 31	31.00		40	01	62½	
Sturt Lane Jct	32.20		41	06	68	
Farnborough	33.20		41	59	71	
Fleet	36.48		44	39	75/77½	
Winchfield	39.83		47	45	30*/20*	sigs/tsr
Hook	42.16		51	51	52½	
Newnham Siding	43.70		53	26	65/71½	
Basingstoke	47.75		57	22	25*	sigs/tsr
Worting Jct	50.30	52.00	61	20	50	
MP 51	51.05		62	11	54½	
Oakley	52.38		63	33	65½	
Overton	55.55		66	11	76	
Whitchurch	59.10		68	58	78	
Hurstbourne	61.14		70	23	83	
MP 62½	62.60		71	30	79	
MP 65	65.10		73	22	82	
Andover	66.35		74	18	83	
Red Post Jct	67.65		75	21	78	
MP 68¾	68.85		76	14	80	
Grateley	72.70		79	18	70/76	

	miles	sched	mins	secs	speed	
Allington Box	75.60		81	42	65	
Idmiston	77.62		85	55	14*	tsr
Porton	78.25		86	38	59	
MP 81	81.10		88	52	80	
Tunnel Jct	82.56		90	20	50*	
Salisbury	83.66	82.00	92	48		
net time	75 minutes					

66.09

Date	Sunday 3rd April 1966
Train	437 pm Bournemouth to Waterloo
Loco	Rebuilt West Country class 4-6-2 No. 34005 *Barnstaple*
Load	10 Pullmans and 1 van, 424½ tons tare, 455 tons gross
Crew	Reuben Hendicott and Bill Stanley. Nine Elms MPD
Timed by	Terry Jackson

	miles	sched	mins	secs	speed	
Southampton	0.00	0.00	00	00		
Northam Jct	1.05	4.00	03	57	18*	
St Denys	2.11		05	46	40	
Swaythling	3.45		07	37	51½	
Eastleigh	5.80	11.00	10	05	59	
Allbrook Box	6.66		11	00	52½*	sigs
Shawford	9.61		14	00	62	
Shawford Jct	10.46		14	44	63	
Winchester City	12.70		16	58	65/63½	
Winchester Jct	14.80		18	58	64½/63	
Wallers Ash Box	17.55		21	30	63½	
Weston Box	19.05		22	53	63	
Micheldever	21.20		24	55	61	
Roundwood Box	23.05		28	10	18½*	tsr
Waltham Box	24.15		31	22	28½	
Wootton Box	26.75		34	49	56/61/58*	
Worting Jct	28.98	40.30	37	07	59/58½	slow line
Basingstoke	31.50		39	31	67/80/75	
Hook	37.08		44	05	76/77	
Winchfield	39.41		46	55	23½*	to fast line
Fleet	42.76		50	42	67½	
Bramshot Halt	43.55		51	28	71	
Farnborough	46.05		53	26	75	
Sturt Lane Jct	47.05		54	15	76	
MP 31	48.25		55	13	75/82	
Brookwood	51.25		57	29	77/73½	
Woking Jct	54.50	70.30	60	05	76	

	miles	sched	mins	secs	speed	
Woking	54.95		60	25	77	
West Byfleet	57.56		62	23	83	
Byfleet & New Haw	58.84		63	19	84	
Weybridge	60.09		64	17	82/77	
Walton	62.16		65	50	80	
Hersham	63.33		66	41	79	
Esher	64.85		67	54	76½	
Hampton Court Jct.	65.90		68	45	75	
Surbiton	67.20		69	49	73/70	
Berrylands	68.26		70	42	72	
New Malden	69.46		72	35	25½*	tsr
Raynes Park	70.60		74	30	40	
Wimbledon	72.05		76	08	56/62½	
Earlsfield	73.66		77	49	60	
Clapham Junction	75.31	89.30	79	42	42*	
Queens Road	76.43		81	22	51	
Vauxhall	77.93		83	03	39*	
Waterloo	79.24	96.30	86	25		
net time	75 minutes					

66.10

Date	Wednesday 1st June 1966
Train	530 pm Weymouth to Waterloo
Engine	Rebuilt West Country class 4-6-2 No. 34001 *Exeter*
Load	10 coaches and 2 vans 430 tns gross (estimated)
Driver	Roy Sloper, Eastleigh MPD
Recorder	Richard Jolliffe

	miles	sched	mins	secs	speed	
Southampton	0.00	0.00	00	00		
Northam jct	1.05	3.00	03	33	15*	
St Denys	2.11		05	24	37½	
Swaythling	3.45		07	22	46	
Eastleigh	5.80	11.00	09	58	57	
Allbrook Box	6.66		10	48	60½	
Shawford	9.61		13	38	63½	
Shawford Jct	10.48		14	23	63	
St Cross Box	11.50		15	23	64	
Winchester City	12.70		16	36	66	
Winchester Jct	14.80		18	32	68½	SVO
Wallers Ash Box	17.55		21	50	41*	sigs
Weston Box	19.05		23	32	53½	
Micheldever	21.20		25	45	58	
Roundwood Box	23.05		27	49	52½	

	miles	sched	mins	secs	speed	
Waltham Box	24.15		29	16	35*	tsr
Steventon Box	25.30		32	03	23½	tsr
Wootton Box	26.75		34	13	50½	
Worting Jct	28.98	39.30	36	29	68	
Basingstoke	31.50		38	30	82	
Newnham Siding	35.55				89/82	
Hook	37.08		42	28	84	
			sigs stop		0*	
Winchfield	39.41		47	29	44	
Fleet	42.76		50	54	69/75	
Farnborough	46.05		53	43	*	
MP 31	48.25		57	48	19*	tsr
Brookwood	51.25		60	53	68	
Woking	54.95	63.30	63	43	82/85	
West Byfleet	57.56		65	39	83½	
Byfleet & New Haw	58.84		66	33	86	
Weybridge	60.09		67	29	79½	
Walton	62.16		69	06	75½	
Hersham	63.33		70	15	30*/19*	tsr
Esher	64.85		73	22	45	
Surbiton	67.20		76	11	61	
New Malden	69.46		78	18	66	
Raynes Park	70.60		79	22	63½	
Wimbledon	72.05		80	33	62	
Earlsfield	73.66		82	19	63½	
Clapham Junction	75.31	89.30	84	10	42*	
Queens Road	76.43		85	48	53½/19½*	sigs
Vauxhall	77.93		87	46	19*	sigs
Waterloo	79.24	96.30	91	30		
net time	72½ minutes					

66.11

Date	Thursday 16th June 1966
Train	635 pm Salisbury to Waterloo
Loco	Rebuilt West Country class 4-6-2 No. 34009 *Lyme Regis*
Load	4 coaches and 5 vans, 260 tons tare, 260 tons gross
Driver	Les Cummings, Nine Elms MPD
Recorder	DB

	miles	sched	mins	secs	speed	
Basingstoke	0.00	0.00	00	00		1 minute late/SVO
MP 46	1.75		02	58	62½	
Newnham Siding	4.05		04	55	76	
Hook	5.59		06	04	82	

	miles	sched	mins	secs	speed	
MP 41	6.75		06	56	84	
Winchfield	7.92		07	45	87	
MP 38	9.75		08	59	93	
Fleet	11.27		09	57	92/93	20% cut off
MP 35	12.75		10	55	90	
Farnborough	14.55		12	10	86	
Sturt Lane Jct	15.60		12	53	87	
MP 31	16.75		13	43	86	
Pirbright Jct	18.26		14	40	90/91	
Brookwood	19.76		15	44	90	
MP 27	20.75		16	26	84	
Woking Jct	23.00		18	56	39*/50	sigs
Woking	23.46	26.00	19	48		
	0.00	0.00	00	00		2 mins early
West Byfleet	2.61		03	49	72	
Byfleet & New Haw	3.89		04	48	81	
Weybridge	5.14		05	48	78	
Oatlands Box	6.17		06	35	76	
Walton	7.21		07	30	63*/21*	tsr
Hersham	8.38		10	05	41	
Esher	9.90		11	53	64	
Hampton Court Jct	10.95	14.00	12	51	68	
Surbiton	12.25		13	58	73	
Berrylands	13.31		14	51	72	
New Malden	14.51		15	54	67	
Raynes Park	15.65		16	55	68/69	
Wimbledon	17.10		18	08	66	
Earlsfield	18.71		19	36	68½	
Clapham Junction	20.36	26.00	21	28	48*	
Queens Road	21.48		22	52	63	
Vauxhall	22.98		24	15	45*/23*	sigs
Waterloo	24.29	33.00	27	18		7¾ mins early
	start to stop average Basingstoke to Woking: 71.09 mph average speed Hook to Brookwood: 88.01 mph Basingstoke to Woking: net time 19 minutes Woking to Waterloo: net time 24 minutes					

66.12

Date	Monday 11th July 1966
Train	6 pm Waterloo to Salisbury
Loco	Rebuilt West Country class 4-6-2 No. 34026 *Yes Tor*
Load	9 coaches, 301 tons tare 325 tons gross
Crew	Fred Hoare and Pete Allen, Salisbury MPD
Recorder	DB

	miles	sched	mins	secs	speed	
Waterloo	0.00	0.00	00	00		½ min late
Vauxhall	1.29		03	34	39	
Queens Road	2.81		05	12	55	
Clapham Junction	3.93	7.00	06	46	38*	
Earlsfield	5.58		09	03	52½	
Wimbledon	7.24		10	50	59	
Raynes Park	8.64		12	10	65	
New Malden	9.78		13	11	68	
Berrylands	10.98		14	15	70	
Surbiton	12.04		15	09	71½	
Hampton Court Jct	13.34	18.00	16	14	74½	
Esher	14.39		17	03	76/77½	
Hersham	15.91		18	16	76	
Walton	17.08		19	18	64*	
Oatlands Box	18.12		21	46	12*	tsr
Weybridge	19.15		24	20	39	
Byfleet & New Haw	20.40		25	57	59	
West Byfleet	21.68		27	11	63/56*	sigs
Woking	24.29		29	51	60	SVO
Woking Jct	24.75	31.00	30	15	63	
Brookwood	27.99		33	14	66½	
Pirbright Jct	29.49		35	08	37*	sigs
MP 31	31.00		37	27	36*	sigs
Sturt Lane Jct	32.15		39	26	36*	sigs
Farnborough	33.20		40	50	52	
MP 35	35.00		42	36	65½	
Fleet	36.48		43	56	71	
MP 38	38.00		45	09	76	
Winchfield	39.83		46	39	73	
MP 41	41.00		47	36	74½	
Hook	42.16		48	33	76/75½	
Newnham Siding	43.70		49	43	79/80	
MP 46	46.00		51	32	75	
			sigs stop			
MP 47¼	47.25		53	33	0*	
			54	58		

	miles	sched	mins	secs	speed	
Basingstoke	47.75	63.00	57	24		5 mins early
		0.00	00	00		One minute early
Worting Jct	2.55	5.30	05	10	48½	
MP 51	3.35		06	03	52	
Oakley	4.63		07	30	61½/63	
MP 53½	5.80		08	36	61	
Overton	7.80		10	22	72½	
Whitchurch	11.35		13	13	77½	
Hurstbourne	13.39		14	42	83	
MP 62½	14.85		15	48	80	
MP 65	17.35		17	40	76	eased
Andover	18.60	23.00	19	23		
	0.00	0.00	00	00		1¼ mins early
Red Post Jct	1.30		03	40	42	SVO
MP 68¾	2.50		05	05	61½	SVO
Grateley	6.35		08	59	58	
MP 73¼	7.00		09	42	56½	
Allington Box	9.25		11	48	70	
Idmiston	11.27		13	25	77½	
Porton	11.90		13	53	82	
MP 81	14.75		15	55	88	
Tunnel Junction	16.21	19.30	18	18	23*/37	sigs
Salisbury	17.31	22.00	20	50		2¼ mins early
net times	Waterloo to Basingstoke: 46 minutes Andover to Salisbury:19¾ minutes					

66.13

Date	Wednesday 13th July 1966
Train	6 pm Waterloo to Salisbury
Loco	Rebuilt West Country class 4-6-2 No. 34032 *Camelford*
Load	9 coaches, 298½ tons taer 325 tons gross
Crew	Fred Hoare and Pete Allen, Salisbury MPD
Recorder	DB

	miles	sched	mins	secs	speed	
Waterloo	0.00	0.00	00	00		½ min late
Vauxhall	1.29		03	30	38	
Queens Road	2.81		05	13	52½	
Clapham Junction	3.93	7.00	06	54	37*/34*	sigs
Earlsfield	5.58		09	30	47½	
Wimbledon	7.24		11	28	53½	
Raynes Park	8.64		12	57	58	
New Malden	9.78		14	06	61	
Berrylands	10.98		15	17	60½	

	miles	sched	mins	secs	speed	
Surbiton	12.04		16	35	39*	sigs
Hampton Court Jct	13.34	18.00	19	16	14*/26*	sigs
Esher	14.39		22	50	0*/0*	sigs stop (2)
Hersham	15.91		29	30	30½	
Walton	17.08		31	17	47½	
Oatlands Box	18.12		33	04	18*	tsr
Weybridge	19.15		35	37	35½	
Byfleet & New Haw	20.40		37	21	51	
West Byfleet	21.68		38	42	58	
Woking	24.29		41	17	63	
Woking Jct	24.75	31.00	41	41	64½	
Brookwood	27.99		44	37	67	
Pirbright Jct	29.49		46	03	68	
MP 31	31.00		47	18	66½	
Sturt Lane Jct	32.15		48	21	70	
Farnborough	33.20		49	14	69½	
MP 35	35.00		50	46	70½	
Fleet	36.48		52	03	70	
MP 38	38.00		53	20	71½	
Winchfield	39.83		54	56	68/67	
MP 41	41.00		55	57	69	
Hook	42.16		56	58	70½	
Newnham Siding	43.70		58	14	74/75½	
MP 46	46.00		60	08	73	
MP 47¼	47.25				37*	sigs
Basingstoke	47.75	63.00	63	17		
		0.00	00	00		4¾ mins late
Worting Jct	2.55	5.30	04	42	50½	
MP 51	3.35		05	32	54	
Oakley	4.63		06	56	61/62	
MP 53½	5.80		08	04	60	
Overton	7.80		09	55	71/76	
Whitchurch	11.35		12	56	73/70½	
Hurstbourne	13.39		14	31	75	
MP 62½	14.85		15	46	70/74½	
MP 65	17.35		17	48	72	
Andover	18.60	23.00	19	34		
	0.00	0.00	00	00		1¼ mins late
Red Post Jct	1.30		03	36	41½	
MP 68¾	2.50		05	05	58½/60	
Grateley	6.35		09	01	59	
MP 73¼	7.00		09	41	60	
Allington Box	9.25		11	41	73	

	miles	sched	mins	secs	speed	
Idmiston	11.27		13	20	74½	
Porton	11.90		13	50	78/82½	
MP 81	14.75		16	01	80	
Tunnel Junction	16.21	19.30	17	34	46*	
Salisbury	17.31	22.00	20	17		½ min early
net time	Waterloo to Basingstoke: 48¼ minutes					

66.14

Date	Friday 19th August 1966
Train	1259 pm Bournemouth to Waterloo
Loco	West Country class 4-6-2 No. 34015 *Exmouth*
Load	6 coaches and 1 van 230 tons gross estimated
Crew	Gordon Porter and Tom Moult, Nine Elms MPD
Recorder	Richard Jolliffe

	miles	sched	mins	secs	speed	
Winchester City	0.00	0.00	00	00		
Winchester Jct	2.10	5.30	04	42	53½	
Wallers Ash Box	4.85		07	24	64½	
Weston Box	6.35		08	42	72½	
Micheldever	8.50		10	23	80½/78½	
Roundwood Box	10.35		11	48	79½	
Steventon Box	12.60		13	47	64	
Wootton Box	14.05		15	16	54½*/31*	tsr
Worting Jct	16.28	25.00	18	36	45½	
Basingstoke	18.80	29.00	21	55		
	0.00	0.00	00	00		
Hook	5.59		06	30	80½	
Winchfield	7.92		08	13	86/97	
Fleet	11.27		10	24	96	
Farnborough	14.55		12	48	75	
MP 31	16.75		14	42	67/70½	
Brookwood	19.76		17	19	69½	
			sigs stop		0*	
Woking	23.46	27.00	23	11		
net times	start to stop average Basingstoke to Woking:60.72 mph Winchester to Basingstoke: 19½ minutes Basingstoke to Woking: 20¼ minutes					

66.15

Date	Monday 22nd August 1966					
Train	635 pm Salisbury to Waterloo					
Loco	BR Standard class 4-6-0 No. 73087					
Load	5 coaches and 4 vans, 268 tons tare 285 tons gross					
Crew	Gordon Porter, Nine Elms MPD and Brian Smith					
Recorder	DB					

	miles	sched	mins	secs	speed	
Basingstoke	0.00	0.00	00	00		15¼ min late
MP 46	1.75		03	03	55½	
Newnham Siding	4.05		05	21	63	
Hook	5.59		06	45	66½	
MP 41	6.75		07	49	67½	
Winchfield	7.92		08	52	70	
MP 38	9.75		10	23	74	
Fleet	11.27		11	37	73	
MP 35	12.75		12	51	74	
Farnborough	14.55		14	19	71	
Sturt Lane Jct	15.60		15	12	71½	
MP 31	16.75		16	13	70	
Pirbright Jct	18.26		17	22	76	
Brookwood	19.76		18	34	80	
MP 27	20.75		19	19	83	
Woking Jct	23.00		21	06	60*	
Woking	23.46	26.00	21	50		
	0.00	0.00	00	00		11 mins late
West Byfleet	2.61		04	00	65	
Byfleet & New Haw	3.89		05	04	74	
Weybridge	5.14		06	09	73½	
Oatlands Box	6.17		06	57	75½	
Walton	7.21		07	45	80	
Hersham	8.38		08	36	83	
Esher	9.90		09	45	82½	
Hampton Court Jct	10.95	14.00	10	30	82	
Surbiton	12.25		11	27	80	
Berrylands	13.31		12	18	77	
New Malden	14.51		13	16	70½	
Raynes Park	15.65		14	15	72	
Wimbledon	17.10		15	29	65½	eased/SVO
Earlsfield	18.71		16	56	70½	
Clapham Junction	20.36	26.00	18	45	45*/26*	tsr
Queens Road	21.48		20	40	48	

	miles	sched	mins	secs	speed	
Vauxhall	22.98		22	23	40*	
Waterloo	24.29	33.00	25	50		2¾ mns late
net time	start to stop average Basingstoke to Woking: 64.47 mph Woking to Waterloo: 24½ minutes					

66.16

Date	Monday 5th September 1966	
Train	635 pm Salisbury to Waterloo	
Loco	Rebuilt West Country class 4-6-2 No. 34026 *Yes Tor*	
Load	5 coaches and 5 vans, 281½ tons tare 305 tons gross	
Crew	Ted Dente and Pete Roberts, Nine Elms MPD	
Recorder	DB	

	miles	sched	mins	secs	speed	
Basingstoke	0.00	0.00	00	00		1¼ mins late
MP 46	1.75		03	33	55½	
Newnham Siding	4.05		05	43	70	
Hook	5.59		06	58	76	
MP 41	6.75		07	53	78	
Winchfield	7.92		09	01	38*/18*	tsr
MP 38	9.75		11	53	57	
Fleet	11.27		13	21	66½	
MP 35	12.75		14	37	74	
Farnborough	14.55		15	59	79	
Sturt Lane Jct	15.60		16	46	82	
MP 31	16.75		17	39	82½	
Pirbright Jct	18.26		18	37	88	
Brookwood	19.76		19	42	90	
MP 27	20.75		20	22	93	
Woking Jct	23.00		23	08	48*/53	sigs
Woking	23.46	26.00	23	48		
	0.00	0.00	00	00		1½ mins early
West Byfleet	2.61		04	35	63½	
Byfleet & New Haw	3.89		05	42	72½	
Weybridge	5.14		06	45	74½	
Oatlands Box	6.17		07	33	77	
Walton	7.21		08	18	82½	
Hersham	8.38		09	08	84	
Esher	9.90		10	13	87	
Hampton Court Jct	10.95	14.00	10	57	88	
Surbiton	12.25		11	52	80	
Berrylands	13.31		12	59	36*/17*	sigs/tsr
New Malden	14.51		16	29	32	
Raynes Park	15.65		18	15	45½	

	miles	sched	mins	secs	speed	
Wimbledon	17.10		19	55	56	
Earlsfield	18.71		21	34	62½	
Clapham Junction	20.36	26.00	23	42	33*	SVO
Queens Road	21.48		25	31	47	
Vauxhall	22.98		27	17	37*/19*	SVO
Waterloo	24.29	33.00	31	30		3¼ mins early
net times	Basingstoke to Woking 20½ minutes Woking to Waterloo:: 25 minutes					

66.17

Date	Saturday 15th October 1966
Train	910 am Special Waterloo to Exeter
Loco	Rebuilt Merchant Navy class 4-6-2 No. 35023 *Holland Afrika Line*
Load	8 coaches, 260 tons tare 280 tons gross
Crew	Bert Hooker and Alan Deadman, Nine Elms MPD
Inspector	Arthur Jupp
Recorder	Terry Jackson

	miles	sched	mins	secs	speed	
Waterloo	0.00	0.00	00	00		
Vauxhall	1.29		04	22	37	
Queens Road	2.65		06	05	51/52	
Clapham Junction	3.93	7.00	07	43	40*	
Earlsfield	5.58		09	56	52	
Wimbledon	7.24		11	44	58	
Raynes Park	8.65		13	08	63	
New Malden	9.78		14	14	66	
Berrylands	10.95		15	16	68	
Surbiton	12.04		16	12	72	
Hampton Court Jct	13.34	17.00	17	16	74	
Esher	14.40		18	07	75½	
Hersham	15.91		19	18	78/77	
Walton	17.08		20	10	79	
Oatlands	18.15		20	59	76	
Weybridge	19.15		21	45	80	
Byfleet & New Haw	20.40		22	42	83	
West Byfleet	21.68		24	11	16½*/11½*	tsr
Woking	24.29		30	50	54	
Woking Jct	24.75	28.00	31	18	58	
MP 26	26.00		32	31	63½	
MP 27	27.00		33	25	67	
Brookwood	27.99		34	18	70	
MP 29	29.00		35	09	71	
MP 30	30.00		35	59	71	

	miles	sched	mins	secs	speed	
MP 31	31.00		36	49	72	
Sturt Lane Jct	32.05		37	46	78	
Farnborough	33.20		38	32	79	
Bramshot Halt	35.70		40	19	83	
Fleet	36.48		40	58	83/86	
Winchfield	39.83		43	19	83	
Hook	42.16		45	46	16½*/69	tsr
Basingstoke	47.75		52	11	67/66	
Worting Jct	50.30	50.00	54	25	68½	
Oakley	52.38		56	09	78	
Overton	55.55		58	28	89/92	
Whitchurch	59.10		60	53	90	
Hurstbourne	61.14		62	09	95	
MP 62½	62.50		63	07	89/101	
Andover	66.35		65	25	100	
Red Post Jct	67.65		66	19	94/96	
Grateley	72.70		69	39	82/80	
Allington Box	75.60		71	45	88	
Idmiston Halt	77.65		73	05	90	
Porton	78.29		73	29	94/98	
Tunnel Junction	82.56	75.30	76	39	55*	
Salisbury	83.66	78.00	79	46		
net time	71 minutes					

66.18

Date	Saturday 15th October 1966
Train	2 10 pm Exeter Central to Waterloo
Loco	Rebuilt Merchant Navy class 4-6-2 No. 35026 *Lamport and Holt Line*
Load	8 coaches 260 tons tare 280 tons gross
Crew	Parsons and Munns, Salisbury MPD
Inspector	Arthur Jupp
Recorder	Terry Jackson

	miles	sched	mins	secs	speed	
Exeter Central	0.00	0.00	00	00		
St James Park Halt	0.45		02	01	23½	
Exmouth Jct	1.05	4.00	03	27	30	
Pinhoe	2.80		05	46	63	
Broad Clyst	4.70		07	22	72½	
Whimple	8.35		10	49	56	
MP 161¼	10.15		12	48	50/60/23*	sigs
Sidmouth Junction	12.15	19.00	15	50	30/58½/49½	
Honiton	16.75		21	22	51½	

	miles	sched	mins	secs	speed	
MP 153½	17.95		22	48	49	
Honiton Incline SB	19.85		24	44	72½/78/60*	
Seaton Junction	23.65		28	10	63/80	
Axminster	26.90	34.00	30	49	75/73	
Chard Junction	32.00		34	59	73½/72/75½	
Hewish Crossing SB	37.45		39	22	72	
MP 133¼	38.25		40	04	69	
Crewkerne	40.10		42	31	82/85/79/83	
MP 126¼	45.35		45	17	77	
Sutton Bingham	46.65		46	19	84	
Yeovil Junction	48.90	55.00	47	56	85/76/80	
Sherborne	53.40	60.00	51	26	69/66	
Milborne Port	57.15		54	29	71	
MP 113½	58.05		55	14	68½	
Templecombe	59.55	66.00	56	26	83/88	
MP 107½	64.10		59	48	68	
Gillingham	66.40		61	36	79	
Semley	70.45		65	17	58/77	
Tisbury	75.45		69	23	75/64	
Dinton	79.75		73	08	75½/78/73/74	
Wilton South	85.55	91.00	78	14	36½*	
MP 85¼	86.45		79	39	38½	
Salisbury	88.05	95.00	83	15		
net time	start to stop average: 63.53 mph 81¼ minutes					

66.19

Date	Wednesday 9th November 1966
Train	629 am Basingstoke to Waterloo
Loco	BR Standard class 4 4-6-0 No.75079
Load	6 coaches and 3 vans, 268 tons tare 285 tons gross
Driver	Les Cummings, Nine Elms MPD
Recorder	DB

	miles	sched	mins	secs	speed	
Woking	0.00	0.00	00	00		1½ mins late
West Byfleet	2.61		04	04	61½	
Byfleet	3.89		05	15	69	
Weybridge	5.14		06	26	65½	
Oatlands Box	6.17		07	20	66	
Walton	7.21		08	14	72	
Hersham	8.38		09	09	76	SVO
Esher	9.90		10	23	77½	

	miles	sched	mins	secs	speed	
			sigs stop		0*	
Hampton Court Jct	10.95		13	28	23/30	
Surbiton	12.25	18.00	16	39		SVO
net time	12¾ minutes					

66.20

Date	Friday 11th November 1966
Train	629 am Basingstoke to Waterloo
Loco	Rebuilt West Country class 4-6-2 No. 34013 *Okehampton*
Load	7 coaches and 2 vans, 274 tons tare 295 tons gross
Driver	Les Cummings, Nine Elms MPD
Recorder	DB

	miles	sched	mins	secs	speed	
Woking	0.00	0.00	00	00		6¾ mins late
West Byfleet	2.61		04	04	64	
Byfleet	3.89		05	12	74	
Weybridge	5.14		06	18	74½	
Oatlands Box	6.17		07	05	78	
Walton	7.21		07	53	83	
Hersham	8.38		08	42	87/90	
Esher	9.90		09	49	81	SVO
Hampton Court Jct	10.95		10	39	72/38*	sigs
Surbiton	12.25	18.00	12	24		
net time	12 minutes					

66.21

Date	Monday 14th November 1966
Train	530 pm Weymouth to Waterloo
Loco	Rebuilt Merchant Navy class 4-6-2 No. 35007 *Aberdeen Commonwealth*
Load	10 coaches and 2 vans, 375 tons tare 405 tons gross
Crew	Gordon Porter and Tom Moult, Nine Elms MPD
Recorder	DB

	miles	sched	mins	secs	speed	
Southampton	0.00	0.00	00	00		14¾ mins late
			sigs stop	25		
MP 78½	0.74		03	12	0*	
			05	08		
Northmam Jct	1.05	3.00	06	54	12*/2*	sigs
St Denys	2.11		11	44	24	
Swaythling	3.45		14	01	46/50	
Eastleigh	5.80	11.00	18	17	18*/32	sigs
Allbrook Box	6.66		19	42	44	

	miles	sched	mins	secs	speed	
Shawford	9.61		23	03	58½	
Shawford Jct	10.46		23	49	61	
St Cross Box	11.50		24	52	63	
Winchester City	12.70		26	03	67	
Winchester Jct	14.80		29	33	21*/30	sigs
Wallers Ash Box	17.55		33	18	54½	
Weston Box	19.05		34	50	61	
Micheldever	21.20		36	49	67½	
Roundwood Box	23.05		38	28	71	
Waltham Box	24.15		39	24	76	
Steventon Box	25.30		40	17	79	
Wootton Box	26.75		41	24	80	
Worting Jct	28.98	39.30	43	19	64*/72	
			sigs stop			
MP 48¾	30.50		44	53	0*	SVO
			45	53		
Basingstoke	31.50		48	37	47	
MP 46	33.25		50	27	70	
Newnham Siding	35.55		52	18	77½	
Hook	37.08		53	27	83	
MP 41	38.25		54	18	85½	
Winchfield	39.41		55	08	87	
MP 38	41.25		56	23	93	
Fleet	42.76		57	23	90	
MP 35	44.25		58	25	87	
Farnborough	46.05		59	37	89	
Sturt Lane Jct	47.05		60	19	90	
MP 31	48.25		61	08	88	
Pirbright Jct	49.60		62	01	94	
Brookwood	51.25		65	10	18*	sigs to slow line
MP 26	53.25		67	40	67½	
Woking Jct	54.50	63.30	69	10	21*	sigs
			sigs stop			
Woking	54.95		70	12	0*	
			72	22		to fast line
West Byfleet	57.56		77	05	65	
Byfleet & New Haw	58.84		78	11	71	
Weybridge	60.09		79	21	67½	
Oatlands Box	61.15		80	13	70	
Walton	62.16		81	02	77½	
Hersham	63.33		81	55	80	
Esher	64.85		83	06	81	
Hampton Court Jct.	65.90	78.30	83	43	78	

	miles	sched	mins	secs	speed	
Surbiton	67.20		84	58	70	
Berrylands	68.26		85	56	63	
New Malden	69.46		87	22	43*	sigs
Raynes Park	70.60		89	53	49	
Wimbledon	72.05		90	28	57	
Earlsfield	73.66		92	09	63	
Clapham Junction	75.31	89.30	94	15	37*	
Queens Road	76.43		97	17	34*	tsr
Vauxhall	77.93		99	24	37½/22*	sigs
Waterloo	79.24	96.30	103	36		21¾ mins late
net time	71 minutes start to stop average MP48¾ to Woking:60.33 mph average speed MP 41 to MP 31: 88.0 mph					

66.22

Date	Tuesday 15th November 1966
Train	530 pm Weymouth to Waterloo
Loco	Rebuilt Merchant Navy class 4-6-2 No. 35007 *Aberdeen Commonwealth*
Load	9 coaches and 2 vans, 375 tons gross estimated
Crew	Gordon Porter and Tom Moult, Nine Elms MPD
Weather	Not recorded
Recorder	Les Kent

	miles	sched	mins	secs	speed	
Southampton	0.00	0.00	00	00		
Northam Jct	1.05	3.00	03	30	26*	
St Denys	2.11		05	17	37½/40	
Swaythling	3.45		09	25	38/45	
Eastleigh	5.80	11.00	11	33	15*	sigs
Allbrook Box	6.66		13	17	37/49	
Shawford	9.61		17	11	48½	
Shawford Jct	10.46		18	06	50	
Winchester City	12.70		21	57	54	
Winchester Jct	14.80		23	23	51½/55½	
Weston Box	19.05		27	06	49	
Micheldever	21.20		31	02	38	
Roundwood Box	23.05		34	25	31½/58	
Wootton Box	26.75		39	11	57	
Worting Jct	28.98	39.30	41	23	68½	
Basingstoke	31.50		43	27	80/96	
Hook	37.08		47	12	91	
Winchfield	39.41		48	40	96/102	
Fleet	42.76		50	43	101/83*	
Farnborough	46.05		52	56	88	

	miles	sched	mins	secs	speed	
MP 31	48.25		55	29	85/90	
			sigs stop		0*	52 seconds
Brookwood	51.25		59	10	26/53½	to slow line
			sigs stop		0*	20 seconds
Woking	54.95		66	46	34/30*	to fast line
West Byfleet	57.56		70	31	59	
Byfleet & New Haw	58.84		71	41	61½	
			sigs stop		0*	3 mins 1 second
Weybridge	60.09		79	11	17½	
Walton	62.16		83	14	49	
Hersham	63.33		84	38	60	
Esher	64.85		85	46	64½	
Hampton Court Jct.	65.90	78.30	86	43	65	
Surbiton	67.20		88	10	58½	
Berrylands	68.26		89	28	54	
New Malden	69.46		90	36	50	
Raynes Park	70.60		91	58	49½	
Wimbledon	72.05		93	38	50½/62	
Earlsfield	73.66		95	18	60	
Clapham Junction	75.31	89.30	97	20	44*	
Queens Road	76.43		98	41	56/30*	tsr
Vauxhall	77.93		101	05		
Waterloo	79.24	96.30	107	19		
	average speed MP 41 to MP 31: 88.0 mph					

66.23

Date	Wednesday 16th November 1966
Train	530 pm Weymouth to Waterloo
Loco	Rebuilt Merchant Navy class 4-6-2 No. 35007 *Aberdeen Commonwealth*
Load	10 coaches and 2 vans, 374 tons tare 400 tons gross
Crew	Gordon Porter and Tom Moult, Nine Elms MPD
Weather	Cold and wet, strong NW wind
Timed by	DB

	miles	sched	mins	secs	speed	
Southampton	0.00	0.00	00	00		12 mins late
Northam Jct	1.05	3.00	03	40	26*	
St Denys	2.11		05	22	39	
Swaythling	3.45		07	18	47/50½	
			sigs stop			
MP 74	5.15		10	15	0*	
			14	6		
Eastleigh	5.80	11.00	16	11	26	
Allbrook Box	6.66		17	45	37½	

	miles	sched	mins	secs	speed	
Shawford	9.61		21	58	48	
Shawford Jct	10.46		22	58	50	
St Cross	11.50		24	14	51	
Winchester City	12.70		25	41	54½	
Winchester Jct	14.80		28	04	55/37*	sigs
Wallers Ash Box	17.55		31	58	46	slipping
Weston Box	19.05		33	51	47	
Micheldever	21.20		36	31	50	slipping
Roundwood Box	23.05		38	48	51	
Waltham Box	24.15		40	01	60	
Steventon Box	25.30		41	11	62	
Wootton Box	26.75		42	39	54/51	
Worting Jct	28.98	39.30	45	02	66/70	
MP 48¾	30.50		47	50	2*	sigs
Basingstoke	31.50		49	50	40	
MP 46	33.25		51	55	63	
Newnham Siding	35.55		53	54	77½	
Hook	37.08		55	04	82½	
MP 41	38.25		55	58	84	
Winchfield	39.41		56	49	88	
MP 38	41.25		58	02	98	
Fleet	42.76		58	58	95	
MP 35	44.25		59	56	93	
Farnborough	46.05		61	09	86½	
Sturt Lane Jct	47.05		61	52	87	
MP 31	48.25		62	42	86	
Pirbright Jct	49.60		63	37	90	
Brookwood	51.25		66	41	22*	sigs to slow line
MP 26	53.25		69	44	58	
Woking Jct	54.50	63.30	71	10	18*	sigs
			sigs stop			
MP 24½	54.75		71	39	0*	
			72	24		
Woking	54.95		74	05	30	to fast line
West Byfleet	57.56		77	09	70	
Byflet & New Haw	58.84		78	12	78	
Weybridge	60.09		79	14	74½	
Oatlands Box	61.15		80	01	77	
Walton	62.16		80	48	82	
Hersham	63.33		81	39	83	
Esher	64.85		82	47	81	
Hampton Court Jct.	65.90	78.30	83	34	80	
Surbiton	67.20		84	34	77½	

	miles	sched	mins	secs	speed	
Berrylands	68.26		85	25	76	
New Malden	69.46		86	25	65½	
Raynes Park	70.60		87	29	64	
			sigs stop			
MP 7¾	71.50		88	36	0*	
			89	11		
Wimbledon	72.05		91	14	28½	
Earlsfield	73.66		93	38	52	
Clapham Junction	75.31	89.30	95	48	43*	
Queens Road	76.43		97	16	53/32*	tsr
Vauxhall	77.93		99	28	34/22*	sigs
Waterloo	79.24	96.30	104	04		19½ mins late
net time	76 minutes average speed Mileposts 24½ to 7¾ = 62.05 mph start to stop average speed Winchfield to Farnborough: 91.8 mph average speed MP 41 to MP 31: 88.0 mph					

66.24

Date	Saturday 10th December 1966
Train	705 am Basingstoke to Waterloo
Loco	Rebuilt Battle of Britain class 4-6-2 No. 34077 *603 Squadron*
Load	4 coaches, 132 ton tare 135 tons gross, increasing to 145 tons
Crew	Gale and A Dedman, Nine Elms MPD
Recorder	David Foale

	miles	sched	mins	secs	speed	
Basingstoke	0.00	0.00	00	00		right time
					78	
Hook	5.59	9.00	07	10		
	0.00	0.00	00	00		
					58	
Winchfield	2.33	5.00	03	53		
	0.00	0.00	00	00		
					34*/56	tsr
Fleet	3.35	6.00	06	00		
	0.00	0.00	00	00		
					64	
Farnborough	3.28	6.00	04	54		
	0.00	0.00	00	00		
MP 31	2.10		03	26	62	
Brookwood	5.21		05	47	84	
Woking Jct	8.45		sigs		*	
Woking	8.91	12.00	10	25		
	0.00	0.00	00	00		

	miles	sched	mins	secs	speed	
West Byfleet	2.61		03	30	74	
Weybridge	5.14		05	19	88	
Walton	7.21		06	41	92	
Hersham	8.38		07	28	88	
Esher	9.90		08	34	86	
Hampton Court Jct	10.95	15.00	09	19	78*	
Surbiton	12.25		10	20	77	
New Malden	14.51		12	04	80	
Wimbledon	17.10		14	14	62	
Earlsfield	18.71		15	51		
Clapham Junction	20.36	26.00	18	10		
Queens Road	21.48		tsr		*	
Vauxhall	22.98		22	27		
Waterloo	24.29	33.00	25	49		7¾ mins early
net times	Farnborough to Woking: 9¼ minutes					
	Woking to Waterloo: 24¼ minutes					

66.25

Date	Monday 12th December 1966
Train	530 pm Weymouth to Waterloo
Loco	Rebuilt Merchant Navy class 4-6-2 No. 35028 *Clan Line*
Load	9 coaches and 2 vans, 348 tons tare 375 tons gross
Crew	Gordon Porter and Bob Lee, Nine Elms MPD
Weather	Rain, SW wind
Timed by	DB

	miles	sched	mins	secs	speed	
Southampton	0.00	0.00	00	00		2 mins late
Northam Jct	1.05	3.00	03	37	27/22*	
St Denys	2.11		05	24	38	
Swaythling	3.45		07	15	51/10*	sigs
Eastleigh	5.80	11.00	12	22	26½	SVO
Allbrook Box	6.66		14	22	21*	sigs to slow line
Shawford	9.61		19	00	52	
Shawford Jct	10.46		19	53	54½	
St Cross Box	11.50		21	02	58	
Winchester City	12.70		22	20	61	
Winchester Jct	14.80		24	27	60½	slipping
MP 63	16.15		25	47	61	
Wallers Ash Box	17.55		27	06	61½	
Weston Box	19.05		28	33	61	slipping
MP 59	20.15		29	43	60	slipping
Micheldever	21.20		30	39	61½	
Roundwood Box	23.05		32	28	63	

	miles	sched	mins	secs	speed	
Waltham Box	24.15		33	32	67	
Steventon Box	25.30		34	31	70½	
Wootton Box	26.75		35	50	63/54½	
Worting Jct	28.98	39.30	38	05	62	
MP 49	30.25		39	11	76	
Basingstoke	31.50		40	07	83½	
MP 46	33.25		41	20	90	
Newnham Siding	35.55		42	51	95	
MP 43	36.25		43	16	92	
Hook	37.08		43	48	94	
MP 41	38.25		44	34	95	
Winchfield	39.41		45	19	98	
MP 38	41.25		46	25	103	
Fleet	42.76		47	18	100	
MP 35	44.25		48	15	93	brakes
Farnborough	46.05		49	40	74*	sigs
Sturt Lane Jct	47.05		50	29	72	
MP 31	48.25		51	31	70½	
Pirbright Jct	49.60		52	41	72½/74	
Brookwood	51.25		54	18	32*	long tsr
Wokiing Jct	54.50	63.30	58	56	60	
Woking	54.95		59	22	66	40% cut off
West Byfleet	57.56		61	33	80	
Byfleet & New Haw	58.84		62	26	86/88½	
Weybridge	60.09		63	21	85½	
Oatlands Box	61.15		64	03	87	
Walton	62.16		64	46	90	
Hersham	63.33		65	30	94	
Esher	64.85		66	01	93	
Hampton Court Jct.	65.90	78.30	67	14	90	
Surbiton	67.20		68	06	86	
Berrylands	68.26		68	53	83	
New Malden	69.46		69	48	75	
Raynes Park	70.60		70	44	70	
Wimbledon	72.05		72	03	63½	even time
Earlsfield	73.66		73	33	67½	
Clapham Junction	75.31	89.30	75	24	43*	
Queens Road	76.43		76	50	58½/19*	tsr
Vauxhall	77.93		79	23	32½	
Waterloo	79.24	96.30	82	50		11¾ mins early
net time	72 minutes average speed Winchfield to Fleet: 101.36 mph average speed MP 46 to MP 35: 95.43 mph					

66.26

Date	Saturday 17th December 1966
Train	718 am Waterloo to Salisbury
Loco	Rebuilt Battle of Britain class 4-6-2 No. 34089 *602 Squadron*
Load	3 coaches and 3 bogie vans, 185 tons gross estimated
Driver	West, Nine Elms MPD
Recorder	Peter Trapp

	miles	sched	mins	secs	speed	
Waterloo	0.00	0.00	00	00		
Vauxhall	1.29		03	11	39	
Queens Road	2.81		04	51	57	
Clapham Junction	3.93	7.00	06	20	45*	
Earlsfield	5.58		08	19	56	
Wimbledon	7.24		09	58	62	
Raynes Park	8.64		11	13	70	
New Malden	9.78		12	12	75½/79	
Berrylands	10.98		13	08	*	
Surbiton	12.04	18.00	14	54		
	0.00	0.00	00	00		
Hampton Court Jct	1.30	3.00	02	32	53	
Esher	2.35		03	41	65	
Hersham	3.87		05	01	73	
Walton	5.04		05	57	79	
Weybridge	7.11		07	32	81	
Byfleet and New Haw	8.36		08	28	85	
West Byfleet	9.68		09	22	83	
Woking	12.25	20.00	12	52	*	sigs to slow line
net time	Surbiton to Woking: 12¼ minutes					

66.27

Date	Saturday 17th December 1966
Train	649 am Salisbury to Waterloo
Loco	Rebuilt West Country class 4-6-2 No. 34013 *Okehampton*
Load	4 coaches, 129 tons tare 140 tons gross
Driver	West , Nine Elms MPD
Recorder	Les Kent and Peter Trapp

	miles	sched	mins	secs	speed	
Woking	0.00	0.00	00	00		
West Byfleet	2.61		03	53	73	
Byfleet and New Haw	3.89		04	51	80	
Weybridge	5.14		05	46	84	
Walton	7.21		07	09	94	even time
Hersham	8.38		07	51	100	
Esher	9.90		08	50	76	

	miles	sched	mins	secs	speed	
Hampton Court Jct	10.95	18.30	09	36	76	
Surbiton	12.25		10	39	74	
Berrylands	13.31		11	30	73	
New Malden	14.51		12	32	64*	sigs
Raynes Park	15.65		13	36	64	
Wimbledon	17.10		14	59	60*	sigs
Earlsfield	18.71		16	42	53*	sigs
Clapham Junction	20.36	30.00	18	49	43*	
Queens Road	21.48		20	22	54	
Vauxhall	22.98		22	08	37*	
Waterloo	24.29	37.00	25	14		
net time	24 minutes					

66.28

Date	Thursday 29th December 1966
Train	638 pm Salisbury to Waterloo
Loco	Battle of Britain class 4-6-2 No. 34057 *Biggin Hill*
Load	4 coaches and 2 vans, 179 tons tare 185 tons gross
Crew	Jim Evans and Dave Davis, Nine Elms MPD
Recorder	DB

	miles	sched	mins	secs	speed	
Basingstoke	0.00	0.00	00	00		5¾ mins late
MP 46	1.75		02	52	63	
Newnham Siding	4.05		04	47	82½	35% cut off
MP 43	4.75		05	20	83	20% cut off
Hook	5.59		05	52	86	
MP 41	6.75		06	42	89	
Winchfield	7.92		07	32	93	eased
MP 38	9.75		08	43	90/84*	slight brakes
Fleet	11.27		09	48	85	
MP 35	12.75		10	52	88	
Farnborough	14.55		12	03	86½	
Sturt Lane Jct	15.60		12	47	88	
MP 31	16.75		13	38	84	slight brakes
Pirbright Jct	18.26		14	39	86	
Brookwood	19.76		15	46	87½	
MP 27	20.75		16	28	83	
Woking Jct	23.00		18	26	55*	
Woking	23.46	26.00	19	14		
	0.00	0.00	00	00		1¾ mins early
West Byfleet	2.61		03	35	70½	
Byfleet and New Haw	3.89		04	36	76	
Weybridge	5.14		05	39	73	
Oatlands Box	6.17		06	28	74	

	miles	sched	mins	secs	speed	
Walton	7.21		07	16	79	
Hersham	8.38		08	07	82½	
Esher	9.90		09	16	80	
Hampton Court Jct	10.95	14.00	10	05	74/38*	sigs
Surbiton	12.25		12	00	44	
Berrylands	13.31		13	18	57½	
New Malden	14.51		14	28	64	
Raynes Park	15.65		15	51	16*	tsr
Wimbledon	17.10		19	17	41	
Earlsfield	18.71		21	06	66½	
Clapham Junction	20.36	26.00	22	51	46*	
Queens Road	21.48		24	45	26*	sigs
Vauxhall	22.98		26	39	44½	
Waterloo	24.29	33.00	29	34		5¼ mins early
	start to stop average Basingstoke to Woking: 73.19 mph average speed MP 41 to MP 27: 86.7 mph net time Woking to Waterloo: 24 minutes					

67.01

Date	Tuesday 17th January 1967
Train	530 pm Weymouth to Waterloo
Loco	Rebuilt West Country class 4-6-2 No. 34098 *Templecombe*
Load	9 coaches and 2 vans, 349 tons tare 365 tons gross
Crew	Gordon Porter and Tom Moult, Nine Elms MPD
Weather	Rain, SW wind
Timed by	DB

	miles	sched	mins	secs	speed	
Southampton	0.00	0.00	00	00		5 mins late
Northam Jct	1.05	3.00	03	50	20*	
St Denys	2.11		05	42	38½	
Swaythling	3.45		07	33	50	
Southampton Airport	4.41		08	31	54½	
Eastleigh	5.80	11.00	09	59	61	
Allbrook Box	6.66		10	50	63/65	
Shawford	9.61		13	37	64½	
Shawford Jct	10.46		14	19	65	
St Cross Box	11.50		15	19	64½	
Winchester City	12.70		16	30	66	
Winchester Jct	14.80		18	27	67	
MP 63	16.15		19	41	67½	
Wallers Ash Box	17.55		21	08	32*	tsr
Weston Box	19.05		25	39	14*	tsr

	miles	sched	mins	secs	speed	
MP 59	20.15		28	07	39½	
Micheldever	21.20		29	24	47	
Roundwood Box	23.05		31	43	52½	
Waltham Box	24.15		32	58	60	
Steventon Box	25.30		34	04	65	
Wootton Box	26.75		35	19	71½/30*	sigs
Worting Jct	28.98	39.30	38	31	44½/29*	sigs
Basingstoke	31.50		42	16	40	
MP 46	33.25		44	36	57½	
Newnham Siding	35.55		46	47	70	
MP 43	36.25		47	26	71½	
Hook	37.08		48	13	74	
MP 41	38.25		48	59	75½	
Winchfield	39.41		49	56	78	
MP 38	41.25		51	17	87	
Fleet	42.76		52	20	85½	
MP 35	44.25		53	23	87	
Farnborough	46.05		54	37	86½	
Sturt Lane Jct	47.05		55	22	85	
MP 31	48.25		56	13	83	
Pirbright Jct	49.60		57	19	88	
Brookwood	51.25		58	17	86	
MP 27	52.25		58	59	90	
MP 26	53.25		59	58	93	
Wokiing Jct	54.50	63.30	60	27	94	
Woking	54.95		60	43	93	
MP 23	56.25		61	35	95	
West Byfleet	57.56		62	28	92	
Byfleet & New Haw	58.84		63	17	93	
Weybridge	60.09		64	19	88	
Oatlands Box	61.15		64	51	86½	
Walton	62.16		65	33	90	
Hersham	63.33		66	19	88	
Esher	64.85		67	26	86	
Hampton Court Jct.	65.90	78.30	68	12	80	
Surbiton	67.20		71	31	3*	sigs
Berrylands	68.26		73	30	44	
New Malden	69.46		74	59	51	
Raynes Park	70.60		76	13	54	
Wimbledon	72.05		77	45	56	
Earlsfield	73.66		81	13	22*	tsr
Clapham Junction	75.31	89.30	84	07	41	

	miles	sched	mins	secs	speed	
Queens Road	76.43		85	37	60	
Vauxhall	77.93		87	14	38*/0*	sigs stop 96 secs
Waterloo	79.24	96.30	93	47		2¼ mins late
net time	72 minutes average speed Hook to Brookwood: 84.46 mph average speed Winchfield to Hampton Court Jct: 87.01 mph					

67.02

Date	Thursday 19th January 1967
Train	530 pm Weymouth to Waterloo
Loco	Rebuilt West Country class 4-6-2 No. 34036 *Westward Ho*
Load	9 coaches and 2 vans, 356 tons tare 380 tons gross
Crew	Gordon Porter and Tom Moult, Nine Elms MPD
Weather	Dry
Timed by	DB

	miles	sched	mins	secs	speed	
Southampton	0.00	0.00	00	00		4¾ mins late
Northam Jct	1.05	3.00	03	31	31½/24*	
St Denys	2.11		05	10	40	
Swaythling	3.45		07	00	53½	
Southampton Airport	4.41		07	53	58	
Eastleigh	5.80	11.00	09	20	64	
Allbrook Box	6.66		10	09	66	
Shawford	9.61		12	44	71	
Shawford Jct	10.46		13	22	70	
St Cross Box	11.50		14	45	37*	sigs
Winchester City	12.70		16	35	42½	
Winchester Jct	14.80		20	26	23*/17*	sigs
MP 63	16.15		24	13	29½	
Wallers Ash Box	17.55		27	04	33	
Weston Box	19.05		31	31	18*	tsr
MP 59	20.15		33	56	36½	
Micheldever	21.20		35	20	44	
Roundwood Box	23.05		37	40	53½	
Waltham Box	24.15		38	55	61	
Steventon Box	25.30		40	01	65	
Wootton Box	26.75		41	18	70/51*	sigs
Worting Jct	28.98	39.30	43	33	61½/46*	tsr
Basingstoke	31.50		46	21	63	
MP 46	33.25		47	56	73½	
Newnham Siding	35.55		49	45	79	
MP 43	36.25		50	16	80	
Hook	37.08		50	52	82½	

	miles	sched	mins	secs	speed	
MP 41	38.25		51	45	82	
Winchfield	39.41		52	36	84	
MP 38	41.25		53	51	90	
Fleet	42.76		54	51	88	
MP 35	44.25		55	51	90	
Farnborough	46.05		57	05	86½	
Sturt Lane Jct	47.05		57	47	87	
MP 31	48.25		58	38	83	
Pirbright Jct	49.60		59	37	87	
Brookwood	51.25		60	46	85½	
MP 27	52.25		61	30	83	
MP 26	53.25		62	25	58*	sigs
Wokiing Jct	54.50	63.30	63	30	67½	
Woking	54.95		63	52	70	
MP 23	56.25		64	56	76	
West Byfleet	57.56		65	57	78	
Byfleet & New Haw	58.84		66	53	80	
Weybridge	60.09		67	53	75½	slight sigs
Oatlands Box	61.15		68	40	76	
Walton	62.16		69	29	80	
Hersham	63.33		70	20	82	
Esher	64.85		71	30	78	
Hampton Court Jct.	65.90	78.30	72	20	76	
Surbiton	67.20		73	23	73½	
Berrylands	68.26		74	15	70	
New Malden	69.46		75	22	62	
Raynes Park	70.60		76	31	55/0*	sigs stop 47 secs
Wimbledon	72.05		81	22	40	
Earlsfield	73.66		85	20	18*	tsr
Clapham Junction	75.31	89.30	88	53	43	
Queens Road	76.43		90	26	58/61	
Vauxhall	77.93		91	55	41*	SVO
Waterloo	79.24	96.30	95	30		3¾ mins late
net time	72 minutes average speed Hook to Brookwood: 85.88 mph					

Date	Saturday 4th February 1967
Train	530 pm Weymouth to Waterloo
Loco	Rebuilt Merchant Navy class 4-6-2 No. 35030 *Elder Dempster Line*
Load	9 coaches and 2 vans, 337 tons tare 365 tons gross
Crew	Roy Sloper and fireman Galleon, Easleigh MPD
Timed by	Terry Jackson

	miles	sched	mins	secs	speed	
Southampton	0.00	0.00	00	00		
Northam Jct	1.05	3.00	03	33	22*	
St Denys	2.11		05	08	43½	
Swaythling	3.45		06	48	54	
Southampton Airport	4.30		07	41	60	
Eastleigh	5.80	11.00	09	05	65	
Allbrook Box	6.66		09	50	66½	
Shawford	9.61		12	28	68	
Shawford Jct	10.46		13	08	69	
St Cross	11.3		14	05	70	
Winchester City	12.70		15	09	72	
Winchester Jct	14.80		16	58	68½	
Wallers Ash Box	17.55		20	24	22*	tsr
Weston Box	19.05		25	05	35	
Micheldever	21.20		26	52	56	
Roundwood Box	23.05		28	44	63	
Waltham Box	24.15		29	48	72½/75½	
Wootton Box	26.75		31	53	69	
Worting Jct	28.98	39.30	34	03	58½*	tsr
Basingstoke	31.50		36	16	77/88/87	
Hook	37.08		40	09	91	
Winchfield	39.41		41	42	94/97	
Fleet	42.76		43	52	85	
Farnborough	46.05		47	06	24*	tsr
Sturt Lane Jct	47.05		49	13	42½	
MP 31	48.25		50	45	52½	
Brookwood	51.25		53	21	81	
Woking Jct	54.50	63.30	55	44	86	
Woking	54.95		56	02	85/79	
West Byfleet	57.56		57	59	84	
Byfleet & New Haw	58.84		58	52	87	
Weybridge	60.09		59	48	85/82	
Walton	62.16		61	16	85	
Hersham	63.33		62	06	83	
Esher	64.85		63	16	75	

	miles	sched	mins	secs	speed	
Hampton Court Jct.	65.90	78.30	64	07	72½	
Surbiton	67.20		65	12	71	
Berrylands	68.26		66	08	65	
New Malden	69.46		67	12	65/64	
Raynes Park	70.60		68	16	66	
Wimbledon	72.05		69	34	62	
Earlsfield	73.66		71	20	47*	tsr
Clapham Junction	75.31	89.30	73	31	44*	
Queens Road	76.43		75	02	53½	
Vauxhall	77.93		77	24	21*	sigs
Waterloo	79.24	96.30	81	20		
net time	72 minutes					

67.04

Date	Thursday 9th March 1967
Train	615 pm Weymouth to Waterloo
Loco	Rebuilt Battle of Britain class 4-6-2 No. 34087 *145 Squadron*
Load	3 coaches and 3 vans, 182 tons tare 195 tons gross
Crew	Bill Anderson and Les Greer, Nine Elms MPD
Weather	Rain
Recorder	DB

	miles	sched	mins	secs	speed	
Winchester City	0.00	0.00	00	00		right time
Winchester Jct	2.10	5.30	03	32	56	SVO
MP 63	3.55		04	52	66½	
Wallers Ash Box	4.85		06	02	72½	
Weston Box	6.35		07	10	78	
MP 59	7.55		09	36	80	
Micheldever	8.50		08	49	82	
Roundwood Box	10.35		10	13	83/85½	
Waltham Box	11.45		11	02	82*	brakes
Steventon Box	12.60		12	04	70*	brakes
Wootton Box	14.05		13	20	68	
Worting Jct	16.28	25.00	15	50	42*/46	sigs
			sigs stop			
MP 48¼	18.30		20	23	0*	SVO
			26	04		
Basingstoke	18.80	29.00	28	10		
	0.00	0.00	00	00		1 minute early
Newnham Siding	4.10		05	18	73	
Hook	5.59		06	29	79½	
MP 41	6.75		07	23	82	

	miles	sched	mins	secs	speed	
Winchfield	7.92		08	15	86½	
MP 38	9.75		09	28	92	
Fleet	11.27		10	28	88	
MP 35	12.75		11	31	87	
Farnborough	14.55		12	46	83	
Sturt Lane Jct	15.60		13	32	84	
MP 31	16.75		14	24	82½	
Pirbright Jct	18.26		15	23	88	
Brookwood	19.76		16	27	92	
MP 27	20.75		17	09	84	
Woking Jct	23.00		20	56	16*	sigs
Woking	23.46	26.00	21	57		
	average speed Milepost 41 to 27: 86.01 mph Winchester to Basingstoke: net time 18 minutes Basingstoke to Woking: net time 19½ minutes start to stop average Basingstoke to Woking: 64.13 mph					

67.05

Date	Wednesday 29th March 1967
Train	916 am Weymouth to Waterloo
Loco	Rebuilt Battle of Britain class 4-6-2 No. 34089 *602 Squadron*
Load	10 coaches, 337 tons tare 370 tons gross
Crew	Reuben Hendicott and Ray McQuade Nine Elms MPD
Also on Footplate	Bill Stanley, Nine Elms MPD
Recorder	David Foale

	miles	sched	mins	secs	speed	
Southampton	0.00	0.00	00	00		12½ mins late
Northam Jct	1.05	4.00	03	20		
St Denys	2.11		04	58	42	
Swaythling	3.45		06	40	54	
Southampton Airport	4.41		07	32	60/0*	sigs stop 138 secs
Eastleigh	5.80	11.00	13	22		
Allbrook Box	6.66		14	35	48	
Shawford	9.61		17	45	62	
St Cross Box	11.50		19	30	64	
Winchester City	12.70		20	39	66/68	
Winchester Jct	14.80	23.00	22	35	63*/40*/44	sigs
Wallers Ash Box	17.55		26	06	42*	sigs
Weston Box	19.05		28	45	29*/18*	sigs
Micheldever	21.20		33	49	35	
Roundwood Box	23.05		36	23	53	
Steventon Box	25.30		38	40	70	
Wootton Box	26.75		39	47	75	

	miles	sched	mins	secs	speed	
Worting Jct	28.98	42.30	41	40	67*	
Basingstoke	31.50		43	38	79	
Newnham Siding	35.55		36	36	89/88	
Hook	37.08		47	38	90	
Winchfield	39.41		49	10	92/96	
Fleet	42.76		51	18	94/95	
Farnborough	46.05		53	24	90	eased
MP 31	48.25		54	57	86/93	
Brookwood	51.25		56	56	92	
Woking	54.95	71.30	59	40	54*/48*	sigs
West Byfleet	57.56		62	54	56*	sigs
Byfleet & New Haw	58.84		65	10	17*	tsr
Weybridge	60.09		68	29	27	
Oatlands Box	61.15		70	10	48	
Walton	62.16		71	17	64	
Hersham	63.33		72	16	72	
Esher	64.85		73	30	77	
Hampton Court Jct.	65.90	86.30	74	20	79/80	
Surbiton	67.20		75	18	79	
New Malden	69.46		77	07	23*	sigs
Wimbledon	72.05		80	58	53	
Earlsfield	73.66		82	43	62	
Clapham Junction	75.31	96.30	84	31	40*/53	
Vauxhall	77.93		87	53	36*/0*	sigs stop 7 seconds
Waterloo	79.24	103.30	93	20		2 mins late
net time	72 minutes average speed Hook to Brookwood: 91.42 mph					

67.06

Date	Wednesday 19th April 1967
Train	638 pm Salisbury to Waterloo
Loco	Rebuilt Merchant Navy class 4-6-2 No. 35003 *Royal Mail*
Load	6 coaches 215 tons approx
Driver	Enticknapp and Gaffney, Nine Elms MPD
Recorder	Les Kent

	miles	sched	mins	secs	speed	
Basingstoke	0.00	0.00	00	00		
Hook	5.59		06	53	85	
Winchfield	7.92		07	41	93/100	
Fleet	11.27		09	45	97	
Farnborough	14.55		12	06	77	
MP 31	16.75		13	56	64/*	sigs

	miles	sched	mins	secs	speed	
Brookwood	19.76		17	05	*	sigs
Woking	23.46	26.00	23	44		
net time	20 minutes					

67.07

Date	Wednesday 19th April 1967
Train	530 pm Weymouth to Waterloo
Loco	Unconverted West Country class 4-6-2 No. 34023 *Blackmore Vale*
Load	11 coaches 358 tons tare 380 tons gross
Driver	Allen, Weymouth MPD
Recorder	David Foale

	miles	sched	mins	secs	speed	
Bournemouth Central	0.00	0.00	00	00		6 mins late
Boscombe	1.20		03	24	38	
Pokesdown	1.75		04	11	52	
Christchurch	3.70		06	05	65/64	
Hinton Admiral	7.00		09	05	66½/62½	
New Milton	9.50		11	24	67/74	
Sway	12.50		13	54	72	
Lymington Junction	14.30		15	31	53*/50*	sigs
Brockenhurst	15.25		16	37	58/67/66	
Woodfidley Box	18.35		19	25	71/73½	
Beaulieu Road	19.95		20	48	69/73	
Lyndhurst Road	22.65		23	04	66/68½	
Totton	25.50		25	42	59*	
Redbridge	26.15		26	21	55/58	
Millbrook	27.90		28	11	52	
Southampton Central	28.80	35.30	30	02		right time
net time	29 minutes					

67.08

Date	Friday 21st April 1967
Train	638 pm Salisbury to Waterloo
Loco	Unconverted West Country class 4-6-2 No. 34102 *Lapford*
Load	5 coaches and 1 van, 194 tons tare 210 tons gross
Crew	Clive Groome, Nine Elms MPD
Recorder	Bryan Benn

	miles	sched	mins	secs	speed	
Basingstoke	0.00	0.00	00	00		7 mins late
MP 46	1.75		03	26	60	
Newnham Siding	4.05		05	23	76	
MP 43	4.75		05	56	76	
Hook	5.59		06	33	79	
MP 41	6.75		07	18	82	

	miles	sched	mins	secs	speed	
Winchfield	7.92		08	15	89	
MP 38	9.75		09	28	93/91	
Fleet	11.27		10	28	92	
MP 35	12.75		11	26	95/98	
Farnborough	14.55		12	31	95	
Sturt Lane Jct	15.60		13	15	97/98	
MP 31	16.75		13	55	93	eased
Pirbright Jct	18.26		14	48	90	
Brookwood	19.76		15	57	81	
Woking Jct	23.00		19	31	*	sigs
			sigs stop			
MP 24½	23.25		20	12	0*	
			22	11		
Woking	23.46	26.00	23	48		
	start to stop aveage to MP 24½: 69.06 mph average speed MP 38 to 31: 94.38 mph net time 19½ minutes					

67.09

Date	Thursday 27th April 1967
Train	638 pm Salisbury to Waterloo
Loco	Rebuilt Merchant Navy class 4-6-2 No. 35003 *Royal Mail*
Load	7 vehicles, 232½ tons tare 245 tons full
Crew	Chapman and Symon, Nine Elms MPD
Recorder	Bryan Benn

	miles	sched	mins	secs	speed	
Basingstoke	0.00	0.00	00	00		
Newnham Siding	4.05		04	51	82	
Hook	5.59		05	55	89	
Winchfield	7.92		07	26	95	
MP 38	9.75		08	36	100	
Fleet	11.27		09	29	100/99	
Bramshott	12.25		10	03	101	
Farnborough	14.55		11	32	91	eased
Sturt Lane Jct	15.60		12	17	93	
MP 31	16.75		12	59	90	
Pirbright Jct	18.26		13	51	94/100	
Brookwood	19.76		14	51	97	
Woking Jct	23.00		17	31	*/56	sigs
Woking	23.46	26.00	18	22		
net time	18 minutes fastest ever known time with steam Basingstoke to Woking start to stop start to stop average: 76.64 mph average speed Winchfield to Brookwood: 95.79 mph					

67.10

Date	Friday 5th May 1967
Train	638 pm Salisbury to Waterloo
Loco	Rebuilt West Country class 4-6-2 No. 34037 *Clovelly*
Load	5 coaches and 2 vans, 235 tons approx
Crew	Dave Davis aand John Gafney, Nine Elms MPD
Recorder	Richard (Joe) Jolliffe

	miles	sched	mins	secs	speed	
Basingstoke	0.00	0.00	00	00		
MP 46	1.75		02	49	65	
Newnham Siding	4.05		04	45	79	
MP 43	4.75		05	16	82	
Hook	5.59		05	46	85½	
MP 41	6.75		06	37	87½	
Winchfield	7.92		07	25	90½	
MP 38	9.75		08	34	97	
Fleet	11.27		09	30	94	
Farnborough	14.55		13	21	27*	tsr
Sturt Lane Jct	15.60		15	00	52	
MP 31	16.75		16	11	63½	
Pirbright Jct	18.26		17	15	78½	
Brookwood	19.76		18	30	83½/84	
Woking	23.46	26.00	22	04		
net time	19 minutes start to stop average: 63.79 mph					

67.11

Date	Monday 22nd May 1967
Train	615 pm Weymouth to Waterloo
Loco	Rebuilt West Country class 4-6-2 No. 34001 *Exeter*
Load	3 coaches and 5 vans, 235 tons tare 260 tons gross
Crew	Jim Evans Nine Elms MPD
Weather	Dry and fine
Recorder	DB from 4th vehicle

	miles	sched	mins	secs	speed	
Winchester City	0.00	0.00	00	00		¼ min late
Winchester Jct	2.10	5.30	03	53	51	
MP 63	3.55		06	00	18*	tsr
Wallers Ash Box	4.85		08	53	45½	
Weston Box	6.35		10	33	61	
MP 59	7.55		11	40	66½	
Micheldever	8.50		12	30	71	
MP 57	9.55		13	22	72½	

	miles	sched	mins	secs	speed	
Roundwood Box	10.35		14	04	73	
Waltham Box	11.45		15	00	74	
Steventon Box	12.60		15	55	76	
Wootton Box	14.05		17	47	38*/0*	sigs stop *
Worting Jct	16.28	25.00	24	46	24/54½	
Basingstoke	18.80	29.00	28	49		
	0.00	0.00	00	00		¼ min early
MP 46	1.75		03	11	60	
Newnham Siding	4.10		05	16	74½	
MP 43	4.75		05	50	74	
Hook	5.59		06	29	79	
MP 41	6.75		07	21	82	
Winchfield	7.92		08	12	85½	
MP 38	9.75		09	29	89	
Fleet	11.27		10	30	86	
MP 35	12.75		11	35	85/86	
Farnborough	14.55		12	50	82½	
Sturt Lane Jct	15.60		13	36	84	
MP 31	16.75		14	28	83	
Pirbright Jct	18.26		15	26	90	
Brookwood	19.76		16	28	90	SVO
MP 27	20.75		17	13	71*	brakes
MP 26	21.75		18	02	74/77½	
Woking Jct	23.00		19	03	74*	SVO
Woking	23.46	26.00	19	50		6½ mins early
	0.00	0.00	00	00		2¼ mins early
West Byfleet	2.61		03	45	70½	
Byfleet & New Haw	3.89		04	47	77½/80	
Weybridge	5.14		05	46	78	
Oatlands Box	6.17		06	31	80½	
Walton	7.21		07	16	84	
Hersham	8.38		08	05	86	
Esher	9.90		09	11	83	
Hampton Court Jct	10.95	16.00	09	58	76	8½ mins early
Surbiton	12.25		11	43	34*	sigs
Berrylands	13.31		13	16	46½	
New Malden	14.51		14	44	52	
Raynes Park	15.65		15	56	60	
Wimbledon	17.10		17	18	65½	
Earlsfield	18.71		19	00	47*/16*	sigs
Clapham Junction	20.36	26.00	23	21	23*	tsr
Queens Road	21.48		25	10	56½	

	miles	sched	mins	secs	speed	
Vauxhall	22.98		26	40	47*/0**	sigs stop**
Waterloo	24.29	33.00	33	32		1½ mins early
	Basingstoke to Woking start to stop average: 70.97 mph average speed MP 41 to 27: 85.14 mph Winchester to Basingstoke net time 20 mins Basingstoke to Woking net time 19¾ mins Woking to Waterloo net time 24 mins					* 21 seconds ** 1 min 57 secs

67.12

Date	Wednesday 24th May 1967
Train	615 pm Weymouth to Waterloo
Loco	Rebuilt West Country class 4-6-2 No. 34001 *Exeter*
Load	3 coaches and 6 vans, 239½ tons tare 260 tons gross
Crew	Jim Evans and C Arbuckle Nine Elms MPD
Weather	Heavy rain
Recorder	DB from 5th Vehicle

	miles	sched	mins	secs	speed	
Winchester City	0.00	0.00	00	00		½ min early
Winchester Jct	2.10	5.30	04	04	51	
MP 63	3.55		06	53	16*	tsr
Wallers Ash Box	4.85		09	58	43	
Weston Box	6.35		11	43	58	
MP 59	7.55		12	52	63	
Micheldever	8.50		13	46	65½	
MP 57	9.55		14	44	67	
Roundwood Box	10.35		15	28	67½	
Waltham Box	11.45		16	26	71	
Steventon Box	12.60		17	22	76/80	
Wootton Box	14.05		18	27	77	
Worting Jct	16.28	25.00	20	55	42*/0*	sigs stop*
Basingstoke	18.80	29.00	27	28		SVO
	0.00	0.00	00	00		½ min early
MP 46	1.75		03	08	61½	
Newnham Siding	4.10		05	08	75½	
MP 43	4.75		05	42	76	
Hook	5.59		06	19	80	
MP 41	6.75		07	13	82	
Winchfield	7.92		08	06	84	
MP 38	9.75		09	21	89	
Fleet	11.27		10	22	87½	
MP 35	12.75		11	23	90	
Farnborough	14.55		12	36	83	eased
Sturt Lane Jct	15.60		13	22	85	
MP 31	16.75		14	14	84	

	miles	sched	mins	secs	speed	
Pirbright Jct	18.26		15	11	90	
Brookwood	19.76		16	13	94	
MP 27	20.75		16	52	83*	brakes
MP 26	21.75		17	45	70*/74½	slight sigs?
Woking Jct	23.00		18	39	63*	
Woking	23.46	26.00	19	34		7 mins early
	0.00	0.00	00	00		1¾ mins early
West Byfleet	2.61		03	36	70½	
Byfleet & New Haw	3.89		04	37	75	
Weybridge	5.14		05	43	70	
Oatlands Box	6.17		06	35	72½	
Walton	7.21		07	25	77	
Hersham	8.38		08	19	74	
Esher	9.90		09	41	62	
Hampton Court Jct	10.95	16.00	10	43	56½	7¼ mins early
Surbiton	12.25		12	07	54	
Berrylands	13.31		13	16	56½	
New Malden	14.51		14	30	60	
Raynes Park	15.65		15	23	61	SVO
Wimbledon	17.10		17	01	60	
Earlsfield	18.71		18	46	54/26*	tsr
Clapham Junction	20.36	26.00	21	41	31½	
Queens Road	21.48		23	36	45	
Vauxhall	22.98		25	26	36/0*	sigs stop**
Waterloo	24.29	33.00	35	00		right time
	Basingstoke to Woking start to stop average; 71.94 mph average speed MP 41 to 27: 87.05 mph Winchester to Basingstoke net time 20½ mins Basingstoke to Woking net time 19½ mins Woking to Waterloo net time 26¼ mins					* 61 seconds ** 4 mins 55 secs

67.13

Date	Thursday 25th May 1967
Train	615 pm Weymouth to Waterloo
Loco	Rblt Merchant Navy class 4-6-2 No.35023 *Holland Afrika Line*
Load	3 coaches and 5 vans, 243 tons tare 265 tons gross
Crew	Bert Fordrey and Tony Cottee, Nine Elms MPD
Weather	Dry but greasy rails
Recorder	DB from 4th vehicle

	miles	sched	mins	secs	speed	
Winchester City	0.00	0.00	00	00		¾ min early
Winchester Jct	2.10	5.30	03	43	53½/56	
MP 63	3.55		05	56	14*	tsr
Wallers Ash Box	4.85		09	15	40	

	miles	sched	mins	secs	speed	
Weston Box	6.35		11	02	58	
MP 59	7.55		12	12	63	
Micheldever	8.50		13	05	67½	
MP 57	9.55		14	00	70	
Roundwood Box	10.35		14	41	71½	
Waltham Box	11.45		15	36	73	
Steventon Box	12.60		16	32	76	
Wootton Box	14.05		17	56	24*	sigs
Worting Jct	16.28	25.00	22	16	41/53/0*	sigs stop *
Basingstoke	18.80	29.00	28	51		
	0.00	0.00	00	00		¾ min late
MP 46	1.75		03	05	60½	
Newnham Siding	4.10		05	08	73	
MP 43	4.75		05	43	74½	
Hook	5.59		06	20	80	
MP 41	6.75		07	15	82½	
Winchfield	7.92		08	04	87	
MP 38	9.75		09	17	94	
Fleet	11.27		10	15	93	
MP 35	12.75		11	13	95	
Farnborough	14.55		12	31	78*	brakes
Sturt Lane Jct	15.60		13	18	82	
MP 31	16.75		14	12	84	
Pirbright Jct	18.26		15	08	90	
Brookwood	19.76		16	09	96	
MP 27	20.75		16	47	93	
MP 26	21.75		17	56	50*/38*	sigs
Woking Jct	23.00		19	34	44½	
Woking	23.46	26.00	20	36		4¾ mins early
	0.00	0.00	00	00		2½ mins early
West Byfleet	2.61		03	54	68½	
Byfleet & New Haw	3.89		04	57	78	
Weybridge	5.14		05	58	77½	
Oatlands Box	6.17		06	43	80	
Walton	7.21		07	27	86	
Hersham	8.38		08	15	88/12*	sigs
Esher	9.90		11	18	48	
Hampton Court Jct	10.95	16.00	12	33	54½	6 mins early
Surbiton	12.25		14	17	40*	sigs
Berrylands	13.31		15	28	53/38*	sigs
New Malden	14.51		17	23	47	
Raynes Park	15.65		18	46	52½	
Wimbledon	17.10		20	26	53	

	miles	sched	mins	secs	speed	
Earlsfield	18.71		22	48	40/26*	tsr
Clapham Junction	20.36	26.00	26	18	34/27*	sigs
Queens Road	21.48		28	34	40/44	
Vauxhall	22.98		30	28	36/10*	sigs
Waterloo	24.29	33.00	35	07		right time
	Basingstoke to Woking start to stop average: 68.33 mph average speed MP 41 to 27: 88.58 mph Winchester to Basingstoke net time 20½ mins Basingstoke to Woking net time 19¼ mins Woking to Waterloo net time 25 mins					* 1 min 31 secs

67.14

Date	Friday 2nd June 1967
Train	530 pm Weymouth to Waterloo
Loco	Rebuilt Merchant Navy class 4-6-2 No. 35003 *Royal Mail*
Load	10 coaches and 1 van, 365 tons tare 395 tons gross
Crew	Gordon Porter and Eddie Presland, Nine Elms MPD
Timed by	Terry Jackson

	miles	sched	mins	secs	speed	
Southampton	0.00	0.00	00	00		
Northam Jct	1.05	3.00	04	19	22*	
St Denys	2.11		06	09	37	
Swaythling	3.45		08	08	45	
Southampton Airport	4.30		09	11	53	
Eastleigh	5.80	11.00	10	44	56	
Allbrook Box	6.66		11	39	57/58½/57½	
Shawford	9.61		14	42	58	
Shawford Jct	10.46		15	30	58	
St Cross	11.3		16	38	58/57½	
Winchester City	12.70		17	57	58	
Winchester Jct	14.80		20	09	57½/16*	tsr
Wallers Ash Box	17.55		26	13	35	
Weston Box	19.05		28	20	45½	
Micheldever	21.20		30	54	53	
Roundwood Box	23.05		32	59	55	
Waltham Box	24.15		34	09	60½/65	
Wootton Box	26.75		36	33	64½/60	
Worting Jct	28.98	39.30	38	48	61½	
Basingstoke	31.50		40	52	78/91/88	
Hook	37.08		44	39	91/90	
Winchfield	39.41		46	13	94/98	
Fleet	42.76		48	18	97	
Bramshot Halt	43.55		48	52	90	

	miles	sched	mins	secs	speed	
Farnborough	46.05		50	36	80	
Sturt Lane Jct	47.05		51	20	72*/47½*	tsr
MP 31	48.25		52	38	49	
Brookwood	51.25		55	23	75/76½/67½*	sigs
Woking Jct	54.50	63.30	58	05	73½	
Woking	54.95		58	24	75	
West Byfleet	57.56		60	23	84	
Byfleet & New Haw	58.84		61	14	89	
Weybridge	60.09		62	09	86/84	
Walton	62.16		63	30	90/92	
Hersham	63.33		64	16	91	
Esher	64.85		65	19	87	
			sigs stop		0*	
Hampton Court Jct.	65.90	78.30	69	03	16½*	to slow line
Surbiton	67.20		71	38	43½/52½	
Berrylands	68.26		72	55	52	
New Malden	69.46		74	58	20*	to fast line
Raynes Park	70.60		76	56	47	
Wimbledon	72.05		78	27	61/63	
Earlsfield	73.66		80	29	49*	sigs
Clapham Junction	75.31	89.30	83	03	29*	sigs
			sigs stop		0*	
Queens Road	76.43		88	18	38	
Vauxhall	77.93		90	27	36	
Waterloo	79.24	96.30	94	19		
net time	74 minutes					

67.15

Date	Tuesday 6th June 1967
Train	638 pm Salisbury to Waterloo
Loco	Unconverted West Country class 4-6-2 No.34023 *Blackmore Vale*
Load	9 vehicles, 290 tons tare 310 tons gross
Crew	Dente and McQuade, Nine Elms MPD
Recorder	Richard (Joe) Jolliffe

	miles	sched	mins	secs	speed	
Basingstoke	0.00	0.00	00	00		
Newnham Siding	4.10		05	27	70	
Hook	5.59		06	38	75	
Winchfield	7.92		08	27	82	
MP 38	9.75		09	46	87/89	
Fleet	11.27		10	46	87	

	miles	sched	mins	secs	speed	
Bramshott	12.25		11	22	89	
Farnborough	14.55		13	05	79/30*	tsr
MP 31	16.75		16	00	43	
Brookwood	19.76		18	54	76/79	
Woking Jct	23.00		21	25	62*	
Woking	23.46	26.00	22	26		
	0.00	0.00	00	00		
West Byfleet	2.61		03	56	68½	
Byfleet & New Haw	3.89		04	58	77	
Weybridge	5.14		05	59	81	
Oatlands Box	6.17		06	43	82½	
Walton	7.21		07	27	87	
Hersham	8.38		08	13	90/91	
Esher	9.90		09	17	85	
Hampton Court Jct	10.95	14.00	10	03	79½/72*	slight sigs
Surbiton	12.25		11	05	75½	
Berrylands	13.31		11	59	79/80	
New Malden	14.51		12	50	79	
Raynes Park	15.65		13	46	75	
Wimbledon	17.10		14	55	70½	
Earlsfield	18.71		16	22	69	
Clapham Junction	20.36	26.00	18	01	46*	
Queens Road	21.48		19	34	59/61½	
Vauxhall	22.98		21	02	42*	
Waterloo	24.29	33.00	24	10		

Basingstoke to Woking start to stop average: 62.75 mph
Woking to Waterloo start to stop average: 60.31 mph
Basingstoke to Woking net time 20 minutes
Woking to Waterloo net time 24 minutes

67.16

Date	Wednesday 7th June 1967
Train	638 pm Salisbury to Waterloo
Loco	Rebuilt West Country class 4-6-2 No. 34100 *Appledore*
Load	6 coaches and 1 van, 235 tons approx
Crew	D Taylor Nine Elms MPD
Recorder	Richard (Joe) Jolliffe

	miles	sched	mins	secs	speed	
Basingstoke	0.00	0.00	00	00		
MP 46	1.75		04	14	71	**
Newnham Siding	4.05		05	20	79½	
MP 43	4.75		05	52	81	

	miles	sched	mins	secs	speed	
Hook	5.59		06	23	83½	
MP 41	6.75		07	16	87	
Winchfield	7.92		08	04	90	
MP 38	9.75		09	15	95	
Fleet	11.27		10	12	94/95	
Farnborough	14.55		12	25	79½	
Sturt Lane Jct	15.60				33*	tsr
MP 31	16.75		15	15	37	
Pirbright Jct	18.26				60½	
Brookwood	19.76		18	37	59*/53*/57	sigs
Woking	23.46	26.00	23	05		
net time	** time and speed at MP 45 start to stop average : 60.98 mph 19½ minutes					

67.17

Date	Wednesday 14th June 1967
Train	638 pm Salisbury to Waterloo
Loco	Unconverted West Country class 4-6-2 No. 34102 *Lapford*
Load	5 coaches and 2 vans, 214 tons tare 235 tons gross
Crew	John Gaffney and Bob Lee, Nine Elms MPD
Weather	Fine
Recorder	DB

	miles	sched	mins	secs	speed	
Basingstoke	0.00	0.00	00	00		right time
MP 46	1.75		03	09	55½	priming
Newnham Siding	4.05		05	18	73	40% cut off
MP 43	4.75		05	51	76	
Hook	5.59		06	28	83	
MP 41	6.75		07	18	87	
Winchfield	7.92		08	05	92	
MP 39	8.75		08	37	94	
MP 38	9.75		09	15	98/97	
MP 37	10.75		09	52	98	
Fleet	11.27		10	10	98½	
MP 36	11.75		10	28	100	40% cut off
MP 35	12.75		11	05	97	
Farnborough	14.55		12	31	64*	
Sturt Lane Jct	15.60		13	34	53*	tsr
MP 31	16.75		14	54	58½	
Pirbright Jct	18.26		16	06	76	
Brookwood	19.76		17	16	88	
MP 27	20.75		17	57	83	brakes

	miles	sched	mins	secs	speed	
MP 26	21.75		19	04	47*	sigs
Woking Jct	23.00		20	37	50	
Woking	23.46	26.00	21	30		
net time	18¾ minutes start to stop average: 65.47 mph average speed MP 39 to MP 35: 97.33 mph					

67.18

Date	Thursday 15th June 1967
Train	638 pm Salisbury to Waterloo
Loco	BR Standard class 4-6-0 No. 73029
Load	5 coaches and 2 vans, 214 tons tare 235 tons full
Crew	John Gaffney and Tom Moult, Nine Elms MPD
Recorder	DB

	miles	sched	mins	secs	speed	
Basingstoke	0.00	0.00	00	00		right time
MP 46	1.75		02	44	63	
Newnham Siding	4.10		04	41	75½	
MP 43	4.75		05	15	75	
Hook	5.59		05	54	77	
MP 41	6.75		06	48	78½	
Winchfield	7.92		07	42	80	
MP 38	9.75		09	04	82½	
Fleet	11.27		10	11	80	
MP 35	12.75		11	20	76	eased
Farnborough	14.55		12	51	63	
Sturt Lane Jct	15.60		13	54	58*	tsr
MP 31	16.75		15	04	63½	
Pirbright Jct	18.26		16	16	73/47*	sigs
Brookwood	19.76		17	53	58½	
MP 27	20.75		18	51	66	
MP 26	21.75		19	45	73/74½	
Woking Jct	23.00		20	46	65*	
Woking	23.46	26.00	21	39		
	0.00	0.00	00	00		right time
West Byfleet	2.61		03	32	70	
Byfleet & New Haw	3.89		04	33	78	
Weybridge	5.14		05	34	76	
Oatlands Box	6.17		06	22	77½	
Walton	7.21		07	08	82	
Hersham	8.38		07	59	80	eased
Esher	9.90		09	16	71	
Hampton Court Jct	10.95	14.00	10	12	69	

	miles	sched	mins	secs	speed	
Surbiton	12.25		11	20	66½	
Berrylands	13.31		12	18	68	
New Malden	14.51		13	22	69	
Raynes Park	15.65		14	21	70	
Wimbledon	17.10		15	40	58*	
Earlsfield	18.71		17	22	61	
			tsr stop			SVO
MP 5	19.29		18	20	0*/16*	tsr
			18	34		
Clapham Junction	20.36	26.00	22	10	37½	
Queens Road	21.48		23	48	54	SVO
Vauxhall	22.98		25	28	39*	SVO
Waterloo	24.29	33.00	28	38		4¼ mins early

Basingstoke to Woking start to stop avearge: 65.02 mph
Woking to MP 5 start to stop average: 63.13 mph
Basingstoke to Woking net time 20 minutes
Woking to Waterloo net time 25 minutes

67.19

Date	Wednesday 21st June 1967
Train	615 pm Weymouth to Waterloo
Loco	Rebuilt Battle of Britain class 4-6-2 No. 34060 *25 Squadron*
Load	3 coaches and 5 vans, 215½ tons tare 235 tons gross
Crew	Reuben Hendicott and Ray McQuade, Nine Elms MPD
Weather	Dry and fine
Recorder	DB

	miles	sched	mins	secs	speed	
Eastleigh	0.00	0.00	00	00		1¼ mins late
Allbrook Box	0.85		02	35	34½	SVO
MP 71	2.50		04	36	53½	
Shawford	3.85		06	02	61	
Shawford Jct	4.55		06	46	64½	
St Cross	5.60		07	43	68	
MP 67	6.50		08	22	70½	SVO
Winchester City	6.95	12.00	09	22		
	0.00	0.00	00	00		¾ min early
Winchester Jct	2.10	5.30	04	48	41½/18*	tsr
MP 63	3.55		08	26	32½	SVO
Wallers Ash Box	4.85		10	07	55½	
Weston Box	6.35		11	32	67	
MP 59	7.55		12	33	71	
Micheldever	8.50		13	21	74	

	miles	sched	mins	secs	speed	
MP 57	9.55		14	13	75½	
Roundwood Box	10.35		14	50	76	
Waltham Box	11.45		15	44	76	
Steventon Box	12.60		16	38	75	
Wootton Box	14.05		17	54	64*/35*	sigs
Worting Jct	16.28	25.00	21	16	52½/0*	sigs stop*
Basingstoke	18.80	29.00	29	40		
	0.00	0.00	00	00		right time
MP 46	1.75		03	14	61	
Newnham Siding	4.10		05	13	78	
MP 43	4.75		05	44	79½	
Hook	5.59		06	20	82	
MP 41	6.75		07	11	86	
Winchfield	7.92		08	00	89	
MP 38	9.75		09	12	93	
Fleet	11.27		10	51	27*	sigs
MP 35	12.75		14	40	23*/2*	sigs
Farnborough	14.55		21	35	31½	SVO
Sturt Lane Jct	15.60		23	10	51	
MP 31	16.75		24	27	60	
Pirbright Jct	18.26		25	40	75½	
Brookwood	19.76		26	52	83½	
MP 27	20.75		27	35	80	eased
MP 26	21.75		28	24	76	SVO
Woking Jct	23.00		29	27	60*	
Woking	23.46	26.00	30	36		
	0.00	0.00	00	00		3¾ mins late
West Byfleet	2.61		03	44	73	
Byfleet & New Haw	3.89		04	42	82	
Weybridge	5.14		05	40	80	
Oatlands Box	6.17		06	24	83	
Walton	7.21		07	07	88	
Hersham	8.38		07	57	82	eased
Esher	9.90		09	10	71	
Hampton Court Jct	10.95	16.00	10	04	72½	2¼ mins early
Surbiton	12.25		12	06	26*	sigs
Berrylands	13.31		13	34	52	
New Malden	14.51		14	49	61	
Raynes Park	15.65		15	55	64	
Wimbledon	17.10		17	17	56½	
Earlsfield	18.71		18	59	61	
Clapham Junction	20.36	26.00	22	07	9*	sigs

	miles	sched	mins	secs	speed	
Queens Road	21.48		24	17	51	
Vauxhall	22.98		26	02	32*/20*	sigs
Waterloo	24.29	33.00	30	17		1 min late
	Basingstoke to Woking start to stop average: 70.97 mph average speed MP 41 to 27: 85.14 mph Winchester to Basingstoke net time 19 mins Basingstoke to Woking net time 19¼ mins Woking to Waterloo net time 26 minutes					* 167 seconds

67.20

Date	Friday 23rd June 1967
Train	6.15 pm Weymouth to Waterloo
Loco	Rebuilt Battle of Britain class 4-6-2 No. 34060 *25 Squadron*
Load	5 coaches and 2 vans, 230 tons tare 245 tons gross
Crew	Reuben Hendicott and Ray McQuade, Nine Elms MPD
Timed by	Terry Jackson

	miles	sched	mins	secs	speed	
Southampton	0.00	0.00	00	00		
Northam Jct	1.05	3.30	03	50	24/16*	
St Denys	2.11		05	32	44½	
Swaythling	3.45		07	10	56/58	
Southampton Airport	4.30	10.00	08	24		
	0.00	0.00	00	00	38	
Eastleigh	1.40	5.00	03	38		
	0.00	0.00	00	00		
Allbrook Box	0.85		02	26	38½	
Shawford	3.85		05	40	64	
Shawford Jct	4.55		06	21	67	
St Cross	5.60		07	19	72/73	
Winchester City	6.95	12.00	08	56		
	0.00	0.00	00	00		
Winchester Jct	2.10	5.30	04	03	43½/17½*	tsr
Wallers Ash Box	4.85		09	34	57½	
Weston Box	6.35		10	56	66	
Micheldever	8.50		12	42	76/77	
Roundwood Box	10.30		14	10	73½*	sigs
Waltham Box	11.45		16	01	30½*	sigs
Wootton Box	14.05		20	05	48½/52½	
			sigs stop		0*	
Worting Jct	16.30	25.00	25	17	49	
Basingstoke	18.80	29.00	30	08		

	miles	sched	mins	secs	speed	
	0.00	0.00	00	00		
Hook	5.60		06	08	83	
Winchfield	7.95		07	45	88/94	
Fleet	11.30		09	58	84	
Bramshot Halt	12.10		10	37	82	
Farnborough	14.55		12	27	77	
Sturt Lane Jct	15.75		13	15	76/61½*	tsr
MP 31	16.80		14	21	62½/75	
Brookwood	19.80		16	51	72/33*	sigs
Woking Jct	23.05		20	46	44	
Woking	23.45	26.00	22	06		
	0.00	0.00	00	00		
West Byfleet	2.70		03	25	75	
Byfleet & New Haw	3.95		04	21	83	
Weybridge	5.25		05	18	84	
Walton	7.25		06	44	90	
Hersham	8.40		07	30	86	
Esher	9.95		08	37	84	
Hampton Court Jct.	11.00	16.00	09	24	75	
Surbiton	12.30		10	29	69	
Berrylands	13.40		11	26	66½	
New Malden	14.60		12	34	60	
Raynes Park	15.70		13	45	59/58	
Wimbledon	17.15		15	09	61	
Earlsfield	18.80		16	50	60	
Clapham Junction	20.45	26.00	18	49	42*	
Queens Road	21.70		20	20	55	
Vauxhall	23.05		22	11	33½	
			sigs stop		0*	
Waterloo	24.35	33.00	28	11		
net times	Winchester to Basingstoke: 19 minutes Basingstoke to Woking: 19 minutes Woking to Waterloo: 25 minutes					

Date	Monday 26th June 1967	
Train	615 pm Weymouth to Waterloo	
Loco	Rebuilt Merchant Navy class 4-6-2 No. 35003 *Royal Mail*	
Load	3 coaches and 2 vans, 164 tons tare 180 tons gross	
Crew	Fred Burridge and R Symon, Nine Elms MPD	
Also on Footplate	Bryan Benn	
Weather	Damp	
Recorder	DB	

	miles	sched	mins	secs	speed	
Basingstoke	0.00	0.00	00	00		right time
MP 46	1.75		02	47	63	
Newnham Siding	4.05		04	36	84	
MP 43	4.75		05	04	86	
Hook	5.59		05	37	90	
MP 41	6.75		06	24	94	
Winchfield	7.92		07	09	98	SVO
MP 39	8.75		07	38	100	
MP 38	9.75		08	13	104/106	
MP 37	10.75		08	47	105	
Fleet	11.27		09	05	100	eased/SVO
MP 36	11.75		09	23	101	
MP 35	12.75		09	59	102	
MP 34	13.75		10	34	100	
Farnborough	14.55		11	07	71½*	brakes
Sturt Lane Jct	15.60		12	02	68*	tsr
MP 31	16.75		13	03	74½	
Pirbright Jct	18.26		14	03	90	
MP 29	18.75		14	27	95	
Brookwood	19.76		15	06	91	
MP 27	20.75		15	49	82*	
MP 26	21.75		16	37	70*	sigs
Woking Jct	23.00		17	52	51*	
Woking	23.46	26.00	18	48		7 mins early
net time	start to stop average: 74.87 mph average speed MP 39 to MP 34: 102.28 mph 17 minutes 24 seconds: 80.9 mph					

67.22

Date	Wednesday 28th June 1967
Train	615 pm Weymouth to Waterloo
Loco	Rebuilt Merchant Navy class 4-6-2 No. 35003 *Royal Mail*
Load	3 coaches and 2 vans, 164 tons tare 180 tons gross
Crew	Fred Burridge and J Roscoe, Nine Elms MPD
Weather	Damp
Recorder	DB

	miles	sched	mins	secs	speed	
Basingstoke	0.00	0.00	00	00		right time
MP 46	1.75		02	50	65½	SVO
Newnham Siding	4.05		04	42	82	
MP 43	4.75		05	11	83	
Hook	5.59		05	46	90	
MP 41	6.75		06	33	95	
Winchfield	7.92		07	17	98½	
MP 39	8.75		07	46	102	SVO
MP 38	9.75		08	20	105	
MP 37	10.75		08	55	103	
Fleet	11.27		09	13	100	eased
MP 36	11.75		09	31	101/103	
MP 35	12.75		10	06	102	
MP 34	13.75		10	41	100	
Farnborough	14.55		11	14	78*	brakes
Sturt Lane Jct	15.60		12	02	60*	tsr
MP 31	16.75		13	13	65½/75	
Pirbright Jct	18.26		14	23	60*	sigs
MP 29	18.75		15	04	48*/28*	sigs
Brookwood	19.76		16	45	48½	
MP 27	20.75		17	55	53	
MP 26	21.75		19	11	45*/46	sigs
Woking Jct	23.00		20	59	34*	sigs
Woking	23.46	26.00	22	07		4 mins early
net time	start to stop average: 63.65 mph average speed MP 39 to MP 34: 102.28 mph 17 minutes 31 seconds: 80.4 mph					

67.23

Date	Thursday 29th June 1967
Train	810 am Waterloo to Weymouth Quay
Loco	Rebuilt Battle of Britain class 4-6-2 No. 34087 *145 Squadron*
Load	12 coaches, 400 tons tare 420 tons gross
Crew	Reuben Hendicott and Ray McQuade, Nine Elms MPD
Recorder	David Foale

	miles	sched	mins	secs	speed	
Basingstoke	0.00	0.00	00	00		right time
Worting Jct	2.51	5.30	05	12	46	
Wootton Box	4.75		07	52	56	
Steventon Box	6.20		09	16	66	
Roundwood Box	8.45		11	16	72	
Micheldever	10.30		12	41	82	
Weston Box	12.45		14	12	89	
Wallers Ash Box	13.95		15	11	93	
MP 63	15.20		15	59	96	
Winchester Jct Box	16.70	21.30	16	55	89	
Winchester City	18.80		18	23	85	
St Cross Box	20.03		19	18	37*	tsr
Shawford	21.92		21	38	48	
Allbrook Box	24.86		24	34	71	
Eastleigh	25.76	29.30	25	15	72	
Swaythling	28.02		27	19	42*	sigs
St Denys	29.43		30	55	*	sigs
Northam Jct	30.49	35.00	32	55	*	
Southampton Central	31.49	38.50	36	29		
net time	31 minutes					

67.24

Date	Thursday 29th June 1967
Train	4 pm Weymouth Quay to Waterloo
Loco	Rebuilt Battle of Britain class 4-6-2 No. 34087 *145 Squadron*
Load	11 coaches and 1 van, 403 tons tare 430 tons gross
Crew	D Shepherd, Eastleigh MPD
Recorder	Richard (Joe) Jolliffe

	miles	sched	mins	secs	speed	
Basingstoke	0.00	0.00	00	00		
MP 45	2.75		04	30	63	
Newnham Siding	4.05		05	45	69	
Hook	5.59		06	56	75	
Winchfield	7.92		08	46	82	
MP 38	9.75		10	03	88/90	
Fleet	11.27		11	04	89	

	miles	sched	mins	secs	speed	
Bramshott	12.25		11	38	92	
Farnborough	14.55		13	19	80	
Sturt Lane Jct	15.60				61½*	tsr
MP 31	16.75		15	16	62½	
Brookwood	19.76		17	52	74	
Woking Jct	23.00		20	30	54½*	
Woking	23.46	26.00	21	41		
net time	20½ minutes start to stop average : 64.92 mph average speed Hook to Farnborough: 86.25 mph					

67.25

Date	Friday 30th June 1967
Train	615 pm Weymouth to Waterloo
Loco	Rebuilt West Country class 4-6-2 No. 34021 *Dartmoor*
Load	3 coaches and 3 vans, 185 tons tare 2015 tons gross
Crew	Fred Burridge and R Symon, Nine Elms MPD
Recorder	Richard (Joe) Jolliffe

	miles	sched	mins	secs	speed	
Winchester City	0.00	0.00	00	00		
Winchester Jct	2.10	5.30	04	50	37/17*	tsr
Wallers Ash Box	4.85		10	41	54½	
Weston Box	6.35		12	09	66	
Micheldever	8.50		13	55	76½	
Roundwood Box	10.35		15	23	79/80	
Waltham Box	11.45		16	15	79/80	
Steventon Box	12.60		17	05	78½/79	
Wootton Box	14.05		18	11	75	
Worting Jct	16.28	25.00	20	10	61½*/0*	sigs stop*
Basingstoke	18.80	29.00	25	26		
	0.00	0.00	00	00		
MP 46	1.75		02	51	67	
Newnham Siding	4.10		04	42	82	
MP 43	4.75		05	10	84	
Hook	5.59		05	43	88	
MP 41	6.75		06	32	92	
Winchfield	7.92		07	17	95	
MP 39	8.75		07	47	98	
MP 38	9.75		08	26	95	
MP 37	10.75		09	05	93	
Fleet	11.27		09	22	96	
Farnborough	14.55		11	35	77½*/62*	tsr
MP 31	16.75		13	31	67	

	miles	sched	mins	secs	speed	
Pirbright Jct	18.26		14	32	80	
Brookwood	19.76		15	47	88	
Woking Jct	23.00		18	22	56*	
Woking	23.46	26.00	19	18		
	Basingstoke to Woking start to stop average: 72.94 mph average speed MP 41 to Fleet: 95.30 mph Winchester to Basingstoke net time 19 mins Basingstoke to Woking net time 18¼ mins					

67.26

Date	Sunday 2nd July 1967	
Train	736 pm Bournemouth to Waterloo	
Loco	Rebuilt West Country class 4-6-2 No. 34037 *Clovelly*	
Load	9 coaches, 302 tons tare 330 tons gross	
Crew	Miles Eastleigh MPD	
Recorder	David Foale	

	miles	sched	mins	secs	speed	
Winchester City	0.00	0.00	00	00		right time
Winchester Jct	2.10	6.30	04	54	39/26*	tsr
Wallers Ash Box	4.85		09	21	50	
Weston Box	6.35		10	59	57	
Micheldever	8.50		13	05	64	
Roundwood Box	10.35		14	47	68	
Steventon Box	12.60		16	43	72	
Wootton Box	14.05		17	56	73	
Worting Junction	16.28	26.00	19	55	63*/64/59*	sigs
Basingstoke	18.80		22	20	66	
Newnham Siding	22.85		25	29	86/85	
Hook	24.38		26	32	87	
Winchfield	26.71		28	09	88	
Fleet	30.06		30	22	92	
Farnborough	33.35		32	41	73/61½*	tsr
MP 31	35.55		34	46	63	
Brookwood	38.55		37	12	82	
Woking	42.25	56.00	39	57	79	
West Byfleet	44.86		41	56	81/85	
Weybridge	47.39		43	48	82/80	
Walton	49.46		45	18	85	
Hersham	50.63		46	07	84	
Hampton Court Jct.	53.20	71.00	48	09	72/71	
Surbiton	54.50		49	15	72/75	
New Malden	56.76		51	07	67	
Wimbledon	59.35		53	36	57½	

	miles	sched	mins	secs	speed	
Earlsfield	60.96		55	13	63	
Clapham Junction	62.61	83.00	57	07	41*/56	26 mins early!
			sigs stop			
Vauxhall	65.23		61	23	0*	
			63	01		
			sigs stops		0*	total 6 mins 4 secs
Waterloo	66.55	90.00	75	04		15 mins early
net time	start to stop average Winchester to Vauxhall: 63.76 mph 60 minutes					

67.27

Date	Monday 3rd July 1967
Train	530 pm Weymouth to Waterloo
Loco	Rebuilt Merchant Navy class 4-6-2 No. 35007 *Aberdeen Commonwealth*
Load	10 coaches and 1 van, 344½ tons tare 370 tons gross
Crew	R Bennett and Dave Deadman, Nine Elms MPD
Recorder	John Clifford

	miles	sched	mins	secs	speed	
Southampton	0.00	0.00	00	00		4¼ mins late
Northam Jct	1.05	3.00	03	38	24*	
St Denys	2.11		05	23	40*	
Swaythling	3.45		07	13	51	
Southampton Airport	4.41		08	09	55	
Eastleigh	5.80	11.00	09	39	61	
Allbrook Box	6.66		10	25	62	
MP 71	8.15		11	57	61	
Shawford	9.61		13	20	61	
Shawford Jct	10.46		14	07	61	
St Cross	11.50		15	12	57*	tsr
Winchester City	12.70		16	37	58/57/60	
Winchester Jct	14.80		18	45	58/30*	tsr
MP 63	16.15		20	45	35	
Wallers Ash Box	17.55		22	38	49	
MP 61	18.15		23	22	53	
Weston Box	19.05		24	16	57	
MP 59	20.15		25	29	60	
Micheldever	21.20		26	24	62½	
MP 57	22.15		27	25	63½	
Roundwood Box	23.05		28	11	64	
Waltham Box	24.15		29	14	67	
Steventon Box	25.30		30	13	71/71½	
Wootton Box	26.75		31	27	70/31*	sigs
Worting Jct	28.98	39.30	34	19	47*	

	miles	sched	mins	secs	speed	
Basingstoke	31.50		36	41	75	
MP 45	34.25		38	49	82½	
Newnham Siding	35.55		39	46	82	
Hook	37.08		40	51	86	
Winchfield	39.41		42	32	87	
MP 38	41.25		43	44	94	
Fleet	42.76		44	41	95/94	
Bramshott	43.74		45	14	95	
Farnborough	46.05		46	48	86	
Sturt Lane Jct	47.05		47	34	78*	tsr
MP 31	48.25		48	26	79	
Pirbright Jct	49.60		49	30	86	
Brookwood	51.25		50	39	87	
MP 26	53.25		52	00	86	
Woking Jct	54.50	63.30	52	54	82	
Woking	54.95		53	12	81/85	
West Byfleet	57.56		55	08	84/87	
Byfleet & New Haw	58.84		56	01	86	
Weybridge	60.09		56	57	82	
Oatlands Box	61.15		57	44	79	
Walton	62.16		58	31	82	
Hersham	63.33		59	20	82/82½	
Esher	64.85		60	29	80	
Hampton Court Jct.	65.90	78.30	61	19	77	13 mins early
Surbiton	67.20		62	21	73	
Berrylands	68.26		63	15	74½	
New Malden	69.46		64	10	73/74½	
Raynes Park	70.60		65	07	72½	
Wimbledon	72.05		66	19	68½	
Earlsfield	73.66		67	48	65½	
Clapham Junction	75.31	89.30	69	35	43½*	
Queens Road	76.43		71	13	53	
Vauxhall	77.93		73	05	35*	
Waterloo	79.24	96.30	76	10		16 mins early
net time	72 minutes average speed Hook to Brookwood: 86.67 mph average speed Hook to Hampton Court Jct: 84.49 mph					

67.28

Date	Tuesday 4th July 1967
Train	245 am Waterloo to Bournemouth
Loco	Rebuilt West Country class 4-6-2 No. 34001 *Exeter*
Load to Woking	3 coaches and 5 vans, 201 tons tare 215 tons gross
Load from Woking	3 coaches and 4 vans, 169½ tons tare 180 tons gross
Load from Basingstoke	3 coaches and 3 vans, 156½ tons tare 170 tons gross
Crew	Gordon Porter and Randall, Nine Elms MPD
Recorder	DB

	miles	sched	mins	secs	speed	
Waterloo	0.00	0.00	00	00		9¼ mins late
Vauxhall	1.29		04	15	15*/38½	sigs to slow line
Queens Road	2.81		05	50	64	
Clapham Junction	3.93	7.00	07	04	56	
Earlsfield	5.58		08	42	67½/70	
Wimbledon	7.24		10	14	63*	
Raynes Park	8.64		11	38	55*	
New Malden	9.78		12	44	63½/65½	
Berrylands	10.98		13	52	61*	
Surbiton	12.04		15	03	55*	
Hampton Court Jct	13.34	18.00	17	05	22*	sigs to fast line
Esher	14.39		18	47	50	40% cut off
Hersham	15.91		20	17	70	
Walton	17.08		21	14	75	
Oatlands Box	18.12		22	03	77	
Weybridge	19.15		22	46	81½	
Byfleet and New Haw	20.40		23	43	87/88	
West Byfleet	21.68		24	35	87	
MP 23	23.00		25	39	70/25*	sigs to slow line
Woking	24.29	37.00	27	56		right time
	0.00	00.00	00	00		7¼ mins late
Woking Jct	0.46		01	27	35	fast line
MP 26	1.71		03	08	55½	
MP 27	2.71		04	05	68	40% cut off
Brookwood	3.70		04	57	72½	
MP 29	4.71		05	45	76	
Pirbright Jct	5.20		06	12	80	
MP 30	5.71		06	30	82	
MP 31	6.71		07	14	83	
Sturt Lane Jct	7.86		08	03	90	
Farnborough	8.91		08	46	85	eased
MP 35	10.71		10	02	90/92	
Fleet	12.19		11	02	90	
MP 38	13.71		12	01	92	

	miles	sched	mins	secs	speed	
Winchfield	15.54		13	13	88½/88	
MP 41	16.71		14	02	89	
Hook	17.87		14	48	90	
MP 43	18.71		15	22	90	
Newnham Siding	19.41		15	48	91	
MP 45	20.71		16	42	83/28*	sigs to slow line
Basingstoke	23.46	29.00	20	43		1 min early
	0.00	0.00	00	00		right time
Worting Jct	2.51	7.00	05	48	33/25*	sigs
Wootton Box	4.75		08	31	60½	
Steventon Box	6.20		09	51	68	
Waltham Box	7.35		10	49	72	
Roundwood Box	8.45		12	15	34*/46	sigs
Micheldever	10.30		14	55	39½/18*	sigs
MP 59	11.35		16	49	22	
Weston Box	12.45		18	15	62½	
MP 61	13.35		18	57	76	
Wallers Ash Box	13.95		19	27	80	
MP 62	14.35		19	42	85	
MP 63	15.35		20	23	90	
MP 64	16.35		21	01	96	
Winchester Jct	16.70	23.30	21	13	98	
Winchester City	18.80	26.30	23	39		
	0.00	0.00	00	00		right time
St Cross Box	1.23		02	33	53/40*	tsr
Shawford Jct	2.47		03	58	47	
Shawford	3.12		04	55	61	
MP 71	4.55		06	03	78	
Allbrook Box	6.06		08	03	23*/40	sigs to slow line
Eastleigh	6.96	11.00	09	47		1¼ mins early
net times	Waterloo to Woking				23 minutes	
	Woking to Basingstoke				19¾ minutes	
	Basingstoke to Winchester				18 minutes	
	Winchester to Eastleigh				9 minutes	
	average speed MP 35 to MP 43: 90.00 mph					
	start to stop average Woking to Basingstoke: 67.95 mph					

67.29

Date	Wednesday 5th July 1967
Train	638 pm Salisbury to Waterloo
Loco	Rebuilt Mechant Navy class 4-6-2 No. 35008 *Orient Line*
Load	6 vehicles 199½ tons tare 205 tons gross
Driver	De'Ath, Basingstoke MPD
Recorder	Bob Grainger

	miles	sched	mins	secs	speed	
Salisbury	0.00	0.00	00	00		
Tunnel Junction	1.10		03	16	48/60	
Porton	5.37		10	33	*/52	tsr
Allington Box	8.06		13	17	67	
Grateley	10.96		15	35	80	
MP 69	14.41		17	54	102	
Red Post Jct	16.01		18	50	82	
Andover	17.31	24.00	20	53		
net time	18¾ minutes					

67.30

Date	Thursday 6th July 1967
Train	530 pm Weymouth to Waterloo
Loco	Rebuilt Merchant Navy class 4-6-2 No. 35007 *Aberdeen Commonwealth*
Load	10 coaches, 337 tons tare 360 tons gross
Crew	F Domm and Dave Deadman, Nine Elms MPD
Timed by	John Clifford

	miles	sched	mins	secs	speed	
Southampton	0.00	0.00	00	00		2½ mins late
Northam Jct	1.05	3.00	03	51	25*	
St Denys	2.11		05	31	44*	
Swaythling	3.45		07	09	56	
Southampton Airport	4.41		08	00	61½	
Eastleigh	5.80	11.00	09	22	65	
Allbrook Box	6.66		10	07	67	
MP 71	8.15		11	29	70	
Shawford	9.61		12	39	71½	
Shawford Jct	10.46		13	18	72	
St Cross	11.50		14	13	71	
Winchester City	12.70		15	20	71	
Winchester Jct	14.80		17	07	70/46*	tsr
Wallers Ash Box	17.55		20	13	55	
MP 61	18.15		20	53	58	
Weston Box	19.05		21	42	62	

	miles	sched	mins	secs	speed	
MP 59	20.15		22	48	64	
Micheldever	21.20		23	39	68	
MP 57	22.15		24	35	69	
Roundwood Box	23.05		25	18	70½	
Waltham Box	24.15		26	15	74	
Steventon Box	25.30		27	06	80/84	
Wootton Box	26.75		28	08	83	
Worting Jct	28.98	39.30	29	53	58*	7¼ mins early
Basingstoke	31.50		34	09	20*	sigs
MP 45	34.25		37	46	68½	
Newnham Siding	35.55		38	49	75½	
Hook	37.08		39	59	81	
Winchfield	39.41		41	41	89	
MP 38	41.25		42	51	95	
Fleet	42.76		43	46	97/98	
Bramshott	43.74		44	19	97	
Farnborough	46.05		45	54	87	
Sturt Lane Jct	47.05		46	38	78/61½	tsr
MP 31	48.25		47	46	63	
Pirbright Jct	49.60		48	56	73	
			stop to examine			
Brookwood	51.25		50	39	0*	
			51	08		
MP 26	53.25		56	10	44	
Woking Jct	54.50	63.30	57	43	52	
Woking	54.95		58	06	56	
West Byfleet	57.56		60	48	64	
Byfleet & New Haw	58.84		61	55	69	
Weybridge	60.09		63	04	68	
Oatlands Box	61.15		63	59	68	
Walton	62.16		64	49	75	
Hersham	63.33		65	43	76	
Esher	64.85		66	55	74½	
Hampton Court Jct.	65.90	78.30	67	47	75	
Surbiton	67.20		68	49	74	
Berrylands	68.26		69	43	75	
New Malden	69.46		70	41	69	
Raynes Park	70.60		71	43	64	
Wimbledon	72.05		73	45	62	
Earlsfield	73.66		74	43	62	
Clapham Junction	75.31	89.30	76	38	36*	
Queens Road	76.43		78	38	41	

	miles	sched	mins	secs	speed	
Vauxhall	77.93		80	52	31*	
Waterloo	79.24	96.30	84	13		9¾ mins early
net time	72 minutes					
	average speed Hook to Farnborough: 90.97 mph					

67.31

Date	Thursday 6th July 1967
Train	451 pm Basingstoke to Salisbury
Loco	BR Standard class 5 4-6-0 No. 73043
Load	4 coaches and 3 vans, 181 tons tare 190 tons gross
Crew	De'Ath, Basingstoke MPD
Recorder	David Foale

	miles	sched	mins	secs	speed	
Basingstoke	0.00	0.00	00	00		4 mins late
Worting Jct	2.55	5.30	03	45	58½	
Oakley	4.63		05	47	64	
Overton	7.80	12.30	09	08		
	0.00	0.00	00	00	52½	
Whitchurch	3.55	6.00	05	44		
	0.00	0.00	00	00		
Hurstbourne	2.04		02	58	67	
MP 62½	3.50		04	14	72/90	
Andover	7.25	11.30	07	22		
	0.00	0.00	00	00		
Red Post Jct	1.30		02	30	59/72	
Grateley	6.35	9.30	07	20		
	0.00	0.00	00	00		
Allington Box	2.90		04	16	66	
Idmiston	4.95	8.30	06	32		
	0.00	0.00	00	00		
Porton	0.60	1.30	02	07		
	0.00	0.00	00	00		
Tunnel Junction	4.32	6.30	04	43	80½/55*	
Salisbury	5.41	9.00	06	45		2 mins early
net time	start to stop average Whitchurch to Andover: 59.06 mph					

67.32

Date		Friday 7th July 1967				
Train		1125 am Weymouth to Waterloo				
Loco		Rebuilt Merchant Navy class 4-6-2 No. 35008 *Orient Line*				
Load		10 coaches 335 tons tare 360 tons gross				
Crew		McClaggon, Nine Elms MPD				
Timed by		Richard (Joe) Jolliffe				

	miles	sched	mins	secs	speed	
Southampton	0.00	0.00	00	00		16 mins late
Northam Jct	1.05	4.00	03	41	27/15*	
St Denys	2.11		05	28	43	
Swaythling	3.45		07	05	56	
Southampton Airport	4.41		07	58	63	
Eastleigh	5.80	11.00	09	13	68	
Allbrook Box	6.66		09	55	72	40% cut off
MP 71	8.15		11	13	73	
Shawford	9.61		12	09	75½	
Shawford Jct	10.46		12	46	74½	
St Cross Box	11.50		13	50	73	
Winchester City	12.70		14	53	74/75½	record time
Winchester Jct	14.80		16	38	68*/42½	tsr
Wallers Ash Box	17.55		19	53	54	
Weston Box	19.05		21	24	61½	
MP 59	20.15		22	31	65	
Micheldever	21.20		23	21	68	
MP 57	22.15		24	17	69	
Roundwood Box	23.05		24	58	71	
Waltham Box	24.15		25	58	69½	
Steventon Box	25.30		26	55	71	
Wootton Box	26.75		28	11	63/58*	sigs
Worting Jct	28.98	40.30	30	24	59/58*	sigs
Basingstoke	31.50		32	54	65	
MP 46	33.25		34	24	75/79½	
Newnham Siding	35.55		36	13	79	
Hook	37.08		37	18	82/80½	
Winchfield	39.41		39	04	82/85½	
Fleet	42.76		41	25	83½	
Bramshott	43.74		42	04	84½	
Farnborough	46.05		43	53	75	
Sturt Lane Jct	47.05		44	44	63/60*	tsr
MP 31	48.25		45	55	60	
Pirbright Jct	49.60		47	04	71½	
Brookwood	51.25		48	31	75	
Woking	54.95	64.30	51	18	79	

	miles	sched	mins	secs	speed	
West Byfleet	57.56		53	17	82	
Byfleet & New Haw	58.84		54	11	82	
Weybridge	60.09		55	20	64*	sigs
Walton	62.16		57	04	76½	
Hersham	63.33		57	56	79	
Esher	64.85		59	11	74½/75	
Hampton Court Jct.	65.90	79.30	60	00	73	
Surbiton	67.20		61	04	72/69½	
Berrylands	68.26		62	02	70½	
New Malden	69.46		63	01	69	
Raynes Park	70.60		64	03	65	
Wimbledon	72.05		65	35	36*	sigs
Earlsfield	73.66		67	55	48½	
Clapham Junction	75.31	90.30	70	00	41*	
Queens Road	76.43		71	39	51	
Vauxhall	77.93		73	23	37*	
Waterloo	79.24	97.30	76	34		8 mins early
net time	71 minutes start to stop average : 62.1 mph					

67.33

Date	Saturday 8th July 1967
Train	245 am Waterloo to Bournemouth
Loco	Rebuilt West Country class 4-6-2 No. 34095 *Brentor*
Load to Woking	3 coaches and 6 vans, 207 tons tare 220 tons gross
Load from Woking	3 coaches and 5 vans, 191 tons tare 205 tons gross
Load from Basingstoke	3 coaches and 4 vans, 178 tons tare 190 tons gross
Crew	Driver Gordon Porter and fireman Randall, Nine Elms MPD
Weather	Rain to Basingstoke then damp and misty
Recorder	DB

	miles	sched	mins	secs	speed	
Waterloo	0.00	0.00	00	00		right time
Vauxhall	1.29		05	10	28½	
Queens Road	2.81		07	16	47	
Clapham Junction	3.93	7.00	08	59	40½*	
Earlsfield	5.58		11	10	55½	
Wimbledon	7.24		12	49	67	
Raynes Park	8.64		14	01	73/75	
New Malden	9.78		14	57	50*	tsr
Berrylands	10.98		16	55	31*	tsr
Surbiton	12.04		18	35	48½	
Hampton Court Jct	13.34	18.00	20	16	34*/0*	sigs stop 85 seconds

	miles	sched	mins	secs	speed	
Esher	14.39		25	17	26½	SVO
Hersham	15.91		27	16	54½	
Walton	17.08		28	26	61	
Oatlands Box	18.12		29	28	62½	
Weybridge	19.15		30	21	67	
Byfleet and New Haw	20.40		31	30	72½	
West Byfleet	21.68		32	34	72/43*	sigs to slow line
Woking	24.29	37.00	35	47		
	0.00	00.00	00	00		4½ mins late
Woking Jct	0.46		01	39	23/22*	sigs to fast line
Brookwood	3.70		06	03	65½	
Pirbright Jct	5.20		07	28	71½	
MP 31	6.71		08	36	75	
Sturt Lane Jct	7.86		09	31	80	
Farnborough	8.91		10	18	82	
MP 35	10.71		11	33	85/87	
Fleet	12.19		12	36	86½	
MP 38	13.71		13	38	90	
Winchfield	15.54		14	52	86½	
MP 41	16.71		15	42	84½	
Hook	17.87		16	32	86½	
MP 43	18.71		17	08	84	
Newnham Siding	19.41		17	36	87	
MP 45	20.71		18	31	83/38*	sigs to slow line
Basingstoke	23.46	29.00	22	16		
	0.00	0.00	00	00		½ min late
Worting Jct	2.51	7.00	04	47	51½	
Wootton Box	4.75		07	04	63½	
Steventon Box	6.20		08	19	72½	
Waltham Box	7.35		09	14	75	
Roundwood Box	8.45		10	08	77	
Micheldever	10.30		11	32	85	
MP 59	11.35		12	12	88	
Weston Box	12.45		13	00	90	
MP 61	13.35		13	32	92	
Wallers Ash Box	13.95		14	01	93	
MP 63	15.35		14	51	92	
Winchester Jct	16.70	23.30	15	47	85	
Winchester City	18.80	26.30	18	13		8 mins early
	0.00	0.00	00	00	footplate	1 min early
St Cross Box	1.23		02	14	59/60	
Shawford Jct	2.47		03	30	44*	tsr
Shawford	3.12		04	21	60½	

	miles	sched	mins	secs	speed	
MP 71	4.55		05	32	78	
Allbrook Box	6.06		07	16	35*/40	sigs
Eastleigh	6.96	11.00	09	08		
	0.00	0.00	00	00		½ min late
Southampton Airport	1.39		02	43	57	
Swaythling	2.35		03	32	68/74	
St Deny	3.69		04	43	65	
Northam Jct	4.75	7.30	05	55	24*/38½	
Southampton	5.80	11.00	08	12		2¼ mins early
net times	Waterloo to Woking Woking to Basingstoke Winchester to Eastleigh average speed MP 35 to MP 43: 86.0 mph start to stop average Woking to Basingstoke: 63.23 mph start to stop average Basingstoke to Winchester: 61.92 mph			26 minutes 21¼ mins 8 minutes		

67.34

Date	Saturday 8th July 1967
Train	830 am Waterloo to Weymouth
Loco	Rebuilt Merchant Navy class 4-6-2 No.35023 *Holland Afrika Line*
Load	11 coaches, 368 tons tare 405 tons gross
Crew	Billy Hughes and Alan Newman, Nine Elms MPD
Weather	Hot and sunny
Recorder	DB, standing in corridor of 1st coach

	miles	sched**	mins	secs	speed	
Woking	0.00	0.00	00	00		1¼ mins late
			sigs stop			
MP 24½	0.21		01	57	0*	
			02	45		
Woking Jct	0.46		03	45	15	
Brookwood	3.70		09	07	51	
Pirbright Jct	5.20		10	57	56	
MP 31	6.71		12	23	58½	
Sturt Lane Jct	7.86		13	32	66	
Farnborough	8.91		14	27	71	
MP 35	10.71		15	53	75	
Fleet	12.19		17	03	77½	
MP 38	13.71		18	12	82	
Winchfield	15.54		19	32	80½	SVO
MP 41	16.71		21	27	80	
Hook	17.87		21	19	81	
MP 43	18.71		21	57	80	
Newnham Siding	19.41		22	27	82/83	
MP 45	20.71		23	25	82	

	miles	sched**	mins	secs	speed	
Basingstoke	23.46		25	32	74½	eased
Worting Jct	25.97	26.30	27	42	64½*/62½	
Wootton Box	28.21		29	50	65	
Steventon Box	29.66		31	08	68½	
Waltham Box	30.81		32	09	70½	
Roundwood Box	31.91		33	07	72	
MP 57	32.81		33	48	75	
Micheldever	33.76		34	35	80	
MP 59	34.81		35	18	82½	
Weston Box	35.91		36	09	85	
MP 61	36.81		36	43	87	
Wallers Ash Box	37.41		37	11	88½	
MP 63	38.81		38	03	92	
MP 64	39.81		38	41	95	
Winchester Jct Box	40.00		38	57	93	
MP 65	40.81		39	20	90	
Winchester City	42.26	45.00	41	17		
	0.00	0.00	00	00		right time
St Cross Box	1.23		02	47	53/48*	tsr
Shawford Jct	2.47		04	03	52½	
Shawford	3.12		04	52	59	
MP 71	4.58		06	10	68	
Allbrook Box	6.06		07	31	74	
Eastleigh	6.96		08	10	75½	
Southampton Airport	8.35		09	17	78	
Swaythling	9.22		09	57	74	SVO
St Denys	10.63		11	12	63*	SVO
Northam Jct	11.71	16.00	12	21	16*/30	
Southampton Central	12.75	19.00	15	20		3¾ mins early
	0.00	0.00	00	00		½ min early
Millbrook	0.90		02	58	35	
Redbridge	2.65		05	19	51	
Totton	3.30		06	00	53½	
MP 85	5.75		08	43	56	
Lyndhurst Road	6.15		09	08	57½	
MP 86	6.75		09	45	65	
Beaulieu Road	8.85		11	42	63	
MP 89	9.75		12	30	73	
Woodfidley Box	10.45		13	05	70½	
MP 90½	11.25		13	46	68	
MP 92	12.75		15	01	74½	
Brockenhurst	13.55		15	42	68	SVO
Lymington Jct	14.50	18.00	16	36	63	

	miles	sched**	mins	secs	speed	
MP 94½	15.25		17	19	58	
Sway	16.30		18	22	64½	
MP 97½	18.25		20	02	73	
New Milton	19.30		20	56	71	
MP 100	20.75		22	04	76	
Hinton Admiral	21.80		22	52	83	
MP 103	23.75		24	13	88	
Christchurch	25.10		25	15	63*	SVO
MP 105	25.75		25	54	63½	
Pokesdown	27.05		27	16	50	
Boscombe	27.60		28	02	45½	
Bournemouth Central	28.80	37.00	29	59		7½ mins early
	** from passing Woking to the Winchester stop: 38 minutes start to stop average Woking to Winchester: 61.42 mph start to stop average sigs stop to Winchester: 65.48 mph average speed Farnborough to Winchester Jct: 76.14 mph start to stop average: 57.63 mph Southampton to Bournemouth					

67.35

Date	Saturday 8th July 1967
Train	4 pm Weymouth Quay to Waterloo
Loco	Rebuilt Merchant Navy class 4-6-2 No.35023 *Holland Afrika Line*
Load	11 coaches and 1 van, 394 tons tare 425 tons gross
Crew	Pearce, Eastleigh MPD
Weather	Fine and dry
Timed by	DB

	miles	sched	mins	secs	speed	
Southampton	0.00	0.00	00	00		2 mins late
Northam Jct	1.05	4.00	03	41	23/18*	
St Denys	2.11		05	41	37	
Swaythling	3.45		07	38	47	
Southampton Airport	4.41		08	40	50	
Eastleigh	5.80	11.00	10	18	54	
Allbrook Box	6.66		11	15	55	
MP 71	8.15		12	56	56	SVO
Shawford	9.61		14	23	56½	
Shawford Jct	10.46		15	12	56½	
St Cross	11.50		16	19	57	SVO
Winchester City	12.70		17	40	58/58½	
Winchester Jct	14.80	26.00	19	54	55	SVO
MP 63	16.15		21	58	33*	tsr
Wallers Ash Box	17.55		24	05	40	
MP 61	18.15		25	04	41½	
Weston Box	19.05		26	13	45	

	miles	sched	mins	secs	speed	
MP 59	20.15		27	44	48	
Micheldever	21.20		28	54	51	
MP 57	22.15		30	04	53½	
Roundwood Box	23.05		31	00	55	
Waltham Box	24.15		32	09	60	
Steventon Box	25.30		33	18	64	
Wootton Box	26.75		34	43	56½	SVO
Worting Jct	28.98	46.30	37	20	40*/22*	sigs
Basingstoke	31.50	50.30	41	54		6½ mins early
	0.00	0.00	00	00		¾ min early
MP 46	1.75		04	01	50	
Newnham Siding	4.05		06	28	62	
MP 43	4.75		07	08	61	
Hook	5.59		07	54	66½	
MP 41	6.75		08	58	67	
Winchfield	7.92		10	00	71	
MP 38	9.75		11	30	74½	
Fleet	11.27		12	42	75	
MP 35	12.75		13	54	76	
Farnborough	14.55		15	18	75½	
Sturt Lane Jct	15.60		16	11	65	
MP 31	16.75		17	29	53*	tsr
Pirbright Jct	18.26		18	53	64/68½	
Brookwood	19.76		20	20	66½	
MP 26	21.75		22	11	63	
Woking Jct	23.00		23	41	35*	
Woking	23.46	26.00	25	04		
	0.00	0.00	00	00		½ min late
West Byfleet	2.61		04	56	56	
Byfleet & New Haw	3.89		06	10	64½	
Weybridge	5.14		07	25	63½	
Oatlands Box	6.17		08	20	66	
Walton	7.21		09	13	72½	
Hersham	8.38		10	08	76	
Esher	9.90		11	20	77½	
Hampton Court Jct	10.95	13.00	12	08	79	
Surbiton	12.25		13	21	71½	Bils held!
Berrylands	13.31		14	07	70	
New Malden	14.51		15	10	67	
Raynes Park	15.65		16	14	60	
Wimbledon	17.10		17	39	58	
Earlsfield	18.71		19	19	61½	
Clapham Junction	20.36	26.00	21	18	38½*	SVO

	miles	sched	mins	secs	speed	
Queens Road	21.48		23	01	52	
Vauxhall	22.98		24	44	33*	SVO
Waterloo	24.29	33.00	28	47		3½ mins early
net times	Southampton to Basingstoke: 38 minutes Basingstoke to Woking : 23½ minutes					

APPENDIX A

SHOWS ENGINES ALLOCATED FOR ALL OR PART OF A DUTY ON MONDAYS TO FRIDAYS FOR THE PERIOD 12TH JUNE TO 7TH JULY 1967

NINE ELMS		DUTY 101	DUTY 102	DUTY 105	DUTY 106	DUTY 108	DUTY 111	DUTY 113	DUTY 113
Monday	12.06.67	41298		80085			82029	76026	76026
Tuesday	13.06.67	82019	41298	80085			82029	76066	76066
Wednesday	14.06.67	41319		80085		41298		76066	34102
Thursday	15.06.67	82019		80085		41312		73029	73029
Friday	16.06.67			80085				73029	73029
Monday	19.06.67	41319	82029		82029	41312		34034	34034
Tuesday	20.06.67	41319	82029	82019		41312		35030	35030
Wednesday	21.06.67	41319	82029	82019		41312		76064	76064
Thursday	22.06.67	41319	41298	82019		41312		34023	34023
Friday	23.06.67							76026	76026
Monday	26.06.67		41319	82019				35007	76026
Tuesday	27.06.67				41319			76064	35007
Wednesday	28.06.67	82029				82019		76064	76064
Thursday	29.06.67							73065	73065
Friday	30.06.67							75074	75074
Monday	03.07.67	82019		82019	41319	41312		75074	75074
Tuesday	04.07.67			82019	41319	41312		35008	75074
Wednesday	05.07.67	80015			41319	41298		76011	35008
Thursday	06.07.67	80015		82019	41319	41298		76011	76011
Friday	07.07.67	80015		82019	41319	41298	80143	73029	73029
								440 and 630 am	638 pm up

DUTY	Booked Engine	
DUTY 101	BR 3 MTT STD	Empy stock and shunting
DUTY 102	BR 4 MTT STD	Empty stock and shunting and 210 pm vans Waterloo to Clapham Junction
DUTY 105	LM 2 MTT	Empty stock and shunting. 436 pm, 506 pm and 536 pm Kensington Olympia to Clapham Junction
DUTY 106	BR 4 MTT STD	Empty stock and shunting. 816 am and 846 am Clapham Junction to Kensington Olympia and 833 am return
DUTY 108	BR 4 MTT STD	Empy stock and shunting
DUTY 111	LM 2 MTT	Nine Elms MPD shunting. Continuous running to Foreman's instructions
DUTY 113	BR 5 MT STD	440 am Waterloo to Woking, 630 am Woking to Salisbury and 638 pm Salisbury to Waterloo
DUTY 135	7P/5F WC/BB	810 am Waterloo to Weymouth and 423 pm return
DUTY 136	7P/5F WC/BB	230 am Waterloo to Portsmouth, 730 am Portsmouth to Eastleigh and 750 pm Eastleigh to Bournemouth

DUTY 135	DUTY 135	DUTY 136	DUTY 136	DUTY 137	DUTY 138	DUTY 145	DUTY 147	DUTY 147	DUTY 148	DUTY 149
35028	35028							34013	34060	35007
35030	35030	35007	35003			35028	34021		34013	34060
35030	35030	34025				35013	35028	35028	34021	35003
D1923	D1923	73043	35028			35030	35013	34102	76007	35007
34087	35028	34060				34036	34021		34102	
34023	34023					35007	35023		34024	35028
35013	35013	34023	75075			35028	35007	35007	34018	34024
35013	35013	34036	34036			35023	35028	34021	35007	34018
35008	35008		75075			35013	35003		34021	35007
						35013	35013			
34060	34060					34090	35013	35013	35023	34087
34060	34060	34036	75075				35023	35023	35013	34087
35030	34025	34095	34018			35007	35030	34093	35023	
34087	34087						34060	75075	34093	35023
35003		34087				35023	34024	34060		34001
34001	34001	34102	34102	34093	34102	35030	35023	35023	34060	35007
34087	34087	73020	34036		34025	35028	34021	34102	35023	34025
34087	35030	34060	34060	34024	35028	35007	35028	34013	34021	35023
35030	35003		34021		34024	35008	34087	34087	34013	35007
35023	35023	34001		34021		35003	35008	34025	34052	34013
810 am down	423 pm up	230 and 730 am	750 pm down			835 am down	251 pm up	654 pm down		

DUTY	Booked Engine	
DUTY 137	7P/5F WC/BB	Freight in the Weymouth and Poole areas and 542 pm Bournemouth to Eastleigh
DUTY 138	7P/5F WC/BB	1254 am Eastleigh to Weymouth, 643 am Weymouth to Bournemouth, 846 am Bournemouth to Waterloo and 622 pm FO Waterloo to Bournemouth
DUTY 145	8P MN	835 am Waterloo to Weymouth, 541 pm Weymouth to Bournemouth and 9 pm Bournemouth to Weymouth
DUTY 146	8P MN	Spare at Weymouth
DUTY 147	8P MN	749 am Weymouth to Bournemouth, 1235 pm Bournemouth to Waterloo and 654 pm Waterloo to Salisbury
DUTY 148	8P MN	649 am Salisbury to Waterloo, 1138 am vans Waterloo to Basingstoke and 706 pm Basingstoke to Eastleigh
DUTY 149	8P MN	530 pm Weymouth to Waterloo

APPENDIX B

SHOWS ENGINES ALLOCATED FOR ALL OR PART OF A DUTY ON MONDAYS TO FRIDAYS FOR THE PERIOD 12TH JUNE TO 7TH JULY 1967

		GUILDFORD					
		DUTY 161	DUTY 162	DUTY 163	DUTY 165	DUTY 166	DUTY 170
Monday	12.06.67					76066*	
Tuesday	13.06.67					35007	
Wednesday	14.06.67				34025	73020	
Thursday	15.06.67				73020	73043	
Friday	16.06.67				73043		
Monday	19.06.67					76067	
Tuesday	20.06.67				76067	75076	
Wednesday	21.06.67					73018	
Thursday	22.06.67						
Friday	23.06.67						
Monday	26.06.67					76007	
Tuesday	27.06.67					76011	
Wednesday	28.06.67					76067	
Thursday	29.06.67						
Friday	30.06.67						
Monday	03.07.67				34095	76011	
Tuesday	04.07.67	73020			73020	76011	
Wednesday	05.07.67				76011	34060	
Thursday	06.07.67				73043	34036	
Friday	07.07.67				73029	75075	
						* 73092 from B'stoke	

DUTY	Booked Engine	
DUTY 161	BR 5 MT STD.	432 am Woking to Basingstoke. Freight and vans
DUTY 162	BR 5 MT STD	As ordered at Basingstoke
DUTY 163	BR 5 MT STD	205 pm Vans Basingstoke to Surbiton
DUTY 165	BR 4 MT STD	451 pm Basingstoke to Salisbury, vans and freight in the Eastleigh area
DUTY 166	BR 4 MT STD	1043 am Southampton to Bournemouth, 108 pm Bournemouth to Weymouth, 446 pm Weymouth to Bournemouth, 651 pm Bournemouth to Woking
DUTY 170	BR 3 MT STD	Woking to Farnham freights
DUTY 254	7P/5F WC/BB	523 pm Waterloo to Bournemouth FO or 523 pm Waterloo to Southampton Docks
DUTY 280	BR 4 MT STD	808 am Christchurch to Brockenhurst (Mondays only), 1013 am Weymouth to Bournemouth, vans and empty stock
DUTY 281	BR 4 MT STD	718 am Waterloo to Salisbury, empty stock and 355 pm Salisbury to Basingstoke

				EASTLEIGH					
DUTY 254	DUTY 280	DUTY 281	DUTY 282	DUTY 283	DUTY 290	DUTY 308	DUTY 313	DUTY 314	DUTY 325
	76031								
		35008							
34018	76064	34102*				80139			
		76064							
34013	80145	73037							
		34037							
	35008								
	73043	35030							
34004								80016	
	34102								
	35030				80016				
	76031	34037							
	34093								
34087									
	73020	73093			73037	80016			
	76031	73065		73029	75075				
	73029	76031		76027	75075				
		75074		76066	75075				
34093	76066	34024		73043	80016	76005			
		* 80145 on 355 pm							

DUTY	Booked Engine	
DUTY 282	BR 4 MT STD	As ordered at Basingstoke
DUTY 283	BR 4 MT STD	420 pm Southanpton to Bournemouth and empty stock working in the Bournemouth area
DUTY 290	BR 4 MT STD	422 pm Eastleigh to Southampton, 516 pm Southampton to Bournemouth, empty stock and freight working.
DUTY 308	BR 4 MTT STD	157 am Eastleigh to Portsmouth, 630 am Fareham to Eastleigh, freight and empty stock, 520 pm Eastleigh to Fratton, 1132 pm Portsmouth to Eastleigh
DUTY 313	BR 4 MTT STD	Basingstoke to Ludgershall freight
DUTY 314	BR 4 MTT STD	134 am Southampton to Eastleigh, freight and vans in Southampton Docks
DUTY 325	3 FT USA	Easteigh MPD coal shunting

APPENDIX C

SHOWS ENGINES ALLOCATED FOR ALL OR PART OF A DUTY ON MONDAYS TO FRIDAYS FOR THE PERIOD 12TH JUNE TO 7TH JULY 1967

					BOURNEMOUTH	
		DUTY 394	DUTY 395	DUTY 396	DUTY 400	DUTY 404
Monday	12.06.67	35023				
Tuesday	13.06.67	34023	35023			
Wednesday	14.06.67	35023				
Thursday	15.06.67	34037	35023			
Friday	16.06.67	35023	34037			
Monday	19.06.67	34093				
Tuesday	20.06.67	34102				
Wednesday	21.06.67	34060				
Thursday	22.06.67	34102				
Friday	23.06.67	34060	34102			
Monday	26.06.67	35003	35030			
Tuesday	27.06.67	35028	35003			
Wednesday	28.06.67	35003	34060			
Thursday	29.06.67	34001				
Friday	30.06.67	34021	34001			
Monday	03.07.67	73020	34037	35030		34087
Tuesday	04.07.67	35030	34001	34037		
Wednesday	05.07.67	34001	35030			
Thursday	06.07.67	34004	73029	34087		
Friday	07.07.67	34095	73092	73018		

DUTY	Booked Engine	
DUTY 394	7P/5F WC/BB	645 am Poole to Bournemouth, 808 am Christchurch to Brockenhurst (not Mondays), 301 pm Bournemouth to Weymouth, 615 pm Weymouth to Waterloo
DUTY 395	7P/5F WC/BB	245 am Waterloo to Weymouth
DUTY 396	7P/5F WC/BB	827 am Weymouth to Bournemouth, 403 pm Brockenhurst to Christchurch and empty stock workings
DUTY 400	BR 4 MTT STD	Empty stock working Bournemouth and Branksome
DUTY 404	BR 4 MT STD	1013 pm Weymouth to Bournemouth and local freight
DUTY 407	BR 4 MT STD	648 am Bournemouth to Brockenhurst and 756 am return and local vans and empty stock
DUTY 409	LM 2 MTT	Empty stock working Bournemouth and Branksome
DUTY 411	BR 4 MTT STD	751 am Bournemouth to Weymouth and 1118 am return

					SALISBURY	
DUTY 407	DUTY 409	DUTY 411	DUTY 412	DUTY 412	DUTY 462	DUTY 463
		34102				
		76005				
		76005				
75076						
		76009				
		76009				
						34089
		76005				
		76005	D6550			
		34037				
		76009	76026	76026		
80146		76006	76026	76026		34052
		76006	34093	76026		
80146		76006	76005	76005		
80011		76006	34004	76005		
			630 pm S'ton			

DUTY	Booked Engine	
DUTY 412	BR 4 MT STD	920 am Bournemouth to Weymouth and 1212 pm return, 152 pm Bournemouth to Southampton and 630 pm return
DUTY 462	7P/5F WC/BB	Salisbury to Basingstoke freight and empty stock
DUTY 463	7P/5F WC/BB	Vans Salisbury, Basingstoke and Portsmouth

APPENDIX D

DO NOT CLIMB ABOVE FOOTPLATE LEVEL WHEN UNDER ELECTRIFIED WIRES

W.C. 25 Oct. 65

ENGINEMEN'S ROSTERS

STAFFING ARRANGEMENTS — PRODUCTIVITY AGREEMENT.

.... M.P. Depot   BRITISH RAILWAYS   Commencing .... 19....   Region ....   B.R. 32711/4

No.	Driver	Fireman	SUNDAY On Duty	SUNDAY Turn/Dia.No.	MONDAY On Duty	MONDAY Turn/Dia.No.	TUESDAY On Duty	TUESDAY Turn/Dia.No.	WEDNESDAY On Duty	WEDNESDAY Turn/Dia.No.	THURSDAY On Duty	THURSDAY Turn/Dia.No.	FRIDAY On Duty	FRIDAY Turn/Dia.No.	SATURDAY On Duty	SATURDAY Turn/Dia.No.
A1	GEE A	BROWN R	1452	464/462	1555	430/236	1452	464/462	1555	456/236	1452	464/462	1455	430/236		
	CUTTING T		R—D	D.7	R—D	D.7	0615	D.7	0440	463/431	0440	463/431	0440	463/431	2332	D.7
	KIFF W	DALEY P	0615	D.7	0615	D.7	0440	463/431	R—D	D.7	0950	463/304	0730	50	0700	A—0
	MOLE H	CHAMBERS J	2344	D.7	2344	D.7	2344	D.7	2344	D.7	2300	A—0	2300	A—0		
	TURPIN P	DOMM A.S	1350	393/250	1350	393/250	1350	393/250	1350	393/250	1330	393	1150	433	0944	247
	ROBINSON J(1)	ROBERTS M	0950	432/304	0950	432/304	0950	432/304	0950	432/304	R—D		R—D			
	HARVEY E	ROBERTS P	2344	D.10	2344	D.10	2344	D.10	2344	D.10	2344	D.10	2100	A—0		
	McCARTHY J	DAVIS D	0440	463/431	0440	463/431	R—D		0615	D.7	0615	D.7	0615	D.10	0844	245
	HOLLOWAY G	GRH C	1555	430/236	1452	464/236	1555	430/236	1452	464/236	1555	430/236	1455	361		
	KING A	HENNINGS P	R—D		R—D		1050	D.16	0950	464/304	0950	A—0	0950	432/304	2332	D.16
	POPE H	MASTERS B	2350	56	2350	56	2350	56	2380	58	2350	58	2336	56		
	NASH L	BELL G	0630	51	0650	51	0950	A—0	R—D		0710	257	0620	257	1750	56/94
	PRICHETT F	DAVIS F	1720	461	1720	461	1720	461	1720	461	1720	461	1505	257	1415	16/244
	CAMP D	CONROY D	1050	D.16	0950	432/304	0630	51	0630	51	R—D		R—D			
	SUTTON C	ROSCOE J	1300	HR	1300	HR	1300	HR	1300	HR	1300	HR	1300	HR		
	HEATH A	LESTER T	0950	A—0	0950	A—0	R—D		1650	D.16	1650	D.16	0750	263	0900	A—0

APPENDIX E

No 2	LINK														
MILLS A.E.	GOLDING L.	1755 VX	507/A-0	1755 VX	507/A-0	1755 VX	507/A-0	1755 VX	507/A-0	1755 VX	507/A-0	1830	C	—	
HOOKER D.	NEWMAN D.	R–D		R–D		0520 VX	501/505	0520 VX	501/505	0520 VX	501/505	0520	501/505	0200	502
ROBINSON J.2	McCARTHY D.	0630	235/234	0800 VX	501/506	0630	235/234	0655 VX	58/431	0655 VX	58/431	0653	261	1800	A-0
DOUST EW	BASSETT. P.	0001	A.0 505	0155	238/385	0001 VX	504/505	0155	238/385	0001 VX	504/501	0155	238/430	1514 VX	501/501
BUDD. A.E.	BARNES. F.	1800	A-0	1800	A-0	1800	A-0	1800	A-0	R–D		R–D		—	
CULL S.	COSTELLO M.	0600	HR	0600	HR	0600	HR	0600	HR	0600	HR	0600	HR	1044 VX	98/433 to.
SUTTON A.C.	JOHNSTON. C.	1.00	A-0	11.00	A-0	R–D		11.20	A.0 506/502	1120	A.0 506/502	1030	A-0	—	
HENDICOTT R	STANLEY W.	0155	238/385	0001	504/505	0155	238/385	0001	504/505	0155	238/385	0001	504/505	—	
BLANCHARD J.	PHILLIPS E.	R–D		R–D		1120	A-0 506/502	1120	A.0 506/502	1410	239	1421	506/502/507	11.00	501/506
MORRIS F	BELL K.3	1330	A-0	1330	A-0	1330	A-0	1330	A-0	1330	A-0	1127	392/62	0844	502/501
HAWKINS W	COOK D.	0653	433/234	0653	433/234	0655	58/B1	R–D		0630	235/234	0920	501/506	1714	506/503
DOMM F.	THOM M.	2120	507/501	2100	C	2120	507/501	2000	A-0	2120	507/501	2359	506/502/507		
ANDERSON. W	SEABY K.	1000	A-0	1120	A-0 506/502	1100	A-0	10.00	A-0	R–D		R–D		—	
HADLEY A.	ARBUCKLE P.	1700	H-K	1700	H-K	1700	H-K	1700	H-K	1700	H-K	1700	H-K	2130	505/503
LLOYD. G	CARSCADDEN. J	2000	A-0	2000	A-0	R–D		2100	C	2100	C	1900	55		
FORDREY. A	SYMON R.	0520 VX	501/505	0520 VX	501/505	0800 VX	501/506	0653	433/234	0653	433/234	0630	235/252		
ROBERTS. D.	RUTHVEN. J	R–D		R–D		2100	C	2120	507/501	2000	A-0	1820 VX	582/508		
PLUMB. W.	MORTLOCK. D.	0500	A-0	0500	A-0	0500	A-0	0500	A-0	0500	A-0	0500	A-0	0820	507/506
HUGHES. W.	PARKER R.	0950	55	0950	55	0950	55	R–D		0950	55	0930	A-0	1700	A-0
TURNER W	TURNER I.	2100.	C	2120	507/501	2000.	A-0	1820	502/504	1800	A-0	1600	A-0	—	
EVANS. J.	PEARCE. M.	0655	58/431.	0630	235/234	0653.	433/234.	0630.	235/234	R–D		R–D.			
HOOPER. G.	McQUADE R.	1120	A.0 506/504	1000	A-0	1000 A.0	0800 VX	501/506	0900	A-0	1020 VX	505/507		0700.	507/502 GR
SKINNER. R.	TURNER. L	0800 VX	501/506	0655	58/431	R–D.		0950	55	0800	501/506	0730	A-0	1544	435

APPENDIX F

No. 3 LINK

JACKSON R.	CLARKSON P.
SAUNDERS L.	ROE A.
DAVIS T.	PAWLEY G.
NOTT M.	BRYCE D.
GAMMON P.	HALE M.
WALKER F.	HUGHES W.
BURRIDGE F.	ARBUCKLE C.
HAMLIN R.	DEDMAN A.
CALLOW B.	COURBROUGH C.
PORTER ?	MOULT T.
CONLON P.	FRENCH B.
SLIMMON C.	BEASLEY R.
KNIGHT R.	REX G.
SULLIVAN T.	SPINCETT V.
MCLAREN B.	ROYCROFT U.
PRIOR N.	HARRIS R.
BOYCE M.	CULVERD C.
O'DELL K.	THOMAS M.
HARRINGTON W.	BRWN M.
WRIGHT A.	ROSSLAND R.
ADAMS G.	MARTIN T.
COLES T.	HOLLOWAY A.
NEVILLE L.	CRONSTOUN
SIGWARD D.	LEE R.

APPENDIX G

ENGINE STOCK POSITION AS AT 4TH OCTOBER 1966

Merchant Navy class 4-6-2		WC & BB class 4-6-2 (Un-Mod)		WC & BB class 4-6-2 (Mod)	
35003	Weymouth	34002	Nine Elms	34001	Nine Elms
35007	"	34006	Salisbury	34004	Bournemouth
35008	"	34015	"	34008	NineElms
35012	"	34019	Nine Elms	34012	Bournemouth
35013	"	34023	Eastleigh	34013	Salisbury
35014	"	34057	"	34018	Nine Elms
35023	"	34102	"	34021	"
35026	"			34024	Bournemouth
35028	"	BR Standard class 4 2-6-0		34025	"
35030	"			34034	Nine Elms
		76005	Bournemouth	34036	"
BR Standard class 5 4-6-0		76006	"	34037	"
		76007	Salisbury	34040	Bournemouth
73002	Weymouth	76008	"	34044	"
73016	"	76009	Bournemouth	34047	"
73018	"	76011	"	34052	Salisbury
73020	"	76026	"	34056	"
73022	Nine Elms	76031	Guildford	34060	Eastleigh
73029	"	76033	"	34071	"
73037	"	76053	"	34077	"
73043	"	76058	"	34087	"
73065	"	76061	Eastleigh	34088	"
73080	Weymouth	76063	"	34089	Salisbury
73085	Nine Elms	76064	"	34090	Eastleigh
73092	Guildford	76066	"	34093	"
73093	"	76067	Salisbury	34095	"
73110	"	76069	Guildford	34098	"
73113	Weymouth			34100	Salisbury
73115	Guildford	BR Class 4 2-6-4 tank		34104	Eastleigh
73117	"			34108	Salisbury
73118	"	80011	Bournemouth		
73119	Nine Elms	80012	Nine Elms	LM class 2 2-6-2 tank	
73155	Eastleigh	80015	"		
		80016	Eastleigh	41224	Bournemouth
BR Standard class 4 4-6-0		80019	Bournemouth	41230	"
		80032	"	41284	Nine Elms
75068	Eastleigh	80085	Nine Elms	41295	Bournemouth
75074	"	80133	"	41298	Nine Elms
75075	"	80134	Bournemouth	41312	Bournemouth
75076	"	80139	Eastleigh	41319	Eastleigh

BR Standard class 4 4-6-0		BR class 4 2-6-4 tank		LM class 2 2-6-2 tank	
75077	Eastleigh	80140	Nine Elms	41320	Bournemouth
		80143	"		
USA class 3 0-6-0 tank		80145	"	BR Standard class 3 2-6-2 Tank	
		80146	Bournemouth		
30067	Eastleigh	80151	Eastleigh	82019	Nine Elms
30069	"	80152	"	82029	"
30071	"	80154	Nine Elms		
30072	Guildford				
30073	Eastleigh	02 class 0-4-4 tanks, 10 at Ryde, Isle of Wight			

APPENDIX H

M.P. Depot   BRITISH RAILWAYS

ALTERATIONS TO ENGINEMEN'S ROSTERS ON .... FRIDAY

MON – FRI   7.7.67

	Driver		Fireman		On Duty	Turn/ Dia. No.				To Wor
MX 108	0012	c	41298							
MO 108	0130	c								
136	0200	W	34001	0035						
101	0200	c		0110						
395	0215	W		0155 OFF 394						
MX 105	0220	c	82019							
MO 102	0305	c								
MX 113	0404	W		OFF						
MO 462	0404	W				SP1	0640	X	41312	14
MO 105	0410	W								
MX 101	0445	c	80015							
111	0600	c	80143	0555		SP8	0720	W	34089	
FX 103	0620	c		0515						
FO 254	0620	c	34025	0515						
281	0651	W	73092	0546						
FO 103	0710	c		0515						
106	0715	c	41319	0610		SP9	1020	W	34021	
135	0735	X	35023	0630	1212					
145	0758	X	34024	0515	1212					
FO 254	0835	W								
105	1020	Neg	82019	BAS		SP10	1500	W	34093	7
148	1055	W								
MO 106	1220	W								
MX 106	1516	c		1456						
105	1528	c	82019	1438						
102	1600	c								
106	1630	W	41319		5					
FO 254 1645	1645	W	34093	1740		102	1815	W	82029	
FO 101	1700	c	80015	1635	3					
FX 101	1725	c		1635						

254	0835	W							
105	1020	NEG	82019	—		SP10	1500	W	34093
148	1055	W		BAS					
MO 106	1220	W		—					
MX 106	1516	C		1456					
105	1528	C	82019	1438					
102	1600	C		—					
106	1630	W	41319	—	5				
254	1645	W	34093	1540		102	1815	W	82029
101	1700	C	80015	1635					
101	1725	C		1635	3				
254	1755			—		138	1755	W	
147	1827	W	34025	1733					
138	1914	W		EX.SQH					
102	1925	W		1705					
102	2020	C		1705					

SERVICE 35030,
EXAM.

W.O. 80085,

APPENDIX I

34023 FINAL WEEK IN SERVICE

Sun 18/06/1967	Railtour (RCTS): Waterloo – Fareham (doublehead with 73029)
	Light Engine to Weymouth
	Weymouth - Eastleigh – Salisbury(doublehead with 34108)
	Light Engine to Nine Elms
Mon 19/06/1967	8.10am Waterloo – Weymouth Quay (except Weymouth Quay branch !!)
	4.00pm Weymouth Quay – Waterloo (except Quay branch)
Tues 20/06/1967	2.30am Waterloo – Portsmouth (via Eastleigh)
	7.30am Portsmouth – Eastleigh
	Eastleigh – Feltham (Goods)
Wed 21/06/1967	9.22am Hemel Hempstead – Southampton Docks
	5.41pm Southampton Docks – Hemel Hempstead
	(both between Willesden and Southampton)
Thurs 22/06/1967	10.43am Waterloo – Southampton Docks
	2.00pm Southampton Docks – Feltham (Goods)
Fri 23/06/1967	4.40am Waterloo – Salisbury
	6.38pm Salisbury – Waterloo
Sat 24/06/1967	2.30am Waterloo – Portsmouth (via Eastleigh)
	6.10pm Fratton – Basingstoke (Vans)
	10.07pm Basingstoke – Waterloo (Vans)
Estimated mileage 1,510	

As the engine was destined for preservation it was then taken out of service on 25/06/1967. It was presumably decided that the last 2 weeks of Southern Steam could manage without it. 34102 then became the only engine remaining in service in original condition.

APPENDIX J

35007 FINAL THREE WEEKS IN SERVICE

Monday 12th June	5.30 pm Weymouth to Waterloo
Tuesday 13th June.	2.30 am Waterloo to Portsmouth. 7.30 am Portsmouth to Eastleigh
Thursday 15th June	5.30 pm Weymouth to Waterloo
Saturday 17th June	8.30 am Waterloo to Weymouth
Monday 19th June	8.35 am Waterloo to Weymouth
Tuesday 20th June	7.49 am Weymouth to Bournemouth. 12.35 pm Bournemouth to
	Waterloo. 6.54 pm Waterloo to Salisbury
Wednesday 21st June	6.49 am Salisbury to Waterloo. 11.38 am vans Waterloo to Basingstoke
	7.06 pm Basingstoke to Eastleigh
Thursday 22nd June	5.30 pm Weymouth to Waterloo
Monday 26th June	4.40 am Waterloo to Woking. 6.30 am Woking to Salisbury
Tuesday 27th June	6.38 pm Salisbury to Waterloo
Wednesday 28th June	8.35 am Waterloo to Weymouth
Monday 3rd July	5.30 pm Weymouth to Waterloo. Exams at Nine Elms MPD
Wednesday 5th July	8.35 am Waterloo to Weymouth
Thursday 6th July	5.30 pm Weymouth to Waterloo
Saturday 8th July	On shed Nine Elms

APPENDIX K

RUNS WITH MAXIMUM SPEEDS OF 90 MPH OR MORE IN 1967

DATE	ENGINE	TRAIN	MAX SPEED	DRIVER
17.01.67	34098	5.30 pm Weymouth	95, 90	Porter
18.01.67	35013	5.30 pm Weymouth	91, 91	Porter
19.01.67	34036	5.30 pm Weymouth	90, 90	Porter
25.01.67	35030	10.30 am Waterloo	96	Hooper
04.02.67	35030	5.30 pm Weymouth	97	Sloper
05.02.67	34021	6.03 pm Bournemouth	90	Porter
14.02.67	35028	5.30 pm Weymouth	92	Parsons
16.02.67	35013	5.30 pm Weymouth	94	Parsons
28.02.67	34044	1.25 pm Weymouth	94, 91	Hooper
03.03.67	35007	5.30 pm Weymouth	90	unknown
09.03.67	34087	6.15 pm Weymouth	92, 92	Anderson
25.03.67	35028	7.22 am Bournemouth	96	Payne
25.03.67	34089	11.25 am Weymouth	92, 92	Dominey
29.03.67	34089	9.16 am Weymouth	96, 92	Hendicott
01.04.67	34024	8.35 am Waterloo	90	unknown
07.04.67	35012	8.35 am Waterloo	94	Parsons
09.04.67	35023	Spl ex Waterloo	93	Doust
19.04.67	35003	6.38 pm Salisbury	100	Enticknapp
20.04.67	35003	6.38 pm Salisbury	98	Groome
20.04.67	34025	6.15 pm Weymouth	90, 90	Hendicott
21.04.67	34102	6.38 pm Salisbury	98	Groome
23.04.67	35003	11.30 am Waterloo	95	Hendicott
26.04.67	34098	6.38 pm Salisbury	93	Chapman
27.04.67	35003	6.38 pm Salisbury	100, 101, 100	Chapman
29.04.67	35028	5.30 pm Weymouth	91	Bramble
05.05.67	34037	6.38 pm Salisbury	96	Gaffney
12.05.67	34024	8.35 am Waterloo	90	McMail
13.05.67	34060	2.30 am Waterloo	95	Grover
13.05.67	34104	8.35 am Waterloo	90	McMail
22.05.67	34001	6.15 pm Weymouth	92	Evans
23.05.67	34093	6.15 pm Weymouth	90	Fordrey
24.05.67	34001	6.15 pm Weymouth	90, 94	Evans
25.05.67	35003	8.35 am Waterloo	97	Mercer
25.05.67	35023	6.15 pm Weymouth	95, 96	Fordrey
26.05.67	35028	11.25 am Weymouth	91, 92, 93	Pilcher
26.05.67	34034	4.22 pm Waterloo	90, 97	Fordrey
26.05.67	34001	6.15 pm Weymouth	90, 91, 95	Evans
28.05.67	35013	7.59 pm Bournemouth	95	Chapman
02.06.67	35003	5.30 pm Weymouth	98, 92	Porter

DATE	ENGINE	TRAIN	MAX SPEED	DRIVER
06.06.67	34023	6.38 pm Salisbury	91	Dente
07.06.67	34100	6.38 pm Salisbury	95	Taylor
09.06.67	35013	11.25 am Weymouth	97, 92	Saunders
12.06.67	35023	6.15 pm Weymouth	90	Wright
13.06.67	34004	5.23 pm Waterloo	90	unknown
14.06.67	34102	6.38 pm Salisbury	100, 93	Gaffney
16.06.67	35023	6.15 pm Weymouth	90	O'Dell
17.06.67	35007	8.30 am Waterloo	95	Evans
19.06.67	35007	8.35 am Waterloo	94	Groome
19.06.67	34034	6.38 pm Salisbury	95	Bennett
19.06.67	34093	6.15 pm Weymouth	95	Hendicott
20.06.67	34024	5.30 pm Weymouth	90	Dente
21.06.67	34060	6.15 pm Weymouth	93	Hendicott
23.06.67	35003	11.25 am Weymouth	90, 90	Groome
23.06.67	34023	6.38 pm Salisbury	95	Bennett
23.06.67	34060	6.15 pm Weymouth	95, 90	Hendicott
26.06.67	35003	6.15 pm Weymouth	106, 95	Burridge
27.06.67	35028	6.15 pm Weymouth	95	Burridge
28.06.67	35003	6.15 pm Weymouth	105	Burridge
29.06.67	34087	8.10 am Waterloo	96	Hendicott
29.06.67	34087	4.00 pm Weymouth	90, 92	Shepherd
30.06.67	34087	2.30 am Waterloo	95	Peyton
30.06.67	34021	6.15 pm Weymouth	98	Burridge
01.07.67	73065	2.30 am Waterloo	90	Peyton
02.07.67	34037	7.36 pm Bournemouth	92	Miles
03.07.67	35007	5.30 pm Weymouth	95	Bennett
04.07.67	34001	2.45 am Waterloo	92, 91, 98	Porter
05.07.67	35008	6.38 pm Salisbury	102, 98	De'Ath, Ainsley
06.07.67	73029	2.45 am Waterloo	90	Porter
06.07.67	73043	4.51 pm Basingstoke	90	De'Ath
06.07.67	35007	5.30 pm Weymouth	98	Domm
08.07.67	34095	2.45 am Waterloo	90, 93	Porter
08.07.67	35023	8.30 am Waterloo	95	Hughes

APPENDIX L

GRADIENT PROFILE-WATERLOO TO SALISBURY

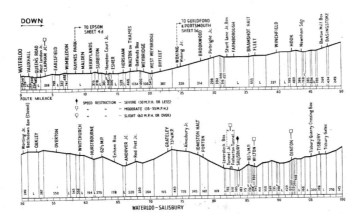

Reproduced by courtesy of the Railway Magazine

GRADIENT PROFILE-WORTING JUNCTION TO WEYMOUTH

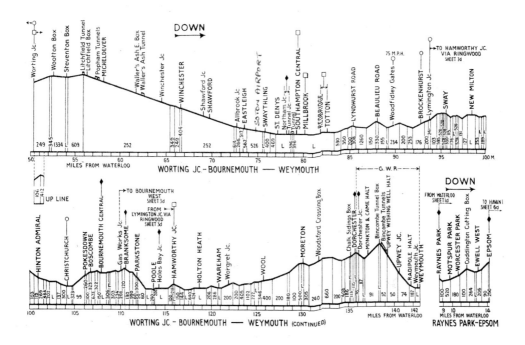

Reproduced by courtesy of the Railway Magazine